India's
FOREIGN
POLICY

India's
FOREIGN
POLICY Retrospect and Prospect

edited by
Sumit Ganguly

OXFORD
UNIVERSITY PRESS

OXFORD
UNIVERSITY PRESS

YMCA Library Building, Jai Singh Road, New Delhi 110 001

Oxford University Press is a department of the University of Oxford. It furthers the
University's objective of excellence in research, scholarship, and education
by publishing worldwide in

Oxford New York

Auckland Cape Town Dar es Salaam Hong Kong Karachi Kuala Lumpur
Madrid Melbourne Mexico City Nairobi New Delhi Shanghai Taipei Toronto

With offices in
Argentina Austria Brazil Chile Czech Republic France Greece Guatemala
Hungary Italy Japan Poland Portugal Singapore South Korea Switzerland
Thailand Turkey Ukraine Vietnam

Oxford is a registered trademark of Oxford University Press
in the UK and in certain other countries

Published in India
by Oxford University Press, New Delhi

© Oxford University Press 2010

ISBN-13: 978-019-569708-7
ISBN-10: 019-569708-1

Typeset in Adobe Garamond Pro 10.5/12.6 by Jojy Philip
Printed in India at De Unique, New Delhi 110 018
Published by Oxford University Press
YMCA Library Building, Jai Singh Road, New Delhi 110 001

To the memory of my father,
Romendranath Ganguly

Contents

List of Tables and Figures   ix

Acknowledgements   xi

List of Abbreviations   xii

1. The Genesis of Nonalignment   1
   Sumit Ganguly

2. India–Pakistan Relations: Between War and Peace   11
   Rajesh M. Basrur

3. When Individuals, States, and Systems Collide: 32
   India's Foreign Policy towards Sri Lanka
   Neil DeVotta

4. Indo-Bangladesh Relations: The Puzzle of Weak Ties   62
   Milind Thakar

5. Evolution of India's China Policy   83
   John W. Garver

6. Southeast Asia in Indian Foreign Policy: 106
   Positioning India as a Major Power in Asia
   Manjeet S. Pardesi

7. Indo-Iranian Relations: What Prospects for Transformation?   132
   C. Christine Fair

8. Indo-Israeli Relations: Emergence of a Strategic Partnership   155
   Nicolas Blarel

9. India: A Growing Congruence of Interests with Korea   175
   Walter Andersen

10. India–Japan Relations: A Slow, but Steady, Transformation   206
    Harsh V. Pant

11. The Evolution of India's Relations with Russia: Tried,   226
    Tested, and Searching for Balance
    Deepa M. Ollapally

12. India and the United States from World War II to   251
    the Present: A Relationship Transformed
    S. Paul Kapur

13. The Evolution of India's Nuclear Policies   275
    Jason A. Kirk

14. India's Foreign Economic Policies   301
    Rahul Mukherji

15. Domestic and International Influences on India's   323
    Energy Policy, 1947–2008
    Dinshaw Mistry

    Select Further Readings   343
    Notes on Contributors   346

Tables and Figures

TABLES

6.1 India's Integration into the Institutional Architecture of Southeast/East Asia   121

9.1 Indian Trade with Asia   184

15.1 India's Oil and Total Energy Production and Consumption   324

15.2 India's Domestic Production and Imports of Energy in 2005   325

15.3 Percentage Share of India's Foreign Suppliers of Oil   327

FIGURES

9.1 India's Trade Partners   185

9.2 Indian Export Destinations   186

9.3 Indian Import Sources   186

9.4 Top Ten Net Oil Importers in 2006   191

9.5 Top LNG Importers in 2006   191

9.6 Korean Energy Consumption   192

9.7 South Korea's 2006 LNG Imports, by Source   192

9.8 Korean Oil Consumption   193

9.9 Korean Natural Gas Consumption   194

9.10 Shipping Routes: Indian Ocean Shipping Routes Connecting the Persian Gulf to East Asia through the Strait of Malacca   195

Acknowledgements

This volume would not have been possible without the support and generosity of a number of organizations and individuals. To that end, I wish to thank the Asia Foundation of San Francisco; the Indian Embassy in Washington, DC; the Office of the Vice-Provost for Research, the Center on American and Global Security, and the Office of the Vice President for International Relations at Indiana University in Bloomington; and Dr Sisir and Heather Dhar and Dr Sanjay and Priyanka Pathak of Terre Haute, Indiana, for their generous support for an author's conference at Indiana University, Bloomington.

I gratefully acknowledge the trenchant comments of Ambassador Ranjendra Abhyankar, formerly of the Indian Foreign Service, and Professor Harrison Wagner of the Department of Government, University of Texas at Austin, on the initial drafts of these chapters. I also wish to acknowledge the invaluable administrative support of Tim Callahan, the Assistant Director of the India Studies Program, and that of Brandon Wilkening, a doctoral candidate at Indiana University, Bloomington, in organizing the conference. I also wish to thank Scott Nissen, my research assistant and also a doctoral candidate in the Department of Political Science at Indiana University, Bloomington, for his timely and substantial assistance in the preparation of this manuscript for publication. I wish to thank Jessica Evans for carefully proofreading the penultimate version of this manuscript. Finally, I wish to thank Manjeet S. Pardesi and Nicolas Blarel, doctoral students at Indiana University, Bloomington for their editorial assistance.

Abbreviations

ADB	Asian Development Bank
AEC	Atomic Energy Commission
AEWC	Airborne Early Warning and Control (Systems)
AIADMK	All India Anna Dravida Munnetra Kazhagam
APEC	Asia-Pacific Economic Cooperation
ARC	Asian Relations Conference
ARF	ASEAN Regional Forum
ASEAN	Association of Southeast Asian Nations
BARC	Bhabha Atomic Research Centre
BIMSTEC	Bay of Bengal Initiative for Multi-Sectoral Technical and Economic Cooperation
BJP	Bharatiya Janata Party
BNP	Bangladesh National Party
BSF	Border Security Force
CANDU	Canada Deuterium Uranium
CAVTS	Combined Acceleration Vibration (Climatic) Test System
CCP	Chinese Communist Party
CECA	Comprehensive Economic Cooperation Agreement
CENTO	Central Treaty Organization
CEPA	Comprehensive Economic Partnership Agreement
CIA	Central Intelligence Agency
CIRUS	Canada India Reactor United States
CM	Chief Minister
CPI (M)	Communist Party of India (Marxist)
CPSU	Communist Party of the Soviet Union
CTBT	Comprehensive Test Ban Treaty
DAE	Department of Atomic Energy
DMK	Dravida Munnetra Kazhagam
DRDO	Defence Research and Development Organisation
EAC	East Asia Community

EAS	East Asia Summit
EPA	Economic Partership Agreement
EU	European Union
E&Y	Ernst and Young
FDI	Foreign Direct Investment
FFYP	First Five Year Plan
FMCT	Fissile Material Cut-off Treaty
FSB	Federal Security Service of the Russian Federation
FSU	Former Soviet Union
FTA	Free Trade Agreement
FYP	Five Year Plan
GAIL	Gas Authority of India Limited
GDP	Gross Domestic Product
GE	General Electric
GNP	Gross National Product
GNPOC	Greater Nile Petroleum Operating Company
HUJI–B	Harkat-ul-Jihad-al-Islami–Bangladesh
IAEA	International Atomic Energy Agency
IAF	Indian Air Force
IAI	Israel Aerospace Industries
IBSA	India–Brazil–South Africa
ICC	International Control Commission
ICSC	International Commissions of Supervision and Control
ILSA	Iran–Libya Sanctions Act
IMB	International Maritime Bureau
IMF	International Monetary Fund
IMO	International Maritime Organization
INA	Indian National Army
INC	Indian National Congress
IPKF	Indian Peace Keeping Force
ISI	Inter-Services Intelligence
IT	Information Technology
ITES	Information Technology Enabled Services
JCE	Joint Committee of Experts
JeM	Jaish-e-Mohammad
JSG	Joint Study Group
JTF	Joint Task Force
JVP	Janatha Vimukthi Peramuna
LCA	Light Combat Aircraft
LDP	Liberal Democratic Party

LeT	Lashkar-e-Taiba
LNG	Liquefied Natural Gas
LoC	Line of Control
LTTE	Liberation Tigers of Tamil Eelam
MDMK	Marumalarchi Dravida Munnetra Kazhagam
MFN	Most Favoured Nation
MIT	Massachusetts Institute of Technology
MoU	Memorandum of Understanding
MTC	Military Technical Cooperation
NAFTA	North American Free Trade Agreement
NAM	Non-Aligned Movement
NASA	National Aeronautic Space Administration
NATO	North Atlantic Treaty Organization
NIGEC	National Iranian Gas Export Company
NNRC	Neutral Nations Repatriation Commission
NPT	Nuclear Non-Proliferation Treaty
NRI	Non-Resident Indian
NSG	Nuclear Suppliers Group
ODA	Overseas Development Assistance
OIC	Organization of the Islamic Conference
ONGC	Oil and Natural Gas Corporation
OPEC	Organization of the Petroleum Exporting Countries
OVL	ONGC Videsh Limited
PL 480	Public Law 480
PLA	People's Liberation Army
PLO	Palestine Liberation Organization
PM	Prime Minister
PMK	Pattali Makkal Katchi
PNE	Peaceful Nuclear Explosive
POSCO	Pohang Iron and Steel Company
PPP	Pakistan People's Party
PRC	People's Republic of China
RAW	Research and Analysis Wing
RSS	Rashtriya Swayamsevak Sangh
SAARC	South Asian Association for Regional Cooperation
SARC	South Asian Regional Cooperation
SAS	Special Air Service
SCO	Shanghai Cooperation Organization
SDF	Self Defense Force
SDR	Special Drawing Right

SEATO	Southeast Asia Treaty Organization
SFYP	Second Five Year Plan
SLFP	Sri Lanka Freedom Party
TELO	Tamil Eelam Liberation Organization
TFYP	Third Five Year Plan
UK	United Kingdom
ULFA	United Liberation Front of Asom
UN	United Nations
UNAMIC	United Nations Advance Mission in Cambodia
UNCIP	United Nations Commission on India and Pakistan
UNP	United National Party
UNSC	United Nations Security Council
UNTAC	United Nations Transitional Authority in Cambodia
UPA	United Progressive Alliance
US	United States
USSR	Union of Soviet Socialist Republics
VHP	Vishwa Hindu Parishad
WTO	World Trade Organization

1

The Genesis of Nonalignment

SUMIT GANGULY

India's foreign policy can be divided into three distinct epochs. The initial phase, which began shortly after Independence, lasted until 1962. The second phase extended from 1962 to 1991. The third and current phase began in 1991 and continues to the present day. The delineation of these historical epochs is far from arbitrary. Instead, it is possible to adduce compelling substantive reasons for their selection.

Personal, national, and systemic factors contributed to India's choice of an ideational foreign policy. At a *personal* level, Prime Minister Jawaharlal Nehru, who was the principal architect of independent India's foreign policy, had sought to pursue an ideational foreign policy. To that end he had been an ardent supporter of multilateral institutions, had placed significant constraints on defence spending, and had strenuously advocated the process of decolonization. These policies had both normative and instrumental underpinnings. At a normative level, Nehru had genuinely hoped to transform the global political order. These goals became embodied in the doctrine of nonalignment. The doctrine called for steering a diplomatic path free from superpower dominance. In practice, however, India's policymakers tended to be more critical of American policies over those of the Soviet Union.[1] This anomaly, in large part, could be attributed to Prime Minister Nehru's propensity to link imperialism with capitalism.[2]

The policy was also in keeping with India's *national* experience of colonialism. As a former colonized state, India was loath to limit its foreign policy options through an alignment with either superpower.[3] Furthermore, the ideas embodied in the doctrine of nonalignment were in keeping with elements of India's historical and cultural legacies. The moral stance of nonalignment against colonization and apartheid neatly dovetailed with India's Gandhian heritage.

Finally, at a *systemic* level, the policy made sense as it enabled a materially weak state to play a role that was considerably more significant than its capabilities would warrant. In effect, the policy made it possible for the state to deftly turn its limitations into a possible asset.

These policies, at least for a while, served India well. The country played a vital role in the United Nations (UN) peacekeeping operations, it was a critical voice in the promotion of decolonization, and also proved to be a driving force for global disarmament. To that end India devoted a significant contingent to the UN peacekeeping operations during the Congo crisis,[4] it highlighted the issue of decolonization in the UN General Assembly, and it introduced along with Ireland the first 'standstill resolution' at the UN in 1954 calling for a complete cessation of nuclear testing.

Though these policies worked to India's advantage at the global level, they had important shortcomings in regional terms. Nehru's staunch opposition to defence spending led to a neglect of India's military preparedness and culminated in a debacle.[5] Shortly after the Communist revolution in the People's Republic of China (PRC), India became embroiled in an important border dispute along the Himalayan frontier. The breakdown of bilateral diplomatic negotiations in 1960 culminated in a short, sharp war in 1962. Indian forces, grossly under-equipped and ill-trained for high altitude warfare, suffered a grievous military defeat at the hands of the battle-hardened People's Liberation Army.[6]

NONALIGNMENT CHALLENGED

In the wake of this war, *personal, national,* and *systemic* factors all contributed to a shift in India's foreign and security policies. At a *personal* level, PM Nehru's unchallenged status in the Indian political arena came under attack. There were widespread calls both from the political opposition in the Indian Parliament and from some members of the country's attentive public for the abandonment of nonalignment. Despite these demands and Nehru's dramatically weakened political standing, India's policymakers did not formally abandon nonalignment.

Nevertheless, at a *national* level, the political outcry and the sense of a perceived threat from the PRC was sufficiently great that despite the professed Nehruvian commitment to hobbling the use of force in international politics, India embarked upon a significant military modernization programme designed to cope with the emergent threat from the PRC.[7]

Finally, at a *systemic* level, India found some support from the United States (US) during and immediately after the China crisis.[8] US assistance to

India obviously stemmed from American concerns about the preservation of the balance of power in Asia.[9]

This programme of military modernization was far from complete when India became embroiled in another war in 1965 with Pakistan over the disputed state of Jammu and Kashmir.[10] The war ended in a stalemate and the Soviet Union brokered a post-war settlement. The Soviets were able to mediate an end to the war as the US had chosen to withdraw from subcontinental affairs and had also become preoccupied with the prosecution of the war in Vietnam. Under the terms of this accord the two sides agreed to return to the status quo ante and abjure from the use of force to resolve the Kashmir dispute.

Six years later, India and Pakistan again became involved in another full-scale war. This war, which had stemmed from the exigencies of Pakistani domestic politics, saw the break-up of Pakistan following India's military intervention in East Pakistan.[11] In the aftermath of this war India emerged as the dominant power in the subcontinent.[12]

Despite India's military predominance in the subcontinent, *personal*, *national*, and *systemic* factors prevented it from playing a significant role in global affairs over the next two decades. At a *personal* level, Indira Gandhi's economic policy choices, which were mostly populist, did little or nothing to promote significant economic growth.[13] Consequently, India's material power remained limited. *Regional* factors also hobbled India's growth prospects and thereby limited its international influence. Specifically, thanks to the Organization of the Petroleum Exporting Countries (OPEC) induced oil crisis in the wake of the 1973 Arab–Israeli conflict, India's economy suffered significantly.[14] Finally, at a *systemic* level, given its material weakness India could play no meaningful role in global affairs. At most, it unsuccessfully flailed away at the inequities of the global economic and trading order.[15]

A REQUIEM FOR NONALIGNMENT?

Indeed, it was not until the collapse of the Soviet Union and the end of the Cold War that India's foreign policy would undergo a fundamental shift and acquire renewed relevance. Once again, *personal*, *national*, and *systemic* factors induced these changes in its foreign policy. There is little question that PM Narasimha Rao, who had assumed the premiership in the aftermath of PM Rajiv Gandhi's assassination, recognized the need for a drastic re-appraisal of India's foreign policy goals and aspirations.[16] Ironically, *national* circumstances and *systemic* forces also induced him to make these changes. Nationally, the country was faced with an unprecedented financial crisis and piecemeal efforts to resolve it would not enable it to address its underlying causes.[17] Systemic forces also induced India to chart a new course.[18] The Soviet collapse meant that India could no longer rely on the support and protection of a veto-wielding superpower. Nor could it count on the principal successor state, Russia, to continue to contain the growth of China's military prowess and possible future revanchism.[19]

The transformation of India's foreign policy was nothing short of dramatic. The country dropped its reflexive, neuralgic hostility towards the US, upgraded its diplomatic ties with Israel, continued cautious attempts to improve its relations with the PRC, and made a major effort to court the countries of Southeast Asia.[20] These shifts in foreign policy orientation also led India to all but abandon its professed commitment to universal nuclear disarmament. Once again, *personal, national,* and *systemic* factors played critical roles in driving India down the path of acquiring an overt nuclear capability. At a personal level, PM Rajiv Gandhi, and subsequently PM Narasimha Rao, had become increasingly convinced that Pakistan's growing nuclear capabilities posed a threat to India.[21] Furthermore, the successful unconditional and indefinite extension of the Nuclear Non-proliferation Treaty (NPT) made even the most ardent exponents of nuclear disarmament in India realize that the nuclear weapons states had little or no interest in containing their own nuclear arsenals, let alone undertake serious steps towards universal nuclear disarmament. Not surprisingly, the country chose to cross the nuclear Rubicon in May 1998.[22] Despite initial and widespread disapprobation from the US and many of the other great powers, India was grudgingly accepted as a de facto nuclear weapons state.[23] More to the point, under the second George W. Bush administration, India successfully negotiated a civilian nuclear deal with the US which effectively enabled it to participate in global nuclear commerce under the aegis of the International Atomic Energy Agency (IAEA) safeguards.[24]

TOWARDS A 'NORMAL' STATE?

An Indian politician, Minister of State for Industry Ashwani Kumar in the United Progressive Alliance government, characterized India's current foreign policy as the pursuit of 'enlightened national-interest'.[25] Once again, *personal, national,* and *systemic* factors will drive this policy. With the exception of the left wing in Indian politics, a consensus seems to have emerged amongst most of the political leadership about the desirability of pursuing a pragmatic foreign policy that enhances India's material capabilities and thereby its standing in the global arena. Also, at a *national* level, there is a shared emphasis on the need for sustaining economic growth and military clout.[26] Finally, at a *systemic* level, given the decline of American power in the aftermath of the acute fiscal crisis, India's hopes of having sufficient freedom of manoeuvre based upon its national size, political stability, and material capabilities may well be realized in an increasingly multipolar world.[27]

ORGANIZATION OF THE VOLUME

The chapters in this volume use the level of analysis framework sketched out in this brief discussion to assess the evolution of India's foreign policy from 1947 to the present day. The volume is thematically divided into four distinct segments. The first segment deals with India's relations with the bulk of its immediate neighbours; the second segment with countries and regions that lie athwart India; the third with several key states in the international order; and finally the fourth segment addresses the country's nuclear, economic, and energy policies.

In Chapter 2, which begins the *first* segment, Rajesh M. Basrur traces the origins of Indo-Pakistani discord. He then proceeds to provide a discussion of how the relationship has evolved over the past 60 years and identifies key turning points. He concludes his analysis with a discussion of possible external and domestic factors which may help to ameliorate the relationship in the future.

In Chapter 3, Neil DeVotta argues that more than any other factor, ties of ethnicity and kinship between India and Sri Lanka have greatly complicated their bilateral relationship. Consequently, he avers that while other factors have, no doubt, influenced the relationship, the role of ethnic affinity has been dominant. His chapter concludes with an analysis of how the Indo-Sri Lankan relationship has improved dramatically in the recent past. However, he cautions that it is still not bereft of difficulties and that the imperatives of ethnic links and concomitant tensions could again pose problems.

In Chapter 4, Milind Thakar discusses the fraught Indo-Bangladeshi relationship. He suggests that the relationship can be broken up into three distinct periods, each with its distinctive characteristics. The latest phase, which he contends started around 1990, coincided with the restoration of democracy in Bangladesh. Despite some improvements, a series of differences continue to bedevil Indo-Bangladeshi relations at multiple levels.

In Chapter 5, John W. Garver traces the origins of India's China policy. Garver outlines the centrality and intractability of the border dispute, discusses the protracted negotiations, and assesses the prospects and limitations of an improvement in bilateral relations.

In Chapter 6, which begins the *second* segment of this volume, Manjeet

S. Pardesi shows that India has long pursued the twin objectives of security and prosperity in Southeast Asia. However, he contends that while these objectives have remained constant, India's ability to realize them has been uneven. Nevertheless, he argues that a variety of factors will propel India to pursue robust ties with the economically dynamic region.

In Chapter 7, C. Christine Fair examines Indo-Iranian relations. She shows how the relationship was mostly hobbled during the Cold War years but has undergone a significant transformation since its end. Nevertheless, she shows that some differences continue to dog the relationship including questions of energy supplies and Iran's pursuit of a clandestine nuclear weapons programme.

In Chapter 8, Nicolas Blarel explains why the Indo-Israeli relationship was so slow to come to fruition during the first 40 odd years of their existence as independent states. He then proceeds to explain the rapprochement that ensued after the Cold War and the growing Indo-Israeli defence and security nexus.

In Chapter 9, Walter Andersen shows that after years of mutual neglect, Indo-South Korean relations are now flourishing. The relationship had been initially developed along mostly economic lines. In recent years, however, it has now taken on other dimensions including an incipient security dimension.

In Chapter 10, which begins the *third* segment, Harsh V. Pant discusses the historic links between India and Japan, their relative lack of contact during the Cold War, and their growing convergence of interests in the recent past. He focuses on their common misgivings about the dramatic rise of China in Asia as one of the driving forces underlying the convergence of their national interests and the coordination of their policies.

In Chapter 11, Deepa M. Ollapally deals with India's evolving relationship with Russia, the principal successor state to the former Soviet Union. She shows that the Indo-Russian defence relationship, despite some ongoing differences, remains robust. Even though the Cold War imperatives that enabled India to forge a close relationship no longer exist, she argues that both states remain interested in fashioning a multipolar global order.

In Chapter 12, S. Paul Kapur examines what is perhaps India's most significant bilateral relationship, namely that with the US. Kapur traces the transformation of this relationship from one of mutual suspicion and distrust to one based upon a convergence of strategic interests and growing cooperation.

In Chapter 13, which begins the *fourth* and final segment, Jason A.

Kirk discusses the evolution of India's nuclear policies. In this chapter Kirk argues that India's acquisition of nuclear weapons, despite the existence of serious security threats, was not inevitable. Rather, he contends that India chose to foreswear its historic commitment to the overt acquisition of nuclear weapons owing to exigent circumstances.

In Chapter 14, Rahul Mukherji provides an account of the evolution of India's foreign economic policies from the era of import-substituting industrialization to the present circumstances of economic liberalization. In tracing this evolution he identifies key turning points and significant epochs in India's foreign economic policy-making process.

In Chapter 15, Dinshaw Mistry discusses India's international energy policies. He shows how India, an acutely energy-short state, has fashioned diplomatic strategies to guarantee its energy security. He also underscores India's increased attempts to secure hydrocarbon supplies in an era of rapid economic growth.

It is important to forthrightly state that the book has some lacunae. It does not cover India's relations with Latin America or Africa.[28] Since the last decade of the twentieth century, India has forged important relationships with two key states in both regions, namely Brazil and South Africa. These relationships have contributed to an informal group referred to as IBSA (India–Brazil–South Africa).[29] However, at this juncture it is difficult to comment at substantial length on the workings of this emergent entity. Prior to the formation of this organization, India's ties to either region were limited and ad hoc. Consequently, there are no chapters on India's relations with either continent.

Additionally, there is no chapter on Indian policy towards West Asia. However, the critical issues affecting India and the region are adequately dealt with in Chapters 7 and 8 which focus on Indo-Iranian and Indo-Israeli relations.

Nor for that matter is there any chapter on India's relations with global multilateral institutions. The decision not to include such a chapter was also quite deliberate, albeit, for different reasons. The theoretical framework utilized in this volume simply did not lend itself to an analysis of India's policies towards multilateral institutions.

NOTES

1.   On the difficult Indo-American relationship, see Andrew Jon Rotter (2002), *Comrades at Odds: The United States and India 1947–1964* (Ithaca: Cornell University Press); for a discussion of the Soviet–Indian relationship, see Robert H. Donaldson (1974), *Soviet Foreign Policy Toward India: Ideology and Strategy*

(Cambridge: Harvard University Press); also see Linda Racioppi (1994), *Soviet Policy Toward South Asia since 1970* (Cambridge: Cambridge University Press).

2.   For Nehru's views, see Jawaharlal Nehru (1963), *Toward Freedom: An Autobiography* (Boston: Beacon Press).

3.   Some Indian hyper-Realists, most notably Bharat Karnad, argue that Nehru used his moral arguments in an instrumental fashion, creating bargaining space for a weak state in the international system. See Bharat Karnad (2002), *Nuclear Weapons and Indian Security: The Realist Foundations of Strategy* (New Delhi: Macmillan).

4.   Rajeshwar Dayal (1998), *A Life of Our Times* (London: Sangam).

5.   On the Indian military debacle, see Major-General D.K. Palit (1992), *War in the High Himalaya: The Indian Army in Crisis* (London: C. Hurst and Company); on the origins of the border dispute; see Steven Hoffman (1990), *India and the China Crisis* (Berkeley: University of California Press); also see John Garver (2001), *Protracted Contest: Sino-Indian Rivalry in the Twentieth Century* (Seattle: University of Washington Press).

6.   On the lack of defence preparedness, see Sumit Ganguly (2001), 'From the Defense of the Nation to Aid to the Civil: The Army in Contemporary India', *Journal of Asian and African Affairs*, 26 (1–2), pp. 11–26.

7.   On the Indian military modernization programme, see Sumit Ganguly (forthcoming), 'Indian Security Policy', in Victor Mauer (ed.), *The Routledge Handbook of Security Policy* (London: Routledge).

8.   Rotter, *Comrades at Odds*.

9.   For the best evidence of American concerns about maintaining a balance of power in Asia and also containing Communist expansion, see *The Foreign Relations of the United States* (South Asia, 1961–3) (1996), vol. XIX (Washington, DC: United States Government Printing). In particular, see Document 175 'Telegram From the Embassy in India to the Department of State', 15 October 1962, pp. 343–4, and Document 181, 'Memorandum From the President's Deputy Special Assistant for National Security Affairs (Kaysen) to President Kennedy', 26 October 1962, pp. 351–2.

10.   The best politico-military analysis of the second Indo-Pakistani conflict remains Russell Brines (1968), *The Indo-Pakistani Conflict* (New York: Pall Mall); for a comparative and comprehensive analysis of the Indo-Pakistani conflicts, see Sumit Ganguly (2001), *Conflict Unending: India–Pakistan Tensions Since 1947* (New York: Columbia University Press).

11.   On the politics of this conflict, see Robert Jackson (1975), *South Asian Crisis* (New York: Praeger) and Richard Sisson and Leo E. Rose (1990), *War and Secession* (Berkeley: University of California Press); for an Indian military perspective on the crisis, see Major-General D.K. Palit (retd) (1972), *The Lighting Campaign* (Tisbury: Compton Press) and Lieutenant-General J.F.R. Jacob (1997), *Surrender at Dhaka: Birth of a Nation* (New Delhi: Manohar Publications). For two Pakistani perspectives, see Siddiq Salik (1977), *Witness to Surrender* (New Delhi: Oxford

University Press) and Hasan Zaheer (1994), *The Separation of East Pakistan: The Rise and Realization of Bengali Muslim Nationalism* (Karachi: Oxford University Press).

12. William J. Barnds (1973), 'India and America at Odds', *International Affairs*, 49 (3), pp. 371–84; also see Steven Hoffman (1972), 'Anticipation, Disaster and Victory: India 1962–71', *Asian Survey*, 12 (11), pp. 960–79.

13. For a particularly trenchant critique, see Jyotindra Das Gupta (1978), 'A Season of Caesars: Emergency Regimes and Development Politics in Asia', *Asian Survey*, 18 (4), pp. 315–49.

14. Prem Shanker Jha (1980), *India: A Political Economy of Stagnation* (New Delhi: Oxford University Press).

15. Lawrence Saez (2006), 'India and the New International Economic Order: A Focus on Trade', in Subrata K. Mitra and Bernd Rill (eds), *India's New Dynamics in Foreign Policy* (Munich: Hanns-Seidel-Stiftung).

16. Sumit Ganguly (1992), 'South Asia After the Cold War', *The Washington Quarterly*, 15 (4), pp. 173–84.

17. Rahul Mukherji (ed.) (2007), *India's Economic Reforms* (New Delhi: Oxford University Press).

18. For a particularly insightful analysis of how systemic forces can induce changes at the domestic level, see Peter Gourevitch (1978), 'The Second Image Reversed: The International Sources of Domestic Politics', *International Organization*, 32 (4), pp. 881–912.

19. On China's military modernization see David Shambaugh (2005), *Modernizing China's Military: Progress, Problems and Prospects* (Berkeley: University of California Press).

20. For a discussion of the transformation of India's foreign policy, see Sumit Ganguly (2003/4), 'India's Foreign Policy Grows Up', *World Policy Journal*, 20 (4), pp. 41–7. For a discussion of the US–Indian rapprochement at the end of the Cold War, see Sumit Ganguly and Andrew Scobell (2005), 'The US and India: Forging a Security Partnership?', *World Policy Journal*, 22 (2), pp. 37–44.

21. Raj Chengappa (2000), *Weapons of Peace: The Secret Story of India's Quest to be a Nuclear Power* (New Delhi: HarperCollins).

22. For a discussion, see Sumit Ganguly (1999), 'India's Pathway to Pokhran II: The Sources and Prospects of India's Nuclear Weapons Program', *International Security*, 23 (4), pp. 148–77.

23. Strobe Talbott (2000), *Engaging India* (Washington, DC: The Brookings Institution).

24. Sumit Ganguly and Dinshaw Mistry (2006), 'The Case for the US–India Nuclear Agreement', *World Policy Journal*, 23 (2), pp. 11–19, and Sumit Ganguly and Dinshaw Mistry (2006), 'The US–India Nuclear Pact: A Good Deal', *Current History*, 105 (694), pp. 375–8.

25. Ramananda Sengupta, 'India will Lead in the Asian Century', http://www.redif.

com/money/2006/mar/20asoc6.htm (accessed on 22 February 2009). Also see http://pmindia.nic.in/speech/content.asp?id=274 and http://pmindia.nic.in/speech/content.asp?id=275 (accessed on 12 April 2009). PM Manmohan Singh had also used the same expression in an interview with Charlie Rose, http://pmindia.nic.in/charlie_rose.htm (accessed on 12 April 2009).

26. On the new economic consensus, see Arvind Panagariya (2008), *India: The Emerging Giant* (New York: Oxford University Press).

27. There is more than an implicit recognition of this trend in National Intelligence Council report, *Global Trends 2025*, http://www.dni.gov/nic/NIC_2025_project.html (accessed on 23 February 2009).

28. Harry G. Broadman (2008), 'China and India Go to Africa', *Foreign Affairs*, 87 (2), pp. 95–109.

29. See the official website: http://www.ibsa-trilateral.org/ (accessed on 10 April 2009).

2

India–Pakistan Relations

Between War and Peace

RAJESH M. BASRUR

India's long drawn-out antagonism with Pakistan has occupied front stage for the best part of its history since independence in 1947. The strings of wars and crises that have erupted in the course of this enduring rivalry have left little room for optimism about its prospects.[1] But after half a decade of continual negotiation and a series of small but significant steps forward in finding common ground, the India–Pakistan relationship shows signs of having reached a new plane. Tracing the evolution of the relationship, this chapter shows how an 'intractable' rivalry has begun to change in substantive ways. In brief, it is argued that the advent of nuclear weapons and the pressures of globalization at the system level, perceptible shifts in national identity and political organization at the state level, and the unprecedented initiatives taken by individual policymakers have combined to alter the trajectory of the relationship. Though a positive outcome is hardly assured as yet, the trend is sufficiently encouraging to evoke expectations of better times. Yet, it will be seen, the process is likely to remain a relatively unhurried and incremental one.

STRUCTURE AND PROCESS AT THE SYSTEM LEVEL

It is important to first distinguish between structure and process in the international system. The former, to present a simplified version of neorealist theory, refers to the distribution of power among states that cannot trust one another because they inhabit an anarchic system.[2] The latter refers to the innumerable interactions that occur continuously among states. The former produces broad patterns of behaviour such as the propensity of states to come into conflicts of interest and power, to form alliances, to engage in arms racing, and occasionally to go to war. The latter, disained by neorealists as negating the possibility of elegant theory because of its complexity, does in fact produce some important overarching patterns. For instance, as the neoliberals point out, the transnationalization of the global economy, a central feature of the system in the current era, makes inter-state conflict more costly and therefore cooperation more likely.[3] Moreover, as the pace of technological change accelerates, the premium on efficiency goes up and the cost of eschewing cooperation rises significantly. Mikhail Gorbachev recognized this and went to great lengths to end the Cold War so that the Soviet state might not be left behind.[4] Similarly, nuclear weapons produce strategic interdependence and induce at least tacit cooperation by raising the costs of war (relative to potential gains) to unacceptable levels.[5]

To refine our understanding of the effects of structure and process, it is useful to distinguish between systemic levels. Thus, the term 'international system' is applied here at the global as well as the regional levels.[6] With regard to structure, it is readily evident that both India and Pakistan are relatively weak states in the global system. In contrast, at the regional level, in what may be called the South Asian or subcontinental system, India is a major power, while Pakistan, though no mean contender, has always been much smaller in terms of size, population, economic strength, and military capabilities. Large or strong powers tend to behave differently from smaller, weaker ones. As Michael Mandelbaum shows, weak states submit to strong states only if they have no viable option. Otherwise, they adopt typical strategies.[7]

First, strong states try and draw closer to their weaker counterparts through enhanced political and economic relationships in order to exploit opportunities to use their power advantage. In contrast, through a strategy of 'moat-building', weak states seek to distance themselves politically and economically from strong states in order to reduce their vulnerability. Second, strong states show a marked preference for bilateral engagement, which places them in an advantageous position, while weak states favour a multilateral framework as it enables them to draw on the support of others in the bargaining process. Third, strong states try to exert their power over weak states to bend them to their will. The latter respond by garnering as much military capability as they can through their own efforts, or what we today call 'internal balancing', and by attempting to bolster their defences with the help of other strong states, that is, by 'external balancing'. It follows that if the weak are successful in obtaining significant support, the balance between the two hostile states may be altered, in which case the stronger state will tend to augment its position by means of its own balancing efforts.

During the period 1947–71, the pattern of behaviour in the South Asian system was mixed. On the one hand, India was clearly a much larger state with all the attributes of a dominant regional power, comprising 73 per cent of South Asia's land area, 77 per cent of its population, and 77 per cent of its gross national product (GNP).[8] Yet, for the first two decades after independence, its actual capacities were limited, whereas the Pakistani military had an exaggerated perception of its relative strength vis-à-vis India.[9] This gave Pakistan the 'false optimism' that caused it to initiate war twice in the expectation of extracting Kashmir by force.[10] The first war, fought in 1947–8, at least partly justified Pakistani optimism, for it left Pakistan in control of about a third of Kashmir. Pakistan's confidence was boosted by its membership of the Cold War alliance system of the United States (US). It became a member of the Southeast Asia Treaty Organization (SEATO) in 1954 and the Central Treaty Organization (CENTO) in 1955, which enabled it to obtain American tanks and fighter aircraft. Its success in external balancing did appear to have given it a fleeting advantage. In the wake of India's poor performance in the 1962 war against China, Pakistan was emboldened to attempt another military venture in 1965, but this time to no avail. The post-war Tashkent Agreement (January 1966) confirmed the 1948 division of Kashmir.

In the early 1970s, India's structural position became uneasy with the emergence of a Pakistan–US–China nexus, but it countered by signing a 'friendship treaty' with the Soviet Union in August 1971. Its confidence buoyed, India took advantage of Pakistan's internal squabbles by intervening militarily. Thus, the use of military power worked in the opposite direction when India used their third war to divide Pakistan and create an independent Bangladesh in December 1971.

This was a turning point. Thereafter, till the mid-1980s, the India–Pakistan relationship conformed to the strong state/weak state pattern. In the structure of the regional system, India was the strong state, the 'local superpower' (as one unbiased if exaggerated view put it), Pakistan the weak one.[11] By the mid-1980s, India's military capabilities far exceeded those of truncated Pakistan. Its total military expenditure in 1985 was US$ 8,921 million against Pakistan's US$ 2,957 million.[12] In relative terms, the cost for Pakistan was much higher. In the same year, India's defence expenditure as a percentage of its GNP was 3 per cent, while Pakistan spent 6.9 per cent of its GNP on defence.[13] To offset its weakness, Pakistan turned to a determined quest for nuclear weapons—the 'great equalizer'—which it eventually obtained by the mid-1980s.

Using strong state strategy, India consistently sought to build closer economic and cultural relations with Pakistan. Accordingly, it favoured higher levels of trade with Pakistan, granted most favoured nation (MFN) status to it in 1995, and welcomed Pakistani cultural figures into India. Pakistan, on the other hand, resisted trade with India, which had declined precipitously from 32 per cent of its imports and 56 per cent of its exports in 1948–9 to a 'mere trickle' by the early 1950s.[14] Official trade, though supplemented by indirect trade and smuggling, was kept to a very low level. By the late 1990s, Pakistan's exports to India were just 0.42 per cent of its total exports and its imports from India only 1.22 per cent of its total imports.[15] In consequence, India's capacity to influence Pakistan was kept to the minimum. Cultural links were shunned. Hindi films and music, popular in Pakistan, were not given access to the Pakistani market. As Pakistani writer Irfan Husain comments, the political leadership 'sought to justify the existence of Pakistan by presenting an image of a country severed from the heritage of culture and history and sealed from the map of South Asia'.[16] But in fact, Pakistan's policy equally reflected the caution of a weak state resisting engagement with a strong one.

Indian bilateralism on Kashmir contrasted with Pakistan's preference for a multilateral approach. India sought to restrict the scope of a possible resolution of the Kashmir question to bilateral negotiations, laying much stress on the Simla Agreement of 1972, which it viewed as a mutual commitment to bilateralism. Pakistan, on the other hand, consistently attempted to drum up support from the United Nations, the Organization of the Islamic Conference (OIC), and individual states, notably the US and China.

From around the mid-1980s, two systemic processes affected the strategic equation in South Asia. The advent of nuclear weapons dramatically altered the India–Pakistan relationship, generating a surge of hostility between them. In the opposite direction, and more slowly, the accelerating pace of global economic change created new incentives for cooperation. With regard to nuclear weapons, the debate over the merits and demerits of nuclear proliferation, while interesting and even useful, stops short of understanding the dynamic processes at work when states enter into a nuclear rivalry.[17] The pattern that all nuclear rivalries display is similar.[18] The level of tension initially shoots up, producing a tendency towards crisis, which in turn brings caution owing to the fear of nuclear war, and negotiations follow. Thereafter, the rivals may repeat the cycle, though not necessarily. India and Pakistan, like the US and the erstwhile Soviet Union, did go through a series of alternations between crisis and negotiation before settling down to negotiate seriously.[19] The tension wrought by rising mutual suspicions and fears was exacerbated by Pakistan's strategy of pushing a low-cost option. With a new confidence gained from the knowledge that India no longer had recourse to war, Pakistan stepped up its support for terrorist groups active in India, especially in Kashmir.[20]

The first crisis occurred in 1990, when both nations were still covert nuclear powers. Both sides mobilized forces, though in defensive configurations, but avoided war. A second crisis took place in 1999, barely a year after both had conducted nuclear tests in the summer of 1998. This time Pakistan pushed the envelope further by sending troops in the guise of *mujahideen* to occupy positions along the Line of Control (LoC) in Kashmir that had been vacated by Indian troops for the winter.[21] Fighting occurred over several weeks from May to July, but both countries exercised restraint at considerable cost. India refrained from crossing the LoC, though this hamstrung its use of air power and slowed down its counter-attack. Pakistan, still claiming that the intruders were 'freedom fighters', did not back up its troops when they were forced to retreat. Both sides took care not to escalate. In December 2001, a third and prolonged crisis broke out when terrorists attacked India's Parliament and an angry India threatened limited war.[22] Both sides mobilized fully along the entire border and resorted to nuclear signalling by carrying out missile tests. The crisis eventually petered out, but left behind a sense of exhaustion. Yet another crisis occurred in late 2008 when a small group of Pakistan-based terrorists ran amuck in Mumbai city, killing some 170 people with small arms.[23] At the time of writing (May 2009), though tension remained, there was a slow drift to normalcy, and the risk of war, which had reared its head again, seemed to have subsided.[24]

Both sides made some gains from the recurring confrontations. India drew the world's attention to Pakistan's risk-taking and its support for terrorism, while Pakistan compelled India to think beyond its status quo approach on Kashmir and come to the negotiating table. Both also saw the limits of their strategies: cross-border terrorism and limited war threats were high-risk gambits that could trigger nuclear war. From this perspective, compromise appeared an acceptable option. In January 2004, India and Pakistan agreed to begin a 'composite dialogue' on a range of issues, including terrorism, nuclear risk reduction, and Kashmir. Most remarkably, they began to think out of the box on Kashmir, abandoning mutually exclusive claims and focusing on the softening of the LoC, expanding communication links between the divided portions of Kashmir, and enhancing trade.[25]

When we turn to the economic aspect of systemic processes, we find developments in the system as a whole had a significant effect on India and Pakistan. The key feature of the system was (and is) what is loosely referred to as 'globalization', a process that was prominent by the mid-1980s. The movement of goods, services, and money grew phenomenally as a result of what Daniel Bell called the 'third technological revolution', an amalgam of developments in electronics, miniaturization, digitalization, and software development.[26] The prominent features of the globalizing economy included transnational production and greatly expanded flows of trade and money. The value of world trade grew from US$ 244.1 billion in 1960 to US$ 3,846.2 billion in 1980.[27] For developing countries, the old Third World–ism of national protection was no longer viable: to get ahead, states had to shift to more open and competitive economies.[28] India, as Rahul Mukherji has shown in Chapter 14 of this volume, entered the brave new world of liberalization reluctantly, dragged into it by a balance of payments crisis that led it to seek a bailout from the International Monetary Fund (IMF), which inevitably compelled it to abandon autarky. Thereafter, its economy shifted gear and quickly achieved a high rate of growth. In the changed environment, with a new focus on obtaining foreign direct investment (FDI) for growth, the economic cost of instability generated by India–Pakistan hostility began to be viewed as unaffordable. During the 2001–2 crisis, there was public criticism to this effect.[29] It was brought home to political leaders that the fast-moving world of information technology was unwilling to tolerate the uncertainty arising from regional tensions and the threat of war.[30]

Political tensions, as we have seen, had long confined India–Pakistan trade to a low level because Pakistan sought to protect itself by keeping India at arm's length. It was only after the 2001–2 crisis was behind them that trade between the two countries began to grow. Along with the growing awareness that nuclear weapons had made confrontation a negative-sum game came the recognition that there was much to be gained through enhanced trade. At the time of writing (May 2009), Pakistan had yet to grant MFN status to India, but that was only part of a bargaining process over the terms of opening up, particularly over the Pakistani demand that India reduce its non-tariff barriers.[31] With talks under way, India–Pakistan trade spurted from US$ 521 million in 2004–5 to about US$ 2 billion in 2007–8.[32] The opening of trade between the separated portions of Kashmir in 2008 brought both economic benefit and a lessening of tension. Talks on a proposed Iran–Pakistan–India gas pipeline were intermittently on, though slowed by the tension between the US and Iran over the latter's nuclear ambitions.[33] Simultaneously, there was a gradual opening up of cultural relations between India and Pakistan. Pakistan permitted the entry of Indian films and cultural troupes after more than four decades. In July

2008, the Pakistani film *Ramchand Pakistani* made history when it was released simultaneously in both countries.[34] Though the Mumbai terrorist attacks of November 2008 marked a sharp setback to relations generally, the 2008–9 crisis was less severe than the three previous ones. One encouraging sign was that, notwithstanding the chill, the rising volume of trade stayed on track, with Indian exports of tomatoes to Pakistan actually increasing during this period.[35]

Although nuclear weapons and economic interdependence impose constraints on the exercise of power in the traditional sense, power does play a significant role in other ways. First, economic power enables a nation to exercise influence over its interlocutors, whether by means of carrots or sticks. Here, India's emergence as a major economic player has occurred precisely at the time when Pakistan's economy has struggled to stay afloat, largely as a result of domestic political turmoil. Nowhere is this more evident than in the relationship between the two states and major international institutions. India's stature has risen sufficiently for it to count as an agenda-shaper on critical issues. For instance, the World Trade Organization's Doha Round of talks collapsed in July 2008 when India (in tandem with China) refused to bow to the US and European pressure to agree to jettison tariff safeguards for its farmers.[36] Similarly, the following month, India (again, along with China) successfully resisted efforts by developed nations at Accra in Ghana to impose greenhouse gas emission cuts on developing nations despite their low per capita contribution to global warming.[37] Clearly, India had demonstrated unprecedented institutional and economic power. In contrast, Pakistan by late 2008 was in dire straits, seeking a massive infusion of cash from lenders as its economy struggled to stem capital flight to the tune of US$ 15 billion annually.[38]

Second, political power still counts, for it determines the success or failure of states in negotiating their way through the institutional framework of international politics. On this front, India made a major breakthrough as a global player when, in the autumn of 2008, the US and the Nuclear Suppliers Group (NSG) agreed to change their restrictive rules and engage in civilian nuclear commerce with it.[39] Washington's insistence that this was a single exception and that Pakistan would not get a similar deal underscored what has come to be known as a policy of 'de-hyphenating' the neighbours and providing only India with special treatment.[40] In effect, the new dispensation recognized India's status as a nuclear weapons power since it involved the acknowledgement of a plan separating the Indian civilian and military programmes. Beneath the expressions of concern about India's need for nuclear energy lay a structural calculus: the interests of India and the US, backed by major components of the NSG, converged over the need to hedge against the new superpower-in-waiting, China.[41] Economics counted as well: the Indian nuclear energy market was enormous, with US Assistant Commerce Secretary David Bohigian estimating it at about US$ 100 billion over a decade.[42]

Though Pakistan's acquisition of nuclear weapons gave it military status comparable to India, the latter's combination of rising economic and political power has widened the gap between them significantly. This gap further encourages (but does not necessitate) long-term cooperation between the two countries. India's strategic horizons have spread well beyond the subcontinent and it needs a modicum of stability in its immediate environs to enable it to play a bigger role in Asia. Pakistan, weakened as never before by internal difficulties, has been placed in a position where the economic cost of challenging India is rising rapidly, while the military and economic incentives to cooperate are growing simultaneously.

Thus, at the systemic level, the structurally driven behaviour of yesteryear was altered as a consequence of fundamental changes occurring in the process of the relationship. The synchronized impact of nuclear weapons and economic transnationalization created the conditions for the shift by (i) providing security from attack to Pakistan and thereby reducing its sense of vulnerability; (ii) producing sufficient risk to encourage leaders to rethink their relationship; and (iii) creating stronger incentives to cooperate, both because nuclear weapons brought a mutual interest in stability and because global economic pressures introduced the prospect of higher returns from cooperation.[43] But the change was not predetermined. Rather, it was made through specific decisions in both countries—decisions that need not have been made. We will return to this later.

IDENTITY AND POLITICS AT THE STATE LEVEL

Contrasting conceptions of national identity were deeply embedded in the hostility between India and Pakistan. Torn apart at the moment of independence, the two countries sought to build very different kinds of nation-states.[44] India under Jawaharlal Nehru sought an inclusive identity, which would give its extraordinarily diverse social segments—both horizontal (ethnic) and vertical (caste/tribe/class)—expression in the making of the collective future. Pakistan, created by Muhammad Ali Jinnah's assertion of Muslim separateness, was less sure of itself and tended to swing between modernist and secular versions of an Islamic identity. The violence of Partition, 'a nightmare from which the subcontinent has not yet fully recovered', persists in the mutual perceptions of the two countries.[45] Its political potency is reflected in the sharply opposing views of ordinary Indians and Pakistanis on Kashmir, the bone of contention between them.[46]

Kashmir remains the symbol of an incomplete parting and a mutually exclusive conception of identity, each country claiming it in its own image. Kashmir's import is multiplied by the centrifugal forces that have threatened to tear both countries apart from time to time. Both, conscious of their internal diversity, fear that the loss of Kashmir will set in motion a process of political disintegration. But while India is relatively status quo-ist, Pakistan has tried hard to alter the status quo. India has been content to retain its portion of Kashmir without making an effort to change the situation on the ground because its control of the Kashmir Valley, a Muslim-majority area, allows it to retain its claim to being a state that can accommodate Muslims. In contrast, Pakistan, always vulnerable and rendered even more so by the breaking away of Bangladesh in 1971, finds the physical alienation of Kashmir deeply hurtful and has repeatedly tried to extract the territory from India by force and by diplomacy. Nowhere has the intensity of the symbolic tug-of-war been more graphically illustrated than in the prolonged military contest for the icy wasteland of northern Kashmir's Siachen glacier, where a hostile geography has exacted a far larger toll than has sporadic fighting since the early 1980s.

Identity is not as straightforward as it is often made out to be. Anthropologists know that ethnic groups are not simply 'etic' or empirically defined aggregations of people with common physical or cultural characteristics, but are more properly 'emic' or self-defining.[47] An individual's sense of affinity with a group is defined externally by the group's separateness from other groups and internally by a sense of belonging arising from participation in the life of the group. Given that a large group is almost always diverse, participation in the collective life of a group (doing) is essential to identification with it (feeling).[48] At the level of the nation-state, this means that a voice, in and therefore a positive contribution to social and political life, is the essential prerequisite of a strong sense of national identity. If the external component of identity is not adequately balanced by the internal, there is an inbuilt tendency to reinforce identity in opposition to a collective external Other. In the case of India and Pakistan, this has been all too evident.

The Kashmir issue was, from the beginning, aggravated by domestic struggles over power sharing that kept the internal component of identity weak and made hostility towards the neighbour an important element of national sentiment. Over time, India's experience was relatively positive. Under Prime Minister Nehru, power was exercised democratically but was nevertheless centralized because of the dominance of the Indian National Congress, which had led the movement for independence under Mohandas Gandhi. Subsequently, Nehru's daughter, Indira Gandhi (no relation of her namesake above) tried to forestall the weakening of the Congress by centralizing power. But barring the aberration of a period of emergency rule (1975–7), an inexorable process of decentralization set in, making coalition governments the rule by the late twentieth century despite the continuing elevation to premiership of members of the Nehru–Indira Gandhi 'dynasty'.[49]

Though pockmarked by recurrent religious, linguistic, and caste conflicts, the Indian polity gradually evolved into a stable democracy in which political power was decentralized and the periodic transfer of power after elections was smooth. The state responded to regular outbursts of secessionist violence with force, but also with a willingness to negotiate. The democratic structure developed a fairly stable process of articulating and negotiating differences.[50] The fragmented character of Indian society ensured that no serious hegemony was possible. The Hindu right under the Bharatiya Janata Party (BJP), which held power from 1998 to 2004, sought with little success to establish Hindutva (or Hindu-ness) as an alternative unifying ethos.[51] Power in India's democratic framework could be attained by even the most powerful groups only through coalitions, which invariably meant compromising political platforms. Since 1989, all general elections have produced multi-party coalition governments.[52] Notwithstanding its multitude of deficiencies, the Indian political system has been built on the participation of an expanding set of players, gradually reaching down towards the most disadvantaged strata. This has engendered the sense of belonging that comprises the domestic element of identity. But the flaws in the system have been evident from its numerous maladies—persistent poverty and hunger, pervasive corruption, a growing Maoist movement in its heartland, and the endless turmoil in Jammu and Kashmir, the last a failure which has intensified the tension with Pakistan.[53] Thus, the internal face of Indian identity is still scarred with a degree of uncertainty and tension.

For Pakistan, the problem was always more difficult because it began with severe handicaps. Grafting a 'fundamentally non-territorial vision of nationality' onto a physically bounded space without the benefit of a history was difficult enough.[54] To attempt it in a society that was ethnically fragmented demanded an effort of Herculean proportions, and neither the leadership (after the early demise of Jinnah and Liaqat Ali Khan) nor the institutional framework for this was available. East Pakistan broke away to form Bangladesh in 1971, and other territories became restless. While the army and the mainstream political parties failed to bring enduring stability, their tensions instead provided political space for Islamic extremism and a 'culture of jihad'.[55] Thanks to its fractured polity, Pakistan has been unable to develop the inner confidence that would have permitted a more sanguine approach towards India, especially Kashmir.

The Pakistani state has tottered between civilian and military control.[56] The army under Ayub Khan overthrew a fractious and unstable government in 1958, but, unable to hold the country together, it gave power back to the civilians following the loss of East Pakistan in 1971. Zulfiqar Ali Bhutto's Pakistan People's Party (PPP) performed no better, resulting in General Zia ul Haq's takeover in 1977. Zia tried and executed Bhutto and reoriented the Pakistani state towards a more severe form of Islam, but he unleashed fundamentalist forces in the process. Civilian rule returned upon Zia's death in 1988 to perform indifferently under the alternating governments of Benazir Bhutto's PPP and Nawaz Sharif's Pakistan Muslim League. But Nawaz's attempt to enervate the army brought a coup in 1999 by General Pervez Musharraf, who ran the country first as chief executive and later as president till yet another popular upsurge led to the revival of civilian authority in 2008. Though Musharraf remained president, the focus of power shifted to the PPP, now under Asif Ali Zardari, who took control of the party following the assassination of his wife Benazir. The hegemony of the army has from time to time been embattled, but has nevertheless remained in place. It has tried to strengthen its position by allying with religious parties, by manipulating extremist groups against opponents, and by obtaining financial and political support from the US.[57] But neither direct nor indirect control has worked very long, and Pakistani politics has been dogged by instability.

Driven by systemic incentives, both India and Pakistan have moved away from their zero-sum approaches to the Kashmir problem and sought to build bridges by loosening controls on the cross-border/LoC movement of people and goods. But factors operating at the state level have ensured that the movement towards peace has been a slow crawl. India has been status quo-ist rather than revisionist, but it has also lacked the capacity to move quickly and substantially towards entente with Pakistan. In an era of coalition governments, the task of hammering out a consensus on virtually any issue requiring a significant shift from established policy has been extraordinarily arduous. Additionally, the rise of 'Hindutva' ideology and its hawkish stance towards Pakistan have made political compromise difficult.

The prospects of a 'democratic peace' between India and Pakistan remain limited for the near future.[58] The truism that democracies do not fight one another applies only to developed capitalist societies, and neither is anywhere close to being that. India is still vulnerable to powerful forces prone to manipulate identity issues for electoral purposes. Pakistan remains a 'hybrid' democracy—an uneasy mix of populism and military power—in which democratic parties are prone to 'outbid' each other in appeasing conservative elements opposed to an India–Pakistan rapprochement and the army has a stake in limiting the prospects for peace when its domestic position is threatened.[59] While India has over the years emerged as a relatively 'self-confident state', Pakistan has not.[60] Yet, India's self-confidence should not be exaggerated. The politics of outbidding has not disappeared. Opposition parties remain alert to the aggrandizing possibilities inherent in conflict with the external other by mobilizing protest against compromise. Thus, BJP's Advani asserted in 2004 that 'the BJP alone can find a solution to problems with Pakistan because Hindus will never think that whatever we have done can be a sell-off', adding the unsurprising corollary that 'the Congress can never do this because Hindus will not trust it'.[61] Ultimately, with neither country's government particularly strong, the prospects of a risk-taking breakthrough based on a compromise over Kashmir remain limited for the foreseeable future.

INDIVIDUALS AND LEADERSHIP

The role of the individual in the making of foreign policy is often over-specified or underspecified as analysts tend either to focus largely on personalities or to treat states as the primary actors in international relations. Gauging the effect that individuals have on large events is difficult. Yet we cannot deny that on occasion they do have a powerful influence in shaping the relations between states. A name that quickly comes to mind is that of Mikhail Gorbachev, who is widely credited with having the political courage and the skill to initiate the end of the Cold War.[62]

How have individual leaders affected the course of the India–Pakistan relationship? In the early years, India had powerful leaders who were able to direct the course of foreign policy with a degree of confidence. Nehru, in particular, was a dominant figure in the making of foreign policy, and the direction that Indian policy took was in large part determined by his personality, preferences, and decisions. His policies were characterized by considerable contradiction between idealism and realism.[63] Thus, his penchant for playing a global role on behalf of India was not backed by a realistic preparation of the hard power capabilities to back it up. This became evident from the Indian army's lacklustre performance against Pakistan in 1947–8 and China in 1962. It took the more realist personalities of Lal Bahadur Shastri and Indira Gandhi to use the military effectively against Pakistan, the former expelling Pakistani forces from India in 1965, the latter decisively defeating and breaking up Pakistan in 1971.[64] Subsequently, till the end of the century, as political power shifted from Congress dominance to a patchwork of coalitions, Indian leaders were too weak to take major initiatives.

On the other side, Pakistan lost its major leaders, Jinnah and Liaqat Ali Khan, shortly after independence, and the intense competition for power did not permit individual leaders to give decisive direction to foreign policy. The populist Zulfiqar Ali Bhutto did not match in practice the expectations he generated and was central to both the loss of East Pakistan as well as to the return of the army soon after. It was the military as a whole rather than individual commanders that shaped the orientation towards India. General Zia directed much of his political energy towards recasting Pakistan in an Islamic mould and keeping India at arm's length. The last quarter of the twentieth century produced no leader of exceptional capability who might have been able to surmount the constraints imposed by systemic and state-level factors to alter the trajectory of India–Pakistan relations. Both Benazir Bhutto and Nawaz Sharif aroused high expectations, but they failed to meet them. As the Pakistani state became bogged down in a morass of inefficiency and corruption, the army entrenched itself, and the populace became increasingly disaffected, all of which fed into a growing turbulence.

With the turn of the millennium, the opportunity for individual initiative was provided by the crises that beset their relationship after India and Pakistan officially went nuclear. Having peered into the abyss, leaders on both sides sought to break new ground. To his credit, Indian Prime Minister Atal Bihari Vajpayee had made the effort almost immediately after the 1998 nuclear tests and travelled to Lahore in early 1999 to attempt a rapprochement. But the response had been shallow, producing the Kargil crisis a few weeks later. A mutual effort to come to terms led Vajpayee and Pakistan President Pervez Musharraf to confer at Agra in 2001, but nothing came of it. After the 2001–2 crisis had subsided, Vajpayee and Musharraf responded symmetrically and a composite dialogue on major issues of dispute began in 2004. Though he was much vilified in India as the brain behind Pakistan's Kargil adventure, Musharraf revealed a remarkable willingness to discard old shibboleths. Vajpayee's successor, Manmohan Singh, showed similar flexibility. By mid-2007, both had indicated obliquely a new readiness to consider dividing Kashmir permanently.[65]

Singh and Pakistan's Zardari maintained continuity, but the peace process was slowed down by Pakistan's internal troubles as well as by the revival of India–Pakistan tensions over the 2008 Mumbai terrorist attacks.

As observed earlier, leadership initiative was curbed by state-level constraints. BJP's Advani, now in opposition, attempted to bridge the divide in the summer of 2005, but was compelled to backtrack quickly when his own followers became critical of his going 'soft' on Pakistan. Similarly, Zardari's criticism of 'terrorists' in Kashmir in the autumn of 2008 aroused a storm of protest in Pakistan. Nevertheless, the composite dialogue was sustained by a succession of leaders on both sides and made significant progress towards improved relations. As a result of leadership persistence, a set of informal principles crystallized to mark the new character of the India–Pakistan relationship. It was understood that the LoC would not be altered but in a sense transcended by expanded communication; there would be a new focus on self-governance on both sides; military forces would eventually be reduced substantially; and India and Pakistan would work together to build a mechanism for implementing the process.[66] Most importantly, both countries shed their old inflexibility and agreed not only to negotiate on all major outstanding disputes, but to discard their non-negotiable and mutually exclusive positions on Kashmir. New thinking was not lacking on either side.

However, it takes a leader of exceptional commitment and skill to override the pressures emanating from factors operating at the system and state levels. The likes of Gorbachev (or, on the negative side, Hitler) are uncommon. In the South Asian context, Vajpayee was unusual in that he had a history of attempting good-neighbourly relations going as far back as the mid-1970s when he had been minister for external affairs. His persistence in the 1990s and thereafter, and certainly the positive response from Musharraf after 2003, were more the products of learning from hard experience that the advent of nuclear weapons had drastically narrowed their options. Indian and Pakistani leaders simply lacked the capacity to override the dictates of state-level pressures. In particular, domestic politics—relatively weak government control and strong opposition to major concessions—did not permit dramatic departures from prevailing policy.

* * *

The India–Pakistan relationship was characterized by unremitting hostility from 1947 till the turn of the millennium. For this entire period, systemic, state-level, and individual-level dynamics pushed in the same direction. Within it, there was one turning point. Till 1971, there was no clear strong state/weak state pattern in the relationship. Though India had the attributes of a strong state, it was relatively cautious. Pakistan was the weaker, yet the more aggressive in initiating war twice. In late 1971, largely owing to the initiative taken by Indira Gandhi, India defeated and broke up Pakistan, thereby producing a well-defined strong state/weak state pattern. This lasted till the late 1980s as Pakistan sought (successfully) to remedy the situation by pursuing the acquisition of nuclear weapons.

By the late 1980s, systemic constraints on conflict and incentives to cooperate gradually began to appear with the covert advent of nuclear weapons and the onset of economic liberalization in the region. Individual leaders, learning from the crises of 1990, 1999, and 2001–2, sought to attune themselves to the systemic changes in progress; major initiatives to break the ice were taken by Vajpayee and Musharraf, with their successors sustaining the new orientation. The setback over the Mumbai terrorist attacks of 2008 significantly slowed but did not derail the peace process. However, state-level politics was not congruent with systemic and leadership shifts. Efforts to build bridges were hampered by the relative weakness of governments, persistent identity politics, and the readiness of powerful groups, such as the religious right in both countries and the army in Pakistan, to block a rapprochement.

Where is the India–Pakistan relationship headed? The systemic pressures for cooperation are powerful and almost certainly cannot be turned back. Individual leaders who have to confront these pressures directly in the process of policy-making are likely to appreciate the need for change and continue to seek resolution. But they are just as likely to be slowed down by state-level politics. Under the existing circumstances, it would take a pair of exceptionally determined and skilful leaders to carry the relationship towards either a high degree of cooperation or the renewal of unremitting hostility. Since it is not in the cards that systemic trends will be reversed, system–state complementarity can only be positive, almost certainly never negative. But for a positive transformation to occur, we will have to await changes at the state level that produce confidence in self-identity and democratization on both sides. The two processes, as we have seen, are closely intertwined. Given the political realities of the subcontinent, they are also likely to be slow-moving. Accordingly, we may expect at worst a persistent but restrained hostility between the two countries and at best incremental and cumulative improvement rather than a dramatic breakthrough in the relationship.

NOTES

1. For a detailed review and analysis, see Sumit Ganguly (2002), *Conflict Unending: India–Pakistan Tensions since 1947* (New Delhi: Oxford University Press). For an extended series of discussions on this 'enduring rivalry', see T.V. Paul (ed.) (2005), *The India–Pakistan Conflict: An Enduring Rivalry* (Cambridge: Cambridge University Press).

2. For a sharp distinction between system structure and process, see Kenneth N. Waltz (1979), *Theory of International Politics* (Lexington, MA: Addison-Wesley).

3. By far the best enunciation of the liberal position in the sense used here is still Robert O. Keohane and Joseph S. Nye, Jr (1977), *Power and Interdependence: World Politics in Transition* (Boston: Little Brown).

4. Mikhail Gorbachev (1988), *Perestroika: New Thinking for Our Country and the World* (New York: Harper and Collins). That he failed does not detract from the validity of his insight.

5. Benjamin Miller (2002), *When Opponents Cooperate: Great Power Conflict and Collaboration in World Politics* (Ann Arbor: University of Michigan Press).

6. For a detailed analysis of the concept and its variable application in different contexts, see Rajesh M. Basrur (2000), *India's External Relations: A Theoretical Analysis* (New Delhi: Commonwealth Publishers).

7. Michael Mandelbaum (1988), *The Fate of Nations: The Search for National Security in the Nineteenth and Twentieth Centuries* (Cambridge: Cambridge University Press).

8. World Bank (2000), *World Development Report 1999–2000* (Washington, DC: World Bank).

9. Stephen P. Cohen (2005), *The Idea of Pakistan* (New Delhi: Oxford University Press), p. 103.

10. Ganguly, *Conflict Unending*, pp. 7–8.

11. Amaury de Riencourt (1982–3), 'India and Pakistan in the Shadow of Afghanistan', *Foreign Affairs*, 81 (2), p. 433.

12. International Institute of Strategic Studies (1999), *The Military Balance, 1999–2000* (Oxford: Oxford University Press).

13. Ibid.

14. R.G. Gidadhubli (2005), 'India–Pakistan Trade: Problems and Prospects', in P.M. Kamath (ed.), *India–Pakistan Relations: Courting Peace from the Corridors of War* (New Delhi: Promilla and Company, in association with Bibliophile Asia), p. 135. On problems relating to trade, see Bidanda M. Chengappa (1999), 'India–Pakistan Trade Relations', *Strategic Analysis*, 23 (3), pp. 443–57.

15. International Monetary Fund (1998), *Direction of Trade Statistics Yearbook, 1998* (Washington, DC: International Monetary Fund).

16. Irfan Husain (1997), *Pakistan* (Karachi: Oxford University Press), p. 12; cited in Maneesha Tikekar, 'Cultural Idiom in the Indo-Pak Conflict', in Kamath (ed.), *India–Pakistan Relations*, p. 196.

17. Scott D. Sagan and Kenneth N. Waltz (2003), *The Spread of Nuclear Weapons: A Debate Renewed* (New York and London: W.W. Norton). The authors specifically debate the issue of stability in South Asia in Chapter 3. See also Sumit Ganguly (2008), 'Nuclear Stability in South Asia', *International Security*, 33 (2), pp. 45–70, and S. Paul Kapur (2008), 'Ten Years of Instability in a Nuclear South Asia', *International Security*, 33 (2), pp. 71–94.

18. Rajesh M. Basrur (2008), *South Asia's Cold War: Nuclear Weapons and Conflict in Comparative Perspective* (Abingdon and New York: Routledge), see especially Chapter 2.

19. P.R. Chari, Pervaiz Iqbal Cheema, and Stephen P. Cohen (2007), *Four Crises and A Peace Process: American Engagement in South Asia* (Washington, D.C.: Brookings Institution Press); Sumit Ganguly and Devin T. Hagerty (2005), *Fearful Symmetry: India–Pakistan Crises in the Shadow of Nuclear Weapons* (New Delhi: Oxford University Press).

20. S. Paul Kapur (2007), *Dangerous Deterrent: Nuclear Weapons Proliferation and Conflict in South Asia* (Stanford, CA: Stanford University Press). See also Peter Chalk (2001), 'Pakistan's Role in the Kashmir Insurgency', *Jane's Intelligence Review*, 1 September, reproduced on the website of the RAND Corporation at http://www.rand.org/hot/op-eds/090101JIR.html (accessed on 14 February 2003), and Praveen Swami (2004), 'Failed Threats and Flawed Fences: India's Military Responses to Pakistan's Proxy War', *India Review*, 3 (2), pp. 147–70. This support was initiated early by way of backing extended to Sikh separatists fighting for an independent 'Khalistan', but was intensified when a popular upsurge occurred in Kashmir.

21. Bruce Riedel (2002), *American Diplomacy and the 1999 Kargil Summit at Blair House* (Philadelphia, PA: University of Pennsylvania, Center for the Advanced Study of India), p. 2; Vikas Kapur and Vipin Narang (2001), 'The Fate of Kashmir: International Law or Lawlessness?', *Stanford Law Journal*, 31 (1), http://www.stanford.edu/group/sjir/3.1.06_kapur-narang.html (accessed on 28 May 2009). Though the events of 1999 are frequently treated as a 'war', I concur with V.R. Raghavan, a former Director-General of Military Operations with the Indian Army, that Kargil was not so much a war as 'a series of local military actions...to clear Indian territory of intruders'. V.R. Raghavan (2000), 'Limited War and Strategic Liability', *The Hindu*, 2 February http://www.hinduonnet.com/thehindu/2000/02/02/stories/05022523.htm (accessed on 21 October 2008).

22. Rajesh M. Basrur (2005), 'Coercive Diplomacy in A Nuclear Environment: The December 13 Crisis', in Rafiq Dossani and Henry Rowen (eds), *Prospects for Peace in South Asia* (Stanford, CA: Stanford University Press); Sumit Ganguly and R. Harrison Wagner (2004), 'India and Pakistan: Bargaining in the Shadow of Nuclear War', *Journal of Strategic Studies*, 27 (3), pp. 479–507.

23. Angela Rabasa, Robert D. Blackwill, Peter Chalk, Kim Cragin, C. Christine Fair,

Brian A. Jackson, Brian Michael Jenkins, Seth G. Jones, Nathaniel Shestak, and Ashley J. Tellis (2009), *The Lessons of Mumbai* (Santa Monica, CA: RAND).

24. While it could be argued that there was no real crisis, such a conclusion cannot be made with confidence. In May 2009, India's Air Force chief, Fali Major, let it be known that an Indian strike had been on the cards immediately after the terrorist attacks, for which Pakistan was widely blamed within India. 'India Came Close to Striking Pak after 26/11: Air Chief', *The Times of India*, 28 May 2009, http://timesofindia.indiatimes.com/India-came-close-to-striking-Pak-after-2611-Air-chief/articleshow/4586233.cms (accessed on 28 May 2009).

25. Verghese Koithara (2007), 'The Advancing Peace Process', *Economic and Political Weekly*, 41 (52), 6 January, pp. 10–13.

26. Daniel Bell (1989), 'The Third Technological Revolution and Its Possible Consequences', *Dissent*, 36 (2), pp. 164–76.

27. International Monetary Fund (1990), *International Financial Statistics Yearbook 1990* (Washington, DC: International Monetary Fund).

28. Nigel Harris (1986), *The End of the Third World: Newly Industrialising Countries and the Decline of An Ideology* (London: Penguin Books).

29. 'War at What Cost?', *The Hindu*, 6 January 2002 http://www.hinduonnet.com/thehindu/2002/01/06/stories/2002010600681500.htm (accessed on 21 October 2008); Sandeep Dikshit (2002), 'Paying the Piper', *The Hindu*, 9 June. http://www.hinduonnet.com/thehindu/2002/06/09/stories/2002060900191600.htm (accessed on 21 October 2008).

30. Thomas L. Friedman (2002), 'India, Pakistan and G.E.', *New York Times*, 11 August, http://query.nytimes.com/gst/fullpage.html?res=940CEED9153AF932 A2575BC0A9649C8B63 (accessed on 21 October 2008).

31. 'Indian Imports to Flood Pak Markets', *News International*, 19 July 2008. http://thenews.jang.com.pk/top_story_detail.asp?Id=16070 (accessed on19 July 2008).

32. The figures for the two dates are taken from separate sources: 'India, Pak Agree on Easing Norms for Cement, Tea Trade', *The Times of India*, 2 August 2007, http://timesofindia.indiatimes.com/India/India_Pak_agree_on_easing_norms_for_cement_tea_trade_/articleshow/2249954.cms (accessed on 2 August 2007) and 'New Pakistan Trade Policy to Double Indo-Pak Trade', *The Times of India*, 24 July 2008, http://timesofindia.indiatimes.com/India/India_Pakistan_trade_policy_to_double_Indo-Pak_trade/articleshow/3274837.cms (accessed on 24 July 2008).

33. Rajesh M. Basrur (2006), 'India's Hard Choice', *Heartland: Eurasian Review of Geopolitics*, 3, pp. 42–7, http://www.heartland.it/_lib/_docs/2006_03_The_ Eastern_challenge.pdf (accessed on 23 October 2008); S.G. Pandian (2005), 'Energy Trade as a Confidence-Building Measure between India and Pakistan: A Study of the Indo-Iran Trans-Pakistan Pipeline Project', *Contemporary South Asia*, 14 (3), pp. 307–20.

34. Zubair Ahmed (2008), 'Pakistan Film Makes India Record', *BBC News*, 14 July,

http://news.bbc.co.uk/go/pr/fr/-2/hi/south_asia/7506364.stm (accessed on 11 August 2008).

35. Dinker Vashisht and Gaurav Sharma (2009), 'One Thing Pak Doesn't See Red Over: Tomatoes from India', *Indian Express*, 1 March, http://www.indianexpress. com/news/one-thing-pak-doesnt-see-red-over-tomatoes-from-india/429352/ (accessed on 1 March 2009).

36. John Miller (2008), 'Global Trade Talks Fail as New Giants Flex Muscle', *Wall Street Journal*, 30 July, p. A.1.

37. Nitin Sethi (2008), 'India, China Join Hands against Rich Countries', *The Times of India*, 28 August, http://timesofindia.indiatimes.com/Climate_talks_India_ China_join_hands/articleshow/3413939.cms (accessed on 21 October).

38. Tariq Butt (2008), 'National Debts [sic] Up by Rs 900 Billion as Rupee Plunges', *News International*, 20 October, http://www.thenews.com.pk/top_story_detail. asp?Id=17906 (accessed on 21 October 2008); Ikram Sehgal (2008), 'The "Hawala" Drain', *News International*, 21 October, http://www.thenews.com.pk/ daily_detail.asp?id=142168 (accessed on 21 October 2008).

39. Siddharth Varadarajan (2008), 'NSG Lifts Sanctions on India', *The Hindu*, 7 September, http://www.thehindu.com/2008/09/07/stories/2008090757400100. htm (accessed on 7 September 2008).

40. Ashley J. Tellis (2008), 'The Merits of Dehyphenation: Explaining US Success in Engaging India and Pakistan', *Washington Quarterly*, 31 (4), pp. 21–42.

41. Stephen Blank (2007), 'The Geostrategic Implications of the Indo-American Strategic Partnership', *India Review*, 6 (1), pp. 1–24.

42. 'India's Nuclear Energy Trade to Touch USD 100 bn in 10 Years: US', *The Times of India*, 9 September 2008, http://timesofindia.indiatimes.com/India/Indias N-energy_trade_to_touch_USD_100_bn_in_10_yrs_US/articleshow/3464364. cms (accessed on 10 September 2008).

43. For a similar argument, see E. Sridharan (2005), 'Improving Indo-Pakistan Relations: International Relations Theory, Nuclear Deterrence and Possibilities for Economic Cooperation', *Contemporary South Asia*, 14 (3), pp. 321–39.

44. Rajen Harshe (2005), 'India–Pakistan Conflict over Kashmir: Peace through Development Cooperation', *South Asian Survey*, 12 (1), pp. 47–60.

45. Sugata Bose and Ayesha Jalal (2004), *Modern South Asia: History, Culture, Political Economy*, 2nd edn (London and New York: Routledge), p. 164.

46. Steven Kull Clay Ramsay, Stephen Weber, and Evan Lewis (2008), 'Pakistani and Indian Public Opinion on Kashmir and Indo-Pakistani Relations', World Public Opinion.org, Washington DC, 16 July, http://www.worldpublicopinion. org/pipa/pdf/jul08/Kashmir_Jul08_rpt.pdf (accessed on 23 August 2008).

47. Thomas Hylland Eriksen (2002), *Ethnicity and Nationalism*, 2nd edn (London and Sterling, VA: Pluto Press, pp. 11–13. The terms 'emic' and 'etic' are derived from phonemics and phonetics. Ibid., p. 12.

48. Maykel Verkuyten (2005), *The Social Psychology of Ethnic Identity* (Hove and New York: Psychology Press), pp. 50–4.

49. Indira's son, Rajiv Gandhi, was PM from 1984 to 1989. His widow Sonia Gandhi led the Congress to victory in the elections of 2004, but preferred to install Manmohan Singh as PM while retaining final authority through her control of the party.

50. Pratap Bhanu Mehta (2006), 'Identity Politics in an Era of Globalization', in A. Kelly, Ramkishen S. Rajan and Gillian H.L. Goh (eds), *Managing Globalization: Lessons from India and China* (Singapore: World Scientific Press).

51. Manjeet S. Pardesi and Jennifer L. Oetken (2008), 'Secularism, Democracy, and Hindu Nationalism in India', *Asian Security*, 4 (1), pp. 23–40.

52. For detailed statistics on India's elections, see the website of the Election Commission of India at http://www.eci.gov.in.

53. On the many challenges remaining before Indian democracy, see Rajesh M. Basrur (ed.) (2009), *Challenges for Indian Democracy* (New Delhi: Oxford University Press).

54. David Gilmartin (1998), 'Partition, Pakistan, and South Asian History: In Search of a Narrative', *Journal of South Asian History*, 57 (4), pp. 1068–95.

55. Jessica Stern (2002), 'Pakistan's Jihad Culture', in Harvey W. Kushner (ed.), *Essential Readings on Political Terrorism: Analyses of Problems and Prospects for the Twenty First Century* (New York: Gordian Knot Books).

56. Irm Haleem (2003), 'Ethnic and Sectarian Violence and the Propensity toward Praetorianism in Pakistan', *Third World Quarterly*, 24 (3), pp. 463–77.

57. Husain Haqqani (2005), *Pakistan: Between Mosque and Military* (Lahore: Vanguard Books).

58. The idea of the democratic peace has a rich intellectual history. For a recent review, see Thomas Jay Nisley (2008), 'The Pugnacious and the Pacific: Why Some Democracies Fight Wars', *International Politics*, 45 (2), pp. 168–81. On its limited applicability in the South Asian context, see Sumit Ganguly, 'War and Conflict between India and Pakistan: Revisiting the Pacifying Power of Democracy', in Mirium Fendius Elman (1997) (ed.), *Paths to Peace: Is Democracy the Answer?* (Cambridge, MA and London: MIT Press).

59. On Pakistan as a 'hybrid democracy', see Rita Chowdhari Tremblay and Julian Schofield (2005), 'Institutional Causes of the India–Pakistan Rivalry', in Paul (ed.), *India–Pakistan Conflict*, pp. 227–37.

60. Christophe Jaffrelot (2002), 'India and Pakistan: Interpreting the Divergence of Two Political Trajectories', *Cambridge Review of International Affairs*, 15 (2), pp. 251–67.

61. Cited in Siddharth Varadarajan (2004), 'BJP may Play Spoiler in Foreign Affairs', *The Times of India*, 14 May, http://timesofindia.indiatimes.com/articleshow/676324.cms (accessed on 14 May).

62. Vladislav M. Zubok (2002), 'Gorbachev and the End of the Cold War:

Perspectives on History and Personality', *Cold War History*, 2 (2), pp. 61–100. See also Jacques Lévesque (1997), *The Enigma of 1989: The Liberation of Eastern Europe* (Berkeley, CA: University of California Press).

63. Jayantanuja Bandyopadhyaya (1979), *The Making of India's Foreign Policy: Determinants, Institutions, Processes and Personalities*, rev. edn (New Delhi: Allied Publishers), pp. 291–8. See also M.S. Rajan, 'Introduction: India's Foreign Policy under Nehru', in M.S. Rajan (ed.) (1976), *India's Foreign Relations during the Nehru Era: Some Studies* (Bombay: Asia Publishing House), p. xvi.

64. Surjit Mansingh (1984), *India's Search for Power: Indira Gandhi's Foreign Policy, 1966–1982* (New Delhi: Sage Publications), pp. 302–8.

65. Iftikhar Gilani (2007), 'Manmohan Speaks of Trisecting Kashmir', *Daily Times*, 25 April 2007, http://www.dailytimes.com.pk/default. asp?page=2007/04/25story_25-4-2007_pgl_1 (accessed on 25 April 2005); Khalid Hasan (2007), 'There is a Need to Identify What is Kashmir: Musharraf', *Daily Times* (Pakistan), 5 June, http://www.dailytimes.com.pk/default. asp?page=2007\06\05\story_5-6-2007_pg7_9 (accessed on 5 June 2007).

66. Koithara, 'Advancing Peace Process'.

3

When Individuals, States, and Systems Collide

India's Foreign Policy towards Sri Lanka

NEIL DEVOTTA

Those studying Indian foreign policy towards its neighbours rightly emphasize Pakistan and China, given that both states have waged war against India and both challenge India's regional dominance and aspirations for great power status. While none would place Sri Lanka at par with Pakistan and China, during the last three decades the small island to India's south has arguably bedevilled Indian leaders as much as any regional nemesis. Indeed, no South Asian country's ethnic politics has adversely affected India as has Sri Lanka's ethnic imbroglio· between the majority Sinhalese and minority Tamils. It led to heavy-handed Indian meddling in Sri Lanka's internal affairs throughout the 1980s and the country's longest war, when the Indian Peace Keeping Force (IPKF) fought the Liberation Tigers of Tamil Eelam (LTTE), which was battling to create a separate state for Tamils in Sri Lanka; prompted the Central government in January 1991 to sack Tamil Nadu's Dravida Munnetra Kazhagam (Dravida Progress Party or DMK) for not cracking down on the LTTE; saw an LTTE suicide bomber assassinate a former prime minister and scion of the Nehru–Gandhi political dynasty in May 1991; and goads politicians in Tamil Nadu to outbid each other when defending the rights of Sri Lanka's Tamils in ways that sometimes embarrass the Indian government and complicate Indo-Sri Lankan relations. Sri Lanka's politics thus not only affects politics in Tamil Nadu, it sometimes destabilizes coalition governments in New Delhi. Indeed, India's elite seem to know how best to engage Pakistan and China, while they appear unsure how to deal with Sri Lanka.

According to neorealism, the international system—and not a country's domestic politics or individual leaders' preferences—dictates opportunities and constraints that all states within a given system (unipolar, bipolar, or multipolar) must negotiate.[1] While the specific strategy that leaders adopt and how effectively they enforce such strategy when negotiating the system-imposed opportunities and constraints cannot be known, neorealism claims that decision-making can be predicted within a given range for the system in place. Kenneth Waltz has argued that neorealism seeks to explain international politics, not foreign policy.[2] But various scholars have utilized realist and neorealist insights to try and explain countries' foreign policies.[3]

In India's case, the country's complex domestic challenges—caste-based violence, communal tensions, widespread poverty, corruption, secessionist pressures, maddening coalition politics, and absence of the rule of law in many areas—combine with its strategic interests and global aspirations to influence foreign policy. Thus, a purely Waltzian approach that privileges the systemic level is inadequate to explain India's foreign policy decision-making. An analysis that incorporates systemic opportunities and constraints and domestic pressures, while also taking into consideration India's changing relative material power capabilities and their influence on threat perceptions, is better suited for the task.[4] How the country's communist parties nearly undermined the United Progressive Alliance (UPA) government in July 2008, when they left the governing coalition in opposition to the India–United States nuclear deal, partly proves the point.

This chapter, consequently, argues that while India acts in accordance with its perceived national interests, those interests are influenced by both systemic and domestic considerations. For instance, Tamil Nadu has long exerted a major influence on India–Sri Lanka relations, just as Indian leaders' personal relations with their Sri Lankan counterparts have.[5] The first section explains why and contextualizes Indo-Sri Lankan relations, while also arguing that India's threat perceptions override the preferences of Tamil Nadu when it comes to the country's foreign policy towards Sri Lanka. The second section evaluates briefly Indian policy towards Sri Lanka during the Nehruvian period, while the following section covers the post-Nehruvian era until 1991. Not before or since has India been so radically involved in the island's affairs. The final section evaluates Indo-Lanka relations since the end of the Cold War, for it contrasts sharply from the 1980s. During this period, Indian policy towards the island has been twofold: promoting a political solution to the ethnic conflict while ensuring the LTTE does not succeed in creating a separate state. In the post-Cold

War era India has sought to maintain its preponderance in the region, while avoiding military ensnarement in Sri Lanka's affairs even when the latter has begged for greater involvement. But this standoffishness too has to do with India's current threat perceptions, relative power capabilities, and enhanced position in an increasingly multipolar world.

CONTEXTUALIZING INDO-SRI LANKAN RELATIONS

The vast majority of Sri Lanka's people are likely of Dravidian (south Indian) stock, although dubious claims and counter-claims have contributed to present Sinhalese–Tamil identities, attendant fissures, and civil war.[6] Even Sinhalese Buddhist mytho-history claims that the Sinhalese came from north India around 2,500 years ago, thus cementing India's progenitor status for the island's inhabitants. And it is clear that Indo-Lankan relations began at least by the time Buddhism spread from India to the island over 2,300 years ago.[7] The earliest references to the two countries go back to the Ramayana, which says that Ravana kept Sita in Lanka and that Hanuman and his monkey army built what is now known as Adam's Bridge so that Rama could cross over to the island and rescue his wife. The Sinhalese chronicle *Mahavamsa* (first written in the sixth century) also discusses numerous invasions from south India.

Sri Lanka's northeast has been economically connected to India since ancient times. There are over a dozen harbours in the northeast, and these were used to trade with especially southern India. Colombo became an important trading hub only around the turn of the twentieth century after the British, partly to ensure a monopoly in trade, conveniently branded Indian and northeast Sri Lankan trade as 'smuggling'. This hardly prevented groups in Sri Lanka's northeast and south India from continuing to trade. Places like Velvetiturai, home to Velupillai Prabhakaran and many other LTTE leaders, long remained famous smuggling posts.

A major reason why the LTTE, which is proscribed as a terrorist group in more than 30 countries (including India), and other Tamil groups were initially able to mobilize seeking *eelam* (a separate Tamil state in Sri Lanka's northeast) was because Tamil Nadu's citizens and politicians supported them. Tamil Nadu has 39 seats in Parliament, and the state's two dominant parties—DMK and All India Anna Dravida Munnetra Kazhagam (AIADMK)—have played an important role propping up coalition governments at the Centre since 1996. Thus, popular sentiment in Tamil Nadu towards the Sri Lankan Tamils' plight, the DMK and AIADMK's political opportunism especially during elections, and the pressure all this exerts on the Indian Central government cannot be discarded when considering India's foreign policy towards Sri Lanka. But Tamil Nadu does not determine Indian foreign policy towards Sri Lanka. The state does have small political parties, like the Marumalarchi Dravida Munnetra Kazhagam (MDMK) and Pattali Makkal Katchi (PMK), which have vociferously supported the LTTE even while being allied with major parties at the Centre. However, they have exerted little influence at the Centre.[8] Just as neorealist proponents dubiously attribute foreign policy decision-making to only systemic influences, certain Sinhalese Buddhist nationalists also mistakenly characterize Tamil Nadu as overly determining Indian policy towards Sri Lanka. They fail to recognize instances when Tamil Nadu's preferences were/are consubstantial with Indian national interest.

Indian civilization has greatly affected all South Asian states, and the accidental borders the British foisted on the region have complicated relations between India and her neighbours. For instance, most South Asian countries have ethnic groups with kinship ties to groups in India. This has caused ethno-religious conflicts in neighbouring states to get diffused into India, as ethnic kin across borders seek help from and provide help to each other. The Bengalis in East Pakistan did this during their civil war with West Pakistan, leading to the creation of Bangladesh; while the Sri Lankan Tamils did likewise when they began fighting for eelam. In the past India used such cross-border ethnic ties to get involved in the affairs of neighbouring states by claiming its security interests were 'coterminous with those of the region as a whole'.[9] Thus, the so-called 'Indira Doctrine' of the early 1980s, loosely modelled on USA's Monroe Doctrine, was said to reflect an Indian national consensus that 'India will not tolerate external intervention in a conflict situation in any South Asian country if the intervention has any implicit or explicit anti-Indian implication. No South Asian government should therefore ask for external assistance with an anti-Indian bias from any country.'[10] Furthermore, whenever the need for external assistance arises, South Asian states should seek help from neighbouring countries 'including India. The exclusion of India from such a contingency will be considered to be an anti-Indian move on the part of the government concerned.'[11] In the 1980s India consequently adapted an aggressive stance when J.R. Jayewardene and the United National Party (UNP) resorted to policies that India considered threatening. The position also dovetailed with sentiment in Tamil Nadu, a state with 50 million Tamils (at the time) who were angered by the discrimination the majority Sinhalese were inflicting on their Tamil cousins in Sri Lanka, although India's highhandedness was also influenced by the cold personal relations between Jayewardene and Indira Gandhi.

In 2000, however, India refused to intervene in Sri Lanka when the island pleaded for help to protect nearly 40,000 soldiers from the LTTE. Prime Minister Atal Bihari Vajpayee dismissed Sri Lanka's entreaties by saying, 'If Jaffna falls to the LTTE it will not be [for] the first time.'[12] The IPKF was considered a blunder; and India, no doubt, was unwilling to get bogged down once more in Sri Lanka's ethnic conflict at a time when its military forces were overstretched within India.[13] But India's disinclination to get involved (at this particular time) was mainly due to the belief that an LTTE take-over of the north as part of a turf war with the Sri Lankan military hardly undermined its regional interests. With no pressure from Tamil Nadu—support for the LTTE in Tamil Nadu dwindled after the group assassinated Rajiv Gandhi in 1991, and, if anything, the group's remaining supporters were urging the government to stay out so the LTTE could retake Jaffna—the Vajpayee government conveniently eschewed renewed military involvement in the island's affairs, although the Indian Navy did make provisions to help evacuate Sri Lankan soldiers on humanitarian grounds.

In the 1980s India was allied with the Soviet Union and viewed the United States (US) suspiciously. The unofficial 'Indira Doctrine' was most certainly influenced by bipolarity, and consequently the neighbouring states allied with the West or pursuing pro-Western policies were eyed disapprovingly. But this was not all. The July 1983 anti-Tamil riots in Sri Lanka, the nearly 1,50,000 refugees that fled to India, the domestic pressure on the Indian government as a result of those riots, and Sri Lanka's rather cavalier pro-Western policies without regard to Indian regional considerations prior to the riots also influenced the manner in which India sought to impose the Indira Doctrine. What merits emphasis here is that, while India sympathized with the Tamils' plight and was exceedingly sensitive to opinion in Tamil Nadu, its anti-Sri Lankan policies in the early 1980s were also influenced by Sri Lanka's pro-Western tilt. In short, it was not just one reason (system-influenced or otherwise) that dictated Indian foreign policy towards Sri Lanka, but a confluence of factors.

By 2000 the Cold War had long ended. India was nearly a decade into pursuing open market policies, and the country had drawn much closer to the world's only superpower and the West. Indeed, analysts in the US and India were starting to contemplate an India–US alliance to stem Chinese influence. India was touted as a potential permanent member of an expanded United Nations Security Council. The country (notwithstanding nearly 140 million Muslims sympathetic to the Palestinian cause) had begun close diplomatic and military relations with Israel. The US had cemented itself as the most preferred destination for Indians going abroad to study and work in specialized fields, and a decade of economic growth had witnessed a rise in India's relative material power capabilities. While India expressed genuine concern about the instability in Sri Lanka—which kept manifesting itself on India's shores with each new wave of refugees[14]—and kept advocating devolution as a solution to the island's ethnic conflict, its enhanced status and reconfigured alliances in a unipolar world reduced its threat perceptions vis-à-vis Sri Lanka's ethnic and foreign policies. But Tamil Nadu and the LTTE's smuggling activities continued to influence decision-making as well, as did personal relations between Indian and Sri Lankan leaders and, to some degree, the nationalist ideologies of political parties in both countries.

What all this means from a theoretical standpoint is that, while a systemic explanation does explain India's policies towards Sri Lanka, it merely represents a partial explanation. It is only those who refuse to recognize that social science theories often sound better than the actual practice of foreign policy who think that Indian leaders always act based on systemic pressures. Indian statesmen, for various reasons, have consistently contravened international (or systemic) pressure to chart their preferred foreign policies, often thumbing their noses at major powers in the process. India's leading role in the Nonaligned Movement and its stubborn opposition to signing the Comprehensive Test Ban Treaty and the Nuclear Non-Proliferation Treaty all bear witness to this.

The upshot is that India's relative power capabilities and ascendant position in global affairs, its leaders' interpersonal relations with foreign counterparts, its unique cross-border ethnic relations, and its threat perceptions—all influence its foreign policy.[15] Indeed, there has long been a rich debate among Indian commentators on what exactly the country's foreign policy and grand strategy ought to be, and these debates highlight that it is not merely systemic influences that dictate the subsequent preferences and recommendations.[16] In recent times, the number of coalition partners constituting the Central government has increased, and the party heading the coalition (Congress or the Bharatiya Janata Party) has had to sometimes balance its partners' preferences with foreign policy exigencies.

It is a cliché to say that a country acts in its national interest because all countries typically act in their national interest. But what needs to be recognized is that the system alone does not dictate a state's national interest; national interest can also be influenced by domestic considerations. India's post-independence relations with Sri Lanka too provide evidence that systemic pressures coupled with perceived and misperceived threat perceptions, domestic considerations, and leaders' camaraderie (or lack thereof), all influenced its foreign policy towards the island nation.

INDO-SRI LANKAN RELATIONS IN THE NEHRUVIAN ERA

Post-independence India viewed itself as Britain's successor in terms of ensuring South Asia's stability and superintending the Indian Ocean. This view was challenged by Pakistan, and it couched India's relations with suspicious neighbouring states. Sri Lanka was no exception. The island's leaders were, in the main, Indophiles and great admirers of Mohandas Gandhi and Jawaharlal Nehru. Nehru visited Ceylon (the country's name until 1972) numerous times prior to India's independence in August 1947 and even holidayed with his family there.[17] Yet, concerns over Indian hegemonic designs prompted Sri Lanka's leaders, led by its first prime minister D.S. Senanayake, to agree to a defence agreement with Britain just prior to the island's independence in February 1948.[18] The agreement allowed the British continued access to Sri Lanka's naval and air bases and temporarily warded off Indian interference. The policy was reversed only in 1957 under S.W.R.D. Bandaranaike's premiership.

The notion that India's defence could only be consolidated by internally organizing the country 'on a firm and stable basis with Burma and Ceylon'[19] had been proposed in the mid-1940s. This idea took on a more hegemonic tone soon after all three states' independence when another strategist declared that 'Burma and Ceylon must form with India the basic federation for mutual defense whether they will it or not. It is necessary for their own security.'[20] Some leftist politicians in pre-independent Sri Lanka had also mulled over such a federation. For instance, the Lanka Sama Samaja Party (Lanka Equal Society Party) had hoped to see the island join India as part of a socialist federation.[21] Certain Sri Lankan Tamil leaders, anticipating eventual independence, had suggested likewise, and Nehru too hinted in 1945 that Sri Lanka could join India 'as an autonomous unit of the Indian Federation'.[22] But Sinhalese Buddhist elites—who considered the island the repository of Theravada Buddhism, valued its separate existence from India over two millennia, and took pride that the British administered the island through the Colonial Office—found such comments unsettling, and this fear of Indian hegemony is partly responsible for their continuing suspicions and ambivalence towards India. In recent times, Sinhalese Buddhist nationalist groups have resorted to agitprop by playing up this notion of Indian expansionism, complicating further India's diplomatic efforts to encourage a political solution to Sri Lanka's ethnic conflict.

Post-independence India, however, faced numerous challenges, with many commentators predicting that the country would disintegrate. Consolidating the Indian Union and cementing India's status as an important world power therefore took precedence over browbeating neighbouring states, although agreements such as the Trade and Transit Treaty with Nepal did seek to emphasize India's dominant status vis-à-vis especially that country.

Jawaharlal Nehru strode the world stage like a colossus, was highly respected and liked, and pursued foreign policy rooted more in conciliation than confrontation. Nehru took pains on numerous occasions to assure Sri Lankan leaders that India had no intention of interfering in the island's affairs,[23] and it appears that India sought to prove this by collaborating with Sri Lanka whenever possible. India thus joined Sri Lanka and three other states in the 1950s to create the so-called Colombo Powers. And while concerned, India did not overreact when in 1963 Sri Lanka and China reached a maritime agreement that granted each other most favoured nation status and promoted mutual commercial interests just one year following India's humiliating war against the Chinese. Sri Lanka desisted from branding China the aggressor in the 1962 war, yet India encouraged the Colombo Conference that saw Sri Lanka take the lead to bring China and India to the negotiating table. In short, India not only respected its small neighbour's independence but also tolerated Sri Lanka's attempts to project itself as an influential Asian state, despite Sri Lanka being nearly one-fiftieth the size of India. Likewise, India hardly responded when Sri Lanka allowed Pakistani civilian aircraft to refuel in Colombo on their way to Dhaka during Bangladesh's war of independence, notwithstanding credible reports that Pakistani military personnel were feigning civilian status to travel on these flights. It is claimed that the India–China border war led to the rise of 'militant Nehruvians' who viewed China, Pakistan, and the US as anti-Indian states and advocated using force to ensure Indian regional hegemony.[24] In this light, India's relations with Sri Lanka, especially given the island's close relations with China, can be characterized as exceedingly friendly.

One major reason that Indo-Sri Lankan relations were so amicable during the first three decades following both states' independence was the camaraderie between the Nehru and Bandaranaike families. S.W.R.D. Bandaranaike had broken away from the pro-Western United National Party to form the Sri Lanka Freedom Party (SLFP), which attained power with Bandaranaike at the helm in 1956. The SLFP pandered to Sinhalese Buddhist preferences and exacerbated Sinhalese–Tamil relations, but it also embraced a more socialist approach to governance and sought closer relations with Asian and communist states. Bandaranaike seems to have trusted the India led by Nehru, but he was uncertain about his unknown successors.[25] When Bandaranaike was assassinated in September 1959, Jawaharlal Nehru declared the day of his funeral (the 26th) a public holiday. Such gestures no doubt laid the foundation for Bandaranaike's wife Sirimavo, who succeeded him as leader of the SLFP and became the world's first elected female head of state in 1960, to develop a close relationship with Nehru's daughter, Indira Gandhi. At a time when females heading states was a novelty, Mrs Bandaranaike and Mrs Gandhi developed a strong personal bond. Both also played leading roles in the Nonaligned Movement.

One bugbear in Indo-Lanka relations was the latter's Indian Tamils (or estate Tamils), whom the British brought to the island beginning in the 1830s to work on coffee and (thereafter) tea plantations.[26] Destitute and marginalized, yet engaged in an industry that was among the main sources of foreign currency, the Indian Tamils were refused citizenship soon after Sri Lanka attained independence, despite the vast majority having been born in Sri Lanka. The Sri Lankan leaders' justification and rhetoric for doing so smacked of racism.[27] Their primary goal in refusing citizenship to the Indian Tamils was to ensure that the Sinhalese Buddhists dominated the central hill areas, although the estate workers' support for leftist/communist parties and the possible dangers this posed for democracy and the free market system were also used deftly to justify the policy. It was left to Nehru's successors to work with Sri Lanka and accommodate the ill-treated Indian Tamils.

THE INTERVENING ERA: A LEGACY OF COOPERATION AND CONFLICT

According to a 1966 survey, Sri Lanka had 9,70,000 Indian Tamils branded stateless, nearly 10 per cent of the island's population.[28] India, under Nehru, refused to take back these Tamils because generations of their ancestors had lived in Sri Lanka, thereby making them Sri Lankans. Furthermore, India did not want a repatriation policy that other states harbouring the progeny of indentured Indian labourers could use as a precedent.[29] Yet in October 1964 Prime Minister Lal Bahadur Shastri and Mrs Bandaranaike signed the Sirimavo–Shastri Pact, under which Sri Lanka agreed to grant citizenship to 3,00,000 Indian Tamils while India agreed to take in 5,25,000. There were around 1,50,000 people not covered by the Pact, and in 1974 Indira Gandhi and Mrs Bandaranaike agreed to their countries taking in 75,000 persons each. Bureaucratic hurdles and the fact that more Indian Tamils preferred to stay on in Sri Lanka complicated the citizenship and repatriation processes; it was only after the Sri Lankan parliament passed the Grant of Citizenship to Stateless Persons (Special Provisions) Act in 1988 that the Indian Tamil citizenship issue was, in the main, resolved.[30] But the willingness of two Congress governments to work with Mrs Bandaranaike to take in nearly 5,00,000 people of Indian origin made clear that India was eager to accommodate Sri Lanka, although this lowered the number of Tamil speakers and emboldened Sinhalese Buddhist nationalists determined to dominate the island's minorities.[31]

The close personal relations Indira Gandhi enjoyed with Mrs Bandaranaike were mainly responsible for India acknowledging Sri Lanka's claims over the small island of Katchchativu in 1974. Indira Gandhi did so despite the DMK in Tamil Nadu demanding that India annex the island and speculation that the nearby area contained deposits of oil.[32] She also did so despite Sri Lanka being one of the last non-Islamic countries to recognize the independence of Bangladesh, a status that India promoted. Katchchativu remains a festering issue for politicians and fishermen in Tamil Nadu, and Indira Gandhi's decision surely represents an instance when she put her friendship with Mrs Bandaranaike above the betterment of her constituents in the south.

Both Mrs Gandhi and Mrs Bandaranaike introduced emergency rule in 1975 and both were defeated in elections held in 1977. Indira Gandhi and the Congress defeated the Janata Party coalition and returned to power in 1980, but the UNP government under J.R. Jayewardene that came to power in Sri Lanka entrenched itself and ruled until 1994. The Janata Party's attempts to hold Indira Gandhi responsible for imposing the Emergency failed, but Jayewardene and the UNP created a commission that found Mrs Bandaranaike guilty of abusing her powers and stripped her of civic rights for seven years. Jayewardene portrayed it as a victory for democracy, but he thus ensured he did not face a strong challenger when seeking re-election. Mrs Gandhi commiserated with Mrs Bandaranaike over the phone during this time and bemoaned in public how the UNP was mistreating her friend.[33]

Jayewardene and Janata Party leader Morarji Desai hit it off, as both were among South Asia's most senior statesmen and because the Janata Party sought to improve relations with other South Asian states; whereas the Congress, especially following Pakistan's defeat in the 1971 war, had adopted a more hectoring and critical stance towards its smaller neighbours.

The UNP's election rallies in 1977 had mocked the Congress' defeat in India and predicted derogatorily that Mrs Bandaranaike and her son, Anura, were heading the way of Mrs Gandhi and her son, Sanjay. When Jayewardene visited India for the first time as Sri Lanka's leader, he used his speech during the official banquet to refer to the periods of emergency in Sri Lanka and India, and highlighted how his party members and India's opposition leaders had been harassed by Mrs Bandaranaike and Mrs Gandhi, respectively.

Indira Gandhi was well known for her strong personality[34] and did not take kindly to those who criticized her. Her return to power in 1980 led to strained relations between India and the Jayewardene government. But such personal disaffection was merely one reason for the downturn in Indo-Sri Lankan relations in the 1980s, although Jayewardene's apologists in Sri Lanka have used it to mask his foreign policy miscues.[35]

The main reason for the strained relations between India and Sri Lanka was Jayewardene's inability to comprehend adequately that while all countries are sovereign, not all are equal; that megalomaniac foreign policies are not the same as megalomaniac domestic policies; and the extent to which Sri Lanka's ethnic politics affected politics in Tamil Nadu and relations between Tamil Nadu and the Indian central government. Consequently, the anti-Tamil policies his government pursued further marginalized moderate Sri Lankan Tamil politicians, radicalized Tamil extremists, and made the Sri Lankan Tamils' plight an election issue in Tamil Nadu, so much so that the main parties in the state began supporting different Sri Lankan Tamil factions (with the DMK rooting for the Tamil Eelam Liberation Organization and the AIADMK supporting the LTTE). But it was not merely pressure from Tamil Nadu politicians that forced the Indian government to interfere radically in Sri Lanka's affairs; it was also the UNP's pro-Western policies that insouciantly disregarded India's regional preponderance and security considerations.

Jayewardene used his massive election victory to defenestrate the SLFP's autarkic and dirigiste policies, and collaborated with the World Bank and the International Monetary Fund (IMF) to institute structural adjustment reforms. It is instructive that Sri Lanka adopted an open market economy two years before China and nearly 15 years before India. Coinciding with the open market economy were massive homebuilding, hydropower, agricultural, and development projects financed through Western and Japanese aid. As Sri Lanka became more and more dependent on the West, it began pursuing policies seeking to further ingratiate itself with Western donors without due regard to Indian strategic designs.[36] For instance, Jayewardene claimed that the 1947 Defence Pact with Britain was never annulled and was therefore still in force, a statement which, while technically correct, disregarded Indian preponderance in the region; he made overtures to leaders from the Association of Southeast Asian Nations (ASEAN), seeking to join the organization, which, if successful, would have allowed Southeast Asian states undue influence in South Asia;[37] he condemned the Soviet invasion of Afghanistan (while India refused to do so) and upon his instructions, Sri Lankan diplomats in the United Nations and other world forums followed the American and Western position; he allowed the Israeli intelligence agencies—Shin Beth and Mossad—a strategic presence on the island when he invited them and ex–Special Air Service (SAS) commandos from Britain to train Sri Lanka's security forces fighting against Tamil militants; he permitted an Israeli interest section to be set up within the US Embassy after disregarding protests by Sri Lanka's Muslims and Indian concerns on the issue;[38] he sought to permit a US concern operating out of Singapore to develop the Tank Farm Development Project in Trincomalee, despite many believing that India would not tolerate an unfriendly power having access to a port so close to her; he permitted recreation and refuelling facilities for US naval ships, including the nuclear-powered aircraft carrier *Kitty Hawk* (at a time when Indians continued to recall angrily the *USS Enterprise* sailing into the Bay of Bengal during the 1971 Indo-Pakistan war); and, he agreed to allow the US to build one of the most powerful Voice of America stations that Indian officials were convinced would be used to monitor Indian intelligence activities in the Indian Ocean. It is debatable whether Jayewardene pursued such policies partly to rile Indira Gandhi, but it is indisputable that all this took place while Indian strategic thinkers hewed to the so-called Indira Doctrine.

Exacerbating ethnic relations between the Sinhalese and Tamils, manifested in the form of anti-Tamil riots and violence in 1977 and 1981, had led to Tamil rebels using south India as a refuge and banking on the strong sympathies of Tamils in Tamil Nadu. The July 1983 anti-Tamil pogrom and the government's complicity in the violence caused over 1,50,000 Sri Lankan Tamils to flee to India.[39] Many Tamils from Tamil Nadu were also holding high positions in the Indian government, and there was much lobbying taking place to crack down on Sri Lanka. Furthermore, the DMK and AIADMK sought to outbid each other by adopting vociferous anti-Sri Lanka positions. The DMK kept demanding that India suspend diplomatic relations with Sri Lanka, impose economic sanctions, take military action against it, and also work to expel the island from the Nonaligned Movement.[40] The AIADMK's Chief Minister M.G. Ramachandran, whose party was allied with the Congress, lobbied Indira Gandhi personally.[41] Indira Gandhi in turn made clear to Jayewardene that India was not 'just another country' when it came to the Tamil issue, leading to fears within Sri Lanka that India was poised to invade the island.

India, however, used the Research and Analysis Wing (RAW) to train, arm, and support Tamil rebels from various organizations.[42] India's goal was to hit back at the Jayewardene government and destabilize Sri Lanka without strengthening the rebels to the point where they could succeed in their separatist quest. It partly did so by playing off Tamil groups against each other and supporting the Tamil Eelam Liberation Organization (TELO) over other groups as TELO was the least ideological and fanatical. The LTTE was the first to realize that the Indian involvement had more to do with regional preponderance than concern for the plight of Sri Lanka's Tamils, which is one reason why the group began secretly organizing its own weapons procurement networks. It did so by raising money in Tamil Nadu and among the Sri Lankan Tamil diaspora, although Tamil Nadu's CM at the time, M.G. Ramachandran, also contributed personal funds and state funds towards the cause.[43] Thus, when RAW ceased supporting the rebels, the LTTE was well set to decimate other groups fighting for secession and proclaim itself the sole representative of Sri Lanka's Tamils.

Indira Gandhi was assassinated in October 1984, but this did not change RAW's activities with the Tamil rebels. Rajiv Gandhi adopted a more tactful approach, and his government helped organize the Thimpu Talks in June and August 1985. Continued violence in Sri Lanka and the intransigent and uncompromising positions of the Sri Lankan government and Tamil rebel leaders led to the talks collapsing.

By 1986, Pakistan, Israel, and the US were providing training, intelligence, and arms in some form to Sri Lanka, which upset India. Such assistance, however, emboldened the Sri Lankan government, and in May 1987 the island's military began an operation to capture part of the Jaffna peninsula. Jayewardene pompously commanded his generals 'to raze Jaffna to the ground, burn the town and then rebuild it'.[44]

India responded in June 1987 by launching Operation Eagle, whereby its air force violated Sri Lanka's air space and dropped food and medicine to Tamils in the north.[45] It thereafter imposed the July 1987 Indo-Lanka Peace Accord. Sri Lanka's total capitulation in this instance and the resultant humiliation was one reason the agreement led to massive protests especially in Colombo. A naval rating almost killed Rajiv Gandhi with the butt of his rifle while the Indian prime minister was inspecting a guard of honour, and that incident captured well the antipathy most Sri Lankans held towards India at the time. Indeed, many Sri Lankans continue to resent the Accord, with some nationalists still claiming that 'Mother Lanka was raped by India in 1987'... It was, however, the ultimate humiliation for J.R. Jayewardene, who looked in vain for his Western friends to come to his aid even as the Accord divided the government and led to massive street protests. In interviews he gave soon after, Jayewardene ruefully noted that 'America won't lift a finger to help me without asking India' and further said, 'In this region the USA is subservient to India. So are all the other countries.'[46]

The Indo-Lanka Peace Accord required the LTTE to hand over its weapons to the IPKF, while the Sri Lankan government agreed to pursue devolution through provincial councils and thereby accommodate fundamental Tamil grievances. The LTTE, however, did not turn over all its weapons. When some LTTE cadre swallowed cyanide to prevent the IPKF from handing them over to Sri Lanka's security forces, fighting began between the LTTE and IPKF, leading to India's longest war that some have branded as 'India's Vietnam'.[47] This ensued even as nationalist Sinhalese kept accusing India of harbouring expansionist ambitions and the IPKF was vilified through the press, posters, and political campaigns. The vain and arrogant behaviour of India's ambassador to Sri Lanka, J.N. Dixit, during this time merely provided the nationalists with additional fodder. The Sri Lankans scornfully referred to Dixit as 'the viceroy' and still bristle when discussing his tenure.[48]

The IPKF began with 6,000 soldiers, but its numbers at one point may have swelled beyond 1,00,000. The Indian government argued that the IPKF's deployment was necessary for India's national security, although many defence analysts were sceptical.[49] It was ironic that many in Tamil Nadu continued to support the LTTE even when the organization was fighting the IPKF. Likewise, malpractice and indiscipline among some IPKF soldiers soon caused Sri Lankan Tamils, who had greeted the Indians as liberators, to loathe them.[50]

In Sri Lanka's December 1988 presidential elections both the UNP and SLFP candidates demanded the IPKF's withdrawal. India initially rejected the argument, claiming that the IPKF was deployed based on a bilateral agreement and therefore could not be unilaterally withdrawn; but, with Lok Sabha elections due in November 1989, Rajiv Gandhi grudgingly agreed to pull back the troops. In Tamil Nadu, DMK leader Muthuvel Karunanidhi harped on IPKF atrocities against Sri Lanka's Tamils to defeat the Congress party.[51] The new government under V.P. Singh relented, and the mission ended in March 1990. Over 1,100 IPKF soldiers were killed in what many now believe was an ill-conceived and ill-starred military venture.

India's agony in dealing with Sri Lanka continued when the LTTE assassinated Rajiv Gandhi in May 1991 while he was campaigning to return as prime minister. The LTTE feared that a victorious Gandhi would re-deploy Indian troops in Sri Lanka, and this fear was the prime motivation for killing him.[52] India soon thereafter became the first state to proscribe the LTTE as a terrorist organization. Killing Gandhi was the single biggest mistake the LTTE made, for the vast majority of Tamils in Tamil Nadu thereafter stopped supporting the group.

POST-COLD WAR RELATIONS

The IPKF would likely have defeated the LTTE had its mission not been curtailed. That noted, nearly all military personnel, analysts, and politicians believe that the IPKF operation was a major mistake and that India should desist from getting militarily involved in Sri Lanka again. But it is not just such opinions that have led India to change its stance towards Sri Lanka: the end of the Cold War, the open market reforms India adopted soon after that enabled a more productive relationship with the US and other Western countries, better relations between Indian leaders and their Sri Lankan contemporaries, and the anti-LTTE sentiment in Tamil Nadu following Rajiv Gandhi's assassination also influenced India's foreign policy.

Soon after the Indo-Lanka Peace Accord was signed an Indian admiral noted that India 'would have had no choice but to treble our naval force' had the US been given the Trincomalee habour for rest and recreation purposes.[53] Post-Cold War India, however, felt more comfortable with the US promoting peace in Sri Lanka and using its Special Forces and Navy Seals to train Sri Lankan military personnel. This change in attitude is understandable given that India and the US now conduct joint military exercises and are touted as natural allies in a potential multi-polar world. While India did not play a direct role in the peace process that began in February 2002, it encouraged Norway to operate as a facilitator. The Sri Lankan government and foreign actors and donors involved kept India abreast of all proceedings throughout. And it is important to recognize that India expects to be briefed about what transpires between Sri Lanka and other foreign states, especially if the issues concerned could have a bearing on Indian security considerations.

Rajiv Gandhi's assassination allowed India and Sri Lanka to pursue common policies, vis-à-vis the LTTE. Both countries were determined to ensure that the LTTE did not succeed in creating a separate state. After all, if a country as small as Sri Lanka can be dismembered to create eelam, why not independence for much larger territories within India? Some Sri Lankan Tamils among the diaspora envision Sri Lanka's northeast merging with Tamil Nadu and becoming a part of India, but the LTTE's decimation and Prabhakaran's death in May 2009 makes the realization of eelam all the more evanescent.[54]

The so-called Gujral Doctrine, with its emphasis on non-reciprocity when dealing with smaller South Asian states,[55] helped mend relations between the two countries. Similarly, the good relations Sri Lanka's President Chandrika Kumaratunga enjoyed with Indian leaders and the late Lakshman Kadirgamar's deft diplomacy as foreign minister also ensured a respectful and predictable relationship between the two states during Kumaratunga's 11-year presidency. Yet it does not take much for Sri Lanka's media to lambaste India for perceived slights. Part of this has to do with India's regional hegemonic status and the sense of distrust stemming from historical involvement.

For instance in April 2004 supporters of the UNP vilified India for supposedly colluding with Kumaratunga to dismiss the UNP-led United National Front government headed by Prime Minister Ranil Wickremasinghe. It was Wickremasinghe who initiated a peace process with the LTTE in February 2002, but Kumaratunga and India became concerned that he was appeasing the rebels unduly. India also seems to have gotten upset that Wickremasinghe secretly negotiated an Acquisition and Cross Servicing Agreement with the US that included the oil farms in Trincomalee while claiming otherwise. Wickremasinghe denied India was involved in Kumaratunga's decision to sack his government, but the accusations led to caustic anti-India articles in the pro-UNP and nationalist press.

Tamil Nadu's political parties that are part of coalition governments at the Centre do have the opportunity to exert some influence over India's policies towards Sri Lanka; but, with numerous political parties constituting such coalitions, national parties leading the coalition (either the Bhartiya Janta Party (BJP) or the Congress) also have more options when picking partners and pursuing foreign policy. This does not preclude coalition partners taking a stance very different from the government, but it is rarely that one coalition partner will succeed in dictating foreign policy to the Centre. The communist parties did enjoy some success in doing so over the Indo-US nuclear agreement, but the fact that the Congress-led United Progressive Alliance (UPA) coalition could cut these parties loose, entice the Samajawadi Party to join it, and thereby maintain its parliamentary majority and pursue the nuclear deal proves the point.

The DMK was the third-largest party in the previous UPA government (2004–9), and in November 2008 it pushed the Indian government to get Sri Lanka to accept donations from India, aid that the International Red Cross distributed among displaced Sri Lankan Tamils in the war zone. DMK parliamentarians, together with most other Tamil parliamentarians, at first threatened to resign their seats and thereby undermine the UPA unless the Indian government got Sri Lanka to agree to a ceasefire with the beleaguered LTTE. The DMK's threat was not taken seriously because, while the party played a vital role propping up the UPA, the Congress in Tamil Nadu played a major role propping up the minority DMK government in the state legislature.

The demands of the DMK and other Tamil Nadu parties must be understood within the context of the barbaric policies the Mahinda Rajapaksa government was pursuing against Sri Lanka's Tamils and the massive protests this unleashed among students, government officials, lawyers, political parties, and the Tamil film industry, which resorted to hunger strikes, fasts, and state-wide human chain demonstrations. The Rajapaksa government's ethnocentrism and hidebound policies were also responsible for the LTTE regaining support in Tamil Nadu during the final phase of the island's civil war. For instance, a survey conducted in mid-2008 by the respected and influential Tamil weekly *Ananda Vikatan* claimed that over 62 per cent in Tamil Nadu believe that India should intervene in Sri Lanka to bring about a solution to the ethnic conflict, and over 54 per cent supported the LTTE.[56]

Some parts of Tamil Nadu never gave up supporting the LTTE. Indeed, in certain areas people name their children after LTTE leader Prabhakaran, hang his picture on walls, and have built bus shelters and housing colonies honouring LTTE martyrs.[57] But the AIADMK under Jayalalitha Jeyaram vociferously opposed the LTTE,[58] which made clear Tamil Nadu's electorate and politicians were divided over the group. With the LTTE now militarily defeated and its leader Prabhakaran dead, Tamil Nadu's politicians and populace should be able to rally together when lobbying for the wellbeing of Sri Lanka's Tamils. The recent past, however, suggests that the DMK and AIADMK are more likely to try and outbid each other on who in Tamil Nadu can best promote the rights of Sri Lankan Tamils, thereby using Sri Lanka's marginalized and humiliated Tamils for their own political ends. This will especially be the case during elections. For instance, during the 2009 Lok Sabha elections Jayalalitha even said she would work to create a separate state for Sri Lanka's Tamils just like Indira

Gandhi created Bangladesh, forcing the BJP (which was allied with the AIADMK) to distance itself from the claim.[59]

In recent years, Sri Lanka's navy, which sought to prevent the LTTE from smuggling materials to the northeast, has been notorious for shooting Tamil Nadu fishermen who cross into the island's waters.[60] Such shootings have led to angry protests in Tamil Nadu and also led to calls for the Indian government to take back the Katchchativu Island that Indira Gandhi gave to Sri Lanka in 1974. The AIADMK's Jayalalitha claims that the transaction was illegal, since it was done via an executive order and not a constitutional amendment, and she has taken the matter to the Supreme Court.

An agreement between the two countries in October 2008 stipulated that Indian fishermen would avoid crossing into Sri Lankan waters and carry government-issued permits for their boats and personal identity cards, while Sri Lanka's navy would cease firing on these fishermen. The measure was apparently designed to placate anti-Sri Lanka sentiment in Tamil Nadu, and only time will tell how effective it is. But the Katchchativu issue has now been resurrected and is likely to feature prominently in the future. One recent proposal calls for Sri Lanka to lease the island to India in perpetuity in exchange for a Defence Cooperation Agreement and a shared military base on Katchchativu.[61]

Sri Lanka lobbied hard for an Indo-Sri Lanka Defence Cooperation Agreement, leading to discussions that began in November 2004. However, pressure from Tamil Nadu forced the Indian government to scupper the deal. Sri Lanka's reluctance to allow India to use the runway at the Palaly army camp in the Northern Province may also have played a role in the deal going sour. Yet India may have to reconsider its decision, given that Pakistan and Sri Lanka exchanged a draft defence pact in August 2008. With the LTTE defeated and Sri Lanka used to receiving a steady supply of weapons from China and Pakistan, it is the island's leaders that now appear disinclined to pursue a defense agreement with India.

Successive Indian governments since the early 1990s have made clear that the Tamil problem was an internal Sri Lankan affair with the caveat that it hoped the island would accommodate the Tamils' legitimate grievances. India has reason to be displeased with the lack of progress made on the political front in Sri Lanka and has occasionally mildly criticized the human rights violations perpetrated by the island's military against Tamils. Sri Lankans, however, consider this position to be hypocritical because Indian soldiers have used aggressive tactics in Kashmir, Nagaland, and many other places to suppress separatist tendencies with little regard to human rights conventions. As one newspaper noted, India's:

concern should be appreciated but how can India forget the fact that the IPKF massacred civilians and gang-raped hundreds, if not thousands, of girls and women under the pretext of helping make peace in this country? Would India tell us how many jawans were court martialled for heinous crimes against civilians? Crabs that move sideways, it is said, want their young ones to walk straight![62]

Successive Indian governments also avoided providing Sri Lanka offensive weaponry since doing so generated protests in Tamil Nadu.[63] However, had the civil war continued, India may have been forced to reverse course so as to limit the influence of Pakistan and China, whose stock in the island has risen sharply thanks to supplying Sri Lanka massive quantities of weapons.

Pakistan had been doing so for awhile. For instance, in May 2000 it was Pakistan that rushed multi-barrel rocket launches to the Jaffna Peninsula and helped rescue nearly 40,000 Sri Lankan soldiers who were close to being overrun by the LTTE. This took place after the Indian government refused to intervene.[64] Pakistan has since stationed around a dozen military personnel in the island, Pakistani pilots may have flown bombing operations for the Sri Lankan Air Force in the country's northeast, and some claim Pakistan also played a role planning the war against the LTTE.[65] Sir Lankan air force officials deny this, although the Pakistani media have claimed otherwise. All this is of concern to India, given especially the country's nuclear facilities in South India.

Both Pakistan and China have also created effective intelligence operations on the island, causing India to worry. India's goal throughout, has been to prevent a hostile power gaining a foothold in Sri Lanka. This was the main reason for its heavy-handed involvement in the island in the 1980s, and the nemeses then were the US and other pro-American interests. India also suspects that steady weapons supplies and diplomatic support from China and Pakistan were major reasons for the Mahinda Rajapaksa government's cocky approach to seeking a military solution to the ethnic conflict. Furthermore, India fears that Pakistan's Inter-Services Intelligence has used *jihadi* elements to build influence among Sri Lankan Muslims in the Eastern Province. This even caused some analysts to argue that India should take a more nuanced approach towards the LTTE, a suggestion that is now irrelevant given the organization's demise in Sri Lanka.

The LTTE consciously avoided making religion an issue in the ethnic conflict, mainly because it took pride in its secular identity and because numerous Tamil Christians played leading roles in the organization.

Should, however, the LTTE's overseas operatives decide to change course and play the 'Hindu card', given that over 90 per cent of Sri Lankan Tamils are Hindu, the group may find enough sympathizers in India's saffron movement to cause a future BJP government to treat it differently. Indeed, the LTTE's supporters have already begun playing this card, and the BJP in Tamil Nadu called for the LTTE to be de-proscribed in India in the run up to the 15th Lok Sabha elections.[66] Many LTTE supporters believe a shift in Indian policy is inevitable, as they are convinced that Sinhalese nationalists, who are typically hostile towards India, are geared to further embrace China and Pakistan and marginalize India. According to them, the day is not far off when India rues its anti-LTTE stand and support for the Sri Lankan government.

Neorealism unduly privileges the most powerful states in the international system even when it is clear that small states can resort to alliances with major powers and gain disproportionate leverage.[67] Israel is a case in point, although Sri Lanka too is a worthy example—for it deftly used Pakistan and China to ward off Indian pressure when seeking aid. Indeed, the reason the Mahinda Rajapaksa government has been able to disregard international concerns about human rights violations is thanks to its close association with states like China—and also Iran, which has provided long-term aid—which are uninterested in making good governance a precondition for developmental aid. For instance, China gave Sri Lanka a billion dollars in 2008 to build three roads, two power plants, and a port in Hambantota. This is worrisome for India, given China's recent agreements with Pakistan, Burma, and Bangladesh to construct roads and ports in those countries as well, all of which is part of a naval strategy to create a 'string of pearls' (or naval bases) stretching from the South China Sea to the Persian Gulf. China has also supplanted Japan as Sri Lanka's largest donor.

It was concerns over how China and Pakistan have used arms sales to build up their influence in Sri Lanka that led Indian National Security Advisor M.K. Narayanan to recently say: 'We are a big power in the region, whatever may be their requirements they should come to us.'[68] His comments were savaged in the Sri Lankan press, with *The Island* newspaper, for example, saying:

India always behaves like a sadist deriving, as she does, immense pleasure from the suffering of her neighbours, like those cheap Indian soap opera characters who are full [of] hatred, envy, jealousy, and hubris. She has a massive ego to nurse, and this she does at the expense of others. She treats her small neighbours like untouchables.[69]

The editorial continued:

It is this kind of arrogance, callousness and coercion that characterized the Nazi regime of Hitler who [sic] always decided what was good for other countries and sought to impose his [sic] will on them. We seem to have a new brand of Nazism across the Palk Straits.[70]

This, of course, is hyperbole; yet it highlights how suspicious Sri Lankans are of India. Many in Sri Lanka believe sincerely that some in India want to ensure that the island stays destabilized. The RAW gets cited as a perennial culprit in this regard. The RAW has been accused of financing the once Maoist and now hyper-nationalist Janatha Vimukthi Peramuna (JVP; People's Liberation Front), which was responsible for two insurgencies in the early 1970s and late 1980 intending to destabilize the island,[71] despite the JVP being one of India's most vociferous critics. In January 2009, some Sri Lankan analysts even speculated that RAW would try and provide refuge to certain LTTE leaders fleeing the military's onslaught so they could be used for future anti-Sri Lanka operations. Sri Lanka may not be as strategically important to India as it was in the Cold War era,[72] but increased Chinese and Pakistani influence could change that.

India has tried to ward off Chinese and Pakistani influence by engaging at varied levels with Sri Lanka. For instance, India provided the island radars to track LTTE aircrafts—which carried out bombing operations (albeit causing minimum material damage) against the island's airport, military camps, and oil refineries—and also provided personnel to man these radars. She (together with the United States) conducted satellite and naval surveillance of Sri Lanka's maritime boundary and helped the country's navy neutralize LTTE shipping operations. Every year Indian military academies train around 800 Sri Lankan officers without cost and even provide the trainees allowances,[73] although both parties rarely tout this arrangement. The Free Trade Agreement that was signed between the two countries in December 1998 and took effect in March 2000 also saw the volume of trade rise from $46 million in 1999 to $516 million in 2008.[74] India currently ranks as the fourth largest investor in Sri Lanka and the signing of the Comprehensive Economic Partnership Agreement in July 2008 is expected to boost bilateral trade to $1.5 billion by 2012. The Indian government provides Sri Lanka long-term loans, is in the process of building a coal-fired power plant, and now also maintains Trincomalee's oil deposit farms. Furthermore, India plans to build roads, station demining teams, and create educational and training institutions in the island.

Private trade and contacts among the countries' citizens too are also on the rise, and this should dissipate suspicions stemming from Indian involvement in Sri Lanka's muddled ethnic conflict. For instance, Indian companies such as Ashok Leyland, Tata, Apollo Hospitals, and Indian Oil Corporation maintain a conspicuous presence in Sri Lanka. There are over 100 flights per week between the two countries, and more Indians visit Sri Lanka as tourists than people from any other country. Indian tourists are also issued visas upon landing in Colombo, a policy India does not reciprocate. Sri Lankans comprise the second-largest contingent of foreign students studying in India (after the US). Importantly, the Indian military was the first among foreign rescue forces on the scene following the December 2004 tsunami, and many Sri Lankans who benefited from this deployment continue to express gratitude.

In addition, both countries are planning an undersea power transmission line so India could sell electricity to Sri Lanka. When Ranil Wickremasinghe was prime minister he proposed building one of the longest bridges in the world, connecting Talaimannar in Sri Lanka with Dhanushkodi in Tamil Nadu. The Tamil Nadu government, however, is more interested in the Sethusamudram project, which would create a 152-km-long, 300-metres-wide shipping canal in the Palk Strait that would allow large container ships heading to south India to save a day of travel. Sri Lanka opposes the project citing environmental concerns, but its principal fear is that the canal would hurt shipping at the Colombo port (the busiest in South Asia). The project has been temporarily halted due to pressure from the BJP and other right-wing Hindu organizations that associate the rock formations in the strait with the mythical bridge in the Ramayana.

In its 2006 Annual Report, India's Home Affairs Ministry for the very first time claimed that the LTTE's naval wing posed a direct threat to the country's security and this assessment no doubt motivated the Mahinda Rajapaksa government's policy of defeating the LTTE militarily—notwithstanding the ensuing carnage that saw upwards of 20,000 Tamils killed between January and May 2009.[75] The LTTE used Tamil Nadu to procure supplies and LTTE cadres captured in India carried maps detailing nuclear and defence areas and the locations of certain information technology companies in Bangalore.[76] India was unhappy that the LTTE acquired airplanes, although it did not fall for Sri Lanka's bait, which claimed the rudimentary LTTE air wing was targeting India's nuclear facilities along the country's southern coast. Indian analysts also accused the LTTE of financing certain Indian politicians, thereby interfering in India's affairs.[77] Most importantly, India feared that the creation of eelam, besides sending a dangerous message to secessionist groups within India, would also encourage pan-Tamil nationalism, given that fringe elements in Tamil Nadu's political universe continue to invoke the dreams of Tamil nationalists like Periyar Ramasamy and aspire to an independent Tamil state.

India had arrest warrants out for Vellupillai Prabhakaran and Pottu Amman, the LTTE's intelligence chief, for Rajiv Gandhi's murder; and soon after Sri Lankan military forces captured the LTTE's administrative capital of Kilinochchi in early January 2009, the ruling Congress party claimed that it would like to see Prabhakaran extradited to India to stand trial for Rajiv Gandhi's murder. Notwithstanding Prabhakaran's death, the LTTE will likely stay proscribed in India so long as the group's overseas supporters continue to clamour for eelam. This suits Sri Lanka. From India's standpoint the LTTE's quest for eelam complicated Indo-Sri Lankan relations and the continuation of that quest in any form and its ramifications in Tamil Nadu stands to prevent bilateral ties from flourishing.

Sri Lankan government officials claim that relations with India have never been better. Indian officials agree, while occasionally grumbling that they must sometimes host Sri Lankan politicians who merely visit South Block to gripe about the island's petty political disputes.[78] Indian officials also believe that a fair political settlement to the island's ethnic problem would further enhance Indo-Sri Lankan relations, and in the post-LTTE era the nature of this settlement is bound to feature prominently between the two countries. This means that India will likely engage Sri Lanka to a greater degree than during the first five years of PM Manmohan Singh's tenure. What is ultimately clear is that Indo-Sri Lankan relations have come a long way since the 1980s and that it is in both states' interest to support this trajectory.

* * *

India's relations with Pakistan, China, Bangladesh, and Nepal range from antagonistic to rivalrous, and she can do without adding Sri Lanka to this list. Thus India should seek to fashion a relationship with Sri Lanka that supersedes the Sinhalese–Tamil ethnic divide and Sri Lankan Tamil–Tamil Nadu consanguineous ties. This would hopefully contribute towards a stable Sri Lankan milieu in which India can cooperate and compete economically with western and Asian states while ensuring her security and military preponderance in the region. It appears India intends on doing so, even if this means occasionally jettisoning its long-standing concern for the island's Tamils. This noted, how Sri Lanka treats its long-suffering

Tamils will affect Indo-Sri Lankan relations, for India cannot completely and insouciantly disregard the plight of this minority.

As already noted, India has long called for a political settlement in Sri Lanka that accommodates Tamils' basic grievances, and the Rajapaksa government repeatedly promised to do just that once it neutralized the LTTE. Sri Lanka, however, now appears to be using China and Pakistan to ward off what it may consider undue Indian influence in the island, and some in India find this cause for concern. Sri Lanka's long-term security and economic promise lies within India's ambit, and this understanding partly forms the basis for India tolerating the island's burgeoning relations with Pakistan and China. But the triumphalism and chauvinism that was unleashed following the LTTE's decimation, the rise of Sri Lanka's military as a major player in the island's affairs, the nexus between the military and civilian leadership and their shared ideology rooted in Sinhalese Buddhist superordination and minority subordination, the Rajapaksa family's determination to create a fearsome political dynasty, and the consequences stemming from all this could very well have an adverse impact on Indo-Sri Lankan relations.

For instance, Sri Lanka's military currently numbers around 1,80,000 personnel but military leaders want to expand the force to 3,00,000 and use these troops to superintend the minorities in the northeast even as they flood the area with Sinhalese settlers. This is partly to ensure that there will never again be another secessionist attempt in the island, although the policy is also dictated by a Sinhalese-Buddhist nationalist ideology that calls for (among other things) Sinhalese Buddhists to become a majority throughout the country.[79] With the LTTE vanquished militarily, India would like to replace China and Pakistan as Sri Lanka's chief military supplier, but doing so within a milieu of ethnic flooding designed to erase Tamils' regional identity is guaranteed to generate opposition within Tamil Nadu. And in a post-LTTE era, it would be easier for those in Tamil Nadu to mobilize to support their Sri Lankan cousins. But India's dilemma stands to see China and Pakistan further expand their influence in the island. Thus there is no reason to assume that the LTTE's military defeat is going to make Indo-Sri Lankan relations rosy.

From a theoretical standpoint, Indo-Sri Lankan relations evidence that it is not merely systemic opportunities and constraints that determine Indian foreign policy; domestic political considerations also play an important role. Indeed, as this chapter hopefully makes clear, it is impossible to comprehend Indian foreign policy towards Sri Lanka without an adequate understanding of ethno-regional politics in both countries.

NOTES

1. Kenneth N. Waltz (1959), *Man, the State, and War: A Theoretical Analysis* (New York: Columbia University Press); Kenneth N. Waltz (1979), *Theory of International Politics* (Reading, Mass.: Addison-Wesley).

2. Kenneth N. Waltz (1996), 'International Politics is not Foreign Policy', *Security Studies*, 6 (1), pp. 54–5.

3. See, for example, Jack Snyder (1991), *Myths of Empire: Domestic Politics and International Ambition* (Ithaca: Cornell University Press).

4. Such an analysis is more in line with neoclassical realism. For how neoclassical realism differs from neorealism, see Gideon Rose (1998), 'Neoclassical Realism and Theories of Foreign Policy', *World Politics*, 51 (1), pp. 144–72.

5. For a historical perspective dealing with south India and Sri Lanka relations, see A. Liyanagamage (1992), 'Pre-Colonial Indo-Sri Lankan Relations with Special Reference to Sri Lanka's Security Problems', in P.V.J. Jayasekera (ed.), *Security Dilemma of a Small State: Sri Lanka in the South Asian Context*, vol. 1 (New Delhi: South Asian Publishers), pp. 28–65.

6. Neil DeVotta (2004), *Blowback: Linguistic Nationalism, Institutional Decay, and Ethnic Conflict in Sri Lanka* (Stanford: Stanford University Press).

7. For a history, see V.L.B. Mendis (1983), *Foreign Relations of Sri Lanka: From Earliest Times to 1965* (Dehiwela, Sri Lanka: Tisara Prakasakayo Ltd).

8. It is instructive that within two weeks of being re-elected to the chief minister's post in Tamil Nadu, Muthuvel Karunanidhi announced: 'The central government's policy (on Sri Lanka) will be the state government's policy', quoted in *The Times of India*, 'Karunanidhi Defines Tamil Nadu Role in SL', 6 June 2006 at http://timesofindia.indiatimes.com/articleshow/1623656.cms (accessed on 7 June 2006).

9. S.D. Muni (1993), *Pangs of Proximity: India's and Sri Lanka's Ethnic Crisis* (New Delhi: Sage Publications), p. 13; N.S. Jagannathan (1990), 'Anatomy of a Misadventure', *Mainstream*, 28 (4), p. 3; Maya Chadda (1997), *Ethnicity, Security, and Separatism in India* (New York: Columbia University Press), p. 97.

10. Bhabani Sen Gupta (1983), 'Regional Security: The Indira Doctrine', *India Today*, 31 August, p. 20.

11. Ibid.

12. *The Times of India* (2000), 'India Rules out Policy Change if Jaffna Falls', 11 May.

13. Neil DeVotta (2003), 'Is India Over-Extended? When Domestic Disorder Precludes Regional Intervention', *Contemporary South Asia*, 12 (3), pp. 365–80.

14. As of December 2007, Tamil Nadu continued to host 80,000 refugees in 117 camps. See Pushpa Iyengar (2007), 'Felines and Felonies', *Outlook*, 17 December, p. 22.

15. Neil DeVotta (1998), 'Sri Lanka's Structural Adjustment Program and Its Impact on Indo-Lanka Relations', *Asian Survey*, 38 (5), p. 457.

16. Kanti Bajpai (2003), 'Indian Strategic Culture', in Michael R. Chambers (ed.), *Future Strategic Balances and Alliances* (Carlisle, Penn: Strategic Studies Institute), pp. 245–303.

17. For details see P. Ramaswamy (1987), *New Delhi and Sri Lanka: Four Decades of Politics and Diplomacy* (Ahmedabad: Allied Publishers Private Ltd), pp. 153–71.

18. P. Sahadevan and Neil DeVotta (2006), *Politics of Conflict and Peace in Sri Lanka* (New Delhi: Manak Publishers Pvt Ltd), p. 348.

19. K.M. Panikkar (1945), *India and the Indian Ocean* (London: G. Allen & Unwin), p. 95.

20. Keshav Balkrishna Vaidya (1949), *The Naval Defence of India* (Bombay: Thacker), p. 30.

21. See Jayadeva Uyangoda (2008), 'The Discreet Charm of India', *Economic and Political Weekly*, 23 February, 43 (8), p. 8.

22. As quoted in W. Howard Wriggins (1960), *Ceylon: Dilemmas of a New Nation* (Princeton: Princeton University Press), p. 399.

23. Shelton Kodikara (1992), *Foreign Policy of Sri Lanka: A Third World Perspective*, 2nd edn (Delhi: Chanakya Publications), p. 23.

24. Subrata K. Mitra (2003), 'The Reluctant Hegemon: India's Self-Perception and the South Asian Strategic Environment', *Contemporary South Asia*, 12 (3) (September), p. 405.

25. Sahadevan and DeVotta, *Politics of Conflict and Peace*, p. 350.

26. The Indian Tamils are different from the Sri Lankan Tamils and are not involved in the island's civil war.

27. See R.R. Sivalingam (1991), 'People of Indian Origin in Sri Lanka', in V. Suryanarayan (ed.), *Sri Lankan Crisis and India's Response* (New Delhi: Patriot Publishers), pp. 48–67.

28. V.P. Dutt (1984), *India's Foreign Policy* (New Delhi: Vikas Publishing House), p. 225.

29. For details on this particular issue, see P. Sahadevan (1995), *India and Overseas Indians: The Case of Sri Lanka* (New Delhi: Kalinga).

30. For details, see Kodikara, *Foreign Policy of Sri Lanka*, pp. 32–8.

31. For concise essays on Sri Lanka's post-independence ethnocentric politics, see Neil DeVotta (2010), 'Politics and Governance in Post-Independence Sri Lanka', in Paul R. Brass (ed.), *Routledge Handbook of South Asian Politics: India, Pakistan, Bangladesh, Sri Lanka, and Nepal* (New York: Routledge); Neil DeVotta (2009), 'Sri Lanka at Sixty: A Legacy of Ethnocentrism and Degeneration', *Economic and Political Weekly*, 44 (5), 31 January, pp. 46–53.

32. K.M. De Silva (1995), *Regional Powers and Small State Security: India and Sri Lanka, 1977–90* (Washington, DC: The Woodrow Wilson Center Press), p. 29.

33. Kodikara, *Foreign Policy of Sri Lanka*, pp. 67–8.

34. See, for instance, Henry Kissinger (1979), *The White House Years* (Boston: Little, Brown & Co.), pp. 879–80.

35. The most notorious in this regard is K.M. De Silva, whose hagiographies of Jayewardene downplay the president's follies and megalomaniac tendencies. See, for instance, his *Regional Powers and Small State Security*.

36. See DeVotta, 'Sri Lanka's Structural Adjustment Program'.

37. Sri Lanka forfeited the chance to join the ASEAN in 1967 as it was unhappy with the anti-China position many ASEAN members adopted at the time. When the UNP-led government applied to join the ASEAN in 1981, there was little enthusiasm for it among ASEAN members and opposition parties, with the latter disapproving of the close military relations between certain ASEAN members and the US. The island ended up joining the South Asian Association for Regional Cooperation (SAARC) after that organization was created in 1985.

38. India did not commence formal diplomatic relations with Israel until 1992.

39. Ramesh Thakur (1994), *The Politics and Economics of India's Foreign Policy* (London: Hurst & Co. Publishers Ltd), p. 185. By 1986 the number of refugees had dropped to 1,25,000 and India even asked Sri Lanka to help defray the costs of taking care of them.

40. Abdur Rob Khan (1986), *Strategic Aspects of Indo-Sri Lankan Relations*, BIISS Papers No. 4 (Dhaka: Bangladesh Institute of International and Strategic Studies), p. 26.

41. For details regarding Tamil Nadu pressure on the Indian government during this time, see Ambalavanar Sivarajah (1992), 'Indo-Sri Lanka Relations in the Context of Sri Lanka's Ethnic Crisis 1976–1983', in Jayasekera (ed.), *Security Dilemma of a Small State*, pp. 514–18.

42. Rajesh Kadian (1990), *India's Sri Lanka Fiasco: Peace Keepers at War* (New Delhi: Vision Books), pp. 100–1.

43. M.R. Narayan Swamy (2003), *Inside an Illusive Mind: Prabhakaran: The First Profile of the World's Most Ruthless Guerrilla Leader* (Colombo: Vijitha Yapa Publications), pp. 106–7.

44. Quoted in J.N. Dixit (2002), *Assignment Colombo*, updated edition (Colombo: Vijitha Yapa Bookshop), p. 96.

45. Sri Lankans derogatorily branded the operation a '*parippu* (or lentil) drop', and the thought of it continues to rankle especially the island's nationalists.

46. Quoted in Amal Jayawardane (1995), 'The Response of External Powers to India's Involvement in Sri Lanka', in Mahinda Werake and P.V.J. Jayasekera (eds), *Security Dilemma of a Small State: Internal Crisis and External Intervention in Sri Lanka*, vol. II, (New Delhi: South Asian Publishers), p. 233.

47. Stephen P. Cohen (2001), *India: Emerging Power* (Washington DC: Brooking Institution Press), p. 149.

48. Thus, over a decade after Dixit left Sri Lanka, a newspaper referred to him as 'another flatulent, petty and pompous Indian bureaucrat making an ass of himself trying to big brother Sri Lanka'. See *Sunday Leader*, '45 Percent Does Not A Summer Make', 18 April 2004 at http://www.thesundayleader.lk/20040418/editorial.htm (accessed on 25 April 2004).

49. See Thakur, *Politics and Economics of India's Foreign Policy*, p. 190.

50. Author interviews conducted with Sri Lankan Tamils settled in Canada suggest that certain IPKF personnel were responsible for the most heinous crimes against northern Tamils up to that point in time, so that when it left Sri Lanka the IPKF was vilified as the 'Innocent People Killing Force'. Also see Sumantra Bose (1994), *States, Nations, Sovereignty: Sri Lanka, India, and the Tamil Eelam Movement* (New Delhi: Sage Publications), pp. 132–3.

51. Narayan Swamy, *Inside an Illusive Mind*, p. 196.

52. The Indian government headed by PM Chandrasekhar used Article 356 of the Constitution and dismissed the DMK government in January 1991 by claiming it was failing to reign in LTTE activities in Tamil Nadu. The DMK was a part of the previous coalition government headed by V.P. Singh between December 1989 and November 1990, and Karunanidhi played a leading role in having the IPKF's mission terminated in March 1990. Many believe it was Rajiv Gandhi, whose Congress was propping up the Chandrasekhar government, who dictated the overthrow of the DMK because he was angry that CM Karunanidhi was highly critical of the IPKF and refused to welcome to Chennai the returning IPKF troops. Some leading Sri Lankan Tamils, during author interviews, have suggested that one reason the LTTE assassinated Rajiv Gandhi was to avenge his involvement in overthrowing the DMK government.

53. Quoted in Dilip Bobb (1987), 'High Stakes Gamble: India's Role in Sri Lanka has Strategic Advantages', *Lanka Guardian*, 10 (16), 15 December, p. 16.

54. See Neil DeVotta (2009), 'Liberation Tigers of Tamil Eelam and the Lost Quest for Separatism in Sri Lanka', *Asian Survey*, 49 (6).

55. Besides non-reciprocity, the Gujral Doctrine also emphasized that South Asian states should not allow their territories to be used against the interests of other countries in the region, there should be noninterference in other states' internal affairs, there should be respect for territorial integrity and sovereignty, and there should be peaceful bilateral settlement of disputes.

56. See *Transcurrents*, 'Tamil Nadu Survey Finds Support for Tamil Eelam and LTTE but Also for Arresting its Leader', 2 August 2008 at http://transcurrents.com/tc/2008/08/tamil_nadu_survey_finds_suppor.html (accessed on 4 August 2008).

57. See Vinoj Kumar (2008), 'Pirabhakaran "Returns" to India', *Tehelka*, 1 November, pp. 24–5.

58. One major reason for this is Jayalalitha's belief that the LTTE tried to assassinate her in the 1990s.

59. *The Gaea News*, 'BJP Distances Itself From Eelam Demand', 9 May 2009, http://blog.taragana.com/n/bjp-distances-itself-from-eelam-demand-57691/ (accessed on 15 May 2009).

60. In 2008 alone, the Sri Lankan navy killed nearly 30 Indian fishermen thought to have crossed into the island's waters. See *The Times of India* (Jaipur edition), 'NSA Summons Lanka Envoy over Violence against Tamils', 7 October 2008, p. 8.

61. V. Suryanarayan (2005), *Conflict over Fisheries in the Palk Bay Region* (New Delhi: Lancer Publishers & Distributors).

62. *The Island*, 'Feline Protests, Crab Walks and Some Questions', 27 November 2006, http://www.island.lk/2006/11/27/editorial.html (accessed on 30 November 2006).

63. For instance, in 2000, Tamil Nadu's CM M. Karunanidhi told the state assembly that 'India should not lend itself to the massacre of Tamils in Sri Lanka. The Indian Army should not be instrumental in the killing of Tamils and Indian military equipment should not be used for it. This is my strong standpoint.' Quoted in T.S. Subramanian (2000), 'Against Assistance', *Frontline*, 17 (10), 13–26 May, http://www.flonnet.com/fl1710/17100160.htm (accessed on 20 May 2000).

64. DeVotta, 'Is India Over-Extended?', pp. 365–6.

65. *LankaNewspapers.com*, 'Reports: Pak Pilots Carry Out all 3,000 Missions in Eelam War', 1 June 2009, http://www.lankanewspapers.com/news/2009/6/44374.html (accessed on 2 June 2009).

66. See, for instance, *TamilNet*, 'Lift Ban on the LTTE: Tamil Nadu BJP', 4 January 2009, http://www.tamilnet.com/art.html?artid=27918&catid=13 (accessed on 6 January 2009).

67. See W. Howard Wriggins and Gunnar Adler-Karlsson (1978), *Reducing Global Inequities* (New York: McGraw-Hill Book Company), pp. 77–85.

68. *The Island*, 'Problem of Being Bully's Buddy—II', 2 June 2007, http://www.island.lk/2007/06/02/editorial.html (accessed on 3 June 2007).

69. Ibid.

70. Ibid.

71. See *Sunday Leader*, 'Mother India Runs Amok', 15 May 2005, http://www.thesundayleader.lk/20050515/editorial.htm (accessed on 20 May 2005).

72. Sahadevan and DeVotta, *Politics of Conflict and Peace*, p. 365.

73. Vinod Kumar (2008), 'Once Bitten, Never Shy', *Tehelka*, 19 July, p. 12.

74. Muralidhar Reddy (2008), 'India, Sri Lanka Finalise Trade Agreement', *The Hindu*, 10 July, http://www.hindu.com/2008/07/10/stories/2008071060741200.htm (accessed on 10 December 2008).

75. India supported Sri Lanka and helped defeat the attempt by the UN Human Rights Council to conduct an international investigation into the killings. This was partly on principle, given that India is averse to outside parties getting involved in its domestic affairs. But there was strong opposition to this stance among Tamils in Tamil Nadu, which suggests that India's position was also influenced by China's support for Sri Lanka. This again confirms the argument in this chapter that while Tamil Nadu influences Indian foreign policy towards Sri Lanka, the state does not dictate foreign policy towards Sri Lanka.

76. See Anjali Sharma (2008), 'That Familiar Southside Pain', *The Pioneer*, 25 October, p. 9.

77. It appears that these were principally politicians who spoke out in support of the LTTE, although the group was also accused of paying Indian lawyers, academics, journalists, and retired diplomats to make favourable speeches. See, for instance, Subramanian Swamy, 'Sri Lanka Post-LTTE', 19 May 2009, http://ibnlive.in.com/blogs/dr.subramanianswamy/2406/53544/sri-lanka-postltte.html (accessed on 1 June 2009).

78. This was especially the case when Chandrika Kumaratunga was president.

79. For details see Neil DeVotta (2007), *Sinhalese Buddhist Nationalist Ideology: Implications for Politics and Conflict Resolution in Sri Lanka*, Policy Studies 40 (Washinton DC: East-West Center).

4

Indo-Bangladesh Relations
The Puzzle of Weak Ties

MILIND THAKAR

Defying expectations in 1972 that the relationship between the emergent state of Bangladesh and its sponsor, India, would be benign and marked by close cooperation, the reality has been a slow and spasmodic decline. While it may not have been possible to maintain the euphoria after the war, the fact that two states that have much to gain from cooperation but have not been able to effect it is a major disappointment for South Asian security. An initial period of amicable cooperation changed with the advent of Ziaur Rahman's military regime in 1975 in Bangladesh, after which the relationship can be said to be characterized by short honeymoon periods of raised expectations, followed by longer periods of disgruntled tolerance.

This chapter will examine the historical evolution of Indo-Bangladesh ties and then analyse the relationship at the systemic, state, and individual levels of analysis. An initial historical section will trace relations between the two states until the present, laying out major events, processes, areas of conflict, and attempts at cooperation. This section will be divided into three periods, the first covering the period from 1971 to 1975 when Mujibur Rahman's government enjoyed highly cordial ties with the Indian government. The second period will be 1975–90 during the military (and quasi-military) interregnum of Generals Ziaur Rahman and H.M. Ershad, when the relationship fluctuated but was noticeably colder. The third phase marks a new era in the post-Cold War world accompanied by the restoration of democracy in Bangladesh and the shedding of welfare socialism for a market economy in both states.

The historical narrative is followed by analytical sections which examine systemic, state, and individual level factors and their role in shaping Indo-Bangladeshi ties, in keeping with the theme of this volume. The systemic level is understood at two levels itself—the global system comprising all the states and the subordinate state system of South Asia, which comprises India, Pakistan, Bangladesh, Nepal, Bhutan, and Sri Lanka.[1]

HISTORICAL EVOLUTION

India's relationship with Bangladesh can trace its roots to the relationship between an *idea of India* and an *idea of Pakistani/Bengali separatism* predating 1947. The All India Muslim League, the political movement and later the party that demanded a separate state of Pakistan, was formed in Dhaka in 1906. However, significantly, an autonomous Bengali political party like the Krishak Prajatantra Party not only competed but defeated mainstream parties like the Indian National Congress and the Muslim League in the provincial elections allowed under limited franchise during British rule. According to Bhardwaj, many Bengali Muslims defined their identity in not just ethnic Bengali but anti-Indian terms, thereby setting the stage for not just the emergence of an antagonistic (to India) East Pakistan, but eventually an antagonistic Bangladesh.[2] While violence marked the partition of united Bengal into West Bengal (India) and East Pakistan, it was much less than the horrific slaughter that occurred in Punjab and did not appear to leave behind the residual hatred that characterized Indo-Pakistan relations. A sizable minority of Hindus remained in East Pakistan and a sizable number of Muslims remained in West Bengal, in contrast to the ethnic cleansing that marked the division of Punjab.

The demand by Bengalis to receive adequate representation and equitable division of resources from the Pakistani state resulted in increasing confrontation by the former and violent reprisal by the latter. In 1970, the victory of the Bengali Awami League party in Pakistan's elections was met by refusal to recognize its claim to form government and later brutal repression in East Pakistan by West Pakistan's minority.[3] The fallout was a near civil war situation with armed Bengalis forming the Mukti Bahini (freedom force) and seeking refuge as well as training and supplies in India. Pakistan's response to the aforementioned Indian assistance was to launch a pre-emptive strike at India, which provided the Indian army the much-needed excuse to attack East Pakistan. Bangladesh emerged as an independent state in December 1971 with India as midwife, and the stage seemed set for a cordial relationship between the two.

The Mujib Era, 1971–5

Bangladesh's charismatic first leader Mujibur Rahman (Mujib) was in power until 1975, when he was assassinated. The leader of the Awami League party,

Mujib had tasted victory in the elections of 1970[4] in undivided Pakistan, and his long years of confrontation and resistance to West Pakistani rule had cemented his dominance of the Bangladeshi polity. His term in office may be thought of as the 'honeymoon' years between India and Bangladesh, when any differences were covered up to show a strong front. Mujib appeared to need India to bolster his position, and there is a belief that this was the reasoning behind the signing of the Indo-Bangladesh Friendship Treaty of 1972.[5] Indian Prime Minister Indira Gandhi was equally popular at home for having won a resounding victory against Pakistan, and her increased stature and confidence, as well as the fraternity of the war time alliance, appeared to make her favourably disposed towards Bangladesh.

However, minor irritants had already surfaced between the two neighbours. Bangladeshis perceived the victory as being an equal partnership with India and consequently were aggrieved at not being equal divisors of the spoils of war, particularly captured arms and ammunition.[6] The Friendship Treaty with India was being viewed with suspicion in Bangladesh as a means of asserting Indian hegemony. A trade pact between the two states also appeared to lead to smuggling across the border and increases in the prices of essentials in Bangladesh, creating misgivings about the fairness of the pact.[7] A more serious complaint against India was the issue of water sharing, since the two states share numerous rivers, in which Bangladesh is the lower riparian, of which the most important are the Ganges and the Brahmaputra.

The Farakka Barrage

Mooted initially in the 1960s, India finished construction of the Farakka Barrage on the Ganges in 1975. The barrage was 75 feet high and 7,000 feet long and also involved a 26.5-mile feeder canal. The aim of this project was to flush out the Hooghly river near Kolkata and keep that port operational.[8] Bangladesh claimed that the Ganges was an international river and therefore the issue of any construction that would affect the flow of water to a lower riparian should be resolved by mutual discussion. In 1972, a Joint Rivers Commission set up between India and Bangladesh for the purpose of carrying out a survey of the shared river systems assisted in the negotiations between the two states. The cooperative spirit ran into problems over the augmentation of the fair weather flow of the Ganges. While India proposed augmentation by diverting water from the Brahmaputra and constructing a feeder canal through Bangladeshi territory, Bangladesh countered with a plan to augment through storage in the Ganges basin. Over the years Bangladesh asked to include Nepal in the process by proposing to build storage dams in India and Nepal to be used in the monsoon season. This demand was, however, not met by India, which preferred to keep discussions bilateral.[9] The two states also disagreed about the amount of water that India could use to flush the Hooghly. The unilateral Indian move to construct the Farakka Barrage therefore became a symbol of India's power vis-à-vis Bangladesh.

Despite the aforementioned disagreement, Indo-Bangladesh ties appear to have been on an even keel during this period. Much of this can be explained by the recent history in which the two states collaborated in the war against Pakistan and shared the euphoria of the largest surrender of troops since World War II when General Niazi of Pakistan capitulated at Dhaka. The leaders of both states were secure in the adulation they received for their victories and had no reason to be wary of the other state.

Mujibur Rahman was assassinated on 15 August 1975 along with members of his family, and Bangladesh was plunged into chaos. A series of coups and counter-coups ended with General Ziaur Rahman, the army chief, becoming president. This ended the 'honeymoon' period and marked a watershed in the Indo-Bangladeshi relationship with a more guarded and cautious relationship emerging in the future.

1975–90: Fluctuations

Bangladesh was under military or quasi-military rule between 1975 and 1990 and was ruled by General Rahman and later General Ershad. During this time, India's political situation also fluctuated tremendously, with the Congress party under Indira Gandhi losing power in 1977 and returning after a three-year gap, in which time the Janata government enjoyed greater success in its relationship with the country's neighbours. While the thaw ended with Indira Gandhi's return, another opening was made possible by her son and successor as PM, Rajiv Gandhi—who embarked on a diplomatic offensive upon his accession. The period ended in 1990 with the removal of General Ershad from office as president and the holding of democratic elections in 1991.

The impact of the assassination of Mujibur Rahman was to dilute ties with India. Reportedly, Indira Gandhi showed her distaste for the military government that succeeded Rahman and even sought to obliquely justify the Emergency imposed by her government in 1975 as a response to a deteriorating regional situation.[10] On the other side, Ziaur Rahman, who consolidated his position as the president of Bangladesh, embarked on a foreign policy that was very different from that of his predecessor—one that challenged India openly.

Specifically, Bangladesh raised the Farakka issue at the Istanbul Islamic Foreign Ministers' Conference in 1976, as well as the Summit conference of the nonaligned countries in the same year at Colombo. Later, it also brought up the issue in the United Nations General Assembly; but there, as at Colombo, various states urged that the matter be resolved bilaterally.[11] These attempts to internationalize the issue were in direct contradiction to the preferred Indian method of bilateral negotiations, particularly sensitive for India due to the possibility of superpower interference during the Cold War.

However, in March 1977, the Congress in India suffered a humiliating defeat and was replaced by the centrist Janata party, which remained in power for two-and-a-half years before succumbing to factional infighting and defeat at a new election. The Janata government led by Morarji Desai appeared to be more amenable to negotiation with Bangladesh and, with Indian Defence Minister Jagjivan Ram serving as an emissary, soon reached an accord on Farakka in November 1977. Interestingly, Ziaur Rahman blamed sections of the Indian government (particularly in West Bengal) for interference in Bangladeshi politics but stopped short of actually naming the Janata government.[12] Indo-Bangladesh ties improved somewhat with the visit of Indian premier Morarji Desai, the first in seven years.[13] While the Farakka accord was some progress on a thorny issue, it was not the only problem between the states. Another irritant was (and remains) unresolved border issues.

Border Disputes
India's border with Bangladesh is long and marked by numerous exclaves and enclaves—the legacy of a well-intentioned but difficult to implement Partition plan. What has made it more difficult has been the terrain of riverine swamp that creates problems of passage for the population. Specific border problems in the 1970s and 1980s included the Tin Bigha Corridor, Muhurir Char dispute, and the New Moore island disputes. The Tin Bigha case revolved around an Indian corridor that would connect a Bangladeshi enclave with the rest of the state. However, a 1974 Indian government agreement to lease the Tin Bigha corridor—which was 178 metres by 85 metres—in perpetuity to Bangladesh found considerable opposition since it would mean that a similar Indian territory would remain cut off from the rest of India. Bangladesh viewed Indian recalcitrance as a betrayal of faith. The matter was eventually resolved in 1982 with India agreeing to the perpetual lease of the corridor by Bangladesh though implementation was delayed by some years.[14]

In 1979, a border clash took place between members of the Indian Border Security Force (BSF) and the Bangladesh Rifles over the newly surfaced land on the Muhuri River. While India viewed the matter as a minor one, to the Ziaur Rahman government it appeared as a major provocation by India. A similar situation arose over the New Moore Island, also called Purbasha or South Talpatty on the Bangladesh side. This island, formed by silt in Haribhanga River's estuary, created the question of a large amount of sea bed that could be claimed by either side on its possession. Both sides provided evidence that the flow of the main branch of the river encapsulated the island, though the Indian navy laid claim to it.[15] The island became another symbol of the fluctuating Indo-Bangladesh relationship, with the issue being raised whenever ties were fractious and being shelved when a rapprochement appeared.

In December 1979, Indira Gandhi returned as India's PM leading a Congress government, and ties with Bangladesh appeared to have deteriorated again. A change in Bangladesh's government also followed through the assassination of Ziaur Rahman in November 1981. This did not have as much of an effect on the relationship as the arrival of his successor, army chief H.M. Ershad, who took over as Chief Martial Law Administrator from the civilian government that replaced Rahman and later became president. Ershad met with goodwill from India. His initial loyalty to the civilian government in Bangladesh from which he took over also buttressed his bona fides.

There was an upswing in India's relations with Bangladesh in 1982, called a 'honeymoon' year by Kathryn Jacques.[16] This may have been due to the smooth transition of power of Ershad as compared to Ziaur Rahman's more unstable rise. Ershad's two-day summit with the Indian leader in October 1982 was the result of diplomatic manoeuvres by both countries' diplomats. The summit involved negotiations on all the contentious matters between the two and significantly produced agreement on the perpetual lease of Tin Bigha to Bangladesh. While similar progress was claimed on the Farakka problem and a memorandum of understanding (MoU) was actually signed, real progress on that issue was stymied by, as usual, differing interpretations of what should be done.

In 1983 two events highlighted the fluctuations in the relationship when within weeks of the creation of a programme of regional cooperation—South Asian Regional Cooperation (SARC)—the Indian government decided to construct a fence around Bangladesh's border to prevent illegal immigrants entering India. The fence was to be a 3,300-km-long barrier to numerous immigrants who had entered India, specifically targeting the changing demographics of the Indian state of Assam, which was reportedly experiencing an increase in its Muslim population through refugee influx.[17] While the fence, being on Indian territory, was within India's rights to construct, Bangladesh responded with outrage over the symbolic barricade that it represented. Matters were not helped by Ershad's (and even current governments') assertions that very few or no Bangladeshi nationals were infiltrating India. This remains a major bone of contention to this day with accounts of illegal Bangladeshi immigrants in India varying from an exaggerated 20 million to about 2 million.[18]

The ascension of Rajiv Gandhi as Indian PM in 1984 following his mother's assassination at the hands of Sikh extremists brought a new flavour to India's relations with its neighbours. His image as 'Mr Clean', his cordial demeanour, and his determination to do away with 'politics' and replace it with a managerial style of operation were initially welcomed, both domestically and internationally. In good dynastic tradition, he exercised personal control over foreign policy decisions and was noted for his enthusiastic diplomacy—visible through visits to 48 countries in his term.[19] More significant for India's neighbours were Rajiv's conciliatory approach and an emphasis on regional relationships. Specifically, Rajiv Gandhi appeared enthusiastic for the new South Asian Association for Regional Cooperation (SAARC)—a fuller version of the earlier SARC—that was to be formally inaugurated in December 1985. He also reached an agreement with Bangladeshi President Ershad to renew efforts to solve the water-sharing problem. The Nassau Accord, as it was called, led to a new MoU between India and Bangladesh, one which seemed more substantial than previous efforts.[20] While retaining certain features of previous agreements, this accord also led to the creation of a Joint Committee of Experts (JCE) that would explore alternative plans for water sharing. Crucially, the JCE would also have a greater mandate and range of options to explore, including building additional barrages, canals, and dams in both the countries. Sweetening the deal further was Rajiv Gandhi's acquiescence in permitting Nepal to be a part of the discussions—a long-standing Bangladeshi demand.

Like other initiatives, these agreements, while exploring new territory, floundered due to a combination of domestic factionalism, pre-existing national positions, and the problems of getting a trilateral arrangement to work. The diverting of the Indian leadership's attention to new problems such as terrorism in Punjab and Assam, the Tamil problem in Sri Lanka, internal problems in various states, and accusations against the PM of being complicit in the Bofors deal displaced the long-standing but non-threatening problem of water sharing from focus. Even SAARC remains a missed opportunity, partly from the very obvious Indo-Pakistan problem, and possibly because other states fear India's natural economic dominance that would dwarf their role.

In sum, the period from 1975 to 1990 was marked by considerable fluctuation in Indo-Bangladesh ties. From a low after the 1975 coups and counter-coups, there appear to have been three periods of hope in the Janata government initiatives, the Ershad summit in 1982, and the Rajiv Gandhi diplomacy—all of which were followed by a progressive deterioration and return to a status quo of discontentment.

THE ERA OF TRANSFORMATION: 1990 TO THE PRESENT

The years 1989–91 saw monumental changes in both South Asia and the world. Globally, communism suffered a loss of internal cohesion and after the break up of the Soviet bloc, market capitalism became entrenched as 'the only game in town'. Regionally, India ended decades of obsession with welfare socialism and liberalized its economy due to both domestic and external compulsions, similar to its neighbours. Additionally, the dominance of the Congress party was threatened for a second time by the appearance of a Janata Dal led government; in its short tenure, it managed to leave a lasting impact by creating a constituency of mobilized lower castes who would increasingly vote for community-based parties rather than a national one. Hindu nationalism arose as a force under the stewardship of the Bharatiya Janata Party (BJP), creating a challenge for the secular and plural identity of Nehruvian India by offering a Hindu-based one. This was mirrored in both South Asia and the world by the rise of Islamic fundamentalism which threatened the autonomy of domestic forces from religious extremism.

In Bangladesh, President Ershad was forced to step down as a result of joint action by the two main opposition political parties, the Bangladesh National Party (BNP) and the Awami League, both led by female dependents of the former leaders—Begum Khaleda Zia (Ziaur Rahman's widow) and Sheikh Hasina Wajed (Mujib's daughter). The elections resulted in the victory of the BNP with Khaleda Zia as PM.

The resumption of democracy in Bangladesh coincided with the return of the Congress in 1991, albeit a non-dynastic Congress under veteran leader Narasimha Rao. Rajiv Gandhi's assassination in 1991 by a Tamil extremist suicide bomber had required the Congress to come up with new leadership, which had paved the way for Rao. Rao's and the Congress' eventual exit from power was mirrored by the BNP which was replaced in the 1996 elections by the Awami League. A coalition of centrist parties took office in India under the name of the United Front until 1998, after which the BJP was able to win two elections and form government until 2004. The Congress returned under new, but not quite dynastic, management in 2004 in an odd arrangement where Sonia Gandhi (Rajiv Gandhi's widow) was the leader of the party but a non-political technocrat, Manmohan Singh, became the PM.

Bangladesh's relations with India did not change substantially under the new democratic regime. The anti-India stance of the BNP and the rise of Hindu nationalism in India seem to have combined to stall any progress. The one major achievement appears to have been the recognition by Bangladesh of Indian sovereignty over the Tin Bigha Corridor, which India leased over to Bangladesh.

The 1990s witnessed the rise of extremism in South Asia, of both Hindu and Muslim variety. The BJP's crusade to build a temple on disputed territory inhabited by a mosque spiralled out of control, with a rampaging mob destroying the four-centuries-old structure. This led to violent retribution by Muslim fundamentalists both within India (blasts in Bombay in 1993) and elsewhere in South Asia (Hindus were targeted in Pakistan and Bangladesh). Indo-Bangladesh ties were affected by this animosity and by the emergence and increasing political relevance of extremist parties and groups such as the BJP and Shiv Sena in India (and the Rashtriya Swayamsevak Sangh (RSS), Vishwa Hindu Parishad (VHP), and Bajrang Dal—extremist Hindu social organizations that urge various versions of a Hindu state) and the Jamaat Islami and recently the Harkat-ul-Jihad-al-Islami–Bangladesh (HUJI-B) in Bangladesh.[21] The rise in terrorist activity in various parts of both countries by such groups has sharpened perceptions of 'Hindu India' and 'Islamic Bangladesh, clouding other pressing issues.

The return of an Awami League government in Bangladesh took place in 1996 with much political drama. Rigged elections held in March 1996 (which returned the BNP) were denounced as a coup, and opposition protests led to the business lobby persuading the president to call for fresh elections in which the Awami League was able to form a government, albeit with help from erstwhile (and imprisoned) President Ershad's Jatiyo party.[22] The Awami League government's return after two decades boded well for Indo-Bangladesh ties. An immediate result was the resolution of one aspect of the water-sharing problem in the shape of a treaty on the Ganges water.[23] The treaty was signed by the minority (and fairly short) government of H.D. Deve Gowda of India and Sheikh Hasina Wajed of Bangladesh. The Indian government appeared to want to strengthen relations with Bangladesh while Hasina's election promise of getting water from the Ganges demanded some creativity and flexibility. The treaty's advantages are in its duration of 30 years, as well as the differential rates of water to be supplied to both countries at different levels of flow. While this has settled (for the duration of the treaty) the issue of the Ganges water, a similar framework has not been applied to the other rivers that the two states share, and so a comprehensive settlement eludes the two states.

Another issue that has exacerbated problems is the issue of Bangladeshi illegal immigrants, both historical and present, whose numbers are disputed, ranging from an estimated 20 million touted by the BJP leader L.K. Advani to no more than 2 million by Bangladeshi official estimates.[24] From India's point of view, East Bengali Muslim leaders had historically tried to settle Muslims in tribal areas which later remained in India (in Assam, Tripura, and other adjoining states). A large number had followed during the Pakistani backlash against Bengali separatism. Since 1971, yet more refugees have crossed over, creating problems in neighbouring Indian states. The reluctance of Bangladesh to address this problem and the fiery rhetoric of Hindu nationalists who paint scenarios of waves of Muslim immigration that would at once overwhelm certain districts and also provide refuge for Islamic terrorists have compounded the issue to one of competing nationalisms. Of particular note is the previously mentioned HUJI–B, a terrorist group that was created in 1992 and has been known to collaborate with Al Qaeda, Jaish-e-Mohammed and Lashkar-e-Toiba. HUJI–B demands an Islamic state in Bangladesh and has been accused by Indians of cooperating with and training ULFA (United Liberation Front of Asom) militants in Assam. Another Islamic militant group, the Asif Reza Commando Force, is held responsible for the attack on the American Center in Kolkata in January 2002.[25] The issue of terrorism in India has grown more acute due to the concerns of numerous illegal immigrants who are spread out across many Indian towns and are indistinguishable from other Indians, especially Bengalis. While Bangladesh disclaims that any such groups are operating on its territory and in turn accuses India of supporting anti-Bangladesh groups, it seems clear that there is a basic lack of cooperation that does not augur well for relations between the two states.

India's problems with Bangladesh have continued over the border enclaves—which saw heavy skirmishing between India's BSF and the Bangladesh Rifles in April 2001, leading to the deaths of numerous soldiers. Though Bangladesh eventually pulled out of the disputed territory, the damage to Indo-Bangladesh ties was considerable.[26]

In the period since 1991, both states have settled into a relationship where expectations appear to be low and frequent minor irritants like border issues create occasional news. There is a sense on both sides that opportunities have been lost and that a more fruitful and cooperative relationship is not only possible but also desirable. Bangladesh's democratic sojourn was interrupted in 2007 when public exasperation with the bitterly competitive two-party system and its increasing irregularities led to a takeover by the military, which installed a caretaker government that was considered more pragmatic and beneficial for the ties with India by a former Bangladeshi diplomat.[27] The return of a Congress-led coalition in India in 2004 may have also reassured India's neighbours who are uncertain about the rhetoric and reality in the BJP's campaign promises.

A final area of both prospects and derived problems lies in the field of economic cooperation. India and Bangladesh have the potential to benefit each other tremendously, but their failure to do so has increased trade costs for both (by trading with distant states) as well as retarded regional cooperation. Bangladesh has failed to use India's burgeoning market as an outlet for its produce, even though figures indicate that it is India's leading regional trade partner.[28] India's attempts to tap into the ample gas reserves in Bangladesh have not made any headway, again due to the distrust that has plagued the relationship. In 2007 this distrust was illustrated by the failure by the Tata group to get its $3 billion investment plan approved after a long wait, and the subsequent cancellation of the project in August 2008 was recognized as a missed opportunity on both sides of the border.[29] The Bay of Bengal Initiative for Multi-Sectoral and Technical Cooperation (BIMSTEC) was an organization founded jointly by India, Bangladesh, Bhutan, Myanmar, Sri Lanka, and Thailand in 1997 with the primary aim of fostering economic integration. Though welcomed by Bangladeshis, BIMSTEC has been another venture that has potential but has not lived up to its name as yet.[30] Even at a smaller level, a proposed free-trade area between the two countries has not taken off though Nepal and Sri Lanka have similar agreements and benefit disproportionately more than India.

The following sections will attempt to examine this troubled relationship from three different levels of analysis by studying the role of systemic, state, and individual level factors.

SYSTEMIC-LEVEL FACTORS

There are two levels of the international system that impact the Indo-Bangladesh relationship. One is the structure of the global system and its processes—this includes the superpowers and the Cold War until 1990, and also their interaction with rising international powers like China. At the more localized level, the states of South Asia themselves form a sub-system that is relatively free of external pressures for most of the time. Over the last six decades, superpower interest in South Asia has been minimal, making a direct appearance only in two periods, during the Soviet invasion of Afghanistan and, more recently, during the US-led war on terror. The relative distance of South Asia from the radar of strategic interests of both the superpowers in the Cold War meant that states in this region formed an autonomous sub-system for the most part. In this secondary system, India has been the regional hegemon by virtue of its size, population, economy, military, and geographic spread and contiguity to other states. For the purpose of analysis from a systemic level, both systems can therefore be considered to have played a role in the Indo-Bangladeshi relationship. In general, global systemic processes appear to have played a very minor role, and the subordinate state system of South Asia carries greater explanatory power for the fluctuating ties between the two countries.

Bangladesh's birth took place at a time of superpower interest in South Asia. The US reliance on Pakistan to forge a rapprochement with China had led to closer ties between the two states, and therefore India's intervention in East Pakistan was resisted by words and action. Barring this indirect instance (since Bangladesh had not emerged as an independent state), there has been no superpower interference or interest in Indo-Bangladeshi ties. However, the global system has exerted an indirect influence on the relationship. Specifically, Jacques makes the claim that there appears to be a pattern where India has been more willing to adopt a conciliatory approach when its relationship with external powers has been better.[31]

A more concrete example of systemic-level process might be the tension between secular globalization and traditional identity that is underway across the world and captured by political scientist Benjamin Barber in the evocative term 'Jihad v. McWorld'.[32] Over the last two decades, India's trajectory is more firmly established in the globalized economy, where national boundaries give way to secular identities (though traditionalist reactions against this are visible in religious and other socially organized resistance), while Bangladesh, perhaps due to its less developed economy, is somewhat more established in the traditional part. This tension may explain the continuing divergence in recent years between the two states. The increasing Islamization of Bangladesh beginning in 1975 with the negation of secularism does clash with both the increasing globalization within India and in the world.

However, much more can be understood from the structure of the South Asian system. Indian dominance has produced a strong state/weak state relationship with all its neighbours, leading to patterns of common behaviour across all of them. Therefore, as a strong state, India has pursued a policy of eschewing great power presence or interference in the region, since that would dilute its strength, but Bangladesh (and other neighbours) has sought external help. Moreover, India has displayed a penchant for resolving problems using a bilateral framework, while Bangladesh has expressed a preference for a multilateral approach. India has also frowned upon the use of international organizations acting as mediating bodies in any dispute, while grievances (notably border and water disputes) have been raised by Bangladesh at various international forums.

The clearest example of this type of differing behaviour is visible in the Ganges water dispute. As recalled earlier, Bangladesh had raised the issue at the Istanbul Islamic Foreign Ministers' Conference, the Non-Aligned Summit in 1976, and the UN. India was able to prevail upon members at the latter two venues to urge both states to keep discussions bilateral. Later, Bangladesh expressed a long-standing preference for examining the water sharing issue in a multilateral framework including Nepal. India's reluctance to agree to this underlines its behaviour as a strong state, though it eventually agreed to Nepal's participation.

The weak state hypothesis also goes a long way towards explaining Bangladesh's disinterest in being involved in a close relationship with India economically. The relative failure of BIMSTEC, as well as other cooperative ventures between the two states, is very likely due to the Bangladeshi concern of being economically dominated by India. It is revealing that the SAARC was born as a Bangladeshi initiative under Ziaur Rahman, and equally so the fact that it has not taken off because of the same fear expressed earlier. If anything, Bangladesh embarked on its own Look East policy of engaging Southeast Asian countries, when an Indian market for its goods remains much closer.

STATE-LEVEL FACTORS

A state-level analysis reveals more about the on–off relationship between India and Bangladesh. This section will not only analyse issues of national identity, and domestic political forces in the shape of political parties, but also non-party pressure groups, as well as the prevailing political conditions in both states.

The nature of India's social system compared to that of its neighbours reveals one major difference: unlike the other states, India is a multi-ethnic, multi-religious, and multi-linguistic society. The other states are generally unified on two of these divides. So Pakistan, Bangladesh, and Nepal are dominated overwhelmingly by one religious group, and only Sri Lanka has one reinforcing cleavage. Linguistically, the first three states are more unified around one national language. Compared to this, India's diversity has resulted in the necessity for a highly accommodative system for minorities. Consequently, the Indian national identity that was manufactured after independence sought to stress a unity amongst the plurality by keeping room for all groups. The composite Indian national identity that emerged was highly inclusive—secular and pluralistic. This immediately put the identities of neighbouring states in competition with the Indian identity, since they shared some commonality. With the exception of Sri Lanka's Sinhalese language and Buddhist heritage (which also can be linked to India), all of India's neighbours share ethnic, religious, or linguistic ties with India. It would, therefore, make sense that their concept of national identity would urge a differentiation from that of Indian identity for fear of irredentist claims from within India. A more significant problem is the possibility of the raison d'etre of a particular state's existence itself being questioned, given commonalities with India.

Therefore, Bangladesh's national identity, though cohesively knit around the Bengali linguistic identity and safe in numerical terms in its Muslim facet, might still be threatened by the larger all-encompassing identity of its largest neighbour India.[33] Given the fact that the Indian state of West Bengal is a mirror-opposite of Bangladesh (the Hindu and Muslim percentages are approximately reversed), all else being similar, it is not unreasonable to understand Bangladeshi concern about being brought formally or informally into the kaleidoscope of the Indian Union.[34] This is an additional explanation for Bangladeshi reluctance to engage with India more closely or in a purely bilateral format and might explain why any overture towards India is viewed with suspicion.

At the level of domestic political forces, a comparison of political parties in India does not reveal any pattern except that centrist Janata Party and similar Janata Dal and United Front governments have enjoyed a better relationship with Bangladesh than their Congress counterparts, producing both the 1977 and 1996 water-sharing agreements. The Desai government had gone out of its way to reassure Bangladesh of India's friendship, as did the V.P. Singh and later Deve Gowda governments. However, any meaningful comparison is difficult to undertake since Janata-type governments have had very short innings and it is difficult to say how much can be attributed to the foreign policy goals of a party as opposed to the approach of a new government for regional rapprochement. In recent years, the formation of coalition governments in India have made any major changes in foreign policy difficult for any one party to effect and, there have been no sharp departures from existing policy. Much more is visible in the clear divide on the other side of the border where the BNP has defined itself as a party that is suspicious of India, while the Awami League, through Mujib's association and later the BNP's accusations, is seen as a pro-Indian force. It is worth noting, however, that the Padua border incident occurred under an Awami League government and that the League has ratcheted up its anti-Indian rhetoric once in power with coalition partners that are not very pro-India.

While political party formation in India is more than a century old and has acquired the hallmarks of a competitive party system (albeit with the South Asian tradition of dynastic succession in many cases), Bangladeshi parties appear to be cultist or dynastic vehicles with little to distinguish by way of policy or ideology. In such a nascent political system where populism rules, differentiation in foreign policy appears to be the easy way of distinguishing a rival party, which might explain the orientation of the BNP. A confrontational approach to a larger power can also appear as a strategy to obtain political gain in the lack of any concrete domestic strategy.

It can be argued that the level of domestic stability appears to be another factor that has cast a shadow on Indo-Bangladesh ties. In 1975, 1983–4, and 1987–9, the ruling Congress was faced with major domestic problems in the shape of the Emergency, Punjab and Assam crises, and Kashmir and Tamil (Sri Lanka) crises, respectively. In the last two cases, both the Indira Gandhi and Rajiv Gandhi's governments faced considerable domestic opposition from rival parties as well as internal disquiet. All these times were marked by the lack of amicability with Bangladesh. Conversely, when the domestic climate seemed stable in 1977 (newly victorious Janata), 1982 (relative calm in Indira Gandhi's second innings in office), 1985 (Rajiv Gandhi's huge mandate in the elections), there appears to have been a spurt of active goodwill diplomacy from the Indian side. Similarly, on the Bangladesh side, with the emergence of Ziaur Rahman in 1976 after a series of coups in Bangladesh, the anti-Indian attitude is more visible than in the bonhomie surrounding Ershad's takeover under much calmer circumstances. The end of competitive party politics between 2007–9 also appears to have brought in stability (albeit at the expense of democracy) and India's relationship with Bangladesh is, if not on the upswing, definitely better than a few years ago.

The rise of militant religious extremists is a third factor that has influenced the two states. Both states are affected by this; Bangladesh's Islamic groups have been mentioned earlier, while India has the Sangh parivar[35] group (as also Islamic groups, but they are not relevant here). The rise of Hindu nationalism and violent outbreaks in Ayodhya, Gujarat, and more recently in Maharashtra have created an impression that the Indian state remains secular in name but Hindu in reality to the detriment of minorities, especially Muslims. This has led to a retaliatory mood in Bangladesh with minority insecurity increasing on both sides.

INDIVIDUAL-LEVEL EXPLANATIONS

The role of individuals in foreign policy depends on the personality of the leader concerned, as well as the nature of the political system—the amount of latitude available to influence policy. Developing countries tend to be more prone to individual actions in foreign policy-making due to the relatively simple and inflexible structure of decision-making. India's foreign policy has always been a prime ministerial prerogative beginning with Jawaharlal Nehru, who shaped it according to his preferences. Much the same could be said of his daughter Indira Gandhi, under whose direction it took a pro-Soviet tilt, and of Rajiv Gandhi, who as mentioned before carried out many visits to foreign countries in his term in office. However, in the realm of framing a policy for Bangladesh, Indian leaders seem to have been reactive to events rather than initiating them. Initiatives have been broad rather than specific, or have been unilateral pronouncements such as the construction of the fence along Bangladesh's border.

While Indira Gandhi and Mujibur Rahman enjoyed a good relationship, this was possibly more due to a commonality of interests—facing Pakistan—that was not available to their successors. Indira Gandhi's disapproval of the coups that installed the military and Ziaur Rahman, found an equally hostile response. However, Indira Gandhi's relationship with Ershad was different, as mentioned before, possibly due to a more stable political climate in 1982. Rajiv Gandhi's initiatives were also welcomed in Bangladesh, leading to a brief spurt in goodwill that also petered out over time. What might explain this lack of attention is the fact that Indian foreign policy remains obsessed with Pakistan at the regional level, and unless a high-profile issue like water sharing turns up, there is not much about Bangladesh on India's strategic radar. In fact, India's foreign policy vis-à-vis Bangladesh appears to be one of benign neglect. Over the years, as major issues have been resolved (Ganges waters), India's individual leadership has had less impact on its policy with Bangladesh. Certainly, the coalition governments since 1991 allow for less personal flavour and more coalitional preferences; hence, there is no discussion here of Narasimha Rao, Atal Bihari Vajpayee, and Manmohan Singh.

The same is not the case with Bangladesh, where individual leadership has been dominant in foreign policy-making. This is possible since, as explained earlier, the political systems consist of parties that are personalized vehicles rather than a platform of leaders. In this situation, a Khaleda Zia can and has had much more impact in defining the tone of policy towards India, while presidential leaders like Ziaur Rahman and Ershad were even less restrained officially.

***

India's relationship with Bangladesh can be explained at all three levels of analysis. India's position as a strong state at the South Asian systemic level encourages a preference for bilateralism and engagement, whereas as the weaker state Bangladesh prefers to hedge its bets via multilateralism and distancing from a giant and (geographically) enveloping neighbour. This explanation for weak ties is supplemented by state-level explanations, notably by questions of national identity and domestic political forces. It is very likely that Bangladesh's exclusivist national identity could be threatened by an inclusivist and plural national identity like that of India. Even in the absence of any concrete threat by India to Bangladesh's existence, the perception of being threatened or intimidated by a larger and more powerful neighbour appears to drive the relationship. Possibly to some extent Bangladesh's identity, like that of Pakistan's, is built around not being Indian, in which case distancing the state from India would become an automatic reflex.

The extent of political stability also appears to have an impact on the relationship. Whenever Bangladesh has appeared unstable in the past—as during the series of coups following Mujib's assassination—or the regime has been vulnerable, the anti-India rhetoric appears to be ratcheted up, possibly to acquire legitimacy by defying a(n) (imagined) threat from India. On the Indian side as well, domestic political instability during the Emergency and later during times of crisis with separatist movements resulted in inflexibility of the Indian government. Magnanimity was more likely when the government was secure and could take a bold step.

While some scholars, notably Jacques, believe that Indo-Bangladesh ties suffered when a Congress government was in power in India, the evidence suggests a mixed record. Other party governments had a better record, such as the Janata Party, Janata Dal, and United Front governments. But the fact that their tenure was relatively short means that meaningful comparison with a long-term Congress (or BJP) government is difficult. Certainly, the BJP's record in office during its six years from 1998 to 2004 was fairly similar to that of Congress governments, in that relations with Bangladesh remained in a rut with no major breakthroughs. On the Bangladeshi side, the nature of political party definitely made a difference, with cordiality having marked the first Awami League government and a long-term water-sharing treaty having marked its second innings. In contrast, the Ziaur Rahman regime and its later avatar BNP were noticeably cooler towards the idea of a stronger relationship with India. The BNP has positioned itself as the 'anti-India' party in the Bangladeshi political spectrum and has sought to define the Awami League as a 'pro-India' party.[36] The use of alignment vis-à-vis India as a definition mechanism points to the lack of well-defined ideological and policy positions between the major parties, something not uncommon in polities where political party formation is hostage to frequent interruptions by autocratic rule and hence does not acquire complexity and sophistication.

Individual-level factors appear to matter less over time, perhaps a reflection of changing and maturing polities, at least on the Indian side. While both Indira Gandhi and her successors until Rajiv Gandhi were more active in foreign policy formulation, and hence initiatives could signal a broad and dramatic shift in course, the formation of coalition governments since the 1990s appears to have lessened an individual's capacity for action. However, in Bangladesh the individual role remains significant, whether the state be under autocratic regime or democratic governance, possibly because of the political parties being personal political vehicles of individuals.

In summing up, it appears that Indo-Bangladesh ties are influenced more by the nature of the state system in South Asia as well as the domestic political forces in both states. The possibility that the strong state/weak state perception can be changed for a more cooperative version depends to some extent on both states. For India, it is incumbent to reassure Bangladesh that its identity, state, and borders are free from Indian domination, which might mean making some concessions on borders. The formulation of a long-term foreign policy that seeks a better relationship over smaller considerations might allow some conciliation on border and water-sharing issues. On its part, Bangladesh must realize the inevitability of India's proximity and also the fact that this can have benefits. For both states, the revival of a multilateral regional initiative like

SAARC assumes tremendous significance since it can provide a forum as well as a mechanism to resolve issues.

In the end, both states have an incentive to cooperate simply because of the porous nature of their border and their proximity. In an era when regional economic cooperation is the norm, India and Bangladesh lag behind without compelling reasons to do so.

NOTES

1. See Michael Brecher (1963), 'International Relations and Asian Studies: The Subordinate State System of South Asia', *World Politics*, 15 (2), pp. 213–25. While Brecher argues for a broader system in southern Asia that includes China, I believe it is possible to have a more restricted system comprising only South Asian states due to their relative isolation from the rest of Asia, both geographically as well as politically. Therefore, the subordinate state system here will comprise only of South Asian states where India, as largest and most powerful state, is the de facto hegemon.

2. Sanjay Bhardwaj (2003), 'Bangladesh Foreign Policy vis-à-vis India', *Strategic Analysis*, 27 (2), pp. 265–6.

3. West Pakistan was a minority in terms of population, though still politically dominant. See Ian Talbot (1998), *Pakistan: A Modern History* (New York: St. Martin's Press), p. 24.

4. The Awami League won half of the seats in that election, giving rise to the prospect of West Pakistan being ruled by an East Pakistan (Bengali) government. See Talbot, *Pakistan*, p. 200.

5. Ishtiaq Hussain (1981), 'Bangladesh–India Relations: Issues and Problems', *Asian Survey*, 21 (11), p. 1116. According to Hussain, while Mujib believed the signing of a treaty would highlight the independence of Bangladesh, he is also suspected of using the treaty to invoke Indian support in case of domestic problems. This may explain why after 1975 Bangladesh remained highly suspicious that India was providing assistance to pro-Mujib elements.

6. Hussain, 'Bangladesh–India Relations', p. 1116.

7. Ibid., p. 1117. Hussain provides an interesting insight into the Bangladeshi psyche, suggesting that automatic suspicion of India having engineered the pact was a throwback to the past when there was a sense of exploitation from Hindu zamindars and business class.

8. For a good background to the Ganges water-sharing problem, see Ashok Swain (1993), 'Conflicts over Water: The Ganges Water Dispute', *Security Dialogue*, 24 (4), pp. 429–39.

9. Hussain, 'Bangladesh–India Relations', p. 1122.

10. Kathryn Jacques (2000), *Bangladesh, India and Pakistan: International Relations and Regional Tensions in South Asia* (New York: St. Martin's Press), p. 30.

11. Hussain, 'Bangladesh–India Relations', p. 1121.

12. Jacques, *Bangladesh, India and Pakistan*, p. 39.

13. Ibid., p. 40.

14. See Bhardwaj, 'Bangladesh Foreign Policy vis-à-vis India'. A Bangladeshi interpretation of these problems is outlined in Lailufar Yasmin, 'Bangladesh–India Tussles', *South Asian Journal*, Electoral Politics in South Asia, 5, pp. 1–12 http:/www.southasianmedia.net/magazine/journal/bangladeshindia_tussels.htm (accessed on 12 September 2008).

15. Jacques, *Bangladesh, India and Pakistan*, pp. 52–3.

16. See Jacques, *Bangladesh, India and Pakistan*, p. 62.

17. See Mohammad Ataur Rahman (1984), 'Bangladesh in 1983: A Turning Point for the Military', *Asian Survey*, 24 (2), pp. 248–9. Also, Jacques, *Bangladesh, India and Pakistan*, p. 73.

18. While the 20 million figure is an exaggerated version heard only on TV news programmes and usually spoken by members of the Hindu right, a figure of 3 million is mentioned specifically in Yasmin, 'Bangladesh–India Tussles', p. 6. Praful Bidwai (2003) attributes the 20 million figure to Indian politician L.K. Advani in 'Beggaring the Neighbour', *Frontline*, 20 (4), 15–28 February, http://www.flonnet.com/fl2004/stories/20030228004410500.htm (accessed on 6 June 2009).

19. Jacques, *Bangladesh, India and Pakistan*, p. 83.

20. Peter Bertocci (1986), 'Bangladesh in 1985: Resolute against the Storms', *Asian Survey*, A Survey of Asia in 1985: Part II, 26 (2), pp. 233–4.

21. See Sreeradha Datta (2003), 'Bangladesh's Political Evolution: Growing Uncertainties', *Strategic Analysis*, 27 (2), for a description of Islamization within Bangladesh, pp. 233–49.

22. Stanley A. Kochanek (1998), 'Bangladesh in 1997: The Honeymoon is Over', *Asian Survey*, A Survey of Asia in 1997: Part II, 38 (2).

23. See Muhammad Mizanur Rahaman (2006), 'The Ganges Water Conflict: A Comparative Analysis of the 1977 Agreement and 1996 Treaty', *Asteriskos*, http://www.igesip.org/asteriskos/1_2/galego/art11.pdf (accessed on 12 September 2008).

24. India has often claimed the 20 million figure; see note 18 as well as a BBC story at http://news.bbc.co.uk/2/hi/programmes/from_our_own_correspondent/4653810.stm (accessed on 14 September 2008). However, Bangladeshi accounts do not address this claim directly, refuting the figure but avoiding mentioning a specific number.

25. From the *South Asian Terrorism Portal*, http://www.satp.org/satporgtp/countries/bangladesh/terroristoutfits/Huj.htm (accessed on 12 September 2008).

26. See, 'A Brush with Bangladesh', *The Hindu*, http://www.hinduonnet.com/fline/fl1810/18100280.htm (accessed on 4 October 2008).

27. Farooq Sobhan (2005), 'Indo-Bangladesh Relations: The Way Forward', http://www.bei-bd.org/docs/fs9.pdf (accessed on 3 October 2008).

28. India accounts for over 15 per cent of Bangladesh's imports and is a major trade partner. Source: *World Bank* report, 'India–Bangladesh: Bilateral Trade', December 2006, Chapter 2, p. 4, http://web.worldbank.org/WEBSITE/EXTERNAL/COUNTRIES/SOUTHASIAEXT/0, contentMDK:21177520-pagePK:146736-piPK:146830-theSitePK:223547,00.html (accessed on 6 June 2009).

29. 'India–Bangladesh Relations: Are the Carrots Working?', *India Post*, http://indiapost.com/article/perspective/3589/ (accessed on 14 September 2008).

30. See Zafar Sobhan (2007), 'Minority Opinion', *Daily Star*, http://www.bilaterals.org/article.php3?id_article=8493 (accessed on 14 September 2008).

31. Jacques, *Bangladesh, India and Pakistan*, p. 68.

32. Benjamin Barber (1992), 'Jihad v. McWorld', *Atlantic Monthly*, March, http://www.theatlantic.com/doc/199203/barber (accessed on 2 December 2008).

33. There are many sources for this line of argument. One such may be found in Hasan Zaheer (1994), *The Separation of East Pakistan: The Rise and Realization of Bengalis Muslim Nationalism* (Karachi: Oxford University Press), pp. 17–18.

34. Source: CIA World Factbook, https://www.cia.gov/library/publications/the-world-factbook/geos/BG.html, which gives Bangladesh's Muslim to Hindu ratio at 83 per cent to 16 per cent and https://www.cia.gov/library/publications/the-world-factbook/geos/IN.html which gives India's Hindu Muslim ratio at 80 per cent to 13 per cent. (Both were accessed on 6 June 2009.)

35. The Sangh Parivar (the family of associations) is the common name given to chauvinistic Hindu groups that advocate the creation of a Hindu, as opposed to secular, state as well as the elimination of personal law provisions that benefit minorities. Particularly targeting Muslims as outsiders who have not accepted India, the Sangh comprises the BJP, the RSS, VHP, and Bajrang Dal.

36. See Bhardwaj, 'Bangladesh Foreign Policy vis-à-vis India'.

5

Evolution of India's China Policy

JOHN W. GARVER

THINKING THROUGH THE UPHEAVAL, 1949–53

Three trends operating at the international system-level of analysis deeply influenced the China policy of newly independent India. First, the decisive victory of the Chinese Communist Party (CCP) in China's civil war led to the establishment in October 1949 of the People's Republic of China (PRC) as a Leninist–Stalinist style state that effectively united China for the first time in decades. That new Chinese state quickly eliminated the Tibetan buffer that had for centuries separated China and India, thereby destroying a central element of the China policy that independent India inherited from Britain.

Second, the accelerating collapse of the European colonial empires that had organized world power over the previous several centuries led to the entry of growing numbers of newly independent Asian and African nations onto the world stage. The collapse of the Japanese empire that had dominated East Asia and the British empire that had dominated South Asia posed the question of what sort of international order would replace those old imperial systems, or more specifically, what roles newly liberated India and China would play in the emerging post-colonial world.

The third trend was the onset of the Cold War between the Soviet and US-led camps, and the expansion of that Cold War to Asia circa 1950. This raised the prospect that Asia's post-colonial order would be defined by the United States (US)–Soviet struggle, with India's efforts to shape the new Asia free of Western domination being overwhelmed by the battles of the American and Soviet superpowers. From India's perspective, both the US and Russia were essentially Western powers.

The collapse of colonial empires paralleled by the onset of the Cold War presented both opportunities and dangers for India's national policies. India's leaders felt that India was a leader of the 'newly emerging nations' (to use the vocabulary of the era), and the situation of great international flux offered India the opportunity to use its influence to shape a new international order based on the indigenous nationalisms of the Asian and African peoples. The danger was that Indian efforts to consolidate the sovereignty of the 'emerging nations' might be overwhelmed by the Cold War between the two post-1945 superpowers. Indian leaders, and especially Jawaharlal Nehru, believed that the PRC's alignment—its support for or opposition to Indian efforts —could be a significant determinant of success of Indian efforts to shape post-colonial Asia.

At the level of national interest, the growing Chinese threat posted to India's national security via an ever-expanding Chinese military presence in Tibet exercised a deep influence on early Indian policy towards China. The CCP moved as swiftly as possible to bring Tibet under its control. In mid-1951, Chinese Communist military forces (the People's Liberation Army, or PLA) entered Tibet, building roads as they advanced. This launched what proved to be a near constant six-decade long drive to strengthen China's military capabilities in Tibet and integrate that region into the PRC. The previously remote, isolated, and militarily null region of Tibet gradually became the base for large and powerful Chinese military forces. For the first time since 1793, when a Chinese-Tibetan army marched on Kathmandu to punish Nepal's rulers, India faced large Chinese armies on its northern border. (Chinese armies withdrew from Tibet after chastizing the Nepalese in 1793.) Moreover, PLA armies in Tibet were supplied by ever-more-robust transport links to China's economic heartland. Preventing exactly such an eventuality had been the rationale for Britain's policy of maintaining Tibet as a buffer. Now that eventuality had materialized. Responding to this altered national security situation became, and has remained, a fundamental determinant in India's China policy.

At the decision-making level of analysis, the dominance of the Congress party on India's national scene deeply influenced the policy towards the PRC. While rejecting British rule over India, the Congress embraced British-derived institutions: parliamentary liberal democracy, rule of law, and civic freedom.[1] In terms of development efforts, the Congress rejected social revolution in favour of non-violent gradualism. From the Congress perspective, class struggle and revolution diverted energy and resources from pressing needs of economic development. This orientation of the Congress contrasted sharply with the CCP's embrace of Stalinist totalitarianism in a quest for a more 'advanced' socialist–communist society and participation in the global Communist Party movement dedicated to replacing 'bourgeois democracy' with revolutionary dictatorships. This stark difference in dominant political cultures contributed to tensions during the 1949–51 period when CCP deemed India's 'bourgeois' government worthy of revolutionary overthrow. It would play an even more important role in the early 1960s when the CCP assumed the role of providing politically correct leadership, non-revisionist (as the CCP then styled itself in its polemics with the Soviet Communist Party) leadership to the Asian and African revolutionaries.

The aspirations and calculations of Jawaharlal Nehru, who dominated India's foreign and security policy-making process in the 1950s, deeply influenced India's China policy. Nehru was the proud leader of what he saw as a historically great nation whose influence had radiated for centuries across Asia before being enslaved by British imperialism, but was now newly liberated. Nehru saw his task as India's leader to restore India to its rightful position as moral leader of Asia and the ex-colonial world. Nehru saw India's epic struggle for independence in the 1920s, 1930s, and 1940s as a key factor in the eventual collapse of European colonialism and found in this further vindication of his quest to establish India in a position of international prominence and influence.[2] Exactly what this meant in terms of relations with the PRC was not clear in the early period of Indian policy. But throughout, Nehru had an awareness of China's influence and potential power. Nehru had followed with sympathy China's anti-Japanese struggles in the 1930s, and was, of course, aware of China's role in Allied war strategy during the 1941–5 period. This meant that winning China to support India's efforts to shape post-colonial Asia—were that possible—would benefit those efforts, from Nehru's view.

There was a second element of Nehru's worldview that would prove an important influence on India's China policy: rejection of power politics. Use of coercion, and especially preparation, threatened use, or actual use of military force in relations among states was, Nehru believed, anachronistic. Reliance on coercion and military force was morally reprehensible and a manifestation of the depraved imperialist style of politics that had led the Western powers to conquer much of the non-Western world. Moreover, Nehru thought that in the nuclear age, the danger of escalation to a nuclear war combined with anti-war public sentiments would act to deter the outbreak of wars. War was a thing of the past, at least as far as enlightened and liberated India was concerned. Nehru accepted the idea embraced by Mohandas Gandhi and Rabindranath Tagore that there was an essential difference between the putatively materialistic, hedonistic, and amoral West and the more spiritual and moral civilizations of the East. It followed that growing influence of the East (India and China) would lead to a more peaceful, moral world.

By the mid-1950s, Nehru's vision of a peaceful, moral world, free of power politics, courtesy of the influence of enlightened 'Eastern' nations, helped inspire his quest for partnership with the PRC. During the early 1960s, it also underpinned the highly unrealistic policies Nehru adopted which contributed greatly to the Indian military debacle of 1962: deploying Indian military forces to far forward positions unsupported by adequate logistic lines and into positions oblivious of tactical consequences of particular terrain, and all underpinned by the assumption that China would not resort to use of military force against India. After India's 1962 defeat, the puncturing of this vision helped fuel the sense of betrayal of India by China. As late as the 1990s, Indian architects of a policy of manoeuvre towards the US would target Nehruvian idealism as a major mental obstacle to such a pragmatic policy of manoeuvre.[3]

Another factor at the decision-making level of analysis that would have a great influence on India's China policies in the 1950s was the death of Vallabhai Patel in 1950. Patel was the key organizational leader of the Congress during 1920s to 40s, who took the lead in securing accession of scores of reluctant princely states to the Indian Union in 1947. His influence within the Congress rivalled Nehru's, and had Patel lived, his more tough-minded approach to China would almost certainly have diluted Nehru's more idealistic policy course. Patel was much more apprehensive about the implications for Indian security of China's military occupation of Tibet and construction of roads to forward frontier regions. Patel favoured vigorous moves—military modernization, road construction, and search for diplomatic partners—to counter China's advances. He was even open to possible cooperation with the US to balance new, revolutionary China. Alone among the top echelon of Congress leaders, Patel had the standing and support to challenge Nehru's direction of foreign policy. His death at the age of 75 in 1950 left Nehru's direction of China policy virtually unchallenged—until that policy began to collapse in the lead-up to the 1962 war. In the years leading up to the 1962 war, the absence within India's top elite of anyone with the stature to challenge Nehru's handling of China policy would be an important, and tragic, factor.

The first period of Indian policy towards the PRC, from 1949 through 1953, was dominated by conflicts over Tibet. India tried to: (i) persuade Beijing to limit the PLA's occupation of Tibet and (ii) maintain its special rights in Tibet (small diplomatic missions in Lhasa and Shigatse) inherited from the British.[4] By 1952–3, however, India began signalling Beijing that

India was unwilling to cooperate with the US in 'containing Communist China'. New Delhi found multiple ways to deliver this message: by conspicuously disassociating India from US positions in the Korean War peace talks; in the Japanese peace treaty negotiations (when India insisted that the PRC, not the Republic of China of Chiang Kai-shek, should sign the treaty); and by arguing in favour of Beijing's representation in the United Nations (UN). By 1954 Nehru realized that Indian protests would not alter, and indeed might accelerate, China's effort to incorporate Tibet and that continued wrangling over Tibet would block the world-history, changing India–China partnership that Nehru envisioned with increasing clarity.

ACCOMMODATION AND PARTNERSHIP, 1954–8
At the level of India's national policy, a turning point came in 1954 with the conclusion of an India–China agreement on Tibet. In that agreement, India relinquished its inherited special rights in Tibet and recognized China's claim to Tibet—the first-ever international agreement to do so. The agreement also contained in its preamble the initial promulgation of what would become known as 'the Five Principles of Peaceful Coexistence', a set of principles intended to guide international relations along a course putatively more fair and just, and different from the predatory 'power politics' putatively practised by the by the Western powers and Japan. In comments to Parliament following the 1954 agreement, Nehru stressed the significance of agreement on the Five Principles; with agreement on these principles, 'this atmosphere of fear which is haunting us will gradually go away'.[5] Five years later, when the India–China partnership began to collapse and the border conflict emerge into public view, critics would condemn Nehru's failure to obtain Chinese recognition of an acceptable border as a quid pro quo for Indian recognition of China's sovereignty over Tibet. All India got in exchange for recognizing China's annexation of Tibet was a set of high-sounding 'principles' and Chinese professions of 'friendship', both of which quickly evaporated. Once granted, however, Indian recognition of China's sovereignty over Tibet could not be withdrawn.

Nehru's vision of India playing a prominent role in Asia and among the 'newly emerging countries' (to again use the nomenclature of that era) in Africa was linked to Indian partnership with China—at least until the India–China relation began to collapse in 1959. Nehru had long followed events in China and sympathized with what he deemed the 'progressive' CCP-led forces there. Nehru also recognized China as a great and ancient leading power in Asia (the Republic of China was, of course, a key member of the Allied coalition against Japan in World War II) and envisioned

India–China joint leadership of post-war, post-colonial Asia. India and China together would lead Asia into a better future, Nehru imagined. Early on, during the 1951–3 UN debates over the Korean War and again during negotiation of a peace treaty with Japan (which India refused to sign because it did not include the PRC), New Delhi found occasion to support Beijing. Nehru hoped that these expressions of Indian goodwill would persuade Beijing to cooperate with India in leading a new Asia. As long as India was at loggerheads with China over Tibet, India's friendship diplomacy towards the PRC yielded little result. With the Indian shift on Tibet embodied in the 1954 agreement, however, Beijing began to reciprocate India's expressions of friendship. By 1954, when Nehru and Chinese Prime Minister Zhou Enlai exchanged visits to each other's capital, 'Hindi Chini bhai bhai' (Chinese and Indians are brothers) was a popular slogan in India. Nehru's vision of Indian–Chinese partnership seemed to be materializing.

Part of India's push for partnership with the PRC was an effort to help China expand ties with the 'newly emerged' countries of Asia and Africa. Because of its intervention in the Korean War, its close alliance with the Union of Soviet Socialist Republics (USSR), and its revolutionary activism as part of the international communist movement (most importantly in Indo-China where the PRC generously supported Vietnam's communist-led anti-French forces starting in late 1949), the early PRC had virtually no diplomatic contacts beyond the socialist camp. Under Nehru, India undertook to help the PRC out of its diplomatic isolation. The first conference of Afro-Asian nations, meeting in Bandung, Indonesia, in 1955 was the most prominent venue for India's role as the PRC's patron. India, and Nehru personally, enjoyed great prestige among the 'newly emerging Afro-Asian nations', and Nehru's recommendation of China and its representative Zhou Enlai at Bandung carried considerable weight.[6]

India's mid-1950s' push for partnership with China was an attempt to convince Beijing of India's friendship in the hope that Beijing would reciprocate on the still-dormant border issue and by limiting China's military build-up in, and direct Chinese rule over, Tibet. Since India was friendly to China, there would be less need for China to militarize Tibet. More broadly, India's mid-1950s push for partnership with the PRC was an effort to form a bloc of Asia's historically great powers, India and China, which could rally the new Afro-Asian nations, along with the 'peace-loving' nonaligned-inclined nations everywhere (for example, Yugoslavia under Tito), to move the world away from the Cold War with its nuclear-war insanity. (The nonaligned movement took an organized form in 1961 with the convention of 25 countries, not including China, in Belgrade.) While these factors operated at the level of the international system, they also represented an effort by Indian national policy to establish India as a major global actor. They were also rooted in the idiosyncrasies of Nehru's view of the world. At the decision-making level of analysis, Nehru's vision of India–China partnership leading the world to a better future proved immensely popular. This popularity in turn strengthened Nehru's and the Congress' electoral appeal.

COLLAPSE OF PARTNERSHIP AND THE ROAD TO WAR, 1959–62

India–China partnership lasted about five years. It floundered over three issues: rivalry for influence in the Afro-Asian world; Tibetan resistance to Chinese rule; and the border. The first two of these are situated at the international system level of analysis, the border at the national level. The impact of all three issues was factored through domestic institutions and personalities.

In terms of rivalry for influence with the 'newly emerging countries', by 1959 CCP leader Mao Zedong had concluded that Soviet leader Nikita Khrushchev was not a fit successor to 'Marx, Engels, Lenin, and Stalin' (in the communist lexicon of the day), and that the Communist Party of the Soviet Union (CPSU) under Khrushchev was misleading rather than correctly guiding the world revolutionary movement. The responsibility to 'correctly' (to continue with Leninist nomenclature) instruct the world revolutionary movement thus fell, Mao concluded, on the CCP—and on himself. The key to revolutionary advance, Mao concluded, was armed wars of anti-imperialist national liberation among the peoples of Asia, Africa, and Latin America. The 'revisionist' leaders of the CPSU were the main target of the revolutionary polemics that now began pouring in a torrent from Beijing. But Indian 'reactionaries' were a secondary target. India, after all, enjoyed considerable influence in the Afro-Asian world, and its emphasis on non-violence, avoidance of revolution, and a 'third way' between capitalism–imperialism and revolution–wars of national liberation, helped mislead the masses, keeping them from revolution, or so Mao concluded. Indian reactionaries and Soviet revisionists were 'working hand in glove' to 'stifle wars of national liberation' in the Afro-Asian world, Mao concluded, and the influence of both needed to be 'smashed'—to use Maoist nomenclature of the day.[7] China's dramatic military defeat of India in 1962 would, in fact, substantially diminish India's, and substantially increase China's, prestige among the newly independent, developing countries.

Tibetan resistance to Chinese rule in Tibet needs to be considered at the international system level because of US involvement in aiding that resistance, the role of this US involvement in leading Mao Zedong to adopt harsh policies towards India, and the Soviet Union's role in further exacerbating Mao's fears. Tibetan resistance, violent and non-violent, to the PLA occupation of Tibet in the 1950s never really ended. Large-scale armed resistance began in south-eastern Tibet in spring 1956, and within months the US Central Intelligence Agency (CIA) had decided to assist that resistance with training, arms, and equipment to be parachuted into Tibet. The scale of US assistance was never large, but it was adequate to convince Mao Zedong that India, the US, and the Soviet Union were conspiring against China in Tibet. Finally, Tibetan resistance to Beijing's steady take-over of Tibet exploded into a general Tibetan uprising in March 1959. Nehru, responding to an eruption of popular sympathy for the Tibetans, granted refuge in India for the Dalai Lama, Tibet's traditional leader, along with thousands of his followers. The refugees clustered in camps in the Indian Himalayan mountains and became a base of support for the CIA-supported anti-Chinese resistance inside Tibet. Mao quickly (and incorrectly) concluded that India was responsible for the uprising and that India's demand for Chinese evacuation of the Aksai Chin plateau (with its important road into Tibet) was part of a Soviet–Indian–American plot to undermine Chinese rule in Tibet.[8] Moscow entered the picture when it declared neutrality in the escalating India–China dispute in spite of the 1950 PRC–USSR treaty of alliance and in spite of a direct request from Beijing that Moscow abide by that treaty and stand behind China against India.

The border issue also erupted about this time, with China's completion and low-key announcement in September 1957 of a road across the Aksai Chin plateau in western Tibet. Indian confirmation of the new Chinese road across Aksai Chin quickly brought to the fore the previously dormant territorial dispute. In negotiations during 1960, Zhou Enlai suggested, unofficially but probably sincerely, that China relinquish its claims in the east (today's Arunachal Pradesh) in exchange for India dropping its claims in the west, Aksai Chin. Nehru adamantly rejected Zhou's proposal, insisting that China must evacuate Aksai Chin. That road was very important to PLA logistic capabilities in Tibet. Nehru's insistence on Chinese withdrawal from Aksai Chin became part of the sinister pattern of conspiracy to undermine Chinese control over Tibet.

Nehru, along with Indian public opinion, was shocked by the ruthless nature of PLA's repression of Tibetan resistance and by the imposition of direct Chinese rule in Tibet in the aftermath of the March 1959 uprising. He was shocked too by the intensity and bitterness of Chinese polemics against him and his policies and by China's attribution of hostile intentions to him.[9] Nehru was also shocked by Beijing's refusal to recognize the McMahon Line (though Zhou Enlai did indicate willingness to accept that line as basis of settlement if India would abandon its claim to Aksai Chin in the west) and by Beijing's willingness—apparent by mid-1962—to use military force to uphold its boundary claims. This was not the way the world was supposed to work, according to Nehru's way of thinking.

As Nehru's policies of friendship with China collapsed and domestic criticism of those policies mounted, factors at the decision-making level of analysis became increasingly important. Nehru's policies had been naïve and weak, his increasingly numerous critics asserted. Nehru had been duped by China. For the first time, Nehru's handling of India's foreign relations came under strong domestic challenge. Confronted with mounting criticism, Nehru defended his policies by seeking to demonstrate his firmness in handling relations with Beijing. Under strong domestic pressure, Nehru welcomed Tibetan refugees—including the Dalai Lama—into India and granted them steadily wider scope of activity. Nehru may have ordered his Intelligence Bureau to turn a blind eye to utilization of Indian air space and territory by the CIA US to organize anti-Chinese operations by anti-Chinese Tibetan rebels.[10] Most consequentially, Nehru attempted to demonstrate his toughness by ordering India's military to assert India's claim to contested territory by actually establishing control over that territory. In November 1961, Nehru ordered Indian forces to assert physical control over territory up to the line claimed by India, pushing out in the process any Chinese forces that might be in those areas.[11]

Here another factor operating at the level of the individual decision-maker—Nehru—played an important role in preparing India's traumatic defeat in 1962. Nehru's disregard for the realities of Chinese power mobilized along the frontier, his belief in the ability of public opinion to deter resort to military force, and, perhaps, even his belief in the obsolesce of war, contributed substantially to the 1962 defeat.[12] By pushing often non-acclimatized Indian troops untrained for high-altitude operations, forward into areas not supported by adequate logistics, all along the contested border, thus disbursing Indian forces and ensuring they would be everywhere thin, in ways often oblivious to the tactical significance of local terrain, Nehru and his Defence Minister (until November 1962) Krishna Menon helped lay the basis for India's defeat. All of this was done on the basis of the assumption that China would not resort to armed force or, at least if it did, such force would be locally very limited. This assumption was not critically examined, and back-up plans, force dispositions, and defensive positions were not prepared in case the assumption proved to be wrong. Even when China's increasingly violent resistance to India's 'forward policy' along the border should have called into question the underlying assumption of Nehru's policy—that China would not resort to large-scale use of force—the strength of Nehru's beliefs prevented him from reconsidering his assumptions. More broadly, while rejecting Beijing's proposal of a compromise settlement to the border involving Chinese acceptance of the watershed principle (that is, McMahon Line) in the east in exchange for India's relinquishing its claim to Aksai Chin in the west, and then ordering the forward policy, Nehru was in effect pursuing a maximal and hard-line policy, but one not backed by equally hard military force. This combination of hard-line policies and military weakness was an invitation to disaster that came in October 1962.[13]

Indian military forces were completely unprepared—tactically, materially, and psychologically—for the powerful Chinese offensive that began in October and continued for a month. The focus of the Chinese offensive was in the eastern sector in what is now known as the Arunachal Pradesh region, especially in the Tawang sector near the Bhutan–Chinese–Arunachal Pradesh tri-juncture. There Indian defences collapsed and Chinese forces advanced almost unopposed to the southern foothills of fringe of the Brahmaputra plain. Chinese forces then halted and, after unilateral declaration of a ceasefire by Beijing, withdrew north of what China claimed represented the status quo ante. As India's military debacle unfolded, panic swept across north India.

THE POST-WAR COLD PEACE, 1963–87

India's defeat by Chinese forces in the 1962 war had a deep and enduring impact on Indian domestic politics, on Indian national policy towards China, and on the international system; that is, at all three levels of analysis. At the level of Indian domestic politics and Indian decision-making, the 1962 war produced a sea change in public opinion.[14] China's attack was nearly universally seen in India as the culmination of China's 'betrayal' of India's offer of friendship. India had made generous concessions (on Tibet) and demonstrations of friendship at the UN, on the Korean War and Japanese peace treaty negotiations, in the Afro-Asian world, and by conspicuously rejecting US invitations to 'contain' China. Beijing had repaid Indian friendship first with hostility and then with outright invasion. China was a war-prone and sinister amoral power, Indian public opinion concluded, that could not be trusted and that could be restrained only by superior force—or so the Indian public opinion concluded.

These popular views were inevitably simplistic and one-sided. They did not include awareness of the CIA operations utilizing Indian air space and territory (the contours of these covert CIA operations in Tibet became public knowledge in the US only in the mid-1970s), and Nehru's probable tacit acquiescence to those operations. Even the classified Indian study of the origins of the 1962 war, not 'leaked' to the public until 2002, avoided discussion of this topic, and indeed of Tibetan developments in general.[15] Nor did Indian opinion understand the Chinese view of developments: that India rejected China's reasonable compromise settlement proposal and then, via the forward policy, pushed Indian forces into territories already under effective Chinese occupation. Regardless of the skewed nature of the Indian public's perceptions, hostile perceptions of China were widespread and deeply rooted. It would take the systemic upheaval of the end of the Cold War to introduce forces adequate to ameliorate the deep popular Indian aversion to China.

Following the 1962 war, Indian leaders would take a much more realistic approach to China, an approach premised on calculations of power. A sort of 'never again' syndrome became dominant among India's leaders: never again would India be caught as unprepared and as unready as in 1962. India's dominant leader for 16 of 18 years between 1966 and 1984, Indira Gandhi, Nehru's daughter and thus heir to the Nehru–Gandhi 'dynasty', was especially hard-headed in such calculations. This newly realistic approach led Indian leaders, and especially Indira Gandhi, to develop a number of strategies to contain and counter China.

In terms of Indian national policy, after the 1962 war India paid far closer attention to the development of Indian military capabilities, with one eye on China. Henceforth, when India found itself in wars with Pakistan (in 1965, 1971, and 1999), Indian leaders kept a close watch on China's moves and levels of support for Pakistan. Many Indian analysts assumed that Pakistan would enter a war between India and China, and Indian defence planning for that contingency included dealing with a two-front challenge.[16] India established (c. 1963) and maintained a division-sized (about 10,000 men) and highly trained and Indian-officered military force of ethnic Tibetans that could operate as a commando force inside Tibet in conjunction with Indian regular forces in the event of a 'second round' war between India and China.[17] One important and overarching policy adopted by Gandhi was insistence that until the border issue was solved, India–China relations could not be normalized.

At the level of the international system, the 1962 war produced two major realignments: (i) of India and the Soviet Union, and (ii) of Pakistan and China. The India–Soviet alignment would persist till the end of the USSR in 1991, while the Pakistan–China alignment endured into the twenty-first century as one of the basic structures of the Asian international system.

With the 1962 war, India turned first to the US, and for a period of perhaps two years it looked as though Washington might prove to be India's major great-power backer against China. However, this incipient Indo-US anti-China partnership was soon aborted. This was most fundamentally due to the fact that the main global rival of the US remained, as it had been since 1945, the Soviet Union, while India's nemesis was the PRC. Meanwhile, the steady and rapid escalation of Soviet–China hostility during the 1960s made Moscow ever more ready to support India against China. By 1971, the Soviet Union was prepared to back an Indian move to partition Pakistan and establish East Pakistan as an independent state, while the US saw China as a potential partner in containing the USSR and was willing to cooperate with China in punishing India for its move against Pakistan.

Regarding the Sino-Pakistan entente, the 1962 war did not immediately produce this result. Mao Zedong had apparently hoped that the severe punishment of India in 1962 would cause India to 'come to its senses' and reach a reasonable settlement of the border issue with China.[18] When that did not happen, and as New Delhi reached out to 'anti-China forces' in Washington and Moscow in the several years after the war, Beijing moved into alignment with Pakistan by endorsing, in February 1964, Pakistan's position on the Kashmir issue (that is, that the people of Kashmir should be allowed a UN-supervised vote about belonging to India or Pakistan). The roots of the Sino-Pakistan entente go back to the 1955 Bandung conference when Pakistan had informed China that Pakistan's alliance with the US was not directed against China.[19] But not until 1964, as Pakistan engineered a 'war of liberation' for Kashmir that would lead to the second India–Pakistan war, did Beijing move decisively into alignment behind Pakistan.[20] By the mid-1960s there existed, what one perceptive analyst termed, the 'fulcrum of Asia': the India–Soviet alignment balanced against the Pakistan–China coalition.[21] Following India's decisive defeat of Pakistan in 1971, China stepped in to help Pakistan rebuild its shattered national capabilities through large-scale assistance—including assistance to Pakistan's nuclear weapons effort.[22]

BEGINNINGS OF RECONCILIATION AND THE END OF THE COLD WAR, 1988–97

Shifting to the national level of analysis, while building up India's position of strength vis-à-vis the PRC, Indian leaders saw overly tense relations with Beijing as disadvantageous to India. Such relations created incentives for China to find ways to injure Indian interests, including the periods of India–Pakistan hostility. Consequently, in 1975, Indira Gandhi ordered India's Tibetan Special Frontier Force drawn back at least 10 km of the border.[23] Gandhi also dispatched an Indian ambassador to Beijing in July 1976, restoring ambassadorial relations that had been broken since 1962. An effort to further improve relations during the Janata Party government (1977–9) received a setback when China invaded Vietnam, a close friend of India's, during a visit (the first to China by an Indian foreign minister in many years) of Atal Bihari Vajpayee to Beijing.[24] A new Indian government resumed the effort to improve relations with China after Indira Gandhi's return to power in 1980, and in June 1981 China's foreign minister Huang Hua made the first visit to India by a high-level Chinese official since 1960. During Huang's visit, the two sides agreed to resume talks on the border issue at the vice-minister level meeting annually in rotating capitals.

An indication of just how costly for India poor relations with China might be came in 1986 and 1987 when India found itself in near simultaneous confrontation with both Pakistan and China.[25] In 1986, the largest-ever manoeuvres by Indian military forces, code-named 'Brass Tacks', led to a Pakistani counter-mobilization and a tense military standoff along the border. As India–Pakistan forces were still facing off, confrontations began to occur between Indian and Chinese patrols in a remote, disputed, and sensitively located canyon, Sumdorung Chu, near the eastern Bhutanese–Chinese–Indian border tri-juncture. Both China and India rushed reinforcements to forward areas, while Beijing reportedly sought assurances from Bangladesh that it would not permit Indian transit of Bangladeshi territory in the event of a China–India war. By fall 1987 the prospect of another war with China, and with Pakistan, stared India in the face.[26]

In the aftermath of the 1986–7 confrontation over Sumdorung Chu, Indian Prime Minister Rajiv Gandhi (who had replaced his mother Indira after her assassination in 1984) reversed earlier Indian policy, opening the way to expanded cooperation with China. Since 1964 Indian governments had insisted that resolution of the boundary issue was an essential precondition for expansion of Sino-Indian ties in other areas. Rajiv Gandhi, in 1988, dropped this and decided to push for expanded cooperation even while the boundary issue remained unresolved. The boundary dispute should be discussed, and indeed discussions over that critical problem should be intensified, Gandhi concluded. But India–China cooperation in other areas should not be held hostage to the border issue. Improved bilateral relations and expanded cooperation in other areas might create a more positive context in which settlement of the boundary issue might be possible. At least that was one key idea underpinning the new Indian approach.

The mindset of Rajiv Gandhi—a factor operating at the decision-making level of analysis in the three-level approach taken here—played an important role in India's decision-making at this juncture. A pilot for Indian Airlines before being called into politics following the death of his brother Sanjay in an airplane crash in 1980, Rajiv Gandhi had extensive knowledge of the greater dynamism of Western economies and was not imbued in the 'socialist' culture of his mother's Congress. He came into the PM's office determined to reform and invigorate the Indian economy, and understood that confrontation with China would run counter to those domestic priorities. Gandhi's relative youth and reforming spirit inclined him towards a bold move such as his summit meeting in Beijing with Deng Xiaoping in December 1988. This was the first visit by a top Indian leader to China since 1954, and finally reciprocated Premier Zhou Enlai's 1957 and 1960 visits to India. (A 1956 visit by Zhou reciprocated a 1954 visit by Nehru to China.) Gandhi's 1988 visit to Beijing ranks with Nikita Khrushchev's 1959 visit to the US, Richard Nixon's 1972 visits to Beijing and Moscow, Anwar Sadat's 1977 visit to Jerusalem, or Deng Xiaoping's 1979 visit to the US, as bold initiatives by individual leaders to reshape the pattern of international relations.

During the 1988 Gandhi–Deng summit, the two sides agreed to accelerate discussion and search for settlement of the border issue. A 'joint working group' was established to meet annually in alternating capitals at the vice-ministerial level. The two sides also agreed that pending solution of the border issue, cooperation in other areas would be expanded. The joint statement resulting from the Gandhi–Deng meeting identified a number of areas of potential cooperation having to do with creation of a new international economic order—a major theme of both Chinese and Indian diplomatic rhetoric over the years. This was an attempt to turn the clock back to the mid-1950s when the two great Asian countries worked together to benefit the Afro-Asian nations, called 'developing countries' or 'the Third World' by the 1980s. This idea did not prove as enticing to India in 1988 as it had been in circa 1955. The Indian approach to China was now much more jaundiced.

Shifts in the international system (and thus at that level of analysis) also influenced Rajiv Gandhi's push for better relations with China. In the USSR, a new, boldly reformist leader, Michael Gorbachev, had taken over in 1985 and was working to deconflictualize the Soviet Union's relations with other countries—including China. One of Gorbachev's steps towards reducing tension with China was to disengage Moscow from Sino-Indian conflicts, draining the 1971 India–Soviet security treaty of its earlier guarantee for India in the process.[27] Indian leaders had increasingly to contemplate confronting China without Soviet support. China, for its part, was very different by 1987 from the China of a decade earlier. Deng Xiaoping had become paramount leader of the CCP in December 1978 and set about scrapping Mao-era policies. Under Deng, China's economy was progressively reformed via marketization and opened via ever deeper participation in the global economy. China was not yet the economic powerhouse it would become by the 2000s, but it was now dedicated to economic modernization and no longer a militant, revolutionary state. China under Deng was less ideological, less militant, and more aware of the costs of war. Deng Xiaoping desired peaceful relations with all of China's neighbours in order to create a favourable environment for a sustained Chinese development drive. On this issue, there was a meeting of minds between Deng and Gandhi.

Between 1989 and 1991 a cluster of events transformed the international system and thus deeply influenced India–China relations. First came the spring 1989 widespread popular challenge to the CCP authority in China, a challenge crushed by brute military and police force in June. With the Beijing massacre, US–PRC relations began to deteriorate, reversing the trend underway since 1971. Later in 1989, the communist governments of Eastern Europe fell before popular anti-communist movements, opening the door to unification first of Germany and then Europe—all within the framework of a continuing transatlantic alliance. Then the communist regime in Russia itself disintegrated, drawing to an end the 74-year history of Soviet socialism. The Russian Federation, successor state to the USSR, displayed little interest in South Asia. Finally, in 1991, the US mobilized a political–military coalition that undid within weeks and at unexpectedly low cost Saddam Hussein's attempted annexation of Kuwait. (Beijing had expected US casualties to be high and the war protracted.) In Beijing, CCP leaders watched these developments with trepidation. Regime survival became the CCP's top-ranking objective. Consolidating 'good neighbourly' relations with surrounding countries, and especially India with its history of troubled relations with China, would minimize the ability of the newly powerful and aggressive (at least so it seemed to CCP leaders) US to undermine CCP rule. Confronting a newly hostile world, Beijing became much more desirous of good relations with India—and, indeed, with all China's neighbours.[28]

The end of the Cold War posed great challenges for India as well. It is paradoxical, but mainstream intellectual opinion in liberal, democratic India had been strongly sympathetic to leftist, so-called progressive causes, and thus watched with dismay the unravelling of East European and Soviet socialism. The USSR had, of course, been India's major backer in the world, while Indian relations with the US, now a unipolar hegemon, were cool. India now lacked a major power backer in a world increasingly dominated by the West and the US. India had also enjoyed a close relation with Saddam Hussein's Iraq. Making matters even worse, the 1991 Gulf War led to collapse of remittances by Indian nationals working in the Gulf and therefore to a monetary crisis of the Indian government. The anti-export orientation of Indian-style socialism thus became apparent, forcing the beginning of a painful reconsideration of India's autarchic economic policies. These economic factors operating at the level of Indian domestic politics had greater influence on India's US (and *not* China) policies in the 1990s—though they would become a significant influence on India's China policies in the 2000s.

It fell to the government of P.V. Narasimha Rao, PM between 1991 and 1996, to begin rebuilding India's position in the international system.[29] Regarding China, Rao decided to respond positively to Beijing's newly ardent desires for more friendly relations. A series of high-level exchanges resulted: by Premier Li Peng to India in December 1991, by President Venkataraman to China in 1992, by Rao himself in 1993, and by paramount leader Jiang Zemin in 1996. Li Peng was one of the key agents behind the Beijing massacre and a target of revulsion and isolation by the West, and India's hosting of him conspicuously demonstrated India's refusal to go along with Western opprobrium of China's rulers. Jiang's visit was the first-ever visit to India by China's paramount leader. New Delhi and Beijing also found common ground in opposing in UN venues Western 'interference in the internal affairs of developing countries' on such issues as Kashmir and the Beijing massacre. New Delhi demanded (in 1990 and 1991), and Beijing granted, modification of China's position on the Kashmir issue, dropping any reference to a UN role in resolution of that dispute.[30] On the border issue, the two sides agreed (in 1993 and 1996) to two sets of confidence-building measures, though absence of an agreed line of actual control rendered those agreements of limited practical value.

There was an abundance of anti-hegemony rhetoric, implicitly directed against the US, in Indian and Chinese statements associated with the denser interactions of the early 1990s. This reflected apprehension in both New Delhi and Beijing of stepped-up Western pressure over human rights issues. Both capitals were hedging against possible increased pressure by the newly more-powerful and US-led West. But both capitals were also apprehensive that the other might align with the US against itself.

While India's foreign policy elite were debating India's response to the end of the Cold War in the mid-1990s, movement towards closer Chinese–US cooperation began to accelerate and created deep concern among Indian leaders. The possibility of a PRC–US coalition to India's disadvantage confronted India by about 1998. Such a coalition did not seem strange to Indian leaders. Indeed, this is what they felt India had confronted between 1971 and 1989. Throughout the 1990s it was clear that Beijing sought strategic partnership with the US. Following the Taiwan Strait crisis of 1996, Washington also began pushing towards such a partnership. A traditional and major US foreign policy objective, preventing the proliferation of nuclear weapons, formed the basis for actual formation of a PRC–US coalition against India on three occasions during the mid-1990s: during the Non-Proliferation Treaty Extension and Review Conference, during the negotiations over the Comprehensive Test Ban Treaty (CTBT), and in the aftermath of India's nuclear tests of 1998. On all three occasions, Beijing and Washington worked together to persuade India to pledge not to develop nuclear weapons and accept status as a non-nuclear weapons state within the Nuclear Non-proliferation Treaty (NPT) framework.[31]

The international system was clearly in great flux with the end of the Cold War structures that had dominated the exercise of power among states since 1945. Certain trends suggested the emerging post-Cold War system could evolve to India's disadvantage, towards a Sino-US coalition that would try to hold India to status of a merely South Asian power equivalent to Pakistan. Effective diplomatic manoeuvre was required to prevent this and nudge developments along lines more compatible with India's national interests.

THE ERA OF TRIANGULAR DIPLOMACY, 1998–2008

The election of March 1998 that brought to power a Bharatiya Janata Party (BJP) government led by Atal Bihari Vajpayee introduced into China policy factors operating at the level of the decision-making process. A new cohort of leaders with new ways of looking at the world came to power.

Vajpayee and his key lieutenants, Jaswant Singh and Brajesh Mishra, who were the first explicit realists to rule India, were deeply critical of what they took to be an earlier Indian propensity to adopt ideological positions that did not well serve Indian power interests and were convinced that India urgently needed to build up a position of greater strength vis-à-vis China, less India be marginalized not only on the global scene but possibly even in South Asia.[32]

The earliest and most controversial manifestation of this new Indian approach was a letter (allegedly written by Mishra) from Vajpayee to US President Bill Clinton, seeking US understanding of India's May 1998 nuclear weapons tests. With bluntness uncharacteristic of earlier top-level Indian-US communications, Vajpayee's letter focused on the Chinese challenge to India, even while avoiding specific identification of China. The letter was leaked by the US side and precipitated a strongly negative Chinese reaction.[33] For the next two years Beijing unfolded a series of measures designed to punish New Delhi for its 'anti-China' stance: lobbying Washington to support strong sanctions against India and weak or no sanctions against Pakistan; cancelling a scheduled meeting of the border joint working group; stepping up arms shipments to Pakistan; re-introducing mention of UN resolutions into China's stance on Kashmir.[34] Beijing lobbied Washington and other capitals to direct sanctions solely at India, rather than targeting Pakistan as well, who had followed India's test with its own tests. Beijing professed to be more concerned about India's 'anti-China' or 'China threat' justification of nuclear weapons than it was about Indian nuclear weapons themselves. That may be, but it suggests that, at bottom, what Beijing feared and what Vajpayee's letter for US 'understanding' suggested, was some sort of India–US alignment against China.

US thinking on India–China issues underwent swift evolution following India's May 1998 nuclear tests. Discussion in the mid-1990s in India and elsewhere of a possible Eurasian bloc to counter US 'unipolarity' and including Russia, China, and India, had raised for some American analysts the question of India's alignment in the post-Cold War world and in a situation of increasingly tense US–China relations. The 1996 Taiwan Strait confrontation and the realization that a Sino-US war over Taiwan was possible, made Washington think about how to deter Beijing from unleashing such a war. Thinking along those lines had not gone very far, however, by the time of India's May 1998 tests. The mainstream US response to intimation in Vajpayee's May 1998 letter of a China threat to India was to dismiss that talk as pure fiction concocted to appeal to US apprehensions. Eventually the bluntness of the letter began to percolate among the US strategic community. The bluntness of Vajpayee's letter deeply irritated Beijing and produced a Chinese campaign to punish India, but the same bluntness helped precipitate the American rethinking that would reorient US policy towards India–China relations later that year. New Delhi's very strongly negative reaction to the US–PRC Joint Presidential Statement of June 1998 also encouraged US rethinking of what approach best served US interests.[35] (The June 1998 joint statement called for India to abandon nuclear weapons, sign the NPT, and accept status as a permanently non-nuclear-weapon state under that treaty. It also suggested that China and the US would work together in South Asia to deal with the security affairs of that region.) Finally, in-depth discussions between Jaswant Singh (then finance minister) and US Deputy Secretary of State Strobe Talbott, beginning in mid-1998 and continuing through the end of the Clinton administration, produced genuine US understanding of India's concerns about China's roles in South Asia and the world. The Singh–Talbott talks led to a new US approach to India–China relations. The US would no longer align with China against India, but would support India's emergence as a major Asian and global power.[36]

One should not exaggerate the role of the China factor in the new Indo-US relations that began emerging in late 1998. 'China' was one factor, and an important one, but it was not the only important factor. The growing influence of the Indian diaspora in the US and, even more, the Indian elite's belated discovery of the wealth-generating potential of participation in the global economy and understanding of the US role in that global economy, were also at work. Discussion along these lines takes us, however, beyond a focus on India's China policy.

By 2000, a situation of Chinese and US competitive cooperation/friendship with India had developed. Beijing watched with apprehension as Washington backed away from cooperation with China in opposing India's nuclear drive (for example, insistence on implementation of Security Council Resolution 1172) and then began steps to advance India–US cooperation. US President Clinton's 2000 visit to India—the first by a US president since 1978—was seen by Beijing as part of a US effort to draw India into a China containment scheme. Developments in India–US military and strategic cooperation, which advanced especially rapidly during the George W. Bush administration, were especially troubling to Beijing. Chinese analysts saw the US as trying to draw India into anti-China containment schemes, and Beijing worked to foil those schemes by courting New Delhi.[37]

By 2000, Beijing ended its post-test campaign to punish India, and quietly began making a series of concessions to New Delhi designed to keep India away from closer alignment with the US. Beijing agreed to a regular strategic dialogue with New Delhi, in which China discussed nuclear issues with India for the first time, starting in March 2000. Previously Beijing had refused to discuss nuclear issues with India on grounds that it was not a nuclear weapons state as recognized by the NPT. Beijing also agreed to hear out Indian concerns about China's missile and nuclear cooperation with Pakistan. Earlier it had insisted such matters were a purely bilateral affair and not a topic of discussion with India, and India had sought to minimize conflict with Beijing by not pressing the issue. In January 2005 Beijing and New Delhi formalized their 'strategic dialogue', and in April of the same year declared formation of a 'strategic and cooperative partnership for peace and prosperity'. Between 2003 and 2005, Beijing incrementally and implicitly but formally recognized Sikkim as a state of the Indian Union, thereby dropping a 30-year-long policy of non-recognition of India's annexation of that territory.[38] Beijing also agreed to permit India to become an observer to the Shanghai Cooperation Organization (SCO). Exchanges between Indian and Chinese military officials increased and a joint naval exercise (targeting maritime rescue operations and named 'Sino-Indian friendship—2005') was conducted in the Indian Ocean during 2005. During a November 2006 visit to India by Chinese President Hu Jintao, India secured—according to foreign secretary Shivshankar Menon—a Chinese promise not to block Indian entry into the UN Security Council as a permanent member. 'China would not be an obstacle' to India's UN aspirations, according to Menon.[39]

India is in the advantageous position of being courted by both Beijing and Washington.[40] This may be a fairly stable state of the post-Cold War international system that India will be able to exploit for perhaps a decade or more. The depth of the suspicion between the US and the PRC, the reigning paramount power and a rapidly ascending global power, is such that both are sensitive to India's alignment. Of course, Indian diplomacy will require skill to identify the requirements of Indian interests and then calibrate diplomatic means to effectively achieve those interests within the context of this new triangle.

NOTES

1. See Sumit Ganguly (2008), 'India's Improbable Success', *Journal of Democracy*, 19 (2), pp. 170–4.
2. Sarvepalli Gopal (1979 and 1984), *Jawaharlal Nehru, A Biography*, volume II: 1947–1956, volume III: 1956–64 (Cambridge, MA: Harvard University Press).

3. Jaswant Singh (1999), *Defending India* (New Delhi: Macmillan India Ltd).

4. Regarding conflict over Tibet, see John Rowland (pseudonym for John Waller, deputy CIA station chief in New Delhi, 1955–7) (1967), *A History of Sino-Indian Relations, Hostile Co-Existence* (Princeton, NJ: Van Nostrand). Tsering Shakya (1999), *The Dragon in the Land of Snows: A History of Modern Tibet since 1947* (London: Pimlico).

5. Rowland, *History of Sino-Indian Relations*, p. 86.

6. John W. Garver (2001), *Protracted Contest; Sino-Indian Rivalry in the Twentieth Century* (Seattle: University of Washington Press) pp. 117–20.

7. Ibid., pp. 133–52. The flavour of the CCP's polemic against CPSU 'revisionism' can be savoured in: *The Polemic on the General Line of the International Communist Movement* (Beijing: Foreign Languages Press, 1965). Studies of Indian–Chinese rivalry to influence the newly independent countries are: B.D. Arora (1981), *Indian–Indonesian Relations, 1961–1980* (New Delhi: Asian Educational Series); Gopal Chaudhuri (1986), *China and Nonalignment* (New Delhi: ABC Publishing House). Regarding Indian–Chinese rivalry in Indo-China see, D.R. SarDesai (1968), *Indian Foreign Policy in Cambodia, Laos, and Vietnam, 1947–1964* (Berkeley: University of California Press).

8. John W. Garver (2006), 'China's Decision for War with India in 1962', in Alastair Iain Johnston and Robert S. Ross (eds), *New Directions to the Study of China's Foreign Policy* (Stanford University Press), pp. 86–100.

9. Regarding the impact of Tibetan developments, see Frank Morales (1960), *The Revolt in Tibet* (Calcutta: Srishti Publishers). Also, Rowland, *History of Sino-Indian Relations*, and Shakya, *Dragon in Land of Snows*.

10. Regarding the extent of Nehru's knowledge of, and/or collusion with, CIA covert operations in Tibet, see John W. Garver (2004), 'India, China, the United States, Tibet, and the Origins of the 1962 War', *India Review*, 3 (2), pp. 171–82; John K. Knaus (1999), *Orphans of the Cold War: American and the Tibetan Struggle for Survival* (New York: Public Affairs).

11. The most detailed study of the Indian decision-making process is Steven A. Hoffmann (1998), *India and the China Crisis* (Berkeley: University of California Press). Also useful is Neville Maxwell (1972), *India's China War* (Garden City: Anchor Books).

12. The most detailed and critical study of the ineptness and lack of realism of Indian policy prior to the 1962 war was the classified history of that war completed by India's Ministry of Defence in 1992 and leaked to the Indian media circa 2002: S.N. Prasad (chief ed.) (1992), *History of the Conflict with China, 1962* (New Delhi: History Division, Ministry of Defence, Government of India), p. 474. URL www.bharat-rakshak.com/LAND-FORCES/Army/History/1962War/PDF/index.html (accessed on 3 June 2009).

13. This critique follows Major General D.K. Palit (1991), *War in the High Himalayas, The Indian Army in Crisis, 1962* (London: Hurst and Co.).

14. On Indian public opinion (1959), see *Dalai Lama and India: Indian Public and Prime Minister on Tibetan Crisis* (New Delhi: The Institute of National Affairs). Also see, Lorne J Kavic (1967), *India's Quest for Security; Defence Policies, 1947–65* (Berkeley, University of California Press).

15. Prasad, *History of the Conflict with China*.

16. For details see Anwar Hussain Syed (1974), *China and Pakistan: Diplomacy of an Entente Cordiale* (Amherst: University of Massachusetts Press).

17. Regarding this Tibetan force, see Kenneth Conboy and James Morrison (2002), *The CIA's Secret War in Tibet* (Lawrence, KS: University of Kansas Press), p. 171.

18. For details, see Garver (2001), *Protracted Contest: Sino-Indian Rivalry in the Twentieth Century* (Seattle: University of Washington Press), Chapters 2 and 3.

19. Satyabrat Sinha (2007), 'China in Pakistan's Security Perceptions', in Swaran Singh (ed.), *China-Pakistan Strategic Cooperation: Indian Perspectives* (New Delhi: Manohar Publications), Chapter 4.

20. Garver, *Protracted Contest*, pp. 190–4.

21. Bhabani Sen Gupta (1970), *The Fulcrum of Asia: Relations among China, India, Pakistan, and the USSR* (New York: Pegasus).

22. The author presents the evidence for this in Garver, *Protracted Contest*, pp. 324–31.

23. Conboy and Morrison, *CIA's Secret War*, p. 257. The US similarly ended covert CIA support for Tibetan resistance in 1969 in order to open the way to improved relations with Beijing.

24. John W. Garver (1987), 'Indian–Chinese Rivalry in Indochina', *Asian Survey*, 27 (1), pp. 1205–19.

25. See note 21.

26. Regarding the 1986–7 crisis, see Kanti P. Bajpai, P.R. Chari, Pervaiz Iqbal Cheema, Stephen P. Cohen, and Sumit Ganguly (1995), *Brasstacks and Beyond: Perception and Management of Crisis in South Asia* (New Delhi: Manohar Publications).

27. Regarding Gorbachev's reinterpretation of the 1971 Soviet–India treaty, see John W. Garver (1991), 'The Indian Factor in Recent Sino-Soviet Relations', *China Quarterly*, 125, pp. 55–85.

28. For details, see Robert G. Sutter (2008), *Chinese Foreign Relations: Power and Policy since the Cold War* (Lanham, MD: Rowman & Littlefield).

29. Regarding India's response to the end of the Cold War, see C. Raja Mohan (2003), *Crossing the Rubicon, The Shaping of India's New Foreign Policy* (New York: Penguin Books).

30. Garver, *Protracted Contest*, pp. 228–9.

31. John W. Garver (2002), 'The China–India–U.S. Triangle: Strategic Relations in the Post–Cold War Era', *NBR Analysis* (Monograph published by the National Bureau of Asian Research), 13 (5), pp. i–67.

32. A manifesto containing this critique was penned by Jaswant Singh shortly before the March 1998 elections: *Defending India* (New Delhi: Macmillan, 1999).

33. For the text of Vajpayee's letter, see 'Nuclear Anxiety: Indian's Letter to Clinton on the Nuclear Testing', *New York Times*, 13 May 1998.

34. John W. Garver (2001), 'The Restoration of Sino-Indian Comity following India's Nuclear Texts', *China Quarterly*, 168, pp. 867–89.

35. For more information on the Chinese reactions to the Indian nuclear tests of May 1998, see Jing-Dong Yuan, 'India's Rise After Pokhran II: Chinese Analyses and Assessments', *Asian Survey*, November/December 2001, 41 (6), pp. 978–1001.

36. Strobe Talbott (2004), *Engaging India: Diplomacy, Democracy and the Bomb* (New York: Penguin Books; Viking Publication). Jaswant Singh (2006), *A Call to Honor: In Service of Emergent India* (New Delhi: Rupa and Company).

37. Garver, 'The China–India–U.S. Triangle'.

38. 'China Map Puts Sikkim in India', *India Abroad*, 14 May 2004, p. 12; 'India's Sovereignty over Sikkim Settled, says China', *News India-Times*, 18 April 2005.

39. 'China will not Block India's U.N. Security Council Bid', *News India-Times*, 1 December 2006, p. 25.

40. This argument is developed in Garver, 'China–India–U.S. Triangle'.

6

Southeast Asia in Indian Foreign Policy

Positioning India as a Major Power in Asia

MANJEET S. PARDESI

The strategic significance of Southeast Asia to India's security was dramatically highlighted when Japan invaded India from Southeast Asia by launching attacks on north-eastern India from land, sea, and air from 1941 onwards during World War II.[1] Noting these developments, K.M. Panikkar, the eminent Indian scholar–diplomat commented that the 'political future' of the countries of Southeast Asia, 'considered in relation to their economic development and their security, is indissolubly bound up with India'.[2] Furthermore, highlighting the centrality of India, Panikkar advocated the creation of a system of 'collective security'[3] for the defence of Southeast Asia as well as the formation of a 'co-prosperity sphere'[4] based on the interdependence between India and Southeast Asia. Jawaharlal Nehru, the first prime minister (and foreign minister) of India, was of the opinion that as a consequence of its actual and latent material power as well as its geostrategic location, India was bound to become the *'pivot of Asia'*.[5]

This chapter will argue that these twin imperatives of security and prosperity, along with the quest for a geostrategic position as a great power in Asia have been the fundamental goals of India's foreign and security policies towards the countries of Southeast Asia ever since its emergence as an independent state in 1947. This is not to argue that India has been successful in achieving these goals or that it has not pursued other important policies towards this region. The claim being made is that India's security and prosperity, and more importantly its standing as a major power in Asia, are dependent on India's role in Southeast Asia and that New Delhi has tried to pursue these very objectives in its relations with the countries of that region.

This essay adopts a 'level-of-analysis'[6] approach to understand the impact of international (or systemic) and domestic factors on, as well as the role of important leaders (and their ideas) in India's foreign and security policy towards Southeast Asia. There have been three major phases in India's relations with Southeast Asia. The first phase began in the late 1940s, when India sought to position itself as a major power in Asia, and ended with its disastrous defeat in the 1962 Sino-Indian border war that temporarily eliminated India from the larger Asian scene and confined New Delhi to South Asia. The second phase began after the end of the Sino-Indian border war and lasted until the implosion of the former Soviet Union in 1991 when the Cold War international architecture dominated India's relations with Southeast Asia, a period during which New Delhi's engagement with this region was limited. The third and the current phase began after the end of the Cold War and with structural reforms in India's economy that were first introduced in 1991, a period during which India has consciously pursued a 'Look East' policy to engage the countries of Southeast Asia (as well as Northeast Asia).

While factors at all three levels of analysis were important during all of these phases, this chapter will demonstrate that individual leaders (and Nehru in particular) dominated India's foreign and security policy towards Southeast Asia during the first phase; that systemic factors dominated India–Southeast Asia relations during the second phase; and that the third phase has witnessed a remarkable confluence of systemic, domestic, and individual level factors in promoting India's interests in Southeast Asia. Before proceeding, it should be noted that Southeast Asia became a widely accepted term only during World War II.[7] As such, this study includes the now prevalent definition of Southeast Asia that comprises the 10 member states of the Association of Southeast Asian Nations (ASEAN)[8] as well as Timor-Leste. Of these 11 countries, India shares land and maritime borders with Burma/Myanmar and maritime borders with Thailand and Indonesia.

LATE 1940s THROUGH 1962: INDIAN LEADERSHIP IN ASIA?

Systemic Factors

The two most important systemic-level developments in the immediate aftermath of World War II in Asia were the process of decolonization and the emergence of the Non-Aligned Movement (or NAM) in response to the Cold War international environment.

Decolonization

India achieved independence in 1947; however, decolonization was a long-drawn affair in much of Southeast Asia. While the Philippines and

Indonesia achieved their independence in the late 1940s, Brunei became independent as late as 1984.[9] The 1940s and 1950s were the most crucial decades for decolonization in Southeast Asia as this period witnessed the emergence of six new states, while Vietnam was divided into communist North and anti-communist South in 1954.[10] One of the most important features of Indian foreign policy towards Southeast Asia in the 1940s and 1950s was the promotion of decolonization.[11]

In the aftermath of World War I, India's nationalist leaders began to oppose imperialism not just in India but across the world. As early as 1928, the Congress declared that 'the struggle of the Indian people for freedom is a part of the general world struggle against imperialism'.[12] There were two important reasons behind India's support for decolonization at home and abroad. First, India's nationalist elite campaigned against imperialism everywhere on moral grounds. Imperialism everywhere was regarded as an evil that not only brought about the political and economic exploitation of the colonized peoples but also promoted racism.[13] Second, India's nationalist elite opposed imperialism on strategic grounds as well. India's nationalist elite believed that India's goal of 'preserving autonomy of action in world affairs could be achieved only in the context of decolonization in the rest of Asia and in cooperation with the genuinely independent governments in the continent's larger and more important states'.[14]

In the immediate aftermath of World War II, India was concerned about the possibility of the continuation of the colonial order in parts of Asia. The first concrete sign of such an eventuality came in 1945–6 when Indian soldiers from the British Indian army were used to restore French colonial rule in Indo-China.[15] As a consequence, independent India came out strongly in support of decolonization in Southeast Asia. This was most dramatically demonstrated during India's support for the Indonesian nationalist movement.

The Dutch tried to reinstall the colonial order in Indonesia in 1945 after the Japanese surrender through what was termed a 'police action'.[16] It took four years of negotiations and the diplomatic efforts of many countries, primarily India and Australia, at the United Nations (UN) that eventually resulted in Indonesia's independence.[17] In fact, during these four years when the Dutch imposed an air blockade on Indonesia, Indian planes made several sorties to Indonesia to provide important supplies and military equipment.[18] Furthermore, Biju Patnaik, a prominent member of the Congress and of the Orissa Legislative Assembly, personally flew to Sumatra to fly Indonesian Prime Minister Sutan Syahrir to India where he was given refuge.[19] In January 1949, India organized the Conference on

Indonesia in New Delhi—the first conference led by an Asian government to deal with a specific issue in Asia—to promote the cause of Indonesia's independence.[20] The resolution passed in Delhi had a definite impact on the final resolution passed by the UN Security Council later that month.[21] Finally, India and Indonesia embarked on defence cooperation soon after the independence of the latter, and Indonesian military officers began to receive training in Indian military bases.[22]

India also played a very active diplomatic role in the decolonization of Indo-China.[23] The Geneva accord on Indo-China had established three International Commissions of Supervision and Control (ICSC), one each for Vietnam, Cambodia, and Laos. Each of these commissions was headed by an Indian chairman. However, India's support for decolonization in Vietnam, while genuine, was nowhere near its championing of Indonesia's freedom movement. This was directly linked to the strategic component of India's decolonization policy. While independent Indonesia had non-aligned leanings, the Vietnamese freedom movement was being spearheaded by the communists. India regarded the Vietnamese communists as genuine freedom fighters; however, India was wary of their ideology as well as of the possibility of increased Chinese influence in Vietnam as a consequence of communist victory there.[24]

India was also concerned about the stability of Asia's post-colonial states as well as their viability as independent states. New Delhi was of the opinion that European powers may use instability in these states as a pretext for intervention and impose a neo-imperial order. Chinese penetration through its revolutionary communist ideology in an alliance with the various communist parties in Southeast Asian states raised similar fears about Chinese expansionism as well. As a consequence, Burma was the first foreign state to receive arms, ammunition, and transport planes from India as early as 1949.[25] Burma was plagued with several insurgencies led by the communists as well as the Karen National Defense Organization soon after its independence. In February 1949, a month after the Conference on Indonesia, New Delhi organized an 'informal' Conference on Burma and invited delegations from several Commonwealth governments to discuss the situation in that country.[26]

Nonalignment and the Non-Aligned Movement (NAM)

Nonalignment was a policy in support of the cornerstone of independent India's foreign policy objective of 'pursuing an independent policy compatible with India's own national interests'.[27] India's nationalist leaders were acutely aware that independence should include domestic autonomy as well as independence in foreign relations. This was critical as India's nationalist leaders were very critical of the British use of Indian troops (raised and supported by taxation in India) in support of British imperial strategy in Asia and beyond. Deriving strength from India's history and its actual and latent power potential, Nehru firmly believed that India 'could not be a mere hanger-on of any country or group of nations',[28] and that 'in no event should India be made to join any war without the consent of her people being obtained'.[29]

However, India's birth as an independent state in 1947 coincided with the onset of the Cold War superpower rivalry between the United States (US) (and its Western allies) and the former Soviet Union (and the socialist bloc). And almost simultaneously, the Cold War threatened to engulf South and Southeast Asia. In order to prevent India from being drawn into rival military blocs and to secure its own interests, India had to shield its immediate neighbours in South and Southeast Asia from superpower rivalry. Thus, India advocated the policy of nonalignment and found ready partners among the most important states in this region—Burma and Indonesia. Both these states readily supported the notion of nonalignment for ideological reasons and for ensuring the stability of their nascent states that were simultaneously facing a number of internal rebellions and even external interference.[30]

India's policy of nonalignment met with some initial successes in the 1950s, but lost its appeal to India in the early 1960s when the meetings of the nonaligned states of Asia and Africa generated no public support for India during the 1962 Sino-Indian border war.[31] The NAM was officially launched as an international organization only in 1961 in Belgrade. Eventually, NAM included members from almost all parts of the world. However, by the 1962 Sino-Indian conflict, nonalignment had become ideologically entrenched in India and in itself had come to signify an independent foreign policy (as opposed to being a strategy that enabled India to pursue an independent foreign policy).

Domestic Factors

India–Southeast Asia Economic Relations

At the time of India's independence, Southeast Asia was India's third-largest trading partner after the United Kingdom (UK) and the US.[32] There were expectations that these trends would continue, for India was more industrialized then than the countries of Southeast Asia.[33] Southeast Asia represented an important consumer market for Indian textiles and other industrial goods. On the other hand, India was dependent on Southeast Asia for natural resources and agricultural produce such as oil, tin, rubber, timber, and rice. While these trends continued for a few years after India's independence, New Delhi's adoption of autarkic economic policies for its industrial development and economic growth began to limit its economic interaction with Southeast Asia at a time when that region began to vigorously pursue export-oriented economic development strategies.[34] Furthermore, the imperative of industrialization vividly demonstrated that the economies of India and Southeast Asia were not complementary (except in a limited sense) as all these countries vied for capital and technological inputs from the West or the former Soviet Union for their development. By the 1960s India had lost its advantageous economic position in Southeast Asia.

People of Indian Origin in Southeast Asia

Another significant concern for New Delhi was the status of the people of Indian origin in different parts of Southeast Asia. Burma had the largest number of Indian immigrants in that region. However, as a consequence of the 'Burma for Burmans' policy, the government of independent Burma passed the Land Alienation Act of 1948 that dispossessed many Indians, especially the Chettiar community from southern India that owned a quarter of best rice lands in Burma.[35] Since Burma was facing internal insurgencies and Chinese communist interference, Nehru raised this issue with Prime Minister U Nu only at the non-official level. As the land nationalization policy continued through the 1950s, several hundred thousand Indian immigrants returned to India. Given the important support of Burma for India's policy of nonalignment, India let strategic concerns override the interests of the Indian community in Burma.

There was a sizeable Indian presence in Malaya since the colonial period. However, as Malaya embarked upon building a modern state, many Malay leaders began to worry about Indian immigration and even feared becoming 'racially overwhelmed' by Indians.[36] The pre-independent voices of prominent Indians advocating a policy of emigration and even colonization of parts of Southeast Asia and Africa did not help matters either.[37] In fact, one prominent Indian scholar even advocated using Indians in Southeast Asia as 'the foreign legion of India'.[38] These policies were never adopted by the Government of India even as they created suspicions about Indian intentions in that region. The government of Malaya passed a number of legislations and began to legally discriminate against their Indian minority.[39] The Government of India took up the issue of fair treatment of its nationals in Malaya as well as equal treatment of all the citizens of Malaya regardless of their racial origins. Nehru also asked Indians living in Malaya (and Singapore) to be loyal to the land they lived in and to integrate themselves with the local communities.[40]

Individual-level Factors: The Pre-eminent Role of Nehru

The cornerstone of India's foreign policy under Nehru was (and still remains) the pursuit of an independent foreign policy. This was translated into nonalignment at the systemic level. In addition to this, an inchoate India-centred pan-Asianism was central to Nehru's approach to Asia. 'India will ... develop as the centre of economic and political activity in the Indian Ocean area, in Southeast Asia and right up to the Middle East',[41] wrote Nehru prior to India's independence. Nehru envisioned India playing a 'leading role in the revival of Asia'[42] and even dreamed up vague and grandiose hopes of two or three Asian federations.[43]

Even before India's independence, Nehru authorized the Indian Council of World Affairs to organize an 'unofficial' Asian Relations Conference (ARC) in New Delhi.[44] Although no specific resolutions were passed and Nehru specifically mentioned that there were no leaders or followers at this conference, Nehru was clearly the star of the show. In the following years India organized the Conference on Indonesia and the Conference on Burma, and provided military and financial assistance to Burma to fight its domestic insurgencies. In the following years, Nehru's India played a very active diplomatic role as the chair of the ICSC for Vietnam, Cambodia, and Laos. In 1955, with the complete backing of Nehru, Indonesia organized the Bandung Conference, an event during which Nehru introduced the People's Republic of China (PRC) and its Premier Zhou Enlai to the countries of Africa and Asia (and indeed the world).[45] Nehru's personal stature in the West was so high that many Western leaders viewed him as their interlocutor with Asia.[46] Nehru's former nemesis, British PM Winston Churchill twice referred to him as the 'Light of Asia'.[47] And finally, the British daily *Manchester Guardian*, while praising Nehru as a world statesman, mentioned that 'Delhi is the school of Asia' just as 'Athens was the school of Hellas'.[48]

However, India and Nehru's bid to play the role of a leader was not well received in many parts of Southeast Asia.[49] As early as 1947, at the ARC, delegates from Malaya and Burma had expressed concern that the end of European imperialism might lead to an era of Indian and Chinese imperialism in Southeast Asia.[50] The discourse on emigration and colonization of parts of Southeast Asia (and Africa) in non-official circles in India, as mentioned earlier, did not help matters in this regard. Furthermore, Indian perceptions of Southeast Asia as an extension of India or *Greater India* were a major cause of concern for the smaller states of this region.[51] Being the dominant thinking in scholarship in his day among both Indian and Western scholars, even Nehru believed that India had colonized Southeast Asia in ancient times.[52] While subsequent scholarship has confirmed that at no time in history did India ever colonize Southeast Asia, and that the transmission of India's culture to Southeast Asia was a peaceful process, the opinions of India's intellectuals and political leaders were viewed with suspicion in Southeast Asia around the time of India's independence.

In other words, during the first phase of India's relations with Southeast Asia, Nehru's self-appointed role of Indian leadership in Asia was viewed with suspicion in that region. Moreover, India's autarkic domestic economic policies meant that India had little to offer to promote growth and development in Southeast Asia. Worse still, the Indian diaspora in these countries was viewed as a potential fifth column doing India's bidding and undermining the nascent Southeast Asian states. Finally, India's disastrous military defeat during the 1962 Sino-Indian border conflict at a time when the Cold War was becoming entrenched in Southeast Asia showed that India would not be able to offer traditional military security to the newly emergent states of Southeast Asia (that is, considering that India would be willing to play such a role in the first place). Following India's loss at the hands of the Chinese, India became a relatively marginal player in Southeast Asia for the rest of the Cold War.

FROM 1962 UNTIL THE END OF THE COLD WAR

Systemic Factors

From the 1960s until the end of the Cold War, India's relations with Southeast Asia were by and large 'derivative' of systemic-level factors dominated by the Cold War international environment.[53] Furthermore, viewed from the perspective of Southeast Asia, this period represented a rapidly changing strategic environment. From 1964 onwards, the US became increasingly embroiled in the Vietnam. India was 'opposed to the Western cause in Vietnam' throughout this period.[54] India's vociferous opposition to US involvement in Vietnam created difficulties in its relations with a number of states in Southeast Asia that had recently formed a regional grouping—Association of Southeast Asian Nations (ASEAN)—that had a pro-Western tilt.[55] In the meanwhile, India's relations with Indonesia, the largest Southeast Asian state, deteriorated significantly when Indonesia supported Pakistan during the 1965 India–Pakistan war. Indonesia had threatened to open a second-front by attacking India's Andaman and Nicobar Islands, thereby diverting India's attention and resources away from Pakistan.[56]

A few years later in 1967, Britain announced its decision to withdraw 'east of the Suez'.[57] The Indian Navy soon announced its intention of assuming the functions of the British Navy after the latter's withdrawal from the region.[58] However, India neither had the resources nor did its political leadership have the vision to assume such a role. Nevertheless, this created suspicions in Indonesia about India's policy towards Southeast Asia.[59] Along with the withdrawal of the British forces came the enunciation of the so-called Guam Doctrine by the US President Richard Nixon. While the doctrine lacked a precise definition, the US was announcing its intention to not get militarily involved on the Asian mainland.[60]

Even before Southeast Asia could come to terms with the meaning of Western disengagement from the region, India signed a 20-year treaty with the (former) Soviet Union in 1971.[61] Within a few months, India defeated and vivisected its South Asian rival, Pakistan, in the 1971 Bangladesh War.[62] India emerged as the pre-eminent power in South Asia with the dismemberment of Pakistan, and to some extent also regained its status as a military power that it had lost after 1962. However, the Southeast Asian states again became suspicious of India's designs for the region as they saw Soviet power lurking behind India's new status at a time when the Western powers were disengaging from that region.[63]

However, Southeast Asia (and the Indian Ocean region) had become vitally important for India's security after the 1971 Bangladesh war as the US had posed a naval threat to India from the Bay Bengal during the war. The US had dispatched the *USS Enterprise* carrier group (believed to be nuclear armed by strategists in New Delhi) from the South China Sea during this war.[64] The strategic environment in South and Southeast Asia had also become more complicated with Sino-American rapprochement in the early 1970s.

All these developments should have prompted New Delhi to 'look East' and to seriously engage its Southeast Asian neighbours given the deleterious effects of the developments over the previous decade on Indian security. However, the 'oil shocks' of the 1970s and the economic boom in the Gulf that followed it caused India to 'look West' towards the oil-rich countries of West Asia (or the Middle East).[65] India was also concerned about the efforts of Iran to play the role of a regional power in South Asia.

In 1972, the Shah of Iran had declared that any attack on Pakistan would be tantamount to an attack on Iran and that Tehran was committed to the territorial integrity of Pakistan.[66]

These international developments prevented India from engaging Southeast Asia in any meaningful sense throughout the 1970s. India's muted response to the Soviet invasion of Afghanistan in 1979 and the recognition by New Delhi of the Heng Samrin government in Kampuchea (Cambodia) after Vietnam invaded that country further alienated India from Southeast Asia. The Kampuchean case in particular was a more serious concern for ASEAN countries which were then concerned about Vietnam's military power (and its links with the former Soviet Union).[67]

Finally, the rapid build-up of India's naval and military power in the 1980s, and its development of a naval (and a possible air) base in the Andaman and Nicobar Islands at the mouth of the Straits of Malacca was a major cause of concern for the Southeast Asian states.[68] India had received an offer for a second aircraft carrier from Britain in 1985.[69] From 1988 to 1991, India also leased a nuclear-powered submarine from the former Soviet Union.[70] The late 1980s further saw the emergence of India as a regional power with military interventions in Sri Lanka and the Maldives.[71] There were concerns in many Southeast Asian states with significant Indian minorities that India might engage in gunboat diplomacy in the region if ethnic Indians in that region were to be harmed or mistreated.

Domestic Factors

India's overall trade with Southeast Asia declined from the early 1950s until about 1970. However, from the early 1970s onwards, Southeast Asia's importance for India grew dramatically, both as a supplier of goods to India and as a market for Indian products.[72] In fact, India's overall trade with Southeast Asia in 1980 was more than 17 times its total trade with that region in 1970.[73] By 1990, this figure had more than doubled.[74] It is also noteworthy that by 1980, India's trade with ASEAN countries was more than twice its total trade with South Asian countries, and by 1990 it was four times as much.[75] In the late 1960s, India had begun to invest in ASEAN countries in the form of joint ventures with local firms in that region.[76] By 1981, almost 40 per cent of India's overseas investment in such ventures was in ASEAN countries.[77]

While the rate of growth in economic interactions was certainly impressive, the closed nature of the Indian economy meant that economic relations between India and Southeast Asia were a minor component of their foreign economic relations. Indeed, as late as 1990, ASEAN accounted for only 6 per cent of India's international trade while India accounted for barely 1 per cent of ASEAN's international trade. Given these economic realities and their different geopolitical orientations, India's economic relations with Southeast Asia did not acquire a strategic dimension during this period.

Individual-level Factors

Lee Kuan Yew

Lee Kuan Yew, the first PM of Singapore, was one of the few Southeast Asian leaders in favour of (and even promoted) a greater Indian role in that region. In the immediate aftermath of China's first nuclear test in 1964, Lee had urged India to conduct a nuclear test to balance Chinese power and had further added that he would have welcomed an Indian naval presence in Southeast Asia.[78] For complex strategic, economic, and moral reasons, India conducted its first nuclear test only a decade later in 1974.[79] Furthermore, India's first significant naval expansion occurred in the 1970s, and even then New Delhi was constrained by financial resources as well as the lack of a strategic vision.

In mid-1960s, Lee had also asked India to train and equip the military of his new city-state that was born in 1965.[80] Singapore wanted India to play an active role in the economic development, political stability, and security of Southeast Asia. Just prior to his first official visit to India in 1966, Lee is even reported to have urged India to adopt an 'Asian Monroe Doctrine' in order to prevent 'poaching' in Asia.[81] However, after suffering a military debacle at the hands of China in 1962 and having fought a major war with Pakistan in 1965 (during which it was subjected to a Western arms embargo), India did not respond to Singapore's request for military assistance. Moreover, India was neither economically strong nor militarily powerful enough to implement its own version of the Monroe Doctrine in Asia.

Indira Gandhi

The renowned Indian diplomat Mohammedali Currim Chagla, who served as Minister of External Affairs in 1966–7 under PM Indira Gandhi, was favourably disposed towards ASEAN on the eve of its formation in August 1967. During his visit to Singapore in May 1967, Chagla declared,

[I]f Singapore chooses to join any regional cooperation [grouping], we will be happy to join such a grouping, if other members want India to do so. If others want to have a small grouping, India will be happy to remain outside and help such a grouping. ... India does not want to dominate any regional grouping.[82]

However, India did not receive an invitation to join ASEAN. There are a number of plausible reasons why India was not invited. It has already been mentioned that Sukarno's Indonesia viewed India as a rival in the region. It is possible that Indonesia wanted to keep India away from the grouping in Southeast Asia. Furthermore, Gandhi came up with the proposal of a regional grouping in Asia in the late 1960s that sounded remarkably similar to the Asian collective security system being proposed by the former Soviet Union.[83] In fact, Chagla had also proposed the idea of this 'Council of Asia' during his Southeast Asian tour. Many Southeast Asian leaders were of the view that India was doing the bidding for the Soviets in South and Southeast Asia. Furthermore, Gandhi herself promoted this idea to Kuala Lumpur during her 1968 visit to Malaysia. The Southeast Asians naturally thought that India was undermining ASEAN by promoting an alternative.[84] It is a widely held but erroneous belief that India was invited to join ASEAN but had declined to do so.[85] On the contrary, India was disappointed that it was not invited in spite of sending out enthusiastic signals.[86]

Indian Diplomacy during the Kampuchean Crisis

India sought to play an active diplomatic role between the countries of the Indo-China and ASEAN during the Kampuchean crisis. Vietnam's invasion of Kampuchea in December 1978 was followed with China's invasion of Vietnam itself in February 1979.[87] 'Gandhi realized that if India were to become the paramount power in South Asia it would have to prevent a Chinese advance into Southeast Asia.'[88] Consequently, Gandhi recognized the Heng Samrin government in opposition to Beijing's preference for the Khmer Rouge clients. After Rajiv Gandhi became India's PM, New Delhi sought to play the role of an 'honest broker' between Vietnam and ASEAN.[89] In January 1987, Vietnam's position was comprehensively formulated for the first time and then communicated to the Indian Minister of External Affairs, Natwar Singh, for transmission to ASEAN. In March–April 1987, Singh visited all six ASEAN states and then visited the three countries of the Indo-China in July 1987. India also made it clear that it would like to be one of the guarantors of an international agreement on Kampuchea.[90] India was a member of the 1989 Paris Accords on Cambodia. India sent military contingents to Cambodia in 1991 as a part of both the United Nations Advance Mission in Cambodia (UNAMIC) as well as the United Nations Transitional Authority in Cambodia (UNTAC). Finally, India was chosen to be the co-chair of the Control Commission to assist UNTAC in implementing the peace accords.[91]

On the whole, India was at best a marginal player in Southeast Asia throughout the Cold War. At worst, India created geopolitical tensions in Southeast Asia as a consequence of its alignment with the former Soviet Union and at times was even perceived as a military (naval) threat in that region. Despite their rapidly growing economic ties between 1970 and 1990 (compared to the 1950s and 1960s), India and Southeast Asia remained marginal for one another in their overall foreign economic relations. Finally, Lee's vision of India playing the role of a major power in Southeast Asia did not come to fruition given the overall economic backwardness and military weakness of India. Indira Gandhi's muddled diplomacy of engagement with ASEAN further caused resentment towards India in that region. The Cold War was a period of 'missed opportunities, mistrust, misperceptions, and bungling diplomacy'[92] in India–ASEAN relations as India lacked an overall policy towards ASEAN as a grouping or towards the Southeast Asian region on the whole.

INDIA AND SOUTHEAST ASIA AFTER THE END OF THE COLD WAR

Systemic Factors

This section will discuss the changing geopolitical landscape, the structure of the emerging international political economy, and the international institutional environment in this part of the world that promoted closer relations between India and Southeast Asia.

The end of the Cold War in 1991 meant that the most serious impediment to India–Southeast Asia relations that had prevented closer and deeper interaction between them since the 1960s was now history. The Soviet Union had already pulled out of Afghanistan by 1989, and the Cambodian question was also in the process of being settled by late 1991. With the implosion of the Soviet Union, the 1971 Indo-Soviet treaty also came to an end. India needed to construct new relationships in the emerging strategic environment in which the US was the most dominant power in the international system. India immediately sought to improve its relations with the US[93] while searching for new friends and partners.

Southeast Asia emerged as a natural candidate as India began searching for new relationships. India was already 'looking East' in the late 1980s as it sought to assuage concerns in that region about its rapid naval build-up. India had opened up its military base in Port Blair (on the Andaman and Nicobar Islands) to visits from naval attachés from Southeast Asia in the late 1980s to demonstrate its benign intentions towards the region.[94] At the same time, India's active diplomacy during the Cambodian crisis had 'provided a worthwhile input into the Indian foreign policy-making process' by enabling India to understand the region while providing her 'with a good indication about which Southeast Asian countries were receptive to Indian diplomatic overtures and which were not'.[95]

Most importantly, there were no sources of bilateral security tensions between India and its immediate neighbours in Southeast Asia,[96] at a time when China was becoming a militarily assertive power in Southeast Asia with its claims to Spratly and Paracel Islands in the late 1980s and early 1990s.[97] Viewed from Southeast Asia, India seemed far less threatening than it had just a few years ago. At the same time, there were some concerns regarding America's continued military presence in Southeast Asia. In late 1991, the Philippines had asked the US to withdraw its military from the Subic Bay naval base by the end of 1992.[98] In this era of strategic uncertainty in Southeast Asia, the region looked towards India as a potential balancer of Chinese power in the region. Noting the opportunity, India began its politico-military engagement with several Southeast Asian states on a bilateral basis.

In 1991–2, India had embarked on a comprehensive 'Look East' strategy and was seeking closer politico-military ties with Southeast Asia.[99] India began conducting joint naval exercises with Indonesia, Malaysia, and Singapore in the vicinity of the Andaman and Nicobar Islands as early as 1991.[100] Singapore made use of India's missile testing facilities at Chandipur to test some guns and missiles in its inventory in 1992.[101] India and Singapore began conducting the Lion King annual bilateral anti-submarine warfare exercises in 1993.[102] India signed a Memorandum of Understanding (MoU) with Malaysia in 1993 to promote defence cooperation between the two countries. This was India's first defence MoU with an ASEAN country. At least 100 Malaysian pilots and ground supporting staff for the MiG-29 aircraft were trained in India. In 1993, the then Indian Foreign Secretary, J.N. Dixit, visited Rangoon to indicate India's desire to meaningfully engage Burma.[103] The then Indian PM Narasimha Rao paid a visit to Thailand in 1993 and to Vietnam in 1994. During Rao's trip to Vietnam, the two sides signed a protocol on defence cooperation.[104] These high-level political visits and the defence diplomacy accompanying them signalled India's intentions to meaningfully engage Southeast Asia.

Since then, India has continued with its politico-military engagement with this region. In 2003, India and Singapore signed a Defence Cooperation Agreement.[105] In 2007, India leased its air base in Kalaikunda (in West Bengal) to Singapore to enable the space-constrained city-state to train its air force personnel in India.[106] This is the first instance of a foreign military being granted training facilities in India on a long-term basis. In 2008, the two countries signed a similar agreement allowing Singapore's army to use the facilities of the Indian Army in Deolali (in Maharashtra) and Babina (in Uttar Pradesh) for training and exercises involving armour and artillery.[107] It has already been speculated in the Singaporean media that the city-state might grant India naval logistics facilities as a quid pro quo.[108] The two countries also held the inaugural India–Singapore Strategic Dialogue in 2008 which is modelled after the Indo–US Strategic Dialogue.[109]

Other Southeast Asian nations have also been on the radar of India's defence diplomacy. In 2000, during his trip to Vietnam, the then Indian Minister of Defence George Fernandes made an offer of joint naval training in combating piracy. India also agreed to help Vietnam in setting up its defence industry, including the manufacture of small and medium weapons. In turn, Vietnam offered to train Indian army officers in jungle warfare and counter-insurgency.[110] After Thailand acquired an aircraft carrier (from Spain) in 2000—the only Asian country apart from India to do so—New Delhi offered to and then trained Thai marine aviators in India.[111]

Structure of the International Political Economy and International Institutions

The first half of the 1990s saw the emergence of three major trading blocs—a single market in Europe under the aegis of the European Union, a free trade area in ASEAN, and the North American Free Trade Agreement (NAFTA). Furthermore, the success of the Uruguay Round of multilateral trade negotiations that eventually led to the creation of the World Trade Organization (WTO) had seemed doubtful for a while.[112] It has already been mentioned that India's trade with the ASEAN countries was four times its trade with the South Asian countries by 1990. The success of the South Asian Association for Regional Cooperation (SAARC) seemed bleak as a consequence of the tensions between India and Pakistan. Given all these factors, New Delhi deemed it imperative to engage ASEAN economically lest it be left out of one of the most dynamic regions of the global economy.

Simultaneously, India began to engage this region in multilateral associations (see Table 6.1). In 1992, India became a 'sectoral dialog partner' of ASEAN, and by 1995 had become a 'full dialog partner'. In 1996, India became a member of ASEAN Regional Forum (or ARF), the most important regional security grouping in the Asia-Pacific.[113] After its nuclear tests in 1998, India endorsed the Treaty on Southeast Asia as a Nuclear Weapon-Free Zone.[114] India was granted the status of a 'summit level partner' of ASEAN in 2002. In 2003, India signed ASEAN's Treaty for Amity and Cooperation. The same year India also agreed to establish a Free Trade Agreement (FTA) with ASEAN within a decade. In 2005, India also became one of the founder members of the East Asia Summit (EAS).

TABLE 6.1: India's Integration into the Institutional Architecture of Southeast/East Asia

Year	India's Organizational Affiliation and Treaties
1992	ASEAN – 'Sectoral Dialog Partner'
1995	ASEAN – 'Full Dialog Partner'
1996	ASEAN Regional Forum
1998	Endorsement of the Treaty on the Southeast Asia as a Nuclear Weapon-Free Zone
2002	ASEAN – 'Summit Level Partner'
2003	ASEAN's Treaty for Amity and Cooperation
2005	East Asia Summit
2008–10	Free Trade Agreement with ASEAN

Source: Manjeet S. Pardesi.

Domestic Factors

Economic Liberalization in India

The end of the Cold War in 1991 also coincided with a serious balance-of-payments crisis in India. In the midst of this crisis, the government led by Rao launched a series of structural reforms in the Indian economy under Finance Minister Manmohan Singh. These reforms introduced a new industrial policy and also led to reforms in India's financial sector. As such, India has begun to embrace the market, and its economy is opening itself to the wider world.[115] More importantly, a number of changes in policies and institutional arrangements related to the conduct of India's external economic relations were implemented along with the reforms of the early 1990s that promoted meaningful economic interaction with Southeast Asia.

The Indian foreign secretary, the highest ranking civil servant in the Ministry of External Affairs, was made an ex-officio member of the Apex Committee of Secretaries on economic policy and also of the Foreign Investment Promotion Board.[116] Heretofore, the Ministry of External Affairs was not involved in economic policy-making in the country. Nor did it deal with the economic aspects of India's foreign relations. These were dealt with on an issue-by-issue basis by specific Indian ministries such as finance or industry dealing with particular concerns. With the inclusion of the foreign secretary in the highest government bodies dealing with economic issues (including reforms), it became clear that India had started to think of the strategic impact of its foreign economic relations. In the early 1990s, the economic cell of the Ministry of External Affairs was strengthened, and India's embassies and missions abroad were charged with the task of interpreting and projecting India's economic policies and objectives in the host countries.

Signalling that Southeast Asia merited special attention in this regard, Dixit, who was the foreign secretary of India when the reforms were implemented, took direct charge of this region in the Ministry of External Affairs. 'There could be no better manifestation, in organizational terms, of the economic rationale behind the diplomatic opening up to Southeast Asian countries.'[117] The success of Indian economic diplomacy in Southeast Asia is demonstrated by the fact that the India–ASEAN trade tripled between 1992–3 and 1996–7.[118] Taking advantage of the favourable economic environment in different ASEAN states, India signed an FTA with Thailand in 2003 and also entered into a Comprehensive Economic Cooperation Agreement (CECA) (that includes an FTA as well as important provisions regarding services and human resources) with Singapore in 2005.[119]

Energy Security

Energy security has emerged as an important component of India's foreign policy towards Southeast Asia, as energy-deficient India is seeking energy resources globally to feed the requirements of its rapidly growing economy.[120] India is exploring the option of importing Burmese natural gas via a pipeline through Bangladesh into India. However, for financial and political reasons this project is still under negotiations.[121] India has also become an investor in Vietnam's offshore gas fields.[122]

Containing Insurgencies and Promoting Development in Northeast India

Many insurgents in north-eastern India such as the Naga rebel groups use sanctuaries in the northern parts of Burma, which are outside of the writ of the Burmese state, to launch attacks on Indian military and paramilitary forces operating in India's north-east. New Delhi's strategy to counter these insurgencies involves their military containment as well as the economic development of these parts of India. In this regard, India and Burma have conducted several coordinated military attacks against these insurgents since 1995.[123] At the same time, India is also building infrastructure to connect this landlocked region of India with Southeast Asia to promote greater economic interaction as well as tourism.[124] Separated from India's heartland by Bangladesh, India's north-east is connected with the rest of the country by a narrow strip of land, the Siliguri Corridor, which is only 21 km wide at its narrowest point. There is growing realization in New Delhi that the development of India's north-east and the containment of the insurgencies there are directly related to the success of India's 'Look East' policy.

Individual-level Factors

Former PM Rao had formally launched India's 'Look East' policy in a landmark lecture that he delivered while visiting Singapore in 1994.[125] However, it must be noted that India was already 'looking East' in the late 1980s as a consequence of its naval expansion during that decade and as a consequence of the diplomatic role that it played during the Cambodian crisis. As a result, at least one scholar has credited Inder Kumar Gujral as the author of India's 'Look East' policy.[126] Perhaps Gujral is regarded as such because he served as India's Minister of External Affairs in PM V.P. Singh's government in 1989–90, the years prior to Rao's enunciation of a comprehensive 'Look East' strategy. However, it was Rao who built on these trends and further added the politico-military dimension to India's engagement with Southeast Asia.

After the departure of Rao's government in 1996, Gujral once again served as India's External Affairs Minister in PM Deve Gowda's government (1996–7) and then served as the PM of India for a year during 1997–8. Through all these years, Gujral continued to take an active interest in India's relations with Southeast Asia. Gujral and his advisor Bhabani Sen Gupta are credited with the so-called Gujral Doctrine, under which India refused to demand reciprocity in its relations with its smaller South Asian neighbours. However, an often overlooked feature of the Gujral Doctrine was his 'attempt to place India at the centrestage in the Asia-Pacific region'.[127] Gujral wanted India to 'go East in search of an Asia-Pacific identity' and to seek 'larger areas of cooperation with the tigers and dragons' of that region.[128] India's subsequent PMs, Atal Bihari Vajpayee and Manmohan Singh, have continued and built upon India's engagement with Southeast Asia that was created under Gujral and Rao.

At the same time, important leaders in Southeast Asia, in particular the leaders of Singapore, have been championing India's enhanced strategic profile in the region. Singapore's former PM Goh Chok Tong generated a 'mild India fever' in Singapore in the early 1990s in order to promote the city-state's economic interaction with its giant neighbour, after having correctly read the economic signals coming out of India.[129] Furthermore, it was Goh's and Singapore's adroit diplomacy that paved the way for India's membership in the institutional and, therefore, the strategic architecture of Southeast Asia. Recognizing his efforts to promote India's cause and stature in Southeast Asia, the Government of India conferred on Goh the 2003 Jawaharlal Nehru Award for International Understanding.[130]

India's comprehensive strategic engagement of Southeast Asia, reflected in its 'Look East' policy, stemmed from India's search for new friends and partners after the loss of its superpower patron in 1991. While it is commonly believed that the underlying rationale behind India's engagement with Southeast Asia has been India's domestic economic liberalization, it must be noted that India had begun to seek purposeful politico-military engagement with Southeast Asia almost simultaneously. At the same time, India was determined to break out of its South Asian strategic box that it had found itself confined to after its defeat in the 1962 Sino-Indian border war. India began to engage Southeast Asia in search for a larger role in Asia and to prevent Southeast Asia from being dominated by Chinese economic and military power. India had the able leadership of Gujral and Rao, as well as important friends in leaders such as Goh during these crucial years.

* * *

This chapter has attempted to explain India's foreign and security policies since its independence towards Southeast Asia through the 'level-of-analysis' approach. India's engagement with Southeast Asia stems from India's search for security and prosperity and from India's quest for a larger role in Asia. In its early years as an independent nation, India sought to position itself as a major power in Asia under the leadership of Nehru. However, as a result of its disastrous defeat in the 1962 Sino-Indian border war, as well as the crystallization of the Cold War security environment in Asia, India became a marginal player in Southeast Asian affairs. However, the end of the Cold War removed the major geopolitical obstacle in India–Southeast Asia relations. At the same time, riding on its domestic economic liberalization and under the visionary and able leadership of Rao and Gujral, India has been able position itself as an important player in Southeast Asia's emerging strategic environment.

However, India needs to continue the process of economic reforms at home to maintain the momentum of its meaningful engagement with Southeast Asia and to position itself as a great power in Asia. While growing rapidly, India's economic ties with Southeast Asia look pale in comparison to China's economic interaction with that region.[131] If the

Indian economy continues to grow and meaningfully integrates itself with Southeast Asia, the next phase in India's interaction with this region is bound to acquire greater strategic significance as India is likely to work in close partnership with the US in that region. Southeast Asian states have already taken a positive view of India's growing ties with the US. But far more interestingly, a senior Indian diplomat recently commented that 'the Pacific facet of the United States should ... be factored into India's Look East policy'.[132]

NOTES

1. Christopher Bayly and Tim Harper (2004), *Forgotten Armies: The Fall of British Asia, 1941–1945* (London: Allen Lane). At the same time, the Azad Hind Fauj (Indian National Army or the INA) was formed in Southeast Asia in 1942 under the leadership of Subhas Chandra Bose. The aim of the INA was to liberate India from British rule with Japanese assistance. See Peter W. Fay (1993), *The Forgotten Army: India's Armed Struggle for Independence, 1925–1945* (Ann Arbor: University of Michigan Press).

2. K.M. Panikkar (1943), *The Future of Southeast Asia: An Indian View* (New York: The Macmillan Company), p. 16.

3. Ibid., p. 11. Panikkar saw a role for all the major powers in the 'collective security' of Southeast Asia. However, India's role was central for any such system, according to him.

4. Ibid., p. 16.

5. Quoted in Sarvepalli Gopal (1979), *Jawaharlal Nehru: A Biography, Volume Two 1947–1956* (London: Jonathan Cape), p. 59 (emphasis added).

6. J. David Singer (1961), '"The Level-of-Analysis" Problem in International Relations', *World Politics*, 14 (1), pp. 77–92.

7. Donald K. Emmerson (1984), '"Southeast Asia": What's in a Name?', *Journal of Southeast Asian Studies*, 15 (1), pp. 1–25.

8. The 10 member countries of ASEAN are Brunei Darussalam, Cambodia, Indonesia, Laos PDR, Malaysia, Myanmar, the Philippines, Singapore, Thailand, and Vietnam.

9. Timor-Leste declared independence from Portugal in 1975 but was attacked and annexed by Indonesia. It finally attained independence in 2002. On the other hand, Thailand was never colonized by the European imperial powers.

10. These six states were the Philippines (1946), Myanmar (1948), Laos (1949), Indonesia (1949), Cambodia (1953), and Federation of Malaya (1957). Malaysia and Singapore were born in 1963 and 1965, respectively. Vietnam was reunified in 1976.

11. Charles H. Heimsath and Surjit Mansingh (1971), *A Diplomatic History of Modern India* (Calcutta: Allied Publishers), p. 225.

12. Quoted in J. Bandyopadhyaya (1970), *The Making of India's Foreign Policy: Determinants, Institutions, Processes, and Personalities* (Calcutta: Allied Publishers), p. 70.

13. Ibid., pp. 69–71.

14. Mohammed Ayoob (1990), *India and Southeast Asia: Indian Perceptions and Policies* (London: Routledge), p. 7.

15. John Springhall (2005), '"Kicking out the Vietminh": How Britain Allowed France to Reoccupy South Indo-China', *Journal of Contemporary History*, 40 (1), pp. 115–30. Also see, T.O. Smith (2006), 'Britain and Cambodia, September 1945–November 1946: A Reappraisal', *Diplomacy and Statecraft*, 17 (1), pp. 73–91.

16. Indonesia had declared independence after Japan's surrender at the end of World War II.

17. On India's support for Indonesian freedom struggle at the United Nations, see Ton That Thien (1963), *India and South East Asia, 1947–1960* (Genève: Librairie Droz), pp. 92–8.

18. Sudhir Devare (2006), *India and Southeast Asia: Towards Security Convergence* (Singapore: Institute of Southeast Asian Studies), p. 71.

19. Ibid.

20. This conference was attended by delegates from a total of 15 countries.

21. On the Conference on Indonesia, see Ton, *India and South East Asia*, pp. 98–102. Also see, A.W. Stargardt (1989), 'The Emergence of the Asian System of Powers', *Modern Asian Studies*, 23 (3), pp. 565–70.

22. Heimsath and Mansingh, *Diplomatic History of Modern India*, p. 233.

23. Gilles Boquérat (2005), 'India's Commitment to Peaceful Coexistence and the Settlement of the Indo-China War', *Cold War History*, 5 (2), pp. 211–34. Also see Heimsath and Mansingh, *Diplomatic History of Modern India*, pp. 252–62.

24. D.R. SarDesai (1968), *Indian Foreign Policy in Cambodia, Laos, and Vietnam* (Berkeley, CA: University of California Press).

25. On the Indian government's military and financial help to Burma, see Ton, *India and South East Asia*, pp. 169–72.

26. Uma Shankar Singh (1979), *Burma and India, 1948–1962* (New Delhi: Oxford University Press and IBH Publishing Co.), pp. 56–9.

27. George E. Jones (1946), 'Nehru Lists Aims in Foreign Policy', *The New York Times*, 1 September.

28. Jawaharlal Nehru (2004 [1946]), *The Discovery of India* (New Delhi: Penguin Books), p. 464.

29. Ibid., p. 461.

30. See Sisir K. Gupta (1965), 'Asian Nonalignment', *Annals of the American Academy of Political and Social Science*, 362, pp. 44–51.

31. Heimsath and Mansingh, *Diplomatic History of Modern India*, p. 79.

32. Ton, *India and South East Asia*, p. 74.

33. N.V. Sovani (1949), *Economic Relations of India with South-East Asia and the Far East* (New Delhi: Indian Council of World Affairs).

34. On the Indian political economy after independence, see Francine Frankel (1979), *India's Political Economy, 1947–1977* (Princeton: Princeton University Press).

35. Heimsath and Mansingh, *Diplomatic History of Modern India*, p. 312.

36. T.A. Keenleyside (1982), 'Nationalist Indian Attitudes Towards Asia: A Troublesome Legacy for Post-Independence Indian Foreign Policy', *Pacific Affairs*, 55 (2), pp. 210–30 (p. 222).

37. Ibid., pp. 226–9.

38. This was the prominent pre-independence Indian scholar of international relations, Lanka Sundaram. Quoted in Ibid., p. 214.

39. On the discrimination in Malaya against Indians, see Ton, *India and South East Asia*, pp. 229–39.

40. Ibid., p. 239.

41. Nehru, *Discovery of India*, p. 597.

42. Judith Brown (2003), *Nehru: A Political Life* (London: Yale University Press), p. 245.

43. Gopal, *Jawaharlal Nehru*, p. 43. On India's idea of Asia, see Giri Deshingkar (1999), 'The Construction of Asia in India', *Asian Studies Review*, 23 (2), pp. 173–80.

44. It was a gathering of over 200 delegates from 30 countries and colonial territories. See A. Appadorai (1979), 'The Asian Relations Conference in Perspective', *International Studies*, 18 (3), pp. 275–85.

45. For a contemporary account of India and Nehru's achievements at Bandung, see 'India: Bandung Balance Sheet', *The Round Table*, 45 (179) (June 1955), pp. 278–81. For an alternative view, see Rahul Mukherji (2006), 'Appraising the Legacy of Bandung: A View from India', *ISAS Working Paper* (Singapore: Institute of South Asian Studies, 8 May).

46. For several examples, see Gopal, *Jawaharlal Nehru*, p. 238.

47. Ibid., pp. 236–7.

48. Quoted in Ibid., p. 193.

49. As will be discussed subsequently, Singapore was a possible exception.

50. Keenleyside, 'Nationalist Indian Attitudes Towards Asia', p. 228.

51. On this, see R.C. Majumdar (1927), *Ancient Hindu Colonies in the Far East* (Lahore: The Punjab Sanskrit Book Depot); R.C. Majumdar (1944), *Hindu Colonies in the Far East* (Calcutta: General Printers & Publishers).

52. See the section titled 'Indian Colonies and Culture in South-East Asia', in Nehru, *Discovery of India*, pp. 211–19.

53. See Kripa Sridharan (1996), *The ASEAN Region in India's Foreign Policy* (Aldershot: Dartmouth Publishing Company).

54. See Ramesh Thakur (1979), 'India's Vietnam Policy, 1946–1979', *Asian Survey*, 19 (10), pp. 957–76 (p. 958).

55. ASEAN was formed in 1967, and its initial members included Indonesia, Malaysia, Singapore, Thailand, and the Philippines. Of these, Thailand and the Philippines were close allies of the US while Malaysia and Singapore had a Western orientation, first through the 1957 Anglo-Malaya Defence Agreement that eventually gave way to the Five Power Defence Agreement in 1971. (The five powers included Britain, Australia, and New Zealand in addition to Malaysia and Singapore). See Michael Leifer (1980), 'Conflict and Regional Order in Southeast Asia', *Adelphi Papers* (London: International Institute of Strategic Studies).

56. Ayoob, *India and Southeast Asia*, p. 41.

57. By 1974, all of Britain's deployments east of the Suez (with the exception of Hong Kong) were withdrawn.

58. This decision was announced in 1969. See Raju G.C. Thomas (1975–6), 'The Indian Navy in the Seventies', *Pacific Affairs*, 48 (4), pp. 500–18 (p. 504).

59. Kirdi Dipoyudo (1985), 'Indonesia–India Bilateral Relations', *Indonesian Quarterly*, 13 (4), pp. 509–23.

60. See J.L.S. Girling (1970), 'The Guam Doctrine', *International Affairs*, 46 (1), pp. 48–62.

61. Linda Racioppi (1994), *Soviet Policy Towards South Asia since 1970* (Cambridge: Cambridge University Press).

62. On the Bangladesh War, see Sumit Ganguly (2002), *Conflict Unending: India–Pakistan Tensions Since 1947* (New York: Columbia University Press), pp. 51–78.

63. Bhabani Sen Gupta (1975), 'Waiting for India: India's Role as a Regional Power', *Journal of International Affairs*, 29 (2), pp. 171–84 (p. 173).

64. Daljit Singh (2002), 'The Geopolitical Interconnection between South and South-East Asia', in Frédéric Grare and Amitabh Mattoo (eds), *India and ASEAN: The Politics of India's Look East Policy* (New Delhi: Manohar Publications and Centre de Sciences Humaines), pp. 21–40 (p. 33).

65. Raju G.C. Thomas, 'Energy Politics and Indian Security', *Pacific Affairs*, 55 (1), pp. 32–53.

66. On Iran's efforts to position itself as a South Asian power, see Gupta, 'Waiting for India', pp. 178–80.

67. The Heng Samrin regime installed by Vietnam was recognized by Indira Gandhi's government in India in 1980. For details, see Ayoob, *India and Southeast Asia*, pp. 53–71.

68. See G.V.C. Naidu (1991), 'The Indian Navy and Southeast Asia', *Contemporary Southeast Asia*, 13 (1), pp. 72–85; and Sandy Gordon (1995), *India's Rise to Power in the Twentieth Century and Beyond* (London: St. Martin's Press), pp. 293–5.

69. Admiral Arun Prakash (2006), 'India's Quest for an Indigenous Aircraft Carrier', *RUSI Defense Systems* (Summer), pp. 50–2.

70. 'Submarine Proliferation: India, Current Capabilities', *Nuclear Threat Initiative* (n.d.), http://www.nti.org/db/submarines/india/index.html (accessed on 14 June 2008).

71. On India's military intervention in Sri Lanka and Maldives with an emphasis on the role of the navy, see Rahul Roy-Chaudhury (1995), *Sea Power and Indian Security* (London: Brassey's), pp. 134–46.

72. Ramesh Thakur (1994), *The Politics and Economics of India's Foreign Policy* (London: Hurst & Company), p. 247.

73. Ibid.

74. Ibid.

75. Ibid.

76. Ayoob, *India and Southeast Asia*, p. 16.

77. Ibid.

78. Baladas Ghoshal (1996), 'India and Southeast Asia: Prospects and Problems', in Baladas Ghoshal (ed.), *India and Southeast Asia: Challenges and Opportunities* (New Delhi: Konark Publishers), p. 96.

79. On an early view of India's 1974 nuclear test, see Onkar Marwah (1977), 'India's Nuclear and Space Programs: Intent and Policy', *International Security*, 2 (2), pp. 96–121.

80. Tim Huxley (2000), *Defending the Lion City: The Armed Forces of Singapore* (St. Leonards, Australia: Allen & Unwin), p. 11.

81. Quoted in V.P. Dutt (1984), *India's Foreign Policy* (New Delhi: Vani Educational Books), pp. 277–8.

82. Quoted in Ayoob, *India and Southeast Asia*, p. 11.

83. Sridharan, *ASEAN Region in India's Foreign Policy*, pp. 69–76.

84. Man Mohini Kaul (2002), 'ASEAN–India Relations During the Cold War', in Grare and Mattoo (eds), *India and ASEAN*, pp. 41–66 (p. 55).

85. For example, see Ibid., p. 55.

86. Ayoob, *India and Southeast Asia*, p. 11.

87. See Les Buszynski (1980), 'Vietnam Confronts China', *Asian Survey*, 20 (8), pp. 829–43.

88. Ayoob, *India and Southeast Asia*, p. 56.

89. Ibid., p. 59.

90. Thakur, *The Politics and Economics of India's Foreign Policy*, p. 252.

91. Ibid., pp. 250–5.

92. Kaul, 'ASEAN–India Relations During the Cold War', p. 62.

93. S. Paul Kapur and Sumit Ganguly (2007), 'The Transformation of US–India Relations: An Explanation for the Rapprochement and Prospects for the Future', *Asian Survey*, 47 (4), pp. 642–56.

94. Admiral R.H. Tahiliani (Retd) (1989), 'Maritime Strategy for the Nineties', *India Defence Review* (July), p. 24.

95. Ayoob, *India and Southeast Asia*, p. 66.

96. India's land borders with Burma were established under the British in 1937. India's maritime boundary with Burma was finalized in 1987, and its maritime

boundaries with Thailand and Indonesia had been agreed upon in a trilateral agreement signed in 1978. Ibid., p. 51 (n. 19).

97. Timo Kivimäki (2002), '"Reason" and "Power" in Territorial Disputes: The South China Sea', *Asian Journal of Social Science*, 30 (3), pp. 525–46.

98. David E. Sanger (1991), 'Philippines Orders US to Leave Strategic Navy Base at Subic Bay', *The New York Times*, 28 December.

99. For a comprehensive account of India's 'Look East' strategy, see Isabelle Saint-Mézard (2006), *Eastward Bound: India's New Positioning in Asia* (New Delhi: Manohar Publications and Centre de Sciences Humaines).

100. G.V.C. Naidu (2004), 'Whither the Look East Policy: India and Southeast Asia', *Strategic Analysis*, 28 (2), pp. 331–46 (p. 338).

101. Ibid., p. 339.

102. Huxley, *Defending the Lion City*, p. 220.

103. I.P. Khosla (2007), 'India and Myanmar', in *Indian Foreign Policy: Challenges and Opportunities* (New Delhi: Foreign Service Institute), pp. 583–612.

104. Carlyle A. Thayer (1997), 'Force Modernization: The Case of the Vietnam's People Army', *Contemporary Southeast Asia*, 19 (1), pp. 1–28 (p. 12).

105. 'Minister for Defence Visits India', MINDEF Singapore, 12 October 2003, http://www.mindef.gov.sg/imindef/news_and_events/nr/2003/oct/12oct03_nr.html (accessed on 15 June 2008).

106. Josy Joseph (2007), 'Singapore "Leases" IAF Base for 5 Years', *Daily News and Analysis*, 10 October.

107. 'India–Singapore Ink Pact for Joint Army Training', *Hindustan Times*, 12 August 2008.

108. David Boey (2003), 'Sky's the Limit with S'pore–India Defence Pact', *The Straits Times*, 17 October.

109. Zackaria Abdul Rahim (2008), 'Singapore and India Explore Ways to Boost Multiple Links', *The Straits Times*, 7 May.

110. On the details of Fernandes' trip to Vietnam, see Nayan Chanda (2000), 'After the Bomb', *Far Eastern Economic Review*, 13 April.

111. Gaurav C. Sawant, 'Indian Expertise and Thai Carrier May Dovetail', *The Indian Express*, 16 April. Also see, Naidu, 'Whither the Look East Policy', p. 340.

112. For details of these trading blocs, see Thakur, *Politics and Economics of India's Foreign Policy*, pp. 255–8.

113. Ibid. See also 'India and ARF', Ministry of External Affairs, India. http://meaindia.nic.in/onmouse/arf1.pdf (accessed on 3 June 2009).

114. Since only official nuclear weapons countries can sign this treaty, India's endorsement was welcomed by Southeast Asian states. See Saint-Mézard, *Eastward Bound*, p. 400.

115. Arvind Panagariya (2008), *India: The Emerging Giant* (New York: Oxford University Press), pp. 95–109.

116. See the chapter titled 'Economic Diplomacy', in J.N. Dixit (1998), *Across Borders: Fifty Years of India's Foreign Policy* (New Delhi: Picus Books), pp. 300–21.

117. Saint-Mézard, *Eastward Bound*, p. 41.

118. Ibid., p. 101.

119. See Jaishree Balasubramanian (2003), 'India, Thailand Sign Free Trade Agreement', *Rediff*, 9 October, http://www.rediff.com/money/2003/oct/09ftal. htm (accessed on 15 June 2008); and 'India (CECA)', *International Enterprise Singapore* (n.d.), http://www.iesingapore.gov.sg/wps/portal/FTA/SingaporeFTAs/ ConcludedFTAs/CECA (accessed on 15 June 2008).

120. Manjeet S. Pardesi and Sumit Ganguly (2009), 'Energy Security and India's Foreign/Security Policy', in Harsh Pant (ed.), *Indian Foreign Policy in Unipolar World* (New Delhi: Routledge).

121. Marie Lall (2006), 'Indo-Myanmar Relations in the Era of Pipeline Diplomacy', *Contemporary Southeast Asia*, 28 (3), pp. 424–46.

122. Faizal Yahya (2003), 'India and Southeast Asia: Revisited', *Contemporary Southeast Asia*, 25 (1), pp. 79–103 (p. 92).

123. Sanjoy Hazarika (1995), 'Indian and Burmese Troops Join to Fight Rebels', *The New York Times*, 4 June. Also see 'Burma "Attacks Separatist Rebels"', *BBC News*, 5 January 2004, http://news.bbc.co.uk/2/hi/south_asia/3369287.stm (accessed on 15 June 2008).

124. Manjeet S. Pardesi (2004), 'India Maps Closer Links with ASEAN', *The Straits Times*, 26 November.

125. P.V. Narasimha Rao (1994), 'India and the Asia-Pacific: Forging a New Relationship', *Singapore Lecture 1994* (Singapore: Institute of Southeast Asian Studies).

126. Deshingkar, 'The Construction of Asia in India', p. 179.

127. Bhabani Sen Gupta (1997), 'India in the Twenty-First Century', *International Affairs*, 73 (2), pp. 297–314 (p. 309).

128. Ibid., p. 309.

129. On this, see Saint-Mézard, *Eastward Bound*, pp. 50–3.

130. Amit Baruah (2004), 'Nehru Award Conferred on Goh', *The Hindu*, 10 July.

131. While India's total trade with ASEAN was a little over $30 billion in 2006–7, China's total trade with ASEAN in 2007 was close to $190 billion. On India's trade with ASEAN, see 'India and ASEAN', India Brand Equity Foundation (January–March 2008), http://www.ibef.org/india/indiaasean.aspx (accessed on 15 June 2008). On China's trade with ASEAN, see 'Vice Premier: China, ASEAN Trade, Economic Ties Enter a New Phase', Chinese Government's Official Web Portal, 28 October 2007, http://english.gov.cn/2007-10/28/content_788198. htm (accessed on 15 June 2008).

132. Ambassador Mr Ronen Sen's address at the CSIS–JIIA Conference on 'Building Strategic Asia: The United States, Japan, and India' (Washington, DC: Embassy of India, 28 June 2007), http://www.indianembassy.org/newsite/press_release/2007/ June/13.asp (accessed on 15 June 2008).

7

Indo-Iranian Relations

What Prospects for Transformation?[1]

C. CHRISTINE FAIR

Since 1993, India and Iran have sought to transform their bilateral relations with limited success. India's efforts to develop closer ties with Iran have always been controversial because Iran's critics believed India's engagement with Iran undermined international efforts to isolate it. However, in recent years, Indo-Iranian relations have drawn considerably more high-level attention because the stakes are higher. Since 2000, the United States (US) and India have embarked upon a serious effort to forge a strategic relationship (see S. Paul Kapur's chapter in this volume). In 2005, the US promised to help India become a global power inclusive of military and nuclear assistance.[2] US nuclear assistance to India required the US Congress to reverse course on decades of non-proliferation legislation, much of which was precipitated by India's 1974 nuclear test, and hoist up an India-specific policy that recognizes India's status as a nuclear power outside of the Nuclear Non-proliferation Treaty (NPT). At the time of the negotiations, some American law-makers were nonplussed by India's relations with Iran, and the US Ambassador to India, David Mulford, even linked the prospects of the deal to Indian cooperation on Iran.[3] One US State Department official pointedly said that Delhi's ties with Tehran are 'the biggest single obstacle to the future of US–India relations and the one issue that could torpedo our strategic partnership'.[4]

Iran's brinkmanship over its nuclear programme has galvanized transatlantic agreement about Iranian intent to weaponize and a consensus on the need to prevent Iran from doing so, requiring India to delicately balance its relations with the US. Due to Iran's refusal to halt uranium enrichment, the United Nations Security Council (UNSC) sanctioned Iran thrice in 2006, 2007, and 2008. The UNSC sanctions required the support of Russia and China, which have championed Iran's right to civilian nuclear technology and have even provided assistance to its programme.[5] US efforts to limit Iran's power remain focused and have intensified due to Iran's backing of Hezbollah in Lebanon and its interference in Afghanistan and in US-occupied Iraq. Some US policymakers expect India, as its new security partner, to help isolate Iran—not provide it with an economic, political, and diplomatic lifeline. The US Congress even tried to condition the US–India nuclear deal upon India's active support for US and international efforts to contain Iran's nuclear programme. In 2007, the George W. Bush administration balked and the final legislation softened this focus but still requires the administration to report to Congress yearly on India's cooperation on Iran, among other items.[6]

Indian leadership's interests in securing this civilian nuclear deal imposed challenges for India's sustained ties with Tehran. Despite controversial statements that India would not betray Iran, India voted 'against Iran' *twice* at the International Atomic Energy Agency (IAEA). First, it voted for the resolutions finding Iran to be in non-compliance in September 2005, and later it voted to refer Iran to the UNSC in February 2006.[7] Those votes did much to chill the Indo-Iranian rapprochement, which irked Indian critics of tight ties with Washington. They opine that New Delhi has relinquished its sovereignty to placate Washington and have called for re-energizing Indo-Iran ties.[8] The debate notwithstanding, India does have several enduring interests in Iran. That country provides India access to Afghanistan and Central Asia. Iran and the Central Asian republics also offer India access to future and current energy markets, as well as prospects for various non-hydrocarbon commercial activities. Ties with Iran and its neighbours also permit India to exert pressure upon Pakistan. Given these important Indian equities in Iran and the constraints of working with Washington, to what extent will India be able to meaningfully transform its ties with Tehran? This is the subject of this chapter.

After providing a brief overview of the present-day Indo-Iranian relationship, this chapter explains the ongoing bilateral efforts to forge significant Indo-Iranian relations using three levels of analyses. First it examines structural factors, especially shifts within the international system. A second level considers domestic developments in Iran and India. At a third level, this chapter considers the role of individual leaders. As will be apparent, Indo-Iran relations appear to be over-determined by structural and domestic factors. However, specific leaders have been important as well. This chapter concludes with a discussion of the future prospects for Indo-Iranian relations.

CONTEMPORARY INDO-IRANIAN RELATIONS

For the first 40 years of independent India's history, its ability to cultivate formal political ties with Iran was constrained by the alignments of the Cold War.[9] While Iran was the first nation to recognize Pakistan and established formal diplomatic relations in May 1948, Iran and India formalized ties on 15 March 1950 when they signed a friendship treaty which called for 'perpetual peace and friendship' between the two states. In principle this document committed the two to amicable relations; however, in reality both states were soon to be ensnared in opposing Cold War alliances that precluded development of robust bilateral ties.[10]

In 1955, Mohammad Reza Shah (or The Shah) joined the US-initiated Baghdad Pact fearing that communism would undermine his regime.[11] India's Prime Minister Nehru denounced the Baghdad Pact (as well as the Southeast Asia Treaty Organization [SEATO]) as a 'wrong approach, a dangerous approach, and a harmful approach'[12] to international relations. While Iran pursued the option of alignment, India emerged as a leading state in the Non-Aligned Movement (NAM) although it certainly tilted towards Moscow. With the first Indo-Pakistan War of 1947/8 and the emergence of an enduring Indo-Pakistan dispute over Kashmir, India and Pakistan became locked in intense enmity. As Pakistan was also a member of the Baghdad pact (later renamed Central Treaty Organization, CENTO), Iran and Pakistan became closer, ostensibly under the security umbrella of the US.[13] During the 1965 and 1971 wars with India, Iran provided Pakistan with military assistance.

Although India largely welcomed Iran's 1979 revolution as an expression of national self-assertion and although the post-revolutionary Iranian leadership was generally well disposed towards India, significant differences persisted. Iran was much more critical of the Soviet invasion of Afghanistan than was India, which avoided public condemnation. During the Iran–Iraq war, India remained ambivalent as it tried to simultaneously protect its oil interests in both states. Under Ayatollah Khomeini, Iran remained isolationist and focused both upon consolidating the gains of the revolution and the strains of the Iran–Iraq war. While the 1970s and 1980s witnessed tensions between the two, there were episodic but notable periods of positive engagement, and the two sustained economic engagement during this period, particularly on energy issues. In 1983, India and Iran forged their first significant institutional mechanism, the Indo-Iran Joint Commission. It convened foreign ministerial level meetings to review progress made chiefly on economic issues.

Throughout the 1980s and 1990s, India and Iran pursued, with various levels of effort, economic and trade dialogues. However, there were surprisingly few high-level activities, such as the 1993 state visit by India's PM Narasimha Rao to Iran and a 1995 reciprocal visit by Iran's President Rafsanjani. Neither visit produced any accord per se, but they were foundational exchanges which laid the groundwork for more substantive future developments. The second major bilateral initiative, the Tehran Declaration, did not occur until 2001. It was signed by Iran's President Khatami and India's PM Atal Bihari Vajpayee during the latter's April 2001 visit to Tehran, it focused upon energy and commercial concerns, and it reaffirmed their commitment to a North–South Corridor and its maximal utilization. (This North–South Corridor will permit facile movement of goods from India by sea, through Iran and into Central Asia and Russia.[14]) Iran and India also agreed to promote scientific and technical cooperation.[15] The so-called India–Iran Strategic Dialogue came out of that agreement and has since met four times. Reflecting the bilateral stall precipitated perhaps in part due to India's votes at the UNSC, it last met in May 2005 and concentrated upon gas pipelines and a bilateral agreement for liquefied natural gas (LNG), which Iran cannot produce.[16] So far, neither side has announced a date to reconvene the Strategic Dialogue.

The most recent and most substantial framework shaping Indo-Iranian relations was the January 2003 New Delhi Declaration, signed when President Khatami visited New Delhi. It included seven additional Memoranda of Understanding and dilated upon international terrorism, shared concerns about the looming US invasion of Iraq, and the mutual need for enhanced cooperation in science and technology. [17] Some reports suggested that space advancements (for example, satellite launch) were discussed, although there is no such mention in the accord.[18] Hydrocarbon and water issues figured prominently, as did close cooperation in efforts to reconstruct and rehabilitate Afghanistan.[19] One of the additional documents signed during Khatami's 2003 visit was the 'Road Map to Strategic Cooperation', which mapped out concrete steps on oil and gas issues (such as the ever-challenging pipeline project), the commitment to expand non-hydrocarbon bilateral trade, and other forms of significant economic cooperation. It also featured India's commitment to help develop the Chahbahar port complex, the Chahbahar–Fahranj–Bam railway link, and a Marine Oil Tanking Terminal at the port. Controversially, it committed the two states to pursue more robust defence cooperation.[20]

Progress in this relationship has been slow.[21] The energy relationship has been stymied by Iranian infrastructure. Iran lacks the capability to produce LNG and India's commitment to help construct an LNG plant in Iran likely falls afoul of the Iran–Libya Sanctions Act (ILSA), which requires sanctions on yearly investments in excess of $20 million in Iran's energy sector.[22] They have continued to make progress on their commitment to build a North–South Corridor with Russia. Russia, Iran, and India signed this agreement (called the Inter-Governmental Agreement on International North–South Transport Corridor) in September 2000 in St Petersburg. This corridor is a part of an Indo-Iranian initiative to facilitate the movement of goods from Indian ports to Chahbahar, across Iran by rail, and onward into Central Asia and Russia.[23] As a part of this agreement, India agreed to help expand the Iranian port of Chahbahar and lay railway tracks that would connect Chahbahar to the Afghan city of Zaranj. India has also committed to upgrading the 215-km road that links Zaranj and Delaran as part of the Ring Road, a circular road network that connects Herat and Kabul via Mazar-e-Sharif in the north and Kandahar in the south. This would permit Indian goods to move into Afghanistan via Delaran and beyond. This access is critical for the movement of Indian products into Afghanistan as Pakistan denies India over-land access.[24]

While these infrastructure and access projects have continued, the two states' efforts to forge strategic relations have yielded few concrete results apart from important joint working groups (for example, counter-terrorism and counter-narcotics) and expanded Indian access to Iran through its long-standing embassy in Tehran and consulate in Zahedan, and most recently its consulate in Bandar Abbas. The Bandar Abbas consulate was built in 2001 and permits India to monitor ship movements in the Persian Gulf and the Strait of Hormuz.[25] The long-established consulate in Zahedan, near the Pakistan border is also, likely, an important listening post.[26] The aforementioned strategic dialogue has met four times between October 2001 and May 2005 but it has not convened since.[27] Despite claims that the forum would permit opportunities for cooperation in defence in agreed areas, little has materialized.[28]

Similarly, the hopes that India would provide expertise in electronics and telecommunications, as well as upgrades for many of Iran's legacy Russian weapons systems have not fructified.[29] There has been some activity in the naval sphere; the two navies carried out their first joint naval manoeuvres in the Arabian Sea in March 2003 during the US build-up to invade Iraq.[30] India and Iran conducted their second naval exercise during 3–8 March 2006, overlapping with US President Bush's trip to Afghanistan, India, and Pakistan.[31] While the exercises themselves, in all likelihood, had little technical significance, their timing had enormous symbolism. The first naval engagement was coincident with the US military build-up in the Gulf to invade Iraq in 2003, and the 2006 visit naval exercise overlapped with US Congress' review of the Indo-US nuclear deal and President George Bush's visit to India and Pakistan.

Bilateral technical cooperation has also been stymied. India had cooperated with Iran on civilian nuclear programmes in the past when the former sought to sell Iran a 10-megawatt research reactor to be installed at Moallem Kalyaeh in 1991, and may have also considered selling Iran a 220-megawatt nuclear power reactor. While both were to be placed under the IAEA safeguards, the US pressured India not to go through with the sales, fearing that Iran would use these facilities to make weapons-grade fissile materials.[32] The issue of nuclear cooperation again emerged in October 2004 during a discussion between then Iranian President Khatami and India's then national security advisor, J.N. Dixit, in Tehran.[33] Reports of Indo-Iranian space cooperation also galvanized small pockets of opposition to the 'other Indo-US deal' on space cooperation, presumably out of concern that US technologies could find their way into the hands of Iranian scientists.[34]

Since 2006, progress in Indo-Iranian relations has stalled in the wake of India's votes 'against' Iran at the IAEA. In an expression of vexation, Iran changed the terms of an important agreement on LNG. In June 2005, India's Petroleum Minister Mani Shankar Aiyar inked a 25-year agreement with Iran, according to which Iran would provide 5 million tons of LNG per year from 2009. While the deal was worth around $22 billion, in actual practice it was dubious. As noted, Iran lacks the capacity to manufacture LNG and is unlikely to develop the capacity to do so as, to date, no LNG facility has ever been made without US patented processes or parts. Despite the largely symbolic nature of the deal, the Supreme Economic Council of Iran, which is the ultimate arbiter of economic agreements, reneged on the agreed-upon price point and demanded renegotiation. Iranians contend that the decision was driven by the skyrocketing price of oil, which also puts upward price pressure on natural gas. However, an equally—if not more—important factor was India's votes against Iran at the IAEA.[35] In addition, Indian officials reported that major infrastructure projects in Iran (for example, the Chahbahar port) had stalled.[36]

The chill was short-lived. India, motivated by energy concerns and access to Afghanistan and Central Asia, has been adamant that its long-standing ties with Iran would not be hostage to its other bilateral relations. Iran, for its part, was keen to resume engagement with India not only because India is an emerging economic power but also because India is an important ally while other countries are seeking to isolate Iran. In April 2008, Iran's controversial president, Mahmoud Ahmadinejad, made a high-profile tour of South Asia, including visits to Pakistan and Sri Lanka. He also visited India although it appears to have been an impromptu visit. Press reports claim that when he made a routine request to refuel his aircraft in India, Indian officials 'pounced on the opportunity to host the Iranian President' in an effort to revive flagging relations. The stop-over became a state visit.[37] Rendering the proposed six-hour stop-over into an extended official visit also afforded the government an opportunity to appease leftist coalition partners who were piqued by New Delhi's alignment with the US, civilian nuclear deal with Washington, and votes against Iran at the IAEA. India also saw an opportunity to revisit the $7 billion Iran–Pakistan–India gas pipeline which has been stalled for numerous reasons, including US opposition, distrust of Pakistan, and commercial non-viability.

REVIVIFYING INDO-IRANIAN TIES

Structural Factors[38]

A number of changes in the international system have expanded and constricted the opportunity space for India and Iran at different points in time despite the long history of shared culture and history. Arguably, their progress in transforming their ties was limited by the political arrangements of the Cold War. The demise of the Soviet Union was an important structural factor that permitted more substantive development. Soon thereafter in 1993, Indian PM Narasimha Rao made a state visit to Iran. He was the first Indian PM to visit post-revolutionary Iran, and Iran's President Akbar Hashemi Rafsanjani called it a 'turning point' in bilateral relations. In 1995, Rafsanjani made a reciprocal visit to India. High-level visits continued since 1995, even though the next state visit did not occur until 2001 when PM Atal Bihari Vajpayee visited Tehran in 2001, culminating in the 'Tehran Declaration'. Signed by PM Vajpayee and Iran's President Mohammad Khatami, this declaration laid the foundation for Indian and Iranian cooperation on a wide array of strategic issues, including defence cooperation.[39]

Two years later, in January 2003, President Khatami travelled to Delhi where he was welcomed as the chief guest at India's 2003 Republic Day celebrations—an honour generally reserved for the most important of personages. Both leaders signed the New Delhi Agreement, which was important both in its timing and substance. India's feting of Khatami, contemporaneously with both the US military build-up in the Persian Gulf in preparation for the second US war in Iraq *and* with an unprecedented qualitative and quantitative expansion in US–Indian military ties, declared the importance that New Delhi attaches to its relationship with Iran. The New Delhi Declaration was also important in its substance. Expanding the Tehran Declaration, this accord further committed the two states to deeper levels of engagement, including military cooperation.[40]

The collapse of the Soviet Union and the conclusion of the Cold War presented both India and Iran with a number of challenges and opportunities. India faced uncertainty as to what would be the fate of its robust and long-standing arms supply relationship with the former Soviet Union. Iran shared this concern because the Soviet Union also supplied Iran with a steady source of arms and technology. In the wake of the end of the Cold War, the US emerged as *the* global hegemon, which unsettled both Iran and India (as well as numerous other states).

As the Soviet Union crumbled, both Iran and India shared security concerns about developments in Central Asia, which comprises Iran's important northern border and India's extended strategic neighbourhood.[41] The new Central Asia states were politically unstable and ill at ease with their neighbours. Both Iran and India wanted to develop commercial access to and political influence in the newly emergent republics. Given hostilities with Pakistan, Iran became the only viable corridor through which India could access the natural resources and economic opportunities of Central Asia and Afghanistan. Central Asia emerged as an open field in which both India and Pakistan sought to secure their political, economic, and diplomatic interests, and jockeyed for influence in the area. Russia, India, and Iran engaged in a number of joint ventures to build infrastructure in Iran, Afghanistan, and elsewhere in support of moving goods between India and Russia, via Iran and/or Afghanistan. India sought to establish robust relationships with the states of Central Asia and Iran at least in part to strategically outmanoeuvre Pakistan, which also had aspirations in that area.

Both Iran and India were discomfited by the upsurge in militant (Sunni) Islamist movements that fanned throughout South Asia and Central Asia in the early and mid-1990s. The consolidation of power by the Pakistan-backed Taliban was a major source of mutual anxiety as both states feared the consequences of unchecked proliferation of the militant Sunni Deobandi/Wahabbist movement throughout their shared neighbourhood. Tehran and New Delhi, working with Russia and Tajikistan among others, helped train and equip Ahmad Shah Massood's Northern Alliance, which was the only meaningful opposition to the Taliban.[42] They also worked to check cross-border terrorism as well as the spread of narcotics from Afghanistan.

Apart from these regional interests, the relationship conferred other benefits in the international arena. Cultivating Iran as a partner could help deflect Pakistan's rhetoric in international forums while India offered Iran a potential means to break out of its isolation. India's value in this regard has only expanded in recent years as it has forged key relations with the US, Israel, the European Union, and the states of Southeast and Northeast Asia. India's growing energy demands also presented attractive markets for hydrocarbons. This general rapprochement of the 1990s resulted in an important, if subtle, shift in Iran's position on Kashmir: in 1991, Tehran first acknowledged Kashmir to be an integral part of India. This was subsequently reiterated when J.N. Dixit, the then Indian Foreign Secretary, visited Iran in 1993, and again with PM Rao's 1993 visit to Tehran.[43]

A second major structural shift in the international arena created further opportunities for Iran and India: the fall of the Taliban regime in Afghanistan (c. 1994–2001). While Iran may have been concerned that it was the US that toppled the Taliban and that the US would have a military presence in yet another neighbouring state, Iran was an important partner at the December 2001 Bonn Conference. Iran encouraged the Bonn Conference to ensure that the final document called for democracy in Afghanistan and acknowledged the war on terrorism. Iran also convinced the Northern Alliance to drop its demands for additional ministries when talks threatened to break down.[44] Only a few weeks later, US President Bush included Iran in his infamous 'Axis of Evil' speech during his 2002 State of the Union address. With the Taliban routed, India worked quickly to become Afghanistan's most important regional partner and to establish an expanded presence that was denied during the Taliban period. India established consulates in Jalalabad, Kandahar, Herat, and Mazar-e-Sharif in addition to its embassy in Kabul. India has recently pledged $450 million in addition to the $750 million already committed. However, it has only disbursed a fraction of this amount according to figures from the Afghan government, cited by the Agency Coordinating Body For Afghan Relief.[45]

Iran too has contributed significant aid (disbursed nearly $251 million) to Afghanistan, more than Australia or even Russia. It has disbursed nearly $251 million.[46] Iran has not only concentrated its aid in the west (near the Iran border) but also in Kabul. It has set up border posts against the heroin trade, built roads and construction projects, established madrassas, provided technical assistance among other projects. It will also help build a rail line linking the two countries. In Kabul, its projects include a new medical centre and a water testing laboratory. Iran is keen that an independent Afghanistan emerges free of both American influence and Sunni militant groups. While Iran hopes for such an Afghanistan and supports President Karzai, it has also begun hedging its bets against alternative, less secure futures by using its radio stations to broadcast anti-American propaganda, funnelling funds to former warlords with ties to Iran, and supplying the Taliban with small arms to antagonize the Americans.[47]

Importantly, India and Iran are collaborating on infrastructure projects such as the aforementioned efforts to link Zaranj and Delaran as part of the Ring Road. The New Delhi Declaration of 2003 makes explicit reference to Afghanistan noting that:

Both sides stressed that the interests of peace and stability in the region are best served by a strong, united, prosperous and independent Afghanistan ... They urge the international community to remain committed on a long-term basis to the reconstruction and development of Afghanistan, to controlling re-emergence of terrorist forces, and spread of narcotics from Afghanistan.

That document also referenced the trilateral agreement between India, Iran, and Afghanistan to develop the Chahbahar route through Melak, Zaranj, and Delaran to facilitate regional trade and transit.[48]

Other changes in the international community impose serious limits to the extent of Indo-Iranian ties. First and foremost, India and the US are cementing unprecedented ties, as noted. While the US and India sought a rapprochement in the early 1980s and late 1990s, those efforts failed bitterly.[49] US President Bill Clinton sought to re-order relations with India in 2000 and achieved some important breakthroughs, with the support of PM Vajpayee. However, Clinton's ability to forge strategic ties with India was hamstrung by his commitment to non-proliferation. President Bush, unrestrained by such commitments, restructured US relations with India and committed Washington to enable India to become a global power. One of the most important elements of this commitment has been the US–India civilian nuclear deal which took around three years to finalize. This has involved contending with their legislatures, placating domestic foes of the deal, and securing international agreement at the IAEA and the Nuclear Suppliers' Groups (NSG). The desire to seal this deal likely persuaded India to vote against Iran at the IAEA. Arguably, the significance of Washington's commitments to India may reshape the relative value of Tehran's offerings.

A second potential constraint is India's relations with Israel. As India has sought deeper ties with Washington and Tehran, it has simultaneously pursued robust defence ties with Tel Aviv.[50] In fact, Israel surpassed Russia to become the largest supplier of military equipment to India.[51] As some of India's defence acquisitions from Israel involve weapon systems co-developed with the US, these deals could move forward only with Washington's blessing (see Blarel's chapter in this volume). Third and equally important, India also seeks better relations with a number of Arab states, which have been nonplussed by recent Iranian adventures in the region and wary of expanding Iranian influence.[52] Unlike Iran, commerce with these Arab Gulf states is not restricted by sanctions.

Fourth and finally, Iran's pursuit of nuclear weapons capability has thrown the relationship into stark relief and has strained the relationship. Iran, unlike India, is a signatory to the NPT. Under that treaty, Iran is entitled to civilian nuclear technology.[53] However, the Indian polity and leadership alike oppose a nuclear-armed Iran. PM Manmohan Singh has consistently stated that Iran must honour its obligations under the NPT and that another nuclear-armed state in the region undermines India's interests.[54] Another important factor explaining India's nuanced view towards Iran is the fact that Iran's nuclear programme benefited from A.Q. Khan's nuclear arms bazaar.[55] Iran discomfited Indian leadership when it equated its nuclear programme to that of India, employed India's aphorism of 'nuclear apartheid' to defend its programme, and argued that the US positions on Indian and Iranian nuclear programmes comprise a double standard.[56]

Domestic Factors

Efforts towards rapprochement with Iran have enjoyed widespread support within India since the 1990s, with all of the mainstream and leftist parties seeking to promote Indo-Iranian ties. Most of the major recent agreements between India and Iran took place during the Bharatiya Janata Party (BJP)-led coalitions governments (1998–2004). Indian commentators frequently explained that these agreements with Iran could help conciliate India's varied Muslim communities which were wary of the Hindu nationalists' agenda. Such developments, coupled with India's increased relations with Israel and its concomitant diminishing of support for the Palestinian cause, have compelled India to bolster its relations with Muslim countries, including Iran. In recent years, under the leadership of Manmohan Singh's Congress-led coalition, India's relations with Iran remain an important means to placate leftist opponents of India's relations with the US. Notably, the February 2007 visit to Iran by India's Minister of Foreign Affairs, Pranab Mukherjee, amid heightened US–Iranian discord and increasing evidence of Iranian involvement in Iraq, helped mollify government critics who object to Delhi's kowtowing to Washington on Iran.[57]

A number of important domestic factors, along with contemporaneous external factors enumerated earlier, helped reshape post-revolutionary Iran's foreign policy priorities. After Ayatollah Ruholla Khomeini died in June 1989, Supreme Leader Ayatollah Ali Khamenei and President Ali Akbar Hashemi governed Iran in tandem. Under Khomeini, Iran's central foreign policy tenet was 'Neither East, nor West'. After his death, under the leadership of reformist and pragmatist Rafsanjani, Iran sought to secure the Persian Gulf by containing Iraq, reconciling with the Arab Gulf Cooperation Council states, and by reaching out to India.[58] The two sought to cultivate their region like 'a common farmland'.[59] While this was driven by security concerns, it was also driven by domestic economic concerns. Rafsanjani was critical of Iran's economic performance since the 1979 revolution. He campaigned with the promise of economic renewal. No doubt, India's economic promise even in the early 1990s drew the attention of Rafsanjani while PM Rao, with his agenda of economic liberalization and growth, looked West and East to secure India's economic future.

Iran had hoped that India would help it fortify and modernize its defences and provide much-needed expertise in electronics and telecommunications. According to the Indian press, India had trained Iranian naval engineers in Mumbai and at Kochi port (Kerala).[60] Iran was also seeking combat training for missile boat crews and simulators for ships and subs. Iran also hoped that India would provide mid-life service and upgrades for its MiG-29 fighters, retrofit its warships and subs in Indian dockyards.[61] There were also reports that Iran believed that Indian technicians would refit and maintain Iran's T-27 tanks as well as its BMP infantry fighting vehicles and the towed 105 mm and 130 mm artillery guns.[62] As noted throughout, Iran had hoped that India would invest in its hydrocarbon infrastructure (for example, develop an LNG capability). It is unlikely that these hopes will materialize any time soon until India can confidently manage its relations with Tehran and Washington.

Both Iran and India are very worried about the domestic ramifications of the recrudescence of the Taliban in Afghanistan. (This is true even though Iran is providing low-level nuisance value support to the Taliban to encourage the US to leave.) Both states are wary about Pakistan's stability and its continued exporting of Sunni militancy. Both Iran and India have been affected by Sunni militant violence. Iran's Baluchistan-o-Sistan province in recent years has suffered a number of such militant strikes. India fears the influence of such extremism not only because it directly and indirectly contributes to the activities of Islamist militants operating in India, but also because it fuels the rhetoric and political positions of Hindu nationalists who seek to make India an explicit home for Hindus. This is anathema to those Indians who prize India's secular values and wish to preserve it.[63] By the same token, India has the second largest Shi'a Muslim population in the world. India was nonplussed by Iran's efforts to export its revolution throughout the 1980s, and no doubt watches with some concern its efforts to shore up Shi'a communities as well as political and militant movements in Lebanon, Afghanistan, Iraq, and possibly Pakistan.

Individual Leadership Factors

Individual leadership factors appear to have less explanatory value in understanding the conditions for and limits to Indo-Iranian rapprochement. Within domestic audiences, Indo-Iranian relations are valued highly and are not controversial. Left to their own devices and unconstrained by developments in the international arena, India and Iran may have been able to achieve more. However, a few leaders have been strongly associated with the renewed efforts to reinvigorate Indo-Iranian relations. PM Rao, who began reshaping India's foreign and domestic policies, drove the move to cultivate Iran, which resulted in his 1993 state visit. (Rao also kept a distance from the Dalai Lama to allay Chinese concerns about India's position on Tibet and housing Tibetan exiles.) His calculations paid off. In 1994, Pakistani PM Benazir Bhutto sought to have a resolution passed by the UN Human Rights Commission in Geneva on the human rights situation in Jammu and Kashmir. She was thwarted at least in part due to a lack of support from China and Iran.[64] Rao's Iranian counterpart, President Rafsanjani, led the rapprochement from Iran's side. Rafsanjani's 1995 visit drew the attention of Washington 'largely because it coincided with—and reportedly upstaged—[US] Treasury Secretary Rubin's visit to India'.[65] Both the 1993 and 1995 visits helped Iran because they undermined US efforts to isolate Tehran and promoted it as a significant actor in broader Asian theatre.[66]

Similarly, both Khatami and Vajpayee were strong leaders. Khatami was elected in 1997 as a reformer and stunned the world with his approach to international relations that focused upon a 'dialogue of civilizations'.[67] Vajpayee is credited with transforming India's foreign policy from its Nehruvian roots of Third Worldism, idealism, and moralism towards one informed by pragmatism and realism. (Others argue that this transition was well underway from 1990 onwards.) [68] Under Vajpayee, India made important strides with numerous capitals, including Washington.

President Ahmedinejad has not overtly and consistently prioritized this relationship with India. While he has applied efforts when needed to ensure that some minimal progress persists, there have been few spectacular developments under his leadership. Instead, his presidency has been marked by international confrontation abroad and economically ruinous policies at home. Iran's emerging support for the Taliban in Afghanistan has vexed Delhi. The Taliban and allied fighters have killed several Indian workers in Afghanistan, which has motivated India to raise this issue with Tehran in recent years.[69] Manmohan Singh, for his part, has demonstrated an adequate ability to maintain India's compleat of complex international relationships. However, he has been less bold than Vajpayee and at times even pusillanimous, as evidenced by his political lethargy in contending with leftist elements seeking to sabotage the Indo-US civilian nuclear deal.[70] Both Ahmedinejad and Singh have focused upon energy politics and Afghanistan rather than the more contentious issues addressed in the countries' various accords.

* * *

Structural factors related to the international system will likely continue restraining the extent of Indo-Iranian ties. Equally important, these structural limitations will accentuate domestic political concerns. Notably, because Iran is likely to become increasingly more isolated, investment in Iran, especially in large hydrocarbon infrastructure, will become more costly and risky for Indian public and private actors. Yet India requires energy resources to sustain its growth and power projection. However, given the challenges of dealing with Iran and ever-tightening sanctions, India may well look elsewhere for immediate energy supplies even while continuing to stay active in Iran in the event that Iran one day normalizes its relations with the international community. (India's competitor China is similarly engaged in Iran and other theatres where India is active such as Sudan, Burma, and Central Asia.)

Apart from energy concerns, both India and Iran are expected to continue working together in Afghanistan; India will likely continue related infrastructure projects at Iran's Chahbahar port complex. However, safety has already impeded progress in Afghanistan, and Iran's continued support to the Taliban may sour Delhi's appetite to do more with Tehran. Clearly, should Iran continue to pursue nuclear weapons or break out of the NPT (for example, by testing), India's astute diplomatic skills surely will be tested. India's own aspirations to be a legitimate nuclear weapons state will also shape its positions on Iranian behaviour in its region. While these structural factors will limit the scope for Indo-Iranian engagement, India's regional interests are enduring and will motivate Delhi to find ways of working with Iran to secure desired access to Central Asia and energy supplies. One should not expect India to abandon its efforts to engage Iran despite these structural limits and the related domestic challenges they impose.

Indo-Iranian ties likely will remain important for domestic reasons, at least over the near term, and that relationship will likely remain a signifier of India's independent foreign policy in a time of ever-closer ties with Washington. However, it is not clear that this will remain the case. It is questionable how much the relationship placates vexed Indian Muslims who are important niche electoral constituencies in India's coalition-driven political system. While Iran has tempered its position on Kashmir at various times, more often than not it has supported Pakistan's position on Kashmir in forums such as the Organization of the Islamic Conference (OIC). Indians dislike the Taliban who have contributed to Islamist terrorism in India. Evidence (however scant) that Iran may have been involved in the 2006 Mumbai train bombings has raised doubts about Iran for some Indians.[71] And there is little support across the Indian government and polity for a nuclear-armed Iran. In contrast, Indo-US relations enjoy widespread support in India despite controversial US policies such as the 2003 invasion of Iraq.[72]

With formidable structural barriers and uncertain domestic motivation for significant transformation of the current status quo, arguably the value of Indian and Iranian leadership will be important wildcards in navigating these challenges. In total, barring the arrival of strong leaders in both capitals who can successfully negotiate these varied impediments and steer a new and more daring course, structural and domestic factors impose real limits to Indo-Iranian rapprochement and render a fundamental transformation of bilateral ties unlikely.

NOTES

1. This paper was drafted in the fall of 2008. The information cutoff for this paper is November 2008.

2. See discussion in Ashley J. Tellis (2005), *India as a New Global Power: An Action Agenda for the United States* (Washington DC: CEIP). See in particular Raaiza Rashid and George Perkovich (2005), 'A Survey of Progress in U.S.–India Relations', in Tellis, *India as a New Global Power*, pp. 5–9.

3. See comments by Representative Tom Lantos and Representative Robert Wexler on this issue made during a hearing of the House of Representatives, Committee on International Relations, on 'The US and India: An Emerging Entente?', 8 September 2005, www.house.gov/international_relations/109/23323.pdf (accessed

on 3 November 2008). See partial transcript in 'India, Iran and the Congressional Hearings on the Indo-U.S. Nuclear Deal', *The Hindu*, 1 October 2005. Also see 'US to India: Shun Iran or Lose Nuclear Help—Nuclear Deal Used as Leverage to Block Support in U.N.', *The Associated Press*, 25 January 2006, www. informationclearinghouse.info/article11669.htm (accessed on 3 November 2008).

4.   Interview with senior US State Department official in Daniel Twining (2008), 'India's Relations with Iran and Myanmar: "Rogue State" or Responsible Democratic Stakeholder', *India Review*, 7 (1), p.1.

5.   United Nations Security Council, 'Security Council Imposes Sanctions on Iran for Failure to Halt Uranium Enrichment, Unanimously Adopting Resolution 1737 (2006)', 23 December 2006, www.un.org/News/Press/docs/2006/sc8928. doc.htm (accessed on 3 November 2008); United Nations Security Council, 'Security Council Toughens Sanctions Against Iran, Adds Arms Embargo with Unanimous Adoption of Resolution 1747 (2007)', 24 March 2007, www.un.org/ News/Press/docs/2007/sc8980.doc.htm (accessed on 3 November 2008); 'U.N. Security Council Passes More Sanctions against Iran', *The Christian Science Monitor*, 3 March 2008, www.csmonitor.com/2008/0304/p25s04-wome.html? page=2 (accessed on 3 November 2008).

6.   Wade Boese (2007), 'Congress Exempts India from Nuclear Trade Rules', *Arms Control Troday*, January/February, www.armscontrol.org/act/2007_01-02/Congress Exempts (accessed on 3 November 2008).

7.   In October 2005, India's then Foreign Minister Natwar Singh declared that India would not support US efforts to refer Iran to the UNSC, which outraged key members of the US Congress. See comments by Representative Tom Lantos and Representative Robert Wexler during a hearing of the House of Representatives, Committee on International Relations, 8 September 2005. Also see C. Christine Fair (2007), 'India and Iran: New Delhi's Balancing Act', *The Washington Quarterly*, 30 (3), pp. 145–59.

8.   See Shebonti Ray Dadwal (2008), 'Re-energizing India–Iran Ties', *Strategic Comments*, 2 May, www.idsa.in/publications/stratcomments/ShebontiRayDadwal 020508.htm (accessed on 3 November 2008); Praful Bidwai (2007), '*India–Iran Ties Jeopardized by US Threats*', 10 February, www.antiwar.com/bidwai/?articleid= 10501 (accessed on 3 November 2008).

9.   Farah Naaz (2001), 'Indo-Iranian Relations: 1947–2000', *Strategic Analysis*, 24 (10), pp. 1911–26; John Calabrese (2002), 'Indo-Iranian Relations in Transition', *Journal of South Asia and Middle Eastern Studies*, 25 (3), pp. 60–82.

10. A.H.H. Abedi (2000), 'Relations between India and Iran: 1947–1979', in A.K. Pasha (ed.), *India, Iran and the GCC States* (New Delhi: Manas Publications), pp. 236–61; Naaz, 'Indo-Iranian Relations'; Calabrese, 'Indo-Iranian Relations in Transition'.

11. Ali Ansari (2003), *A History of Modern Iran since 1921: The Pahlavis and After* (London: Longman), pp. 125–46.

12. Quoted in Naaz, 'Indo-Iranian Relations', p. 1914.

13. Naaz, 'Indo-Iranian Relations' and Calabrese, 'Indo-Iranian Relations in Transition'.

14. Jian Yaping (2003), 'Why India Attaches Importance to Central Asia', *Alexander's Gas and Oil Connections*, 11 December, http://www.gasandoil.com/GOC/news/ntc35023.htm (accessed on 3 November 2008); Rizvan Zeb (2003), 'Gwadar and Chabahar: Competition or Complimentarily', *Central Asia-Caucasus Analysts*, 22 October, www.cacianalyst.org/?q=node/1578 (accessed on 3 November 2008); Stephen Blank (2003), 'The Indian–Iranian Connection and Its Importance for Central Asia', *Eurasianet.org*, 12 March, www.eurasianet.org/departments/business/articles/eav031203.shtm (accessed on 3 November 2008).

15. Government of India, Ministry of External Affairs, 'New Delhi Declaration Text', 16 October 2001, http://meaindia.nic.in/speech/2003/01/25spc01.htm (accessed on 3 November 2008).

16. Government of India, Ministry of External Affairs, 'India Iran Strategic Dialogue', 16 October 2001, http://meaindia.nic.in/pressrelease/2001/01/16pr01.htm (accessed on 3 November 2008); 'Iran, India Hold 4th Round of Strategic Dialogue', 5 May 2005, http://www.payvand.com/news/05/may/1006.html (accessed on 3 November 2008).

17. Government of India, Ministry of External Affairs, 'Documents Signed between Islamic Republic of Iran and India New Delhi—25 January 2003 in Hyderabad House, New Delhi, India', 25 January 2003, http://meaindia.nic.in/tratiesagreement/2003/btjan25.htm (accessed on 3 November 2008).

18. Government of India, Ministry of External Affairs, 'President Mohammad Khatami's Visit to India 24–28 January 2003 New Delhi', http://meaindia.nic.in/event/2003/01/25events01.htm (accessed on 3 November 2008); 'India, Iran have Co-operation in Space Research', *The Times of India*, 1 February 2003, http://finance.indiainfor.com/news/2003/01/01indiiran.html (accessed on 3 November 2008); Government of India, Ministry of External Affairs, 'Documents Signed between Islamic Republic of Iran and India'; Ramananda Sengupta (2003), 'Yes, India is a Friend of Iran, So What?',13 November, www.rediff.com/news/2003/nov.13ram.htm (accessed on 3 November 2008).

19. Press Information Bureau (of India) (2003), 'India Iran Discuss Modalities for Execution of S&T Agreement', 28 January, http://pib.nic.in/archieve/lreleng/lyr2003/rjan2003/28012003/r280120036.html (accessed on 3 November 2008).

20. C. Raja Mohan (2003), 'India, Iran Moving Towards Defence Cooperation', *The Hindu*, 20 January, http://www.hinduonnet.com/2003/01/20/stories/2003012003921100.htm (accessed on 3 November 2008).

21. Fair, 'India and Iran'; Fair (2007), 'Indo-Iranian Ties: Thicker Than Oil', *Middle East Review of International Affairs Journal*, 11 (1); Fair (2004), 'Indo-Iranian Relations: Prospects for Bilateral Cooperation Post 9–11', in Robert Hathaway (ed.), *The 'Strategic Partnership' Between India and Iran* (Washington: Woodrow Wilson International Center for Scholars).

22. Information provided in personal communications with Henry Rowen, Mark Hayes, Mojan Movassate, and Medhi Varzi in April 2006. All of these individuals are well-reputed authorities on this issue. See also Energy Information Administration (2007), *Country Analysis Brief: Iran* (EIA, October), http://www.eia.doe.gov/cabs/Iran/pdf.pdf (accessed on 3 November 2008).

23. Regine A. Spector (2002), 'The North–South Corridor', *Central Asia-Caucus Institute Analyst*, 3 July, http://www.cacianalyst.org/?q=node/165 (accessed on 3 November 2008); Sushil J. Aaron (2003), *Straddling Faultlines: India's Foreign Policy Towards the Greater Middle East*, CSH Occasional Paper, No. 7 (New Delhi: Centre de Sciences Humaines de New Delhi); Sudha Ramachandran (2002), 'India, Iran, Russia Map out Trade Routes', *The Asia Times Online*, 29 June, http://www.atimes.com/ind-pak/DF29Df02.html (accessed on 3 November 2008).

24. Yaping, 'Why India Attaches Importance to Central Asia'; Zeb, 'Gwadar and Chabahar'; Zeb (2003), 'The Emerging Indo-Iranian Strategic Alliance and Pakistan', *Central Asia-Caucasus Analysts*, 12 February, www.cacianalyst.org/?q=node/902 (accessed on 3 November 2008); Aaron, *Straddling Faultlines*, p. 30.

25. Donald L. Berlin (2004), *India–Iran Relations: A Deepening Entente*, Asia-Pacific Center for Security Studies Special Assessment (Honolulu: Asia-Pacific Center for Security Studies).

26. Author fieldwork in Zahaden in April 2001, which included a visit to the Indian consulate there. See also Berlin, *India–Iran Relations*.

27. Government of India, Ministry of External Affairs, 'India Iran Strategic Dialogue'; 'Iran, India Hold 4th Round of Strategic Dialogue'.

28. Ramananda Sengupta (2003), 'Advantage: India', 30 January, www.rediff.com/news/2003/jan/30ram.htm (accessed on 3 November 2008); Ramtanu Maitra (2003), 'Why Courting Russia and Iran Makes Sense', *Asia Times Online*, 2 October, www.atimes.com/atimes/South_Asia/EJ02Df04.html (accessed on 3 November 2008). For a reputable view from Pakistan, see Khaled Ahmed (2005, 'India's Relations with Iran', *The Friday Times*, 16 (49), and M.P. Zamani (2004), 'Indo-Iran Strategic Cooperation', *Iran Daily*, No. 2119, 21 October.

29. Stephen Blank, 'India's Rising Profile in Central Asia', *Comparative Strategy*, 22 (2), pp. 139–57; Calabrese, 'Indo-Iranian Relations in Transition', Sengupta, 'Yes, India is a Friend of Iran'; Anthony Cordesman (2004), *Iran's Developing Military Capabilities* (Washington, DC: Center for Strategic and International Studies); Zeb, 'Gwadar and Chabahar'; Zeb, 'Emerging Indo-Iranian Strategic Alliance and Pakistan', Ehsan Ehrari (2003), 'As India and Iran Snuggle, Pakistan Feels the Chills', *Asia Times*, 11 February, http://www.atimes.com/atimes/South_Asia/EB11Df01.html (accessed on 3 November 2008).

30. Fair (2004), *The Counterterror Coalitions: Cooperation with India and Pakistan* (Santa Monica: RAND); Fair, 'Indo-Iranian Relations'.

31. There has been considerable acrimony over the precise nature of this engagement. See Vivek Raghuvanshi and Gopal Ratnam (2006), 'Indian Navy Trains Iranian

Sailors', *Defense News*, 27 March, http://www.congress.gov/cgi-bin/cpquery/?
&sid=cp109QuAhF&refer=&r_n=sr288.109&db_id=109&item=&sel=TOC_
801810& (accessed on 3 November 2008); Vijay Sakhuja (2006), 'Iran Stirs
Indian–US Waters', *Institute of Peace and Conflict Studies*, 10 April, http://www.
ipcs.org/US_related_articles2.jsp?action=showView&kValue=1999&military=10
16&status=article&mod=b (accessed on 3 November 2008); Sridhar Krishnaswami
(2006), 'Iran not Getting Military Training from India: Rice', 6 April, http://www.
rediff.com/news/2006/apr/06ndeal3.htm (accessed on 3 November 2008). See
comments of Under-Secretary of State for Political Affairs, R. Nicholas Burns, on
the US–India Civilian Nuclear Deal at the Carnegie Endowment for International
Peace on 16 May 2006, Audio-file available at www.carnegieendowment.org/
events/index.cfm?fa=eventDetail&id=884&&prog=zgp&proj=znpp,zsa,zusr
(accessed on 3 November 2008). Burns claimed that the exercise was little more
than a few hundred Iranian naval cadets playing volleyball with Indians.

32. See Nuclear Threat Initiative (2005), 'Iran Profile', August, www.nti.org/e_
research/profiles/Iran/1825_1864.html (accessed on 3 November 2008); Mark
Skootsky (1995), 'US Nuclear Policy Toward Iran', 1 June, http://people.
csail.mit.edu/boris/iran-nuke.text (accessed on 3 November 2008); Jehangir
Pocha (2003), 'Concern Increases over Ties between India, Iran: Nuclear Arms
Proliferation Worries US', *San Francisco Chronicle*, 14 October; 'India Helping
Iran with Nuclear Energy Programme: Foreign Minister', *Agence France Presse*
(AFP), 13 December 2003, www.accessmylibrary.com/coms2/summary_0286-
19717763_ITM (accessed on 3 November 2008).

33. India has been consistent in its support for Iran's right to nuclear energy while
rejecting Iranian pursuit of nuclear weapons. In November 2008, External
Affairs Minister Pranab Mukherjee said that Iran has every right to develop
nuclear energy for peaceful purposes, but insisted that this be consistent with
its international obligations and commitments. See 'India–Iran relations are
Important in Themselves: Pranab', *The Indian Express*, 1 November 2008.

34   Richard Speier (2006), 'India's ICBM—On a "Glide Path" to Trouble?', The
Nonproliferation Policy Education Center, 7 February, www.npec-web.org/
Essays/060207SpeierICBM.pdf (accessed on 3 November 2008); 'Iran Watch
Round Table', February 2006, www.iranwatch.org/ourpubs/roundtables/
rt-indiadeal-022806.htm (accessed on 3 November 2008); *The Times of India*,
'India, Iran have Co-operation in Space Research'; Ramananda Sengupta (2003),
'India–Iran Gas Pipeline: A Transit Challenge', 22 January, http://us.rediff.com/
news/2003/jan/22ram.htm (accessed on 3 November 2008). In the 1970s, India
and Iran began a joint venture project named Zohreh to launch four Iranian
communications satellites into a geostationary orbit. At that time, they negotiated
with NASA for launching satellites, according to Yiftah S. Shapir (2005), 'Iran's
Efforts to Conquer Space', *Strategic Assessments*, 8 (3), www.inss.org.il/publications.
php?cat=21&incat=&read=160 (accessed on 3 November 2008).

35. See discussion in P.R. Kumaraswamy (2008), 'Delhi: Between Tehran and Washington', *Middle East Quarterly*, 15 (1), pp. 41–7, http://www.meforum. org/1821/delhi-between-tehran-and-washington (accessed on 9 June 2009); Fair, 'Indo-Iranian Ties'.

36. Interviews with officials in the Indian Ministry of External Affairs in February 2008.

37. Nilofar Suhrawardy (2008), 'Ahmadinejad's Visit not a Refueling Stop', *Arab News*, 28 April, www.arabnews.com/?page=4&section=0&article=109367&d=28 &m=4&y=2008 (accessed on 3 November 2008); Madhur Singh (2008), 'India and Iran: Getting Friendly?', *Time*, 24 April.

38. This section draws from Fair, 'India and Iran', 'Indo-Iranian Relations', and 'Indo-Iranian Ties'.

39. Fair, 'Indo-Iranian Relations'.

40. Ibid.

41. Juli MacDonald (2002), *Indo-US Military Relationship: Expectations and Perceptions* (Falls Church: Booze Allen Hamilton). See Chapter 2, 'Views of the Strategic Environment'.

42. C. Christine Fair (2008), 'Pakistan's Relations with Central Asia: Is Past Prologue?', *Journal of Strategic Studies*, 31 (2), pp. 201–27.

43. Calabrese, 'Indo-Iranian Relations in Transition', p. 69.

44. Michael Connell and Alireza Nader (2006), *Iranian Objectives in Afghanistan: Any Basis for Collaboration with the United States? A Project Iran Workshop* (Alexandria, VA: The CNA Corporation), www.payvand.com/news/07/jan/1354. html (accessed on 3 November 2008).

45. Aid that is pledged is often not committed (for example, budgeted). Once aid is committed, it is often not executed or disbursed in the recipient country for a number of reasons including insecurity, poor absorptive capacity of the recipient, poor execution capacity of the donor, among others. An exact accounting of aid disbursed is very difficult to determine and thus exact figures are not generally available. However, according to Afghan government figures cited by Matt Waldman in his study for the Agency Coordinating Body For Afghan Relief, India has only disbursed about one-third of its commitment for 2002–8. In contrast, the US has disbursed about half, whereas the European Commission and Germany have disbursed about two-thirds. See Matt Waldman (2008), *Falling Short: Aid Effectiveness in Afghanistan* (Kabul: ACBAR), p. 1 available at www. acbar.org/ACBAR%20Publications/ACBAR%20Aid%20Effectiveness%20 (25%20Mar%2008).pdf (accessed on 9 June 2009). For an alternative but similar accounting, see cumulative data on aid committed and disbursed available through the Donor Assistance Database for Afghanistan. For a discussion of Indian aid to Afghanistan, see Shanthie Mariet D'Souza (2007), 'Change the Pattern of Aid to Afghanistan', *IDSA Strategic Comments*, 28 June, www.idsa.in/publications/ stratcomments/ShanthieDSouza280607.htm (accessed on 3 November 2008);

Shanthie Mariet D'Souza (2007), 'India's Aid to Afghanistan: Challenges and Prospects', *Strategic Analysis*, 31 (5), pp. 833–42.

46. Using cumulative amounts of disbursed aid, Iran has disbursed about $251 million of its $252 million pledged. India has pledged or committed much more, nearly $1 billion. However, it has disbursed only about $250 million. See graphic in Waldman, *Falling Short*, p. 8. For alternative but similar figures, see data in the Donor Assistance Database for Afghanistan.

47. Author fieldwork in Afghanistan between June and October 2007.

48. See Government of India, Ministry of External Affairs, 'New Delhi Declaration Text'.

49. Fair, *Counterterror Coalitions*.

50. See, for example, P.R. Kumaraswamy (1998), 'India and Israel: Evolving Strategic Partnership', *Mideast Security and Policy Studies*, 40, http://www.biu.ac.il/SOC/besa/publications/40pub.html (accessed on 9 June 2009). See also Blarel's chapter in this volume.

51. Yaakov Katz (2009), 'Israel Now India's Top Defense Supplier', *Jerusalem Post*, 15 February, http://www.jpost.com/servlet/Satellite?cid=1233304779410&pagename=JPost%2FJPArticle%2FShowFull (accessed on 6 June 2009).

52. Aaron, *Straddling Faultlines*.

53. Some analysts argue that Iran's deception, a violation of Article II of the NPT, obviates its rights to a full nuclear fuel cycle under Article IV of the NPT. See text of the Nuclear Nonproliferation Treaty, available at www.fas.org/nuke/control/npt/text/npt2.htm (accessed on 3 November 2008); International Crisis Group (2006), *Iran: Is There a Way Out of the Nuclear Impasse?* (Brussels: ICG).

54. On 18 April 2006, the PM declared that 'Iran has had a clandestine nuclear programme for several years and it is not in India's interest to have another nuclear weapon state in the neighbourhood'. See 'Ties with US in India's interest: Prime Minister', *The Hindu*, 19 April 2006, http://www.hindu.com/2006/04/19/stories/2006041906741200.htm (accessed on 3 November 2008); C. Uday Bhaskar (2005), 'Vote at IAEA Not Anti-Iranian But Pro-India', *IDSA Strategic Comments*, 6 October, http://www.idsa.in/publications/stratcomments/cudaybhaskar61005.htm (accessed on 3 November 2008).

55. K. Subrahmanyam (2005), 'Vote for Iran a Yes for Khan', *The Indian Express*, 19 October.

56. For a thoughtful discussion of this issue, see P.R. Kumaraswamy (July 2008), 'India's Persian Problems', *Strategic Insights*, http://www.ccc.nps.navy.mil/si/2008/Jul/kumaraswamyJul08.asp (accessed 6 June 2009) and Daniel Twining (2008), 'India's Relations with Iran and Myanmar: "Rogue State" or Responsible Democratic Stakeholder?', *India Review*, 7 (1), pp. 1–37.

57. T.P. Sreenivasan (2007), 'Pranab's Iran Visit a Signal to the US', 12 February, http://in.rediff.com/news/2007/feb/12tps.htm (accessed on 3 November 2008).

58. Cited in R.K. Ramazani (1992), 'Iran's Foreign Policy: Both North and South', *The Middle East Journal*, 46 (3), p. 394.

59. Cited in Ibid., p. 395.

60. Vijay Sakhuja (2006), 'Iran Stirs India-US Waters', IPCS Article No. 1986, 10 April http://www.ipcs.org/article_details.php?articleNo=1986 (accessed on 6 June 2009); Indo-Asian News Service (2003), 'India, Iran begin naval exercise off Mumbai', 10 March. http://www.siliconindia.com/shownews/India_Iran_begin_naval_exercise_off_Mumbai___-nid-18814.html (accessed on 6 June 2009); Vivek Raghuvanshi and Gopal Ratnam (2006), 'Indian Navy Trains Iranian Sailors', *Defense News*, 27 March; Rahul Singh (2007), '"Non-aligned" India trains Iran's Sailors', *Hindustan Times*, 5 September. Available online at http://www.hindustantimes.com/StoryPage/StoryPage.aspx?sectionName=&id=d6e13f01-a5ff-4acb-ab07-51031ca9ea5e&Headline='Non-aligned'+India+trains+Iran%e2%80%99s+sailors (accessed on 6 June 2009).

61. Calabrese, 'Indo-Iranian Relations in Transition', pp. 75–6.

62. Zeb, 'The Emerging Indo-Iranian Strategic Alliance and Pakistan'.

63. Conversation with a high-ranking Indian diplomat in Washington in August 2008.

64. See 'Narasimha Rao: Our Finest PM Ever?', 27 December 2004, www.rediff.com/news/2004/dec/28raman.htm (accessed on 3 November 2008).

65. Stephen Grummon (1995), 'Iran and India: Assessing the Rafsanjani Trip', The Washington Institute for Near East Policy, Policy Watch No. 150, 26 April, www.washingtoninstitute.org/print.php?template=C05&CID=2870 (accessed on 3 November 2008); David Sanger (1995), 'Treasury Chief Goes to India and is Upstaged by Iranian', *New York Times*, 19 April.

66. In the days and weeks before the visits by Rubin and Rafsanjani, Washington squashed a deal between Conoco Inc. and Iran to develop a part of Iran's oilfields. Washington had been trying to stop American companies from buying Iranian oil and selling it to third countries. A few days before the visit, Secretary of State Warren Christopher failed to persuade China to stop supplying nuclear goods to Teheran. Sanger, 'Treasury Chief Goes to India and is Upstaged by Iranian'.

67. See address by Mohammed Khatami (2000), 'Dialogue among Civilizations', Speech delivered at the United Nations, New York, 5 September, http://www.unesco.org/dialogue/en/khatami.htm (accessed on 3 November 2008).

68. Vajpayee is often credited with this transition because of India's nuclear test. However, the lineaments of India's foreign policy had been steadily shifting at least since 1990 with both the collapse of the Soviet Union (see Ollapally's chapter in this volume) and economic crisis of 1990 (see Mukherji's chapter in this volume). For a discussion of India's transition from moralism and idealism as principles of foreign policy to realism, see C. Raja Mohan (2003), *Crossing the Rubicon: The Shaping of India's New Foreign Policy* (New Delhi: Viking Publication). For an empirical critique of these moves, see S.S. Chaulia (2002), 'BJP, India's Foreign

Policy and the "Realist Alternative," to the Nehruvian Tradition', *International Politics*, 39 (2), pp. 215–34.

69. In 2008, the British government asked both Russia and India to raise with Tehran the issue of its support to the Taliban. See Mark Townsend (2008), 'Special Forces Find Proof of Iran Supplying Taliban with Equipment to Fight British', *The Guardian*, 22 June.

70. Rama Lakshmi and Emily Wax (2008), 'India's Government Wins Parliament Confidence Vote', *Washington Post*, 23 July, p. A12.

71. One of the culprits flew to Iran, travelled to the border town of Zahedan, and then crossed into Pakistan. Others fled to Bangladesh. See Praveen Swami and Anupama Katakam (2006), 'Gaps to Fill', The *Hindu* (e-book), 20 October, http://pay.hindu.com/ebook%20-%20ebfl20061020part3.pdf (accessed on 3 November 2008).

72. WorldPublicOpinion.org (2006), 'Most Indians Believe Iran is Trying to Develop Nuclear Weapons: Think UN Should Try to Stop Nuclear Proliferation, Muslim and Hindu Indians Concur', 1 March, http://www.worldpublicopinion.org/pipa/articles/brasiapacificra/170.php?nid=&id=&pnt=170 (accessed on 3 November 2008).

8

Indo-Israeli Relations

Emergence of a Strategic Partnership

NICOLAS BLAREL

O n 29 January 1992, India became the last major non-Arab and non-Islamic state to establish full and normal diplomatic relations with Israel, almost 42 years after recognizing it as a sovereign state. In pursuing this normalization, New Delhi rectified what appeared to be a blind spot of India's foreign policy that had existed from 14 May 1948, the independence of Israel. Since the early 1950s, both India and Israel maintained only limited contacts with each other despite not having any direct conflict. In fact, the two former British territories shared some common features as newly sovereign nation-states, as they both dealt with a difficult partition linked to religious identities and both emerged as relatively stable democracies in very volatile neighbourhoods. As a consequence, it seems paradoxical that there was no real attempt to reappraise India's West Asia policy until the early 1990s.[1]

After 1992, the normalization of relations helped the two countries explore many areas of cooperation such as agriculture, culture, tourism, and especially trade and military exchanges. Almost non-existent for 40 years, trade and economic relations took an upward swing after 1992 when the Indian government decided to liberalize and open its economy to international investments. The signing of various free-trade agreements paved the way for an enormous growth in the volume of bilateral trade,[2] which increased fivefold between 1992 and 2000 to reach $1 billion, and is expected to reach $12 billion by 2012.[3] Although both governments are still reluctant to talk openly about cooperation in this sensitive area, arms sales are a major component of this flourishing partnership. India has become Israel's largest arms export market in the world for the last four years (replacing China), with sales representing roughly $1.5 billion in 2006.[4] Judging from an assessment by the audit firm Ernst & Young (E&Y), Israel is today on the verge of becoming India's largest arms supplier, overtaking the traditional Russian partner.[5] This fast burgeoning relationship that has developed over the last 15 years demonstrates that there had always been a potential for fruitful and complementary cooperation between the two nations.

Why have Indo-Israeli relations moved from almost naught to a rapid and substantial development in certain sensitive sectors like defence cooperation and, in particular, hi-tech weaponry in only a few years? By analysing changes at the international, national, and individual levels after 1991,[6] this chapter aims to go beyond existing empirical explanations to bring a more theoretical understanding of the reorientation of India's policy towards West Asia and Israel.[7]

Existing studies emphasize the obvious link between the convergence of Indo-Israeli interests in 1991–2 and the almost sudden change of global politics from a bipolar world to a unipolar world, characterized by the disappearance of India's traditional Soviet partner and the emergence of the United States (US) as the sole superpower after the Gulf Crisis of 1990–1. The dramatically changed structure of global politics of 1991 pushed India to modify its foreign policy towards the US and the Western bloc, and most notably towards Israel. Numerous domestic factors equally shaped India's West Asia policy after 1991. The existence of complementary national security interests with Israel pushed the Indian government to modify its West Asia policy. Finally, individual leadership in India also played an important role in the sudden establishment of a strong and stable strategic partnership with Israel. It is important to analyse the pivotal role of the Narasimha Rao government in moving Indo-Israeli strategic relations from rhetoric to substance in the post-Cold War setting.

This chapter proceeds in five parts. First, it is necessary to present a background of the nature of Indo-Israeli contacts from the time of Indian and Israeli independence to the end of the Cold War. The chapter will then describe the important evolutions at the structural level that facilitated a reappraisal of India's policy towards West Asia and Israel. The third section will explore the existing domestic incentives in India for a strategic partnership with Israel. The fourth section will examine the role of Indian political leaders in taking the bold and necessary steps to create favourable and decisive conditions for the establishment of a strong and durable strategic partnership in the last 15 years. Finally, the chapter will conclude that it is the combination of these different levels of changes that

can accurately explain the quality, the timing, and the new intensity of
Indo-Israeli relations.

HISTORICAL BACKGROUND

Relations between the Indian and Israeli communities existed well before
they became independent from the British Empire after World War II. The
roots of India's Israel policy can even be dated back to the 1920s, when the
leaders of the Indian nationalist movement started supporting the Palestinian
cause against the British rule.[8] It was through this shared opposition to
British imperialism that the first political links were established between
Indian and Arab leaders. Nehru held discussions with Arab nationalists in
various anti-imperialist meetings, such as the 1927 Brussels Conference
of Oppressed Nationalities.[9] As a consequence, India's attitude towards
Israeli national aspirations has long been opposed to that of the Western
countries. Nehru found similar features between the partitions of Palestine
and the Indian subcontinent. He believed that both were the results of
a division between two nationalisms encouraged by the British tactics of
divide and rule.[10] As a result, the Jewish problem was a minority problem
and Nehru envisaged a single Palestinian state based on federal principles,
a solution which was consistent with his own domestic position in regard
to the Muslim League's demand for Pakistan.[11]

Although India was one of the few countries where there was no record
of any persecution of the Jewish communities,[12] Indian nationalists did
not support the Zionist movement. The Zionists were seen by the Indian
National Congress (INC) as Westerners, backed by imperialist forces to
create a neo-colonial state at the expense of Arab nationalism. The INC
could not support a nationalism based exclusively on religion, which
was at variance with its professed secular form of nationalism. Mahatma
Gandhi summarized India's position in one quote: 'Palestine belongs to
the Arabs in the same sense that England belongs to the English or France
to the French'.[13]

When the question of the partition of Palestine became an issue at
the United Nations (UN), New Delhi, along with the rest of the newly
independent countries, rejected the 'two nation' theory and instead
supported an alternative plan envisaging a federal Palestine with an
autonomous status for the Jewish population. Regardless of this initiative,
the UN General Assembly approved by a large majority the plan creating
the State of Israel on 29 November 1947. Indian recognition was not
immediate as Nehru admitted he did not want to 'offend the sentiments of

our friends in the Arab countries'.[14] Nevertheless, on 17 September 1950, India finally recognized the State of Israel after two years of its existence, including UN membership.[15] Having become a *fait accompli* recognized by a large number of states, of which some had an important Muslim population like Iran and Indonesia, Nehru conceded that the de jure recognition of the State of Israel could not be 'indefinitely' deferred.[16]

Although some efforts to establish links were partly successful with the creation of an Israeli Consulate in Bombay (now Mumbai) in 1953 and the Indian support for Israel's participation to the Bandung Conference in 1955,[17] the recognition was not followed by the establishment of full diplomatic relations. This policy was characterized by a deliberate refusal by New Delhi to reciprocate Israeli requests to set up diplomatic relations.[18]

The sources of this policy could be traced to domestic and international considerations. From the very beginning, Indian Prime Minister Nehru and his successors did not want to antagonize the large Muslim minority at home (who constituted over 11 per cent of the country's population) and Arab states in the region.[19] The sentiments of India's domestic Muslim population were always an integral part of the country's West Asia policy calculations. For instance, Muslim members of the Constituent Assembly openly showed their opposition to the recognition of the State of Israel during parliamentary debates.[20] Maulana Abdul Kalam Azad, a Muslim leader who had a strong influence on Nehru, equally questioned full-fledged diplomatic contacts with Israel as it could have an unsettling effect on Indian Muslims.[21] Since Muslims had regularly voted for the Congress, Nehru did not want to jeopardize this vote bank by any hostile action, such as engaging Israel.[22]

This pro-Arab bias in dealing with West Asia was also seen as a way to maintain good relations with Arab and Muslim states. A strong personal relationship united Nehru and Egyptian President Gamal Abdel Nasser and influenced India's relations with Israel. As a socialist and secular leader who espoused the doctrine of nonalignment, Nasser was an attractive partner for Nehru. Support from Arab States in West Asia against Pakistan was also interpreted as decisive in the Kashmir issue. From the onset of the Kashmir dispute, Pakistan tried to internationalize the issue, especially by trying to obtain religious solidarity from the Muslim world by the intermediary of the Organization of the Islamic Conference (OIC). Although Israel had always supported the Indian position on Kashmir, New Delhi decided to support the Palestine cause and the Arab demands, hoping in exchange to gain their backing or to the least their neutrality on the Kashmir dispute.[23]

This pro-Arab policy was illustrated by India's support of Egypt in the Suez crisis (1956) against Great Britain, France, and Israel. Nehru was very critical about this venture and condemned the Sinai campaign as a 'clear naked aggression'.[24] The fact that Israel collaborated with ex-colonial powers such as France and Britain in attacking a nonaligned country revived anti-imperialist sentiments and further dissipated what little sympathy the Indian leadership had for the Jewish state. As former Defence Minister Krishna Menon testified, this ended any possibility of opening relations with Israel as sending an ambassador to Tel Aviv would now be perceived by the Arabs as a hostile action.[25] The official excuse, invoking financial and personnel difficulties, for delaying the institution of diplomatic relations was no longer relevant. Furthermore, lacking Nehru's strong personal ties to regional leaders such as Nasser, successive Indian PMs tried to compensate this deficit of individual connections by a more aggressive position against Israel and a more unequivocal support of the Arab cause.

However, it quickly became apparent that Indo-Arab relations were only one-way as the unambiguous Indian support against Israel in 1956 and in the crises of 1967 and 1973 was never reciprocated by the Arab states, which failed to back India in its regional conflicts against China in 1962 and against Pakistan in 1965 and 1971.[26] Moreover, with the third-largest Muslim population at that time after Indonesia and Pakistan and with a repeated and unambiguous support to the Palestinian cause during the Arab–Israeli wars, India hoped it had a legitimate right to participate at the meeting of the OIC in Rabat in September 1969. As this conference was summoned to 'condemn Israel's destruction of the holy shrine', India felt its important domestic Muslim population was as concerned with the Palestinian situation as any other Muslim country.[27] Although India was officially invited to the conference, opposition from Pakistan kept the Indian delegation from seating and participating at the conference.[28] This was a serious blow to the Indira Gandhi government that sought in the future, albeit with little success, to demand more reciprocity in its relations with the Arab and Muslim states.[29] In spite of the lack of success of India's pro-Arab policy, Indo-Israeli relations still deteriorated in the 1970s and 1980s as other domestic and regional factors affected India's position.

Aside from the need to entice Arab sympathies on the Kashmir dispute, India's pro-Arab policy was also shaped by its growing energy needs. Since it lacks hydrocarbon reserves in its territory, India is perennially dependent on energy imports.[30] India must import 70 per cent of its crude and is therefore strongly dependent on Gulf energy exports.[31] Furthermore, the oil shocks of 1973 had put New Delhi in a more vulnerable position towards the Arab states. The fourfold increase of oil prices in 1973 by the Organization of the Petroleum Exporting Countries (OPEC), which PM

Indira Gandhi described as 'just', severely affected India by provoking shortages that inhibited agricultural and industrial production.[32] To meet these challenges, Indira Gandhi decided to further strengthen political links with Arab states, supporting their diplomatic positions against Israel but also by offering engineering services and manpower. This policy did bring some relief to India's energy dilemma, thanks to help from Iraq and the United Arab Emirates, as well as from non-Arab, but Muslim, Iran.

The remittances from the growing Indian expatriate community in West Asia also became important elements in the formulation of India's West Asia policy. The number of these immigrants, ranging from labourers to skilled technicians, employed in the Arab states has increased tremendously since the 1970s, going from 1,23,000 in 1975 to approximately 3.3 million in 2008.[33] Since these workers send to India about 70 per cent of their income, the Gulf remittances have an important impact on India's economy, and particularly in Kerala where most of these non-resident Indians (NRIs) originate from.[34] In discussions with Arab states, India equally took into account the presence and well-being of this population.

This historical background can explain why Israel did not have any place in India's West Asia policy from 1948 to 1991. Indian foreign policymakers considered it too risky to establish relations with Israel because such a decision could jeopardize its traditional links with Arab partners. However, by finally normalizing relations with Israel, the Narasimha Rao government corrected what had become a controversial characteristic of India's West Asia policy. This chapter analyses the combination of structural, domestic, and individual leadership factors that has shaped this abrupt change.

STRUCTURAL FACTORS

The emergence of India and Israel as sovereign states respectively on 15 August 1947 and 14 May 1948 coincided with the start of a struggle for power between two big global players, the US and the Union of Soviet Socialist Republics (USSR). Inter-state relations were ineluctably defined by this new international environment and peripheral states such as India and Israel were limited to three options: to align with Washington, to align with Moscow, or to try to have amicable relations with both superpowers. The Soviet collapse, events in West Asia in 1991–2, and the resulting systemic changes pushed India to modify its foreign policy towards the West, and particularly vis-à-vis Israel.

Dependent diplomatically and financially on US support to survive, Israel logically joined the Western bloc. India took a different direction by deciding to side with neither superpower during the initial years of the

Cold War and by devising an independent foreign policy.[35] For the first two decades after its independence, India accepted financial and military assistance from both the USSR and the US. In spite of this initial Indo-US cooperation, India and Nehru were more attracted to the socialist, anti-imperialist leanings of the USSR, and India's diplomacy repeatedly gave the impression of siding with the Soviet Union and other Third World countries on many international issues until the mid-1960s. In August 1971, the signing of the 'India–Soviet Union Treaty of Peace, Friendship, and Cooperation' for 20 years finally confirmed India's diplomatic and military dependence on the USSR.[36] This further reduced any opportunity for cooperation with the Western bloc and Israel.

As a consequence, the bipolar structure dominating international relations had some long-term consequences on India's military ties and prevented New Delhi from establishing closer ties with Tel Aviv. Although Israel supported India in its 1971 war by offering limited military assistance consisting of small arms and ammunition, India's almost exclusive military reliance on its Soviet partner became evident following 1971.[37] Because it lacked the defence–industrial infrastructure, India realized it needed external help, and the Soviet assistance in hardware and technology became vital. Since the US and most nations from the Western bloc had placed an arms embargo vis-à-vis India after the Indo-Pakistan Kashmir war of 1965 and because of very favourable financial conditions offered by the USSR, India did not have to look for alternative weapons' suppliers.[38] Systemic factors thus explain this Indian dependence on Soviet diplomatic support and military aid, and subsequently the lack of reciprocity to Israeli diplomatic overtures for four decades.

Global changes in the early 1990s were decisive to help understand the difficult situation in which India was when its ally, the Soviet Union, collapsed. Because of this induced military dependence, the USSR had been India's largest arms supplier since the early 1960s. In 1991, 70 per cent of India's military equipment was of Soviet origin, including 400 Mig-29 in the Indian Air Force (IAF).[39] Almost overnight, India had to deal with a military industry that was dispersed in 15 countries that emerged following the disintegration of the USSR and with less favourable financial conditions offered by the Russian Federation. This new unipolar world that surfaced in 1991 presented new challenges but also new opportunities for India. The end of the bipolar confrontation offered India more strategic leeway than in the Cold War era. As a consequence, India sought assistance from all countries that could help improve its precarious regional and international security situations threatened by a nuclear Pakistan and a rising China. The strategic rapprochement with Israel became logical as the Israeli military–industrial complex had the capacity to modernize and upgrade the obsolete Soviet military equipment that India had purchased.

Regional developments in the early 1990s also permitted India to transform its relations with Israel. The Kuwait crisis of 1990–1 and its consequences modified Israel's status vis-à-vis Arab states. Internal opposition within the Arab world and widespread criticism regarding the Palestine Liberation Organization's (PLO) support of Iraq during the war limited the negative implications of opening up to Israel. The Iraqi intrusion into Kuwait diverted attention from Israel as the Saddam Hussein regime became the new source of concern in the region.[40] India no longer needed to systematically condemn Israel to obtain Arab sympathies. Following the Gulf war, where Israel showed military restraint in spite of Iraqi attacks, many countries from the region even sought new ties with the Jewish state. A series of West Asian peace initiatives, such as the Madrid Conference of October 1991, created a new era in the region where coexistence and negotiations with Israel were possible. The result of this peace process was the Oslo Accord signed on 13 September 1993 which institutionalized talks between Tel Aviv and the PLO.[41] As a result, this created a window of opportunity for India to revise its traditional pro-Arab policy and subsequently to develop a strategic partnership with Israel.

Another systemic change was the emergence of the US as the sole superpower in the international arena. In this new context, the rapprochement with Israel was also a way for India to indirectly engage the new preponderant power. Given the insurmountable asymmetry of power and the strategic leverage a rapprochement with Washington could bring to India in its relations with China, New Delhi understood that it was in its temporary self-interest to establish more cordial relations with the US. The liberalization of the Indian economy and the increase of US investment further encouraged the reorientation of Indian policy towards Washington. Good relations with the Jewish state seemed to be a pre-requisite to the easing of prevailing Indo-US tensions. As a result, India decided first to join the move to revoke the UN General Assembly Resolution 3379 equating Zionism with racism in December 1991, then to normalize ties with Israel, which was finally announced just as Indian PM Narasimha Rao was visiting the US in January 1992.[42]

US approval of Indo-Israeli relations was equally necessary for the development of strong bilateral security cooperation, particularly in sensitive areas such as anti-missile and radar technologies.[43] In this respect, the Chinese precedent has deeply shaped India's military negotiations with

Israel and the US. Since the 1990s, Washington and Tel Aviv have often diverged over the transfer of Israeli weapons and technology to China. This culminated in an important diplomatic showdown in 2000. Under intense pressure from the Clinton administration, Israel was forced to cancel the sale of the Phalcon radar system to China despite talks that began in 1996 and the loss of a potential billion dollar contract.[44] To avoid such an outcome, India coordinated its efforts with high-ranking US officials during the Phalcon talks between India and Israel. After four years of negotiations, Washington finally authorized the Phalcon sale in 2004.[45] This deal was finalized only 12 years after the normalization of bilateral relations and symbolized the total reorientation of India's foreign policy towards the West and Israel in a new US-dominated world.

As a consequence, structural factors seem to have shaped India's Israel policy. In a bipolar world where alliances were rigid, India's only option was an almost exclusive partnership with the USSR to obtain security and diplomatic guarantees. The end of the Cold War liberated India from these structural constraints: New Delhi took advantage of the 'looseness' of the new international system to diversify its partners. In West Asia, certain events like the Gulf War and the Israel–Palestine peace process made it possible for India to redefine its priorities and finally engage Tel Aviv.

However, after 1991, the remodelling of India's foreign policy to adapt itself to the new international structure was gradual and never consensual. Some political parties, such as the Communist Party of India (Marxist) (CPI(M)), remain sceptical vis-à-vis any strategic negotiations with Israel and demand a continuation of India's pro-Palestinian policy.[46] The collapse of the Soviet Union and the end of the Cold War facilitated a redefinition of India's foreign policy priorities, but other factors can help explain why India specifically turned to Israel for help in 1991.

NATIONAL FACTORS

Domestic-level factors have also been important in facilitating Indo-Israeli rapprochement in the post-Cold War environment. Similar to the structural changes analysed previously, national factors dictating India's West Asia policy since 1947 seemed to have lost some of their relevance in the early 1990s. The negative response of Saudi Arabia, the United Arab Emirates, and Iran to back India's counter-insurgency struggle in Kashmir in 1990 put an end to India's expectations of reciprocal support on Kashmir in exchange for its pro-Palestine stance.[47]

In the domestic arena, there were always important economic and military incentives for cooperation with Israel. However, because it pursued its socialist economic development policies, India's domestic market was not integrated in the global economic order, and there were only a limited number of investments from Israel. Compelled to introduce economic liberalization in 1991, the Rao government developed strong trade relations with Israel, especially in fields where Israeli experience and expertise were decisive such as software technology and agriculture. Although both sides have been reluctant to discuss them in public, military technology imports have boosted the trade between the two countries since 1992 to the point that today Israel is India's second-largest military supplier after its abiding partner—Russia. Between 1992 and 2000, there have been 50 exchanges of military missions, a figure that demonstrates the intense military interaction and discussion between the respective military staffs.[48] Although bilateral military trade only began in 1992, it expanded significantly after 1998. This was the combined result of the policy of the Bharatiya Janata Party (BJP), which came to power in India in 1998, and of the military embargo that followed the Indian nuclear tests of May 1998.[49]

For political, economic, and security reasons, India has always wanted to develop an important and diversified domestic military industry. This encouraged negotiations with Israel, which had developed a domestic high-technology military industry capable of rivalling the Western powers.[50] This emphasis on national production is a consequence of intermittent supply problems that both countries have endured because of military embargoes during their conflicts with regional adversaries. But the two countries have met different fates in their quest for military independence. If the Israeli military–industrial complex today is of international fame and has become the fifth-largest international arms supplier, the Indian military industry has encountered more difficulties.[51]

Consequently, the Israeli experience offered some advantages to India's domestic military industry. Many ambitious strategic weapons programmes in India launched in the early 1980s were still in development because its military industry lacked expertise in certain advanced technological systems. The most ambitious Indian military programme had been the construction of a Light Combat Aircraft (LCA) which was expected to replace the ageing MiGs in the IAF. The difficulties that the LCA programme encountered were actually very similar to the ones Israel had while building its Lavi fighter jet in the 1980s.[52] For the last 15 years, Israel Aerospace Industries (IAI) and Elbit Systems Ltd have therefore offered their assistance to Hindustan Aeronautics Ltd to complete the construction of India's LCA, particularly in radar technology.[53] There are other military programmes where New Delhi and Tel Aviv have started to work together. The Indian

Defence Research and Development Organisation (DRDO) has long wanted to build a main battle tank, the Arjun prototype, to replace the obsolete Vijayanta.[54] Israeli expertise was also considered to be decisive because the Israelis had developed a comparable tank, the very reputed Merkava.[55] A parallel was equally drawn between the two national Agni and Barak missile programmes. Frustrated by the slow pace of development of its indigenous ballistic missile programme and troubled by Pakistan's relative success in that area, India has sought Israeli expertise.[56]

Finally, another domestic factor that can explain the increase of Indo-Israel military cooperation is the fact both countries also share comparable internal problems with minority ethno-religious communities. Even though terrorism has taken diverse forms in local conflicts (Hamas and Islamic Jihad in Palestine, Kashmiri separatists in India), there has always been a potential for cooperation. The 1999 Kargil conflict has, for instance, put in perspective the Indian border management control problem and has finally convinced the Indian government of the necessity to emulate Israel's counter-terrorism tactics. Tel Aviv's handling of cross-border terrorism and border infiltration caught former interior minister L.K. Advani's attention in particular, and was one of the reasons that motivated his Israel visit in 2000.[57] As a result, Israel has extended strong logistical support to India with the sale of surveillance equipment for the Line of Control (LoC), including thermal sensors or night-vision devices that had been used by the Israeli Army in the Golan Heights and in the Negev Desert.[58] In September 2000, an Israeli team of counter-insurgency experts was invited by Advani to assess India's security needs. The Israelis were asked to determine the areas in which Israel could offer assistance to India to help reduce the incidence of terrorist incursions into Jammu and Kashmir from Pakistan.[59] These regular security meetings were finally institutionalized with the creation of an annual Joint Working Group on counter-terrorism in Jerusalem in January 2002.[60]

Important strategic complementarities between India and Israel can explain the development of a productive strategic partnership. There were strong domestic reasons for India to look for Israeli assistance. There was in India an important military market in search of new solutions to fill the qualitative gap it had compared to its regional adversaries. On the other hand, there was in Israel a prestigious military industry in crisis, looking for funds to maintain a technological edge against its regional adversaries. But Indian policymakers have always known it was in the national interest to establish strategic and military contacts with Israel as they pursued an ambiguous and dual policy with Tel Aviv. For instance, covert military contacts had already been established after the Sino-Indian war of 1962. Following the border debacle, India showed willingness to consult Israeli military specialists and to purchase artillery and ammunition.[61] There were also talks and exchange of information between India's Research and Analysis Wing (RAW) and its Israeli counterpart, the Mossad.[62] Domestic factors can explain why there was an important potential for a stable strategic partnership but only the analysis of the interplay of structural and national factors with individual decisions is decisive to understand the abrupt evolution of Indo-Israeli relations after 1991.

POLICY-LEVEL FACTORS

Systemic changes brought about by the end of the Cold War were important in explaining how India had greater autonomy to choose between new alternative strategic options. Long-existing domestic incentives from the Indian side also facilitated the acceleration of bilateral relations and could help us understand the specific nature of this partnership. However, individual leadership in New Delhi after 1991 has played a decisive role in analysing and exploiting these structural changes to finally establish this long overdue strategic partnership with Israel.

As mentioned earlier, individual decisions played an important role in shaping India's relations with West Asia in the past. Personal relationships between PM Nehru and some Arab leaders such as Egyptian President Nasser had a significant impact on India's refusal to establish normal diplomatic relations with Israel. In 1990–1, the role of leadership still proved crucial as only the Narasimha Rao government showed a strong comprehension of the ongoing developments in West Asia. The previous fragile coalition governments from 1989 to 1991 failed to properly assess the long-term changes in the Gulf region caused by the Kuwait Crisis of 1990–1 and the end of the Cold War.[63] As a consequence, the Rao government pushed for a profound foreign policy adjustment in order to appropriately defend India's interests in the region.

As Foreign and Defence Minister in the Indira Gandhi and Rajiv Gandhi governments in the 1970s and 1980s, Rao had already been involved in India's foreign policy decision-making process. What changed in 1991 is the fragile and divided situation of the ruling Congress, which pushed an uncharismatic Rao to the PM's position. After Rajiv Gandhi's assassination in 1991, his nomination was mostly a compromise between two warring camps within the Congress. As he was dismissed as a low-profile political leader without any electoral base, it was widely believed that his appointment would not last long.[64] Because he was heading an apparently weak government of transition, Rao did not feel constrained by the Congress' long-established ideological positions and by traditional domestic voting constituencies such as the Muslim vote. As a consequence of this greater flexibility, he gradually pushed for a reformist agenda, especially in the foreign policy field.

The end of the Cold War left Indian decision-makers facing a completely uncertain situation where the parameters of a new emerging global order were still undefined. Rao's response was to discern some broad directions of the transformations taking place. In response to these projections, he sought to radically modify India's strategic and security priorities. Taking advantage of this greater political uncertainty at the international and domestic levels, PM Rao and his Foreign Secretary Jyotindra Nath Dixit reoriented New Delhi's diplomatic priorities by redefining Indian national interests in the new post-Cold War equilibrium. In this context, the normalization of relations with Israel was a calibrated move with three key factors taken into consideration.

First, the disappearance of the Cold War military blocs, the irrelevance of nonalignment in the emerging world order, and India's economic crisis led Rao to encourage better relations with the US. In fact, the success of Rao's development strategy based on market reforms depended greatly upon investment and technological assistance from the West, and especially the US. As Washington had been pressuring New Delhi to adjust its Israel policy since 1948, Rao was conscious that establishing diplomatic relations with Israel was a necessary step to a meaningful engagement with the US as an important and necessary economic and strategic partner. This correction of India's Israel policy was consistent with Rao's policy of opening up relations with the US. Symbolically, Rao announced the establishment of diplomatic relations with Israel on the eve of a visit to the United Nations (UN) in New York to speak with George H.W. Bush in January 1992.

After the fall of the USSR, New Delhi's new foreign policy priorities also included ensuring India's defence capabilities.[65] As discussed earlier, Indo-Israeli relations have had a strong military dimension as Israel was considered an attractive strategic partner to upgrade India's obsolete Soviet-origin military equipment and to quickly acquire hi-tech military weaponry. The question of defence cooperation was first raised by Dixit during his March 1993 visit to Tel Aviv, and in May 2003 the delegation accompanying Israeli Foreign Minister Shimon Peres during his visit to New Delhi included chief executives from the Israeli industrial–military complex.[66] In its rationale for improving relations with Israel, the Rao government also expressed a strong interest in Israel's expertise in counter-terrorism operations.[67] Only a month after the establishment of full diplomatic relations, Rao publicly confirmed India's interest in learning from Israeli's experience in dealing with terrorism.[68]

Finally, PM Rao and Foreign Secretary Dixit openly expressed their frustration with the lack of support from their Arab partners with regard to the Kashmir issue and decided that establishing diplomatic relations with Israel was a way to indirectly warn its traditional West Asian partners that India's diplomatic support could not be taken for granted.[69]

Transforming India's Israel policy took important courage and foresight from PM Rao and his government as this new diplomatic orientation was not consensual. Some policymakers and elements of the foreign policy bureaucracy considered the normalization of relations with Israel as a rushed and unprepared initiative in seeming contradiction with more than 40 years of India's West Asia policy, which could have disoriented Arab allies. Yet today, some political parties such as the CPI(M) still see this reorientation of India's Israel policy as a betrayal of the Palestinian cause.[70] Even in Rao's own party, some influential leaders such as Arjun Singh or Mani Shankar Aiyar disagreed with his move to engage Tel Aviv as a departure from the 'Nehruvian framework of [India's] foreign policy'.[71] It is highly probable that other governments would have been more cautious in their dealings with Israel than a pragmatic Rao government that had analysed beforehand the strategic benefits of this partnership.

If the normalization of bilateral relations can be credited to the Congress in 1992, another example of the important role of individual leadership is the BJP's Israel policy after 1998. For the BJP, Israel became a logical and natural partner since it shared the same concerns about terrorism. The two countries have dealt with Islamic and transnational terrorism in their border issues with Palestine and Kashmir. Hindu nationalists have also been interested by the highly militarized nature of the Israeli society and by their leaders' strong will in using force against Palestinian terrorists. As a consequence, the BJP has always given priority to strengthening relations with the State of Israel and has long criticized the Congress' pro-Arab policies.

A real evolution began with the visits of India's Deputy PM L.K. Advani and Foreign Minister Jaswant Singh to Israel in 2000 and of Israeli PM Ariel Sharon to India in September 2003. During these visits, both Indian and Israeli authorities condemned cross-border terrorism and encouraged intelligence-sharing on Islamic extremism. The BJP also expressed a strong interest in Israel's tough legislation directed against elements that assist in financing, incitement, family support, or state support of terrorists.[72]

Finally, the BJP government also suggested and advocated the creation of a triangular forum composed of the US, India, and Israel to combat a similar terrorist threat.[73] The BJP was convinced that Israeli military expertise and its experience of 'zero-tolerance' legislation could help them against the new terrorist threats and thus encouraged a significant expansion of military trade between the two countries after 1998, concluding deals worth billions of dollars, such as the purchase of the Israeli airborne early-warning and control (AEW&C) Phalcon systems in 2003.[74]

THE FUTURE OF INDO-ISRAELI RELATIONS

Structural, domestic, and individual factors are crucial in understanding the timing and nature of the Indo-Israeli partnership. This chapter argues that a confluence of structural, domestic, and individual leadership factors has been responsible for a radical shift in Indo-Israeli strategic relations. At the structural level, the end of the Cold War fundamentally altered India's strategic calculus and made it possible for New Delhi to engage Israel. At the domestic level, there were strategic complementarities between India's growing military market in search of new solutions to replace the traditional Soviet supplier and Israel's prominent military industry looking for resources to maintain a technological edge. At the individual level, political leaders broke with past ineffective and irrational policies in ways that helped transform the trajectory of Indo-Israeli relations.

In spite of internal political risks linked to contentious diplomatic initiatives, both the Narasimha Rao and BJP governments were committed to improving relations with a state they considered as a valuable strategic and economic partner. It is only in a progressive fashion that opposing parties realized the benefits of cooperation with Israel and encouraged this new orientation of India's West Asia policy. In fact, from mainly military exchanges, Indo-Israeli relations have now diversified to include knowledge-intensive sectors like information technology (IT) and software, space research, medical technology and biotechnology; India's quest for improving production and productivity in its agricultural sector has also created space for cooperation in this vital sector of its economy.[75]

This relationship became so strategically crucial for India that the traditionally pro-Palestinian Congress party pursued negotiations with Tel Aviv when it returned to power in 2004. There were initial doubts about the endurance of this new privileged partnership as the United Progressive Alliance's[76] electoral programme had evoked a new beginning in relations with West Asia with a confirmation of India's support of the Palestinian cause.[77] Similar to the Rao government, the Manmohan Singh government was aware of the new international context and the need to diversify its alliances by engaging important Western partners like Israel and the US.[78]

Limits of the Relationship

There are still many historic and regional factors that could endanger this promising relationship. For instance, India has maintained good relations with one of Israel's declared enemies, Iran.[79] For some time now, Israel has expressed its concerns regarding the increasing military ties between India and Iran. In October 2003, these qualms were made public by Ariel Sharon, who threatened to put an end to military technology transfer to India that could be redirected towards Tehran.[80] India's aspirations to engage very diverse allies like Iran or Israel are a vital trait of its new realist foreign policy with regard to West Asia. The Indian government has tried to maintain good relations with Iran to respond to internal and external critics of its ideological rapprochement with Israel.

As the absence of anti-Semitism throughout its history had been a source of pride in India, events in November 2008 in Mumbai and the attack on Nariman House, the Jewish community centre, initially raised doubts about future Indo-Israeli cooperation. Nevertheless, following these terrorist attacks, India sought out Israeli assistance in setting up an elaborate intelligence network specifically aimed at neutralizing terror activities.[81]

It is difficult to clearly envisage the impact of the Iran factor and of the Mumbai terrorist attacks on the future of Indo-Israeli relations, but it seems improbable that they can put an end to a very prolific and now institutionalized strategic cooperation between the two nations.

NOTES

1. Rejecting the Eurocentric terms 'Near East' or 'Middle East', PM Jawaharlal Nehru had an Asia-centric worldview and therefore referred to this region as 'West Asia'.

2. See Embassy of Israel in India website, Economic Department, http://delhi.mfa. gov.il/mfm/web/main/document.asp?SubjectID=2540&MissionID=93&Lan guageID=0&StatusID=0&DocumentID=-1 (accessed on 18 April 2008), and 'India–Israel FTA may be in Place by Nov', *Business Line*, 26 February 2008.

3. 'India, Israel likely to start formal talks for FTA soon', *The Hindu Business Line*, 5 July 2008.

4. Bruce Riedel (2008), 'Israel and India: New Allies', *Middle East Bulletin*, Brookings Institute, 1 April.

5. Josy Joseph (2008), 'Israel may Emerge Top Arms Supplier', *Daily News and Analysis*, 20 February.

6. For more details on the three levels of analysis approach, see the first chapter of Kenneth Waltz (1959), *Man, the State, and War* (New York: Columbia University Press).

7. The pioneering scholar to make significant contributions to the study of Indo-Israeli relations is Dr P.R. Kumaraswamy who has published many helpful articles I have cited in this study. Other scholars such as Prithvi Ram Mudiam (1994) in *India and the Middle East* (London: British Academic Press) have also investigated this topic but only as one element of India's broader position towards West Asia.

8. Leonard Gordon (1975), 'Indian Nationalist Ideas about Palestine and Israel', *Jewish Social Studies*, 37.

9. Najma Heptulla (1992), *Indo-West Asian Relations: The Nehru Era* (New Delhi: South Asia Books), p. 38.

10. Jawaharlal Nehru (1989), *Glimpses of World History* (New Delhi: Oxford University Press), pp. 763–5.

11. The former PM's position is cited in a publication from India's Ministry of External Affairs, *India and Palestine: The Evolution of a Policy*, Ministry of External Affairs, New Delhi, 1968, pp. 69–70.

12. The three Jewish communities in India are the Baghdadi, Bene Israeli, and Cochini, which are mainly settled in Maharashtra and Kerala. For more, see Opra Slapak (ed.) (1995), *The Jews of India: A Story of Three Communities* (Jerusalem: The Israel Museum).

13. Mohandas K. Gandhi, *The Collected Works of Mahatma Gandhi*, vol. 68 (New Delhi: Publications Divisions, Indian Government, 1958), p. 137.

14. G. Parthasarathi (ed.) (1986), *Jawaharlal Nehru, Letters to Chief Ministers 1947–1964*, vol. 2, 1950–2, (New Delhi: Oxford University Press), p. 217.

15. P.R. Kumaraswamy (1995), 'India's Recognition of Israel, September 1950', *Middle Eastern Studies*, 31 (1), pp. 124–38.

16. Ibid.

17. Arthur G. Rubinoff (May 1995), 'Normalization of India–Israel Relations: Stillborn for Forty Years', *Asian Survey*, 35 (5), pp. 487–505.

18. Michael Brecher (1963), *The New States of Asia: A Political Analysis* (London: Oxford University Press).

19. Arthur G. Rubinoff (1995), 'Normalization of India–Israel Relations: Stillborn for Forty Years', *Asian Survey*, 35 (5).

20. K.P. Misra (1996), *India's Policy of Recognition of States and Government* (New Delhi: Allied Publishers), p. 35.

21. Micheal Brecher, *New States of Asia*.

22. Rubinoff, 'Normalization of India–Israel Relations'.

23. The Kashmir conflict erupted in 1947 because of competing projects of nation-building between India and Pakistan. New Delhi insisted on holding on to Kashmir in order to show that the Muslim province could thrive in a secular state. In opposition, Islamabad believed that Kashmir, whose population is mostly

Muslim, belonged in Pakistan, homeland of the Muslims of South Asia. For more on the Kashmir conflict, see Sumit Ganguly (1997), *The Crisis in Kashmir: Portents of War, Hopes of Peace* (Cambridge: Cambridge University Press).

24. Cited in Jacob Abadi (2004), *Israel's Quest for Recognition and Acceptance in Asia: Garrison State Diplomacy* (London: Frank Cass), p. 267.

25. Cited in an interview with Michael Brecher, *India and World Politics: Krishna Menon's View of the World* (London: Oxford University Press, 1968), p. 79.

26. Rubinoff, 'Normalization of India–Israel Relations', pp. 495–8.

27. Ibid., p. 498.

28. Ibid.

29. Ibid.

30. Gulshan Dietl (2000), 'The Security of Supply Issue: The Growing Dependence on the Middle East', in Pierre Audinet, P.R. Shukla, and Frederic Grare (eds), *India's Energy: Essays on Sustainable Development* (New Delhi: Manohar Publications), pp. 209–24.

31. 'Does India Need Strategic Oil Reserve', *Business Standard*, 13 November 2002.

32. Dietl, 'The Security of Supply Issue'.

33. Girijesh Pant (2001), 'Gulf NRIs: From Expatriates to Entrepreneurs', *World Focus*, March 2001, 22 (3), pp. 9–11, and Rajendra Abhyankar (ed.) (2009), *West Asia and the Region: Defining India's Role* (New Delhi: Academic Foundation), p. 199.

34. K.P. Kannan and K.S. Hari (2002), 'Kerala's Gulf Connection: Emigration, Remittances and Their Macroeconomic Impact 1972–2000', Working Paper No. 328, March, Centre for Development Studies, Thiruvananthapuram.

35. See Stanley Wolpert (1996), *Nehru: A Tryst with Destiny* (New York: Oxford University Press) and Robert J. McMahon (1994), *The Cold War on the Periphery: The United States, India, and Pakistan* (New York: Columbia University Press).

36. Ramesh Thakur and Carlyle Thayer (1992), *Soviet Relations with India and Vietnam* (London: Macmillan Publishers and St. Martin's Press).

37. P.R. Kumaraswamy (1998), 'India and Israel: Evolving Strategic Partnership', *Mideast Security and Policy Studies*, No. 40, Begin-Sadat Center for Strategic Studies (September), p. 62.

38. See Dennis Kux (1992), *India and the United States: Estranged Democracies* (Washington, DC: National Defense University Press), and P.R. Chari (1979), 'Indo-Soviet Military Cooperation: A Review', *Asian Survey*, 19 (3), pp. 230–44.

39. Amit Gupta (1995), 'Determining India's Force Structure and Military Doctrine', *Asian Survey*, 35 (5), pp. 441–58.

40. P.R. Kumaraswamy (2005), *Israel's New Arch of Friendship: India, Russia and Turkey* (Dubai: Gulf Research Center, Research Papers).

41. P.R. Kumaraswamy (1995), 'India and Israel: Prelude to Normalization', *Journal of South-Asian and Middle Eastern Studies*, 19 (2), pp. 53–73.

42. Edward Gargan (1992), 'India Announces Full Israeli Ties', *New York Times*, 30 January.

43. P.R. Kumaraswamy (1996), 'The Limitations of Indo-Israeli Military Cooperation', *Contemporary South Asia*, 5 (1), pp. 75–84.

44. Wade Boese (2000), 'Israel Halts Chinese Phalcon Deal', *Arms Control Today*, September, http://www.armscontrol.org/act/2000_09/israelsept00 (accessed on 2 June 2009).

45. Arieh O'Sullivan (2004), 'Phalcon Deal Signed with India', *The Jerusalem Post*, 6 March.

46. 'Snap the Growing Ties with Israel, says Karat', *Rediff India Abroad*, 5 March 2008.

47. Mudiam, *India and the Middle East*, pp. 173–4.

48. Ilan Berman (2002), 'Israel, India and Turkey: Triple Entente?', *Middle East Quarterly*, 9 (4), pp. 33–40.

49. Stephen Blank (2005), 'Arms Sales and Technology Transfer in Indo-Israeli Relations', *The Journal of East Asian Affairs*, 19 (1), pp. 200–41.

50. Amit Gupta (1997), *Building an Arsenal: The Evolution of Regional Power Force Structures* (Westport: Praeger Publishers), pp. 173–4.

51. Ibid.

52. Lt Col James P. DeLoughry (1990), 'The United States and the LAVI', *Airpower Journal*, 4 (3), pp. 34–44.

53. Ravi Sharma (2007), 'Israeli Knowhow for LCA Radar', *The Hindu*, 29 June.

54. P.R. Kumaraswamy, 'India and Israel: Evolving Strategic Partnership'.

55. Ibid.

56. 'India, Israel to Jointly Develop Anti-Aircraft Missiles', *Agence France Presse*, 27 February 2008.

57. Yossi Melman (2000), 'India's Visiting Strongman Wants to Expand Nuclear Cooperation with Israel', *Haaretz*, 16 June.

58. Harsh V. Pant (2004), 'India–Israel Partnership: Convergence and Constraint', *The Middle East Review of International Affairs*, 8, pp. 60–73.

59. 'Israeli Experts in Kashmir to Assess Security Needs', *The Times of India*, 22 September 2000.

60. Ramananda Sengupta (2002), 'India Walks the Tightrope with Israel', *Rediff.com*, 11 January http://www.rediff.com/news/2002/jan/11ram.htm (accessed on 2 June 2009).

61. Subhash Kapila (2003), 'India–Israel Relations: The Imperatives for Enhanced Strategic Cooperation', *South Asia Analysis Group Papers*, No. 777, 9 September, http://www.southasiaanalysis.org/papers2/paper131.html (accessed on 20 November 2008).

62. P.R. Kumaraswamy, 'India and Israel'.

63. Mohan Malik (1991), 'India's Response to the Gulf Crisis: Implications for Indian Foreign Policy', *Asian Survey*, 31 (9), pp. 847–61.

64. K. Shankar Bajpai (1992), 'India in 1991: New Beginnings', *Asian Survey*, 32 (2), pp. 207–16..

65. J.N. Dixit (2003), *India's Foreign Policy 1947–2003* (New Delhi: Picus Books), pp. 225–6.

66. Rahul Bedi (1993), 'India Eyes Israeli Arms Upgrades', *Jane's Defense Weekly*, 13 November, p. 37.

67. P.R. Kumaraswamy, 'India and Israel'.

68. Ibid.

69. Sumit Ganguly (2003–4), 'India's Foreign Policy Grows Up', *World Policy Journal*, XX (4), http://www.worldpolicy.org/journal/articles/wpj03-4/ganguly.html (accessed on 2 June 2009); and P.R. Kumaraswamy (2004), 'Israel–India Relations: Seeking Balance and Realism', in E. Karsh (ed.), *Israel: The First Hundred Years: Israel in the International Arena* (London: Frank Cass), pp. 254–73.

70. Sreenivas Janyala (2008), 'CPI Passes Resolution on Palestine, Condemns Israel', *The Indian Express*, 25 March.

71. J.N. Dixit (1996), *My South Block Years: Memoirs of a Foreign Secretary* (New Delhi: UBS Publishers).

72. Martin Sherman and M.L. Sondhi (1999), 'Indo-Israeli Strategic Cooperation as a US National Interest', Ariel Center for Policy Research, Policy Paper No. 39.

73. Christophe Jaffrelot (2003), 'Inde-Israël, le Nouvel Elément-Clé de l'Axe du Bien?', *Critique internationale*, No. 21 (October), pp. 24–32.

74. Stephen Blank, 'Arms Sales and Technology Transfer in Indo-Israeli Relations'.

75. In December 2004, the Indian Minister for Commerce & Industries Kamal Nath established a Joint Study Group (JSG) in order to boost bilateral trade, see 'India, Israel set up joint study group to boost bilateral trade', *The Hindu Business Line*, 9 December 2004.

76. United Progressive Alliance (UPA) is the ruling coalition of political parties that has been heading the Government of India since June 2004. The coalition is led by the Congress.

77. P.R. Kumaraswamy (2004), 'Uncertainties about Indo-Israeli Ties', *The Deccan Herald*, 15 June.

78. P.R. Kumaraswamy (2005), 'Indo-Israeli Ties: The Post-Arafat Shift', *The Power and Interest News Report* (PINR), March.

79. P.R. Kumaraswamy (2004), 'Indo-Iranian Ties: The Israeli Dimension', in The 'Strategic Partnership' between India and Iran, Asia Program special report, *Woodrow Wilson International Center for Scholars* (April), p. 28.

80. Ibid.

81. See Jeremy Kahn (2008), 'Jews of Mumbai, A Tiny and Eclectic Group, Suddenly Reconsider Their Serene Existence', *New York Times*, 2 December, and Siddharth Srivastava (2008), 'India Sets Sights on Pakistani Camps', *Asia Times*, 6 December, http://www.atimes.com/atimes/South_Asia/JL06Df04.html (accessed on 6 December 2008).

9

India

A Growing Congruence of Interests with Korea

WALTER ANDERSEN

Structural changes in world politics brought on by the end of the Cold War in the early 1990s made possible a significant improvement in ties between the Republic of Korea and India.[1] Korea and India earlier had perceived each other on the wrong side of the Cold War and had minimal contacts. New Delhi had viewed Seoul as closely linked to American strategic objectives in Asia, and Seoul was suspicious of New Delhi's close ties to the former Soviet Union (USSR). Moreover, each country had adopted an inward-looking orientation that limited contacts with each other from the mid-1950s for Korea, and the early 1960s for India. With the end of the Cold War, the security situation of each country improved. Korea's confrontation with the USSR and China was over, providing Seoul greater room for foreign policy manoeuvre. Korea's major foreign policy goals now are to pursue a peaceful reunification with North Korea, increase free market trade, and achieve nuclear disarmament.[2]

The United States (US)–Korea alliance, based on the 1953 Mutual Defense Treaty, is still a central feature in Korea's security policy, though it has not limited its moves to broaden its international presence in the past decade, including independent efforts to improve relations with North Korea.[3] For India, the threat from China receded as Indian ties to Russia lost any security dimension that the Chinese would find threatening. Pakistan moreover was no longer of significant security relevance to the US with the Soviet departure from Afghanistan in the late 1980s. However, subsequent to 9/11, Pakistan again became a 'frontline' state in the fight against terrorism, though this has not slowed the trend towards a closer strategic relationship between the US and India. These developments similarly enhanced India's room for foreign policy manoeuvre, and a key initiative was to deepen ties with countries, like Korea, that could help it attain a faster economic growth rate.[4] For the first time since the Korean War in the early 1950s, the path was clear for India and Korea to develop closer relations.

Changes at the state level in the 1990s in both countries provided concrete incentives to take advantage of the end of the Cold War. India adopted market reforms and began to look outwards for trade, high technology, and investment. Korea, presently the world's eleventh-largest economy, had experienced 8 per cent annual GDP (gross domestic product) growth rates in the 1980s and was also looking outwards for markets for its high-technology industries and for places to invest. The India–Korea relationship has been led by trade, which since 2003 has increased at about 25 per cent annually, and the two countries are currently building an institutional framework for increased economic interaction.[5] The importance of trade as a driver in foreign policy is consistent with India's relationships elsewhere in Southeast Asia and East Asia. The countries of Asia, especially those to the east of India, are India's fastest growing trading partners.

Korean and Indian dependence on imported oil and gas, mainly from the Persian Gulf region, to sustain their robust economies has created a potential basis for geostrategic cooperation in securing the Indian Ocean sea lanes, as well as such key choke points as the Straits of Malacca and the Hormuz Straits. With over half the world's known reserves of oil and some 40 per cent of known reserves of gas in states around the Persian Gulf, Indian and Korean dependence on energy imports from this area will almost certainly increase.[6] There are, however, presently very few effective multilateral mechanisms to provide security against the growing threats of piracy, terrorism, and the drug trade along these vital sea lanes and their key choke points.[7] While all the major East Asian states—Korea, Japan, and China—would gain from improved security arrangements along these sea lanes, Korean participation in a multilateral security arrangement would be more acceptable to India and the states of Southeast Asia than that of Japan or China.

At the level of leadership, Korea and India in the 1990s—and beyond— had pragmatic leaders who recognized the importance of trade diplomacy and membership in multilateral associations in defence of national interests. In both cases, economic strength has become the central element shaping policy in foreign affairs and national security, replacing the inward-looking security orientation of the Cold War era. Korea has moved away from the conservative military focus of its political leadership, especially after the 1997 financial crisis. The current President, Lee Myung-bak (February

2008–), was a leader in Korea's globalized construction industry before he entered politics and has pursued a policy of economic globalization since coming to office.[8] India had a core of economists around a visionary prime minister in the early 1990s who laid the framework for market reforms and a more globalized economy. The positive economic results of those reforms have prompted every successoral Indian government to expand the scope of the reforms. The operative question for most Indian leaders has not been whether market reforms are good for India, but what should be the pace of the reform process. The global financial crisis during the last half of 2008, however, has triggered a debate over whether the pace has been too fast and thus exposing the Indian economy to the crisis in the developed economies such as the US.[9]

Several developments at the international level, however, could slow the bilateral Korea–Indian relationship. Among the more serious would be a significant slowdown in international trade that might result if the 2008 financial crisis deepens appreciably. Still another might be India's approach to nuclear non-proliferation, an issue of importance to Korea because of the threat posed by North Korea's nuclear weapons potential. Given North Korea's nuclear testing on 25 May and its subsequent belligerent statements, this issue is likely to become even more pressing. Still another might be India's approach to nuclear non-proliferation, an issue of major importance because of the threat posed by North Korea's nuclear capability. Korea with no great enthusiasm backed the US-sponsored proposal at the Nuclear Suppliers Group (NSG) meeting in early September 2008 that would exempt India from the prohibitions on sale of nuclear fuel and technology to countries, like India, that had not signed the 1970 Nuclear Non-proliferation Treaty (NPT). Korea, with North Korea's nuclear programme in mind, very likely will push for international treaties that ban nuclear testing and the production of fissile fuel. India might oppose both as unacceptable limitations on its security.

INDIA AND KOREA: COLD WAR INTERVENES IN EARLY ENGAGEMENT

India's relative neglect of Korea (and the rest of East Asia) was not the intention of the country's first Prime Minister, Jawaharlal Nehru (1947–64), who promoted a vision of Asian solidarity aimed at ending colonial exploitation, a commitment informed by India's own long colonial experience. Even prior to independence in 1947, he had engaged with other Asian nationalists. Nehru believed that Chinese involvement in the diplomacy of Asia was necessary to achieve the goals of nonalignment in Asia.

Within a year of India's recognition in late 1949 of the new People's Republic of China, the North Korean aggression of South Korea challenged Nehru's vision of a closer China–India relationship. India voted for the United Nations (UN) resolution which identified North Korea as the aggressor and demanded a withdrawal of its troops from below the 38th parallel, the de facto boundary between the two Koreas. However, Nehru was to explain the later Chinese intervention in Korea as a defensive measure and advocated Chinese inclusion in international bodies, stands that were to reduce Chinese suspicions of India, though simultaneously were to enhance suspicions of Indian neutrality in the Cold War by the US and among American allies in Asia.[10] While opposed to the North Korean aggression, Nehru did not subscribe to the Western policy objectives in the Korean War.[11] He did not commit Indian troops to Korea, and spoke out against the movement of UN troops north of the 38th parallel, fearing—as it turned out, rightly—that the move northwards would bring the Chinese into the war.[12]

Nehru saw an opportunity to get diplomatically involved in late 1952 when the peace talks stalled on the issue of how to determine the fate of prisoners of war. He tasked his foreign policy advisor, V.K. Krishna Menon, to try to break the stalemate. Menon devised a formula for 'non-forcible' repatriation to be carried out by a body composed of 'neutral' states, a proposition that was accepted by the UN.[13] India became chair of the Neutral Nations Repatriation Commission (NNRC) and supplied the troops that would control some 22,000 prisoners. India came off relatively well in this very difficult task where China and the US and its allies had very different objectives. This diplomatic activism underscored Nehru's goal of playing a role to mediate disputes on the basis of nonalignment. However, India was excluded from the conference which met in Geneva in April 1954 to seek a resolution of the Korean issue, in large part due to opposition from the US and South Korea.

Following up on the significant role India played in the NNRC, Nehru took a diplomatic interest in the resolution of the Indo-China crisis to prevent it from developing into another source of Cold War tensions. He again sent his closest confidante on foreign policy, V.K. Krishna Menon, to the May 1954 discussions in Geneva on Indo-China, even though India was not a formal participant.[14] Menon, on the margins of the formal deliberations in Geneva, clearly made a favourable impression and, to implement the peace process, India was named the key member of the International Control Commission (ICC) composed of Canada, Poland, and India. India was designated the chair, and it provided an overwhelming share of the ICC's administrative personnel. India was thus entrusted with the supervision of the Geneva settlement on Indo-China, which included ceasefire arrangements for its three constituent parts (Laos, Cambodia, and Vietnam), the independence of the three successor states, steps that would lead to the eventual union of the two 'temporary' Vietnamese administrations, the withdrawal of French troops, and the exchange of prisoners.

India's key role in the ICC guaranteed that it would have a role in the diplomacy involving Vietnam and Laos for the next several years. SarDesai in his classic study of India's active involvement in the Indo-China issue, however, points out that India found itself in the unenviable position of a nonaligned state having to make decisions on issues where the other two participants often had differing views and thus risked the charge of partisanship by one side or the other.[15] As India's relations with China improved in the wake of the conference on Indo-China, SarDesai notes that India increasingly focused its efforts on obstructing US influence—and by extension the role of Southeast Asia Treaty Organization (SEATO)—in Southeast Asia, a stance that seemed to associate it with Chinese objectives and thus made India suspect in the eyes of several Asian states, such as Korea, which were concerned about Chinese foreign policy objectives. He writes that 'India was unwittingly drawn into a pro-Chinese and anti-American position, which was not her objective at the time of her initial intervention in Indochina'.[16] Still another move that brought China and India closer together was the 1955 Asian–African Conference meeting at Bandung, Indonesia, attended by 29 states. Nehru took advantage of the opportunity offered by the Bandung Conference both to advance support for nonalignment and to try to break China's diplomatic isolation.[17]

The proximate cause of India's withdrawal from active diplomatic involvement in the affairs of Southeast and East Asia was the marked deterioration of relations with China, on which Nehru had placed such high hopes for cooperation. After an initial period of Chinese coolness towards India in the late 1940s, the bilateral relationship was placed on an amicable footing with the April 1954 Sino-Indian agreement on Tibet and by the Panchsheel declaration of peaceful coexistence issued on the occasion of the visit of Chinese Premier (and Minister of Foreign Affairs) Zhou Enlai to India two months later. It was also confirmed by India's handling of the NNRC, the ICC, and the Bandung Conference. However, this policy of engagement on areas of tension in Asia was undermined by the rising border tensions with China.

Indian patrols in 1958 discovered that the Chinese had completed a road through the Aksai Chin area of north-eastern Kashmir that linked the province of Xinjiang with Tibet. Starting in 1959, a series of border clashes erupted in both the Aksai Chin area of Kashmir and also the border area further to the east—a border which the Chinese said needed to be renegotiated because it was the result of British 'imperialist' action. Nehru in turn moved to strengthen India's troop presence at the frontier. The Chinese in October 1962, perhaps to force India into negotiations on a border the Indians considered legitimate, attacked in both the eastern and western frontier areas. After defeating Indian forces with relative ease on both fronts, China declared a unilateral ceasefire on 20 November 1962, and withdrew its forces to 'the line of actual control of November 7, 1959', except for a few pockets that it continued to occupy in the north-eastern area of Kashmir. The Chinese action shattered Indian influence in the world, which may have been one of its objectives, and even India's nonaligned partners were relatively silent on the Chinese action.

China's victory—coming at a time of growing Cold War tensions in Asia, India's pre-occupation with Pakistan, and economic troubles at home—worked to limit Indian engagement with Southeast Asia and East Asia for three decades. India did not, for example, establish full diplomatic relations with Korea until the end of 1973, and ties with it remained rather thin for the next 25 years.[18] All the Southeast and East Asian powers (with the exception of Vietnam) were somewhat cool to India, in part because of its Soviet tilt from the late 1960s to the late 1980s, thus inhibiting closer ties with them until after the Cold War. India's closer ties to the USSR was a logical development as New Delhi sought to counter an unfriendly China that supported Pakistan, without becoming dependent on the US and the West.[19] The USSR similarly sought to counter China by developing a closer relationship with India. Moscow became India's major supplier of sophisticated military equipment at what amounted to subsidized prices, consistently supported India at the UN (thus blocking any adverse resolution on Kashmir in the Security Council), and demonstrated sensitivity to Indian prestige. New Delhi responded favourably by generally adopting a sympathetic stand towards Soviet policy, even its invasion of Afghanistan in 1979 that brought the Cold War to South Asia itself.

Symptomatic of the anaemic Indian ties with East and Southeast Asia was the fact that not a single full-time correspondent from the vigorous and influential Indian print media was in the region until the late 1990s. They were in Europe, the USSR, and the US—the main sources of trade, the main areas of security interest, and the cultural and intellectual front for much of the post-independence political elite class. India's new policy of focusing on relations with countries to the east represents a more comprehensive move away from a Eurocentric cultural and media orientation. The Indian media is now represented throughout Asia.

INDIA: NEW CIRCUMSTANCES LEAD TO FOREIGN POLICY INNOVATIONS

The end of the Cold War, along with the Soviet withdrawal from Afghanistan in the late 1980s and the termination of US military assistance to Pakistan in the early 1990s due to its nuclear weapons programme, had a profound impact on India's foreign policy. No longer was there a basis for the strategic links to the USSR, a fact that registered quickly in China, which moved to improve relations with India. The US, in addition, came courting during the second Clinton administration (1996–2000) and India was pursued even more vigorously in the two presidential terms of George W. Bush (2000–4 and 2004–8).

The Bush administration had looked at a rising India as a balance to a rising China and as a stabilizing factor in the critically important region stretching from east Africa around the Indian Ocean to Indonesia. The Bush approach worked on the proposition that a strong India, whether linked to the US militarily or not, is a strategic asset. This policy assumption was most dramatically demonstrated by bipartisan action of the US Congress in late 2006 to back legislation proposed by the Bush administration to make India an exception to American nuclear non-proliferation laws and thus enable it to import nuclear fuel and nuclear technology. The Bush administration also lobbied the international community to follow the American lead in the International Atomic Energy Agency (IAEA) and the 45-nation NSG, of which the Republic of Korea is a member.[20] Korea was one of several countries concerned by the implications of the proposed American nuclear waiver on North Korea (and Iran), though Seoul did not oppose the waiver, either at the 1 August 2008 IAEA meeting or at the 6 September 2008 NSG discussions on the Indian waiver proposal.

The end of the Cold War and the tensions generated by it provided India an opening to forge a new foreign policy aimed at enhancing the country's goal of faster economic growth. The virtually simultaneous adoption of market reforms in the early 1990s forced the country to look outwards for trading partners, for high technology, and for sources of investment. The rising economic powers of Asia east of India were of immediate interest to achieve these important objectives. An economically robust Korea was one of those countries.

INDIAN LEADERSHIP LOOKS EAST FOR ECONOMIC GROWTH

At the 2005 East Asia summit, Indian PM Manmohan Singh announced specifically that India's 'Look East' foreign policy initiative dictated its participation in the summit. He declared that this new policy orientation was an important part of a larger outward-looking approach to world affairs, representing a strategic shift in India's vision of the world.[21] He should know. Manmohan Singh was involved in the creation of the 'Look East' policy some 15 years earlier when he served as the powerful Finance Minister under PM Narasimha Rao (1991–6). Its original goal was to develop a robust trading relationship with the countries of Southeast Asia, though the scope of this policy has been expanded to include the East Asian states of China, Japan, and Korea. This decision to deepen ties with the rising economies to the east of India was largely shaped by domestic economic concerns, specifically the desire for a higher annual GDP growth rate. The country's earlier rather poor performance (about 3 per cent per annum since independence in 1947—and sarcastically referred to by some as the Hindu rate of growth) was viewed as far too low to satisfy the growing demands of vast numbers of newly politicized groups. The country's political class at that time determined that higher growth rates required acquiring foreign markets for Indian products, high technology, foreign direct investment, and additional sources of oil and gas.[22] All this meant scrapping much of India's socialist economic orientation and what had been a half-century of looking inward towards the South Asian subcontinent. Inspiration for resulting reforms was the success of the East Asian economies, including that of Korea. Indian planners were well aware of the policy process used to transform Korea from a developing country in the 1950s to a high-income country starting in the 1970s with a substantial per capita income.

The 'Look East' policy was conceived as an incremental programme focusing on strengthening trade and security ties, initially with the countries of Southeast Asia and later with East Asia. In the crucial first stage, its chief goal was to establish Indian bona fides as a worthy trading partner. That meant getting over a bad economic brand name and suspicions generated by its earlier pro-Soviet tilt during the Cold War. Even its friends had begun to conclude that the cantankerous Indian democracy doomed the country to poor governance and economic stagnation. Years of autarky had generated low growth rates, a reputation for shoddy products, among the highest tariff rates in the world, and a heavily bureaucratic system generally unfriendly towards business of any kind. The business-oriented Asian leadership was highly sceptical. Despite the efforts to change in the early

1990s, the Chinese remained somewhat contemptuous of India, and Japan had a minimal presence and interest. Korea, an exception, took notice and began to invest in a significant way. Foreign direct investment (FDI) from Korea, for example, expanded from a meagre $2.5 million in 1991, the year initiating Indian market reforms, to over $3 billion of approved investment, with several billion more dollars of likely investment waiting for approval at the end of 2008. Korea has become the fifth-largest investor in India, after the US, Mauritius, the UK, and Japan.[23]

In sum, however, India's 'Look East' policy did not meet with instant success. Just as it was launched in earnest, two events at the international level blocked significant forward movement. The first was the economic meltdown in the Southeast Asian states in the late 1990s. The second was the widespread negative reaction to India's nuclear tests in May 1998, which provoked the US to impose sanctions and elicited tough criticism from China, Japan, Korea, Australia, and many other Asian states.

India had to prove itself economically to earn the respect of sceptical Asian leaders. Manmohan Singh, finance minister during the first surge of market reforms, moved quickly to put the Indian economy on a faster growth track. Among his first acts was to abolish an intrusive licensing system that had placed severe constraints on Indian industry. The reforms permitted private investment in many areas reserved for public enterprises, lowered tariffs, and opened the country incrementally to FDI. Successive Indian governments have stuck to the market reforms because the economic results have been positive, producing sufficient political support domestically to sustain a new foreign policy orientation. Major successes include:

- The average annual increase in the GDP between 1994 and 2007 was double the earlier annual average growth rate of about 3.5 per cent. In the early years of the new millennium, India's annual economic growth rate has edged upwards to over 9 per cent, though the slowdown in the international economy in the last half of 2008 could slow it to 7.8 per cent for 2008 and 6.3 for 2009, according to projections of the International Monetary Fund.[24]
- Indian hard currency holdings moved from less than $1 billion in 1990 to over $250 billion in 2008. From January 2007 to January 2008, India's foreign currency assets jumped from $170.2 billion to $266.8 billion, an increase of nearly 57 per cent, though there has been an estimated decline of some 10 per cent in the fall of 2008.[25]
- With the liberalization of trade policy, overall volume has expanded rapidly over the past few years, with two-way trade tripling since

2002–3 from $124 billion to over $414 billion for 2007–8.[26] After an initially sluggish start, the rate of trade expansion with Southeast Asia and East Asia has averaged over 30 per cent growth per year since 2002. Partly this trade surge is due to the slashing of customs tariff rates from peak levels of 150 per cent in 1991–2 to 15 per cent in 2005–6; in addition, import licensing was dismantled and quantitative restrictions in imports have been phased out.

TABLE 9.1: Indian Trade with Asia (US$ Million)

	2003–4	2004–5	2005–6	2006–7	2007–8
Trade with Asia	42,915.49	57,950.65	73,908.58	98,586.31	1,31,725.10
Total Trade	1,41,991.66	1,95,053.39	2,52,256.27	3,11,866.77	4,14,343.32

Source: Government of India, Ministry of Commerce and Industry website, http://commerce. nic.in/eidb/default.asp (accessed on 17 February 2009).

'LOOK EAST' PAYS OFF ECONOMICALLY

Since the adoption of market reforms in the early 1990s India has supported the notion of free-trade zones to create a more favourable trade environment for its robust economy.[27] PM Manmohan Singh, for example, has been personally involved in resolving the various outstanding issues that have delayed finalizing a free-trade agreement with the 10-member Association of Southeast Asian Nations (ASEAN) since the negotiations started in 2005.[28] Prompting Singh's government to push for such a trade relationship with ASEAN and the states of East Asia is the surge of Indian trade with these countries over the past few years.[29] India's fastest growing trade partners are in fact the ASEAN states and the East Asian states, including Korea. In the past seven years, trade between India and the ASEAN states, for example, has jumped from about $10 billion to about $39 billion in fiscal year 2007–8, about 40 per cent of that (or about $15.5 billion) with Singapore, India's largest trading partner in the region. India and Singapore are now engaged in trade talks that envision two-way trade to expand to some $50 billion in 2012.[30]

With the other major states of East Asia, as well as Australia, the growth of Indian trade has been even faster, increasing from $10 billion in 2001–2 to almost $81 billion in 2007–8. The expansion of trade with China over this time period has been dramatic, expanding from $3 billion (or about the amount with Japan in 2001–2) to almost $47 billion in 2007–8 (if Hong Kong figures are included); while trade with Japan, less spectacularly, has almost tripled over the same period from $3.5 billion to $10.2 billion. The level of Japan's trade and investment could change dramatically as

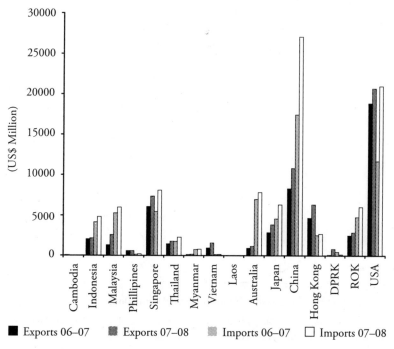

FIGURE 9.1: India's Trade Partners

Source: Government of India, Ministry of Commerce and Industry (Trade Statistics), updated 16 October 2008 (accessed on 17 February 2009).

Japanese companies, with encouragement from Tokyo, appear poised to increase significantly both their investment and trade with India, especially in infrastructure projects. Japanese contractors are thus likely to be competitors with Korean construction companies for Indian infrastructure projects.[31]

Trade with Korea has similarly gathered momentum. Bilateral trade has quadrupled from a relatively small base of $1.5 billion in 1997–8 to almost $8.9 billion in fiscal year 2007–8, of which some 68 per cent in the most recent year is Korean exports to India, reflecting a consistent trade balance in Korea's favour. Two-way trade since 2003 has been growing at about 25 per cent.[32] Korean exports are a diversified basket of goods, consisting mainly of electronics (39 per cent), machinery (14 per cent), and transport equipment (9 per cent), while India's exports have been dominated by a relatively narrow range of items of petroleum products and raw materials. India's booming service sector is only marginally represented in its exports to Korea, and there is considerable scope for a broad range of

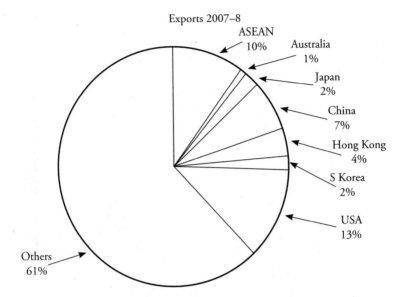

FIGURE 9.2: Indian Export Destinations

Source: Government of India, Ministry of Commerce and Industry (Trade Statistics), updated 16 October 2008 (accessed on 17 February 2009).

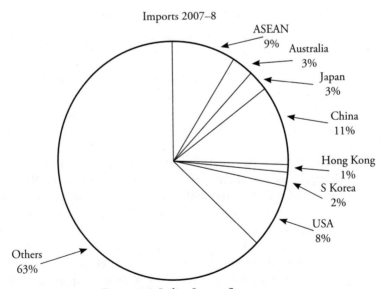

FIGURE 9.3: Indian Import Sources

Source: Government of India, Ministry of Commerce and Industry (Trade Statistics), updated 16 October 2008 (accessed on 17 February 2009).

Indian services once its negotiated Comprehensive Economic Partnership Agreement (CEPA) with Korea goes into effect in 2009. Korean exports to India increased by almost 26 per cent in 2007–8 over the previous fiscal year, while Indian exports to Korea grew by a more modest 13.5 per cent, a major decline from the previous year's 37.5 per cent jump in Indian exports to Korea. In fiscal year 2007–8, the dollar value of Korean exports to India was $6 billion (of total Korean exports worldwide worth $371.4 billion), and the dollar value of Indian exports to Korea was $2.9 billion (of a total Indian export value of $162.9 billion).[33]

Since the two economies inherently complement each other, the potential exists for significantly increased trade. India's cost-effective human resources could complement the growing labour scarcity and rising wages in Korea. Korean companies are already looking at India as an ideal location for global outsourcing. Hyundai India, for example, is a regional manufacturing hub for its parent company in Korea. Other opportunities for expanding business linkages exist in engineering, design engineering, and construction services. As the Indian economy continues to expand, even at the lower projected 7–8 per cent range for 2009, there will be a continuing demand for high technology products from Korea. In services, Korea has a competitive edge in hardware while India has the advantage of cutting-edge software. Korean construction firms are already heavily engaged in India's ambitious highway construction programme. This gives Korean construction firms an added advantage in bidding for other infrastructure development projects. India over the next decade will likely invest several hundred billion dollars for development of its ports, railroads, airports, electrical generating facilities/transmission lines, and utilities. Still another area where Korea has an advantage in India is naval construction. As India expands its navy, the technologically advanced Korean shipbuilding industry stands out as a potential supplier. India has already expressed interest in this Korean technology, particularly as a source to replace the now out-of-date warships from the Soviet Union/Russia.

India's liberal market reforms have had a similar positive impact in attracting direct investments from Korea. This increase comes at a time of a dramatic and sudden increase in overall FDI into India from about $7.6 billion in 2005–6 to $19.7 billion in 2006–7, and $23 billion in 2007–8.[34] When most other potential investors in the early years of India's market reforms were sceptical of whether the sluggish Indian political system would really permit a dynamic economy to flourish, Korean investors seemed more willing to take a risk. They gambled that the economy would take off and that India's autarkic system would be transformed. Others took almost a decade before deciding that market reforms in India would last.

A significant indication of Korea's growing interest in India's vast mineral resources is the pending $12 billion investment by a Korean steel company, Pohang Iron and Steel Company (POSCO), close to one of India's largest reserves of iron ore adjacent to the Bay of Bengal. This integrated project would include the construction of a 12-million-ton integrated Greenfield steel project, a township for workers, and transportation facilities to a dedicated port on the Bay of Bengal.[35] Domestic opposition to this huge project, the largest single investment to date in India, has delayed construction. Since the signing of a memorandum of understanding (MoU) between the state of Orissa and POSCO in mid-2005, POSCO has engaged in patient commercial diplomacy. It has scaled back the land usage from 5,000 to 3,000 acres in response to protests over the displacement of farmers; it has promised jobs and training to displaced farmers and their children; it is offering investment in general educational projects in the area. This is beginning to pay off. POSCO has recently granted contracts to over a dozen Indian firms for feasibility studies on the various parts of the steel project. The successful completion of this project will almost certainly serve as a positive sign to many other Koreans and other investors interested in developing India's huge mineral reserves.

Yet, complications involved in getting the POSCO project off the ground underscore the problems of dealing with the robust Indian democracy. Formerly disadvantaged groups are demanding dignity and an improved style of living. And they are voting and expressing their views in a variety of ways. Farmers and forest workers refuse to be denied their livelihood without compensation and some reasonable means of alternative employment. The days of meekly following orders from above are over as these newly assertive groups use the Indian political system to protect their interests. That phenomenon suggests that these groups have confidence that the political system will work to their benefit. But the process makes for much debate, many protests, and the necessity of compromise.

A major hurdle was cleared in August 2008 when India's Supreme Court lifted all legal hurdles involving POSCO's acquisition of some 3,000 acres of forest land in Orissa. This decision will permit the company to begin construction.[36] POSCO has confronted the realities of Indian democracy and seems to have adjusted well—and quickly—to making necessary compromises. Indeed, they seem to have been more aware of Indian political and cultural sensitivities than many European and American investors, perhaps because of a common Asian cultural context. By contrast, a case study of how not to go about responding to these social–political problems of displacement was the $2 billion American-funded Enron power project in the 1990s. At that time, this was the largest single foreign investment in India. Enron's inability to deal with or understand local grievances created major delays in construction. Ultimately, it was a key factor in the decision to sell the complete project to Indian investors before any electricity was generated.

The POSCO project is significant not only because of its size, but also because it reflects the likely future trend in Korean investment in, as well as trade with, India. India possesses a cornucopia of minerals. Production costs are relatively low, and the resources are relatively close to coastal areas for easy sea transport. Anticipating a continued expansion of trade, Indian PM Manmohan Singh and Korean President Roh Moo-hyun met in New Delhi on 6 October 2004 to authorize establishment of a Joint Study Group for comprehensive study of their bilateral economic linkages. The study group was mandated to examine the feasibility of a comprehensive economic partnership agreement.[37] Following up on this start, Indian External Affairs Minister Pranab Mukherjee and his Korean counterpart, Song Min-soon, decided that the two countries would conclude a CEPA by the end of 2007, a deadline that was missed because of differences over rules of origin, services, and trade in agricultural products. On the margins of the July 2008 G-8 Summit in Japan, Korean President Lee Myung-bak and PM Manmohan Singh discussed the CEPA, and they agreed to establish a negotiating mechanism at the vice-ministerial level to quicken the negotiating process.[38]

The two sides moved quickly to resolve their differences and at the conclusion of the 12th round of CEPA talks on 26 September 2008 announced an agreement stipulating that India would open up 85 per cent of its market to Korea, which in turn will give India access to 95 per cent of its market at either zero duty or at concessional rates. A major benefit to India is likely to be a greater share of Korea's services imports, which amounted to some $85 billion in 2007, only a small part of that from India. The two sides announced that the formal agreement would be signed before the end of 2008 and go into force in early 2009.[39]

INDIA AND KOREA: STILL LIMITED SECURITY INTERACTION

India has a relatively sparse security interaction with Korea. Therefore, the existing bilateral institutional framework is considerably less defined than with the countries of Southeast Asia, or even Japan. Indian engagement with East Asia is generally still peripheral to the region's major security issues, such as Taiwan or North Korean nuclear capabilities. India is not a member of the six-party talks with North Korea, though it has a stake in a positive resolution of the issue. There was allegedly a Pakistan–North Korean trade-off involving Pakistani assistance to North Korea's nuclear weapons programme in return for North Korea's reported assistance to Pakistan's missile programme aimed against India.[40]

India has a similar marginal relationship with other East Asian multilateral organizations. While it does have observer status in the Shanghai Cooperation Organization (SCO)—an organization set up by China and Russia to work out ways to handle their relations with the Central Asian republics—it plays a limited role in the SCO deliberations, with relatively low-ranking officials being sent to SCO meetings. India had representation at the East Asia Summit held in December 2005, convened to consider the creation of an East Asia Community (EAC) similar to the European Community. But this contentious meeting, with China and Japan struggling for pre-eminence in the projected EAC, proved symptomatic of the national rivalries that have blocked the emergence of effective multilateral institutions in Asia. In fact, concerns about a rising China led other participants to push for the inclusion of India and Australia in the Summit as a balance to China, a move China unsuccessfully opposed on grounds that neither is an East Asian power.[41]

Similarly, Korea's involvement in key security issues in the Indian Ocean littoral or even in South Asia is very limited. It was granted observer status in the South Asia Association of Regional Cooperation (SAARC) in 2006, along with the US and the European Union, though SAARC has a very thin record of achievement and activity. Protection of the sea lanes from the oil/gas-rich Persian Gulf states, however, could form a basis for greater strategic cooperation in the future between India and Korea, as both depend heavily on the Persian Gulf region for their energy needs. About 75 per cent of India's oil requirement is imported; of that, some 73 per cent is imported from the Persian Gulf region. India, the third largest consumer of oil in Asia after Japan and China, increased its oil imports 11 per cent from 2006–7 to 2007–8, reflecting the robust growth of its economy.[42] India's liquefied natural gas (LNG) imports were an estimated 353 billion cubic feet in 2007, mostly from the Middle East, which is roughly one-fourth of India's domestic natural gas consumption.[43]

Compelling reasons exist for the energy-deficient countries of East Asia, which include Korea, to be as concerned as India with the security of Indian Ocean sea lanes because they are all heavily dependent on oil and gas from the Persian Gulf region. Almost two-thirds of Korea's energy

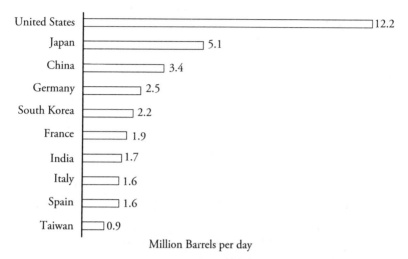

FIGURE 9.4: Top Ten Net Oil Importers in 2006

Source: EIA Short-term Energy Outlook (May 2007).

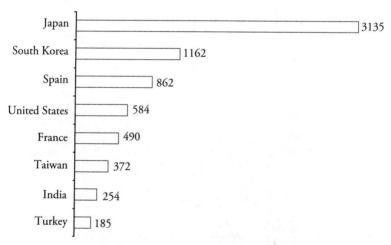

FIGURE 9.5: Top LNG Importers in 2006

Source: EIA International LNG Import Tables (posted 20 November 2007).
Note: Values are in billion cubic feet, http://www.eia.doe.gov/emeu/international/gaslngimports.html (accessed on 14 January 2009).

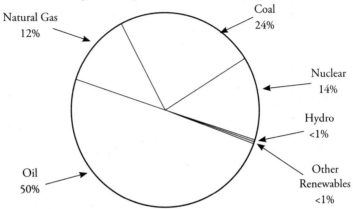

FIGURE 9.6: Korean Energy Consumption

Source: EIA International Energy Annual 2004.

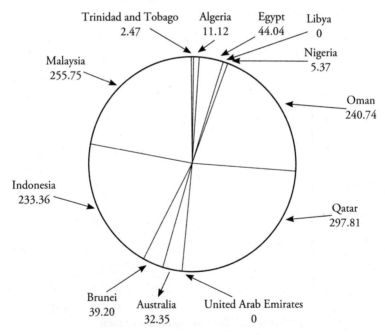

FIGURE 9.7: South Korea's 2006 LNG Imports, by Source

Source: EIA International LNG Import Tables (posted 20 November 2007).
Note: Values are in billion cubic feet http://www.eia.doe.gov/emeu/international/gaslng imports.html (accessed on 14 January 2009).

consumption comes from oil and LNG, almost entirely from imports.[44] Korea is the world's fifth-largest net importer of oil (after the US, Japan, China, and Germany), importing some 2.2 million barrels per day. It is also the world's second-largest importer of LNG, after Japan.

The Persian Gulf is the source of some two-thirds of Korea's imported oil and about one-half of its LNG. Almost all of it comes by tanker through the Indian Ocean and the Straits of Malacca to the South China Sea. Korea's dependency on the Gulf states, as is the case of India, is likely to grow, despite efforts to diversify. The Persian Gulf region contains well over one-half the world's known reserves of oil and over 40 per cent of the known gas reserves. The figures are likely to go up with increased offshore gas and oil exploration, such as the vast Pars Gas Field off the southern coast of Iran.

This deepening dependence on Gulf oil and gas raises important security issues because of escalating political, social, and ethnic tensions within and around the unstable Persian Gulf area. Moreover, the oil and gas traffic must pass through several vulnerable maritime choke points, such as the Hormuz Strait, the Gulf of Aden, the Suez Canal, and the Straits of Malacca, subject to attack by both rogue states and non-state actors. A blockage of any of

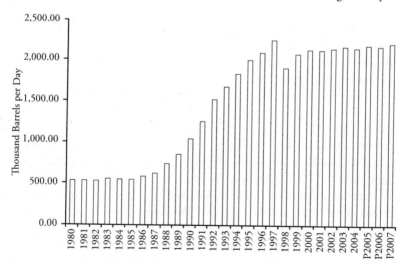

FIGURE 9.8: Korean Oil Consumption

Source: International Petroleum Consumption Tables (posted 7 November 2008).
Note: P stands for preliminary data.
http://tonto.eia.doe.gov/cfapps/ipdbproject/IEDIndex3.cfm?tid=5&pid=54&aid=2
(accessed on 15 January 2009).

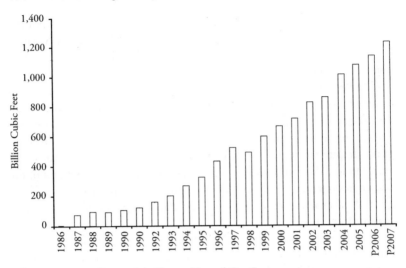

FIGURE 9.9: Korean Natural Gas Consumption

Source: EIA International Natural Gas Consumption Tables (posted 30 June 2008).
Note: P stands for preliminary data, http://tonto.eia.doe.gov/cfapps/ipdbproject/IEDIndex3.
cfm?tid=3&pid=26&aid=2 (accessed on 15 January 2009).

these choke points would create a world economic crisis. Problems of gun-running, drug trafficking, piracy, and terrorism constitute major non-state threats to maritime security.[45] Almost one-third of the attacks in the waters off Southeast Asia have been against bulk carriers. While tough Indonesian and Malaysian action against piracy in 2007–8 has significantly reduced the level of hijackings in the Malacca Straits area, this has not been the case for the other side of the Indian Ocean. A spike in piracy has occurred off the north-eastern coast of Africa, especially in the sea lanes close to Somalia. Fifty-five ships have been subject to pirate attacks off the coast of Somalia since January 2008, according to the International Maritime Board.[46]

International efforts have been launched to address the various security threats to the Malacca Straits. In 2007, the International Maritime Bureau (IMB) launched a 24-hour global hotline for maritime security information, particularly information linked to maritime terrorism, piracy, and organized crime. The Japan International Cooperation Agency funds Japanese Coast Guard seminars to train maritime officials in Southeast Asia. Japan has also funded efforts of the International Maritime Organization (IMO) to track and study piracy incidents, and Japan's Ship and Ocean Foundation has provided seed money for the IMO-sanctioned Anti-Piracy Center in Kuala Lumpur. Proposals by the US to deploy special forces to counter terrorism

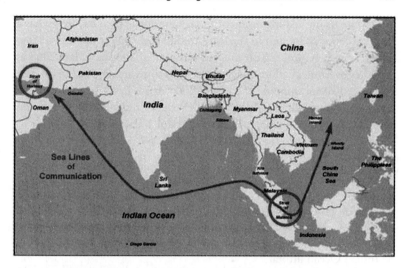

FIGURE 9.10: Shipping Routes: Indian Ocean Shipping Routes Connecting the
Persian Gulf to East Asia through the Strait of Malacca

Source: Walter Andersen.

Note: Potential choke points are circled.

and sea piracy in the Straits of Malacca under a Regional Maritime Initiative
were rejected by Indonesia and Malaysia, fearful that such deployments
would compromise sovereignty. This reluctance underscores the general
lack of multilateral agreements to counter acts of terrorism and piracy that
take place in the Indian Ocean sea lanes. The US has assumed primary
leadership for securing the sea lanes of the Indian Ocean, though it is
looking for cooperative arrangements to share the burden and to respond
to the growing challenges.

In the wake of 9/11, the US established Task Force 150, drawing mainly
on ships of the US Fifth Fleet deployed in the western reaches of the Indian
Ocean, to patrol the sea lanes leading from the Persian Gulf. India and
Korea were not participants. The spike in ship hijackings off the coast of
Somalia during 2008, including Korean and Indian ships, reflected the
inadequacy of existing ad hoc arrangements. Several countries have reacted
by sending war ships to protect their own vessels, given the lack of multilateral
agreements on the issue. India has deployed warships; the European Union
has sent warships, as has Russia.[47] The head of the IMB's Piracy Reporting
Center, reacting to the spike in hijacking, advocated greater cooperative
efforts among concerned nations and warned that 'as long as there is no firm
deterrent, piracy will continue in the African waters'.[48]

Despite its limited involvement in sea lane defences so far, Korea has a definite economic interest in the issue, and in late 2008 it was considering a more activist stance. A Korean team was sent to Somalia in late 2008 as part of a government effort to determine if its ships are required in the area to protect Korean shipping.[49] India and Korea are in the early phase of a strategic understanding, starting with the visit of President Roh Moo-hyun to India in 2004 and Indian President Abdul Kalam's reciprocal visit to Korea in early 2006. The first ever bilaterals by their defence ministers were held in May 2007, and sea lane security was a topic of discussion. Indian Defence Minister A.K. Antony proposed to his Korean counterpart, Kim Jang-soo, that the two countries hold joint naval exercises with anti-piracy and anti-terrorism objectives.[50] They also discussed Coast Guard cooperation. These proposed naval exercises with Korea and Coast Guard cooperation would fit a pattern of recent Indian joint exercises throughout the Indian Ocean littoral.

Korea is in the process of creating a blue-water navy that could operate in the Indian Ocean. Korean President Kim Dae-jung in 2001 announced that Korea would create a 'strategic mobile fleet' consisting of destroyers, submarines, and anti-submarine aircraft, with the first Aegis destroyer for this proposed 'mobile fleet' launched in mid-2007 and a second (of three planned) in late 2008.[51] On the occasion of the launching of the destroyer, the Korean Navy's Public Affairs Office said the projected 'mobile fleet' would enable Korea to conduct 'independent and joint naval operations' with its allies for 'securing southern sea lanes for energy supplies and peacekeeping'.[52] While the projected blue-water capability is a decade or more away, Korea has the industrial capacity to speed up its naval programme if it decides to do so.

In addition to naval exercises in May 2007, the Korean defence minister reportedly has asked India to add a military attaché to its embassy staff in Seoul, as well as form regular military consultation bodies, mainly to identify likely Korean military items for export to India.[53] This still modest India–Korea military supply relationship could mark the beginning of a closer strategic relationship between the two democracies with very similar strategic visions. Despite a push for indigenous production, India still relies heavily on imported equipment. With increased arms trade in mind, India and Korea held the first India–Korea Defense Committee meeting in March 2007 at Seoul.[54] Korea proposed joint projects for manufacture of a range of equipment, including 5,000-ton class frigates and minesweepers, armoured vehicles, and K-9 self-propelled guns. Underscoring the serious prospects for such military sales, the two sides signed a MoU on ensuring the quality of the defence products that would be jointly manufactured in India and Korea.[55]

Total Korean defence exports reached a record of $1.1 billion in the first nine months of 2007, and, considering the substantial increase in the allocation of funds for research and development, it is possible that Korea could achieve its goals of becoming among the 10 top weapons exporters, with India becoming a major customer.[56] India's defence spending has been on an upward trajectory for the past several years, including a dramatic increase in the import of sophisticated military hardware. Its proposed defence budget for 2007–8 was about $22 billion, an increase of about 8 per cent over the previous year. While defence spending as a percentage of GDP has declined over several years, to arrive at a figure of 2.1 per cent of the expected GDP for 2007–8, the absolute amount has increased due to a robust Indian economy. Much of this funding is for military imports, expected to reach some $30 billion over the next five years, according to India's Associated Chambers of Commerce and Industry in a study of the subject.[57] In the past three years, 2005–7, India has spent almost $11 billion on radar equipment (largely from Israel, a growing supplier of sophisticated equipment), submarines and helicopters (from France), and tanks (from Russia)—all making India the largest importer of military equipment in the developing world. Korea, the US, and Israel—relatively recent suppliers of sophisticated military equipment to India—could overtake traditional suppliers like Russia, the UK, and Sweden.[58]

There are challenges to a deepening of the security relationship, the most important being the regional focus of each country's security interests, though both India and Korea are broadening their strategic horizons. Among the other challenges is the implicit American acceptance of India's nuclear weapons status at a time when delicate six-party negotiations to end North Korea's nuclear weapons capabilities are being conducted. The agreements signed in July 2005 and March 2006 at summit meetings between Indian PM Manmohan Singh and US President George W. Bush, with subsequent Congressional legislation, pledged the US to make India a special case among countries that have not signed the NPT. Opponents of the nuclear deal with India in the US and elsewhere fear that this exception for India will make it more difficult to deal with nuclear proliferators like North Korea and potential proliferators like Iran. While Korea did not formally oppose the waiver for India at either the IAEA or the NSG, the two countries might be on opposite sides of new international efforts to get more countries to support a Comprehensive Test Ban Treaty (CTBT) and a fissile fuel cut-off treaty.

* * *

The Asian states have relatively few real achievements so far in economic or strategic cooperation. While national rivalries continue to be a significant limiting factor, some advances have been made to foster trade and investment because greater cooperation in these areas fits domestic goals of economic growth. The increasingly international activity of Korea and India, by way of example, is motivated largely by economic considerations. The rapid growth of bilateral trade, some 25 per cent plus annual growth since 2003, makes each among the fastest growing economic trade partner of the other. This rapid growth was the motivating factor for the India–Korea CEPA that goes into effect in 2009. There is a natural fit. India has enormous infrastructure needs that provide a market for Korea's sophisticated and internationally oriented construction industry. Korea is already a major investor in India and the level is likely to grow significantly. India for its part is a source of affordable information technology that is beginning to compete in the Korean market. It is also a source of many of the minerals that Korean industry requires. The international economic crisis that emerged in 2008 may affect the rate of trade growth over the short term, but the political leadership in both countries are committed to economic globalization and thus likely to resist domestic demands for protectionist barriers, as demonstrated by their support of concrete measures to stabilize the international financial system at the mid-November 2008 G-20 meetings in Washington, DC.

Regional cooperation in security generally has far fewer achievements—and this applies to Korea and India. Protection of vulnerable Indian Ocean sea lanes, however, is a likely area for bilateral cooperation because the economies of both countries are increasingly dependent on oil and gas from the Persian Gulf. There are presently very few multilateral agreements that address the common threats of piracy, terrorism, drug trafficking, and smuggling on the high seas. The thin record of achievement in this area provides an opportunity for Korea and India to take creative steps on an issue that is critically important to their respective economies. The alternative is uncoordinated unilateral action, which is what is taking place in response to the dramatic spike in piracy off the Somalia coast in 2008. Korea and India have the naval capacity to respond to this crisis. India would almost certainly welcome Korea as a partner in maritime security as Korea, in contrast to China, another East Asian state increasingly dependent on oil and gas from the Persian Gulf region, is not perceived as a potential threat to its security interests.

As the Asian states move to address issues of importance, such as trade and investment, peacekeeping, global warming, nuclear non-proliferation, scarcities of energy and water, piracy, and terrorism, the process of integration is likely to gain greater political traction. India will not want to be left out of this process as it was when the organization for Asia-Pacific Economic Cooperation was formed in 1989. It was similarly left out of the six-party talks on North Korea's nuclear programme and has not been included in the several Track-II efforts on security in northeast Asia. Neither Korea nor India has hegemonic political goals in Asia and thus are potential partners to ensure that no other Asian state, such as China, gains a hegemonic position in the integrating process very likely to take place over the next few decades in Asia.[59] Chinese, Japanese, and American proposals for multilateral cooperation in Asia have a thin record of achievement due in large part to mutual distrust among these powers and suspicions about their larger security goals by smaller states. By way of contrast, Korea and India, two middle-level powers with excellent bilateral relations, are much less likely to arouse such suspicions and could be the nucleus for broader Asian economic and security cooperation. Their active involvement in efforts to move the integrative process along would also reduce the chances that these efforts would degenerate into power struggles among the larger states, as has been the tendency so far.[60] The first step in such Korean–Indian security cooperation might be joint action to establish a multilateral agreement addressing the safety of the Indian Ocean sea lanes and their choke points.

NOTES

1. We will use Korea for all future references to the Republic of Korea.

2. A comprehensive analysis of the Korea–America relationship in the post-Cold War period is S. Han (2007), 'Korea–U.S. Alliance and Korean Security', in Taek Hyun, Kyudok Hong, and Sung-han Kim (eds), *Asia-Pacific Alliances in the 21ˢᵗ Century* (Seoul: Oreum Publishing House).

3. For a discussion of the declining significance of the US–Korea alliance, see P. Morgan (2007), 'The U.S.–ROK Alliance: An American View', *International Journal of Korean Studies*, 11 (1). The author proposes that the alliance is of diminishing utility to the US as well as Korea because it limits American leverage with North Korea on the nuclear issue.

4. A comprehensive analysis of the changes in India's post-Cold War foreign policy is in C. Raja Mohan (2003), *Crossing the Rubicon: The Shaping of India's New Foreign Policy* (New Delhi: Penguin Books India).

5. India's two-way trade with the Republic of Korea was $8.9 billion in 2007–8, nine times the size of Indian two-way trade with North Korea. *Trade Statistics*

(Government of India: Department of Commerce), 16 October 2008, http://commerce.nic.in/eidb/default.asp (accessed on 13 February 2009).

6. Energy Information Administration (2007) (Department of Energy: US Government, June). Presently, the Persian Gulf region produces about 28 per cent of the world's oil. Of the 18.2 million barrels per day (bbl/d) exported, about 17 million bbl/d went by sea and the rest by pipeline.

7. A comprehensive review of the multiple challenges to the Indian Ocean lines of communications can be found in V. Sakhuja (2001), 'Indian Ocean and the Safety of Sea Lines of Communication', *Strategic Analysis*, 25 (5), pp. 689–702.

8. See a comprehensive biography of President Lee Myung-bak in *JoongAng Daily* (Seoul), 21 August 2007.

9. See a review of the arguments about whether the market reforms have exposed the Indian economy to negative consequences of the global financial crisis in a set of articles, including a positive analysis of the reform process by India's economist PM, titled 'India's Leaders Promise Policy Action to Sustain Growth, Protect the Poor', in *Wall Street Journal (Eastern Edition)*, 22 November 2008. Dr Rakesh Mohan, Deputy Governor of the Reserve Bank of India, has argued, like the Indian PM, that the global financial crisis has had a relatively limited impact on India so far and that India has the tools to protect the country from the negative international consequences of the crisis. For the transcript of his talk, see 'Global Financial Crisis and Key Risks: Impact on India and Asia', Reserve Bank of India, 9 October 2008, http://www.rbi.org.in/scripts/BS_speechesView.aspx?Id=402 (accessed on 27 February 2009).

10. Nehru's ambassador to China during this period, K.M. Panikkar, in his book describing the Indian relationship with China at that time does so in a very sympathetic manner towards China and its foreign policy goals. See K.M. Panikkar (1955), *In Two Chinas: Memoirs of a Diplomat* (London: G. Allen and Unwin).

11. The most comprehensive analysis of the Indian involvement in the Korean War is the unpublished doctoral dissertation of Charles H. Heimsath (1956), *India's Role in the Korean War* (New Haven: Yale University).

12. Charles H. Heimsath and Surjit Mansingh (1971), *A Diplomatic History of Modern India* (Calcutta: Allied Publishers).

13. Ibid., p. 71.

14. A comprehensive discussion of Nehru's involvement in the Vietnam issue is in D.R. SarDesai (1968), *Indian Foreign Policy in Cambodia, Laos and Vietnam 1947–64* (Berkeley: University of California Press).

15. Ibid., p. 55.

16. Ibid., pp. 56 and 234. SarDesai further notes that Indian moral force in Asia dropped sharply in the wake of China's victory in October 1962 against India. He notes, for example, that the Southeast Asian states ceased to seek an Indian mediating role in regional disputes.

17. For a review of Nehru's hopes for the relationship with China, see Heimsath and Mansingh, *Diplomatic History of Modern India*.

18. Relations were simultaneously established with the Democratic Republic of Korea (North Korea). India maintains diplomatic relations with both of the Korean states concurrently.

19. A review of the geostrategic factors in the 1960s that led to the closer Indian relationship with the USSR is in Stephen Phillip Cohen (2001), *India: Emerging Power* (Washington: Brookings Institution Press).

20. The governing board of the International Atomic Energy Agency unanimously gave its approval to the exception for India on 1 August 2008, and the Nuclear Suppliers Group did so by consensus on 7 September 2008.

21. For a personal sense of the important economic consequences PM Manmohan Singh expected of his 'Look East' policy, see 'Media Briefing by Prime Minister Dr Manmohan Singh on-board Special Aircraft to Kuala Lumpur to attend 4th India-ASEAN Summit and 1st East Asia Summit', Ministry of External Affairs, 11 December 2005, http://meaindia.nic.in/pressbriefing/2005/12/11pb01.htm (accessed on 25 January 2009).

22. While there was a general sense among senior policymakers that globalization was needed for the higher rates of economic growth, there was a vigorous political debate about the pace of change and the degree of foreign involvement in the Indian economy.

23. See 'India–South Korea Economic Relations', Economy Watch on-line, 19 October 2007, http://www.economywatch.com/world_economy/south-korea/indp-south-korea-trade-relation.html (accessed on 29 January 2009). Actual investment inflows from Korea are only about $800 million as of 2005, with the remainder representing investments approved, but funds not yet expended. This figure, however, does not include a multi-billion dollar iron-ore refinery project in Orissa, which, when completed, would be the largest single FDI project in India.

24. These are the projected figures of the International Monetary Fund in its update of the world economy prepared for the G-20 meeting in Washington, DC, in mid-November 2008. World Economic Outlook Update (2008), 'Rapidly Weakening Prospects Call for New Policy Stimulus', (Washington DC: International Monetary Fund), Table I.

25. 'Weekly Statistical Supplements', Reserve Bank of India, 21 September 2008, http://www.rbi.org.in/scripts/WSSViewDetail.aspx?TYPE=Section&PARAM1=2 (accessed on 1 March 2009).

26. Statistics available on the website of the Ministry of Commerce, Export Import Data Bank, at http://commerce.nic.in/eidb/default.asp (accessed on 5 February 2009).

27. India has negotiated several free-trade agreements over the past decade. Among the multilateral agreements are (i) Bay of Bengal Initiative for Multi-Sectoral Technical and Economic Cooperation (BIMSTEC, 1997) which includes Bangladesh, Bhutan, India, Myanmar, Nepal, Sri·Lanka and Thailand, (ii) The

South Asia Free Trade Agreement (2004) including the regional states of South Asia, and (iii) the 10-member ASEAN (2008). India is also negotiating a free-trade agreement with the European Union. There are also several bilateral free-trade agreements, including with almost all the regional states of South Asia, as well as with Myanmar, Singapore, and Korea.

28. For discussion of these talks, see 'India–ASEAN FTA likely to be finalized by May 2008', *The Economic Times*, 22 November 2007.

29. A free-trade agreement between India and ASEAN was signed in December 2008.

30. Government of India, Ministry of Commerce and Industry, Department of Commerce: Export-Import Data Bank. http://commerce.nic.in/eidb/iecnt.asp. (accessed 14 February 2009). See also 'India-ASEAN summit postponed due to Thailand unrest', *The Times of India*, 2 December 2008. This projection calculated to take trade to the $50 billion level by 2012 was made during the second phase of the implementation of the Indo-Singapore CECA in August 2008. For a report of those meetings, see Neha Pal (2008), 'India, Singapore Seek to Take Bilateral Trade to $50 Billion', *Financial Express*, 29 August.

31. Ibid.

32. Ibid. The most comprehensive study of trade between India and Korea is the study of the Joint India–Korea Study Group, which was mandated by the PM of India and the President of the Republic of Korea, under the aegis of the CEPA between the two countries. The figures, which only go to 2004–5, are slightly out of date, though the analytical section is still relevant. The Study Group submitted its report in February 2006 on the occasion of the visit of Indian President Abdul Kalam to Korea. The two countries at that time mandated a Joint Task Force (JTF) to develop a CEPA aimed at increasing volume of trade. As of this writing, six meetings of the JTF have been held.

33. Ibid.

34. Data taken from 'Work Investment Report', United Nations Conference on Trade and Development, 2007, www.UNCTAD.org/wir (accessed on 27 February 2009).

35. The website for this project in India called POSCO–India can be accessed at http://POSCO-India.com

36. Information on the challenges and the ultimate legal resolution are nicely summarized in Rakesh Bhatnagar (2008), 'SC Clears Way for POSCO Sterlite Projects', *Daily News and Analysis*, 9 August.

37. 'India, Korea iron out CEPA differences, to ink pact by year-end'. *The Financial Express*, 26 September 2008. The Indian press reported in late 2007 that Korea is reluctant to open up its services' industry through a CEPA agreement with India.

38. Information on the state of negotiations on this issue can be found online at http://www.Bilateral.org. This is a website on trade agreements and negotiations (accessed on 7 August 2008).

39. See report on the agreement, 'India, Korea Iron out CEPA Differences, to Ink Pact by Year-End', *Financial Express*, 26 September 2008.

40. Sharon A. Squassoni (2006), 'Weapons of Mass Destruction: Trade between North Korea and Pakistan.' CRS Report for Congress, 28 November.

41. For an excellent discussion of the rivalries that got in the way of any effective action, see Mohan Malik (2006), 'China and the East Asia Summit: More Discord than Accord', *Asia-Pacific Center for Security Studies* (February).

42. Statistics taken from the 'Report on Petroleum Statistics', Ministry of Petroleum and Gas, Government of India, 2007–8. Also see *World Energy Outlook 2007* (Paris: OECD/International Energy Agency).

43. Information on LNG imports from Energy Information Administration, 2 August 2008, http://www.eia.doe.gov/international/RecentNaturalGasImportsBCF.xls (accessed on 9 February 2009). Even though India's domestic extraction of natural gas is increasing, it still does not meet the growing demand of a rapidly expanding economy. For this reason, India is exploring the import of gas by pipeline from Iran, Myanmar, and Turkmenistan.

44. Statistics in this section drawn from *Country Analysis Briefs: South Korea*, Energy Information Administration, June 2007.

45. There is a large and rapidly growing literature analysing and identifying threats to commercial shipping lanes. Among the most comprehensive is the 'Weekly Piracy Report', *Commercial Crime Services, International Chamber of Commerce*, http://www.icc.ccs.org/prc/piracyreport.php. The International Maritime Bureau (UK) also provides an updated reporting of threats to shipping which is available at http://wordpress.com/tag/intgernational_martime_bureau/2/. The Jamestown Foundation, located in Washington, DC, also has a number of publications that address terrorism, including terrorism at sea. They include *Spotlight on Terror, Terrorism Focus*, and the *Terrorism Monitor*. In the last of these, for example, is an excellent analysis of the danger terrorism poses to shipping in John C.K. Daly (2008), 'Terrorism and Piracy: The Dual Threat to Maritime Shipping', 6 (16), http://www.jamestown.org/programs/gta/single/?tx_ttnews[tt_news]=5112&tx_ttnewsbackPid]=167&no_cache=1 (accessed on 13 February 2009). Still another very useful source is the MIPT Terrorism Knowledge Base, an online portal on terrorist incidents. This is a non-profit organization funded by the Department of Homeland Security. It can be accessed at http://www.mipt/org.

46. From news reported in an online service of *The Times of India*, http://timesofindia.indiatimes.com/india/hijackedship_captain_contacts_family/articleshow/3501060.cmw (accessed on 9 February 2009).

47. See 'India Sends Warships to Somali Waters', *Mail & Guardian Online*, 17 October 2008, http://www.mg.co.za/article/2008-10-17-india-sends-warships-to-Somali-waters (accessed on 10 February 2009). Indian commandos on an armed helicopter operating from an Indian warship had already gone into action off the coast of Somalia in a set of anti-piracy operations in early November. The

press reports that on 11 November 2008 the commandos gave chase to pirates attacking a Saudi Arabian chemical tanker and rescued a nearby Indian ship under attack by a different set of pirates. This was a significant assertive step by Indian forces, operating 1,800 miles from the home port, to translate military power into political clout, 'Indian Navy Fights off Pirates in Gulf of Aden', http://www.chinadaily.com.cn/world/2008-11/19/content_7220687.htm. Related to this greater Indian activism, the Indian press also reports that PM Manmohan Singh during a visit to the Gulf signed a bilateral maritime security framework agreement with Qatar. Reported in Atul Aneja (2008), 'Navy Foils Bid to Hijack Indian Ship in Gulf of Aden', *The Hindu*, 12 November.

48. Noel Chou, the head of the IMB's Piracy Reporting Service, quoted in 'Follow India's Approach: Maritime Body Chief', *Hindustan Times*, 22 November 2008. Chou praised the assertive policy of the Indian Navy in challenging the piracy menace in the waters off Somalia and noted that UN Security Council Resolution 1816, passed on 2 June 2008, with the consent of the Somalian government, gave the right to naval ships to engage in anti-piracy efforts in the territorial waters of Somalia for up to six months.

49. 'South Korea Likely to Send Warship to Somalia', TMCnet, 29 October 2008, http://tmcnet.com/ususubmit/2008/10/29/3741740.htm (accessed on 13 February 2009).

50. See 'Korea, India Agree on Naval Drills, Defense Exchanges', *The Korea Herald*, 31 May 2007.

51. A report of the increased capabilities of the Korean Navy in Globalsecurity. org, available at http://www.globalsecurity.org/military/world/dprk/navy.htm (accessed on 15 February 2009).

52. Jung Sung-ki (2007), 'South Korea's Navy Cruises Toward Oceangoing Force', *The Korea Times*, 28 May. This is likely a reference to the sea lanes of the South China Sea.

53. See 'S. Korea, India to Hold Joint Military Drills', *Korea Times*, 30 May 2007.

54. See 'Korea Seeks Joint Production of Arms with India', *The Korea Herald*, 20 March 2007.

55. See an analysis of this meeting in S.K. Mishra (2007), 'Korea–India Defense Committee Meet and Implications', online at Korea.net, 11 March; also see online 'India, South Korea Agree to Cooperate', *BBC Monitoring South Asia*, 30 May 2007, http:///www.korea.net/news/News/NewsView.asp?serial_no=200705 11024&part=111&SearchDay= (accessed on 17 February 2009).

56. See an analysis of Korea's efforts to expand its defence exports in an online report, 'S. Korea's Defense Exports Reach $1.1. Billion', *DefenseNews.com*, 5 November 2007 (accessed on 27 February 2009).

57. See 'India's Military Imports to Hit $30USb: Study', *Business Times Singapore*, 15 May 2007.

58. Siddharth Srivastava (2007), 'India flies the red flag', *Asia Times Online*, 5 December, http://www.atimes.com/atimes/South_Asia/IL05Df03.html.

59. Two scholars in Korea have used this theme to analyse what they see as a significant future development of Korea–India relations. Lakhvinder Singh (2008), 'The Importance of Korea: A Strategic Perspective on India's Engagement with Northeast Asia', *The Korean Journal of Defense Analysis*, 20 (3), pp. 283–94; Ra Yoon-dho (2007), 'India as a Rising Power and the Credibility of U.S. Diplomacy', *Korean Observations on Foreign Relations*, 9 (2).

60. For a discussion proposing involvement of middle-level powers in building security mechanisms in north-east Asia, see Ok-Nim Chung (2000), 'Solving the Security Puzzle in Northeast Asia: A Multilateral Security Regime', Brookings, September, http://www.brookings.edu/papers/2000/090/diplomacy_chung.aspx?p=1 (accessed on 1 March 2009).

10

India–Japan Relations
A Slow, but Steady, Transformation

HARSH V. PANT

It has been suggested that Japan has a slow metabolism.[1] Because changes in Japanese policies tend to occur gradually, they often go unnoticed. One of the changes that are gradually shaking up Japanese foreign policy, however, has not gone unnoticed. Japan's growing ties with India over the last few years have generated significant interest as they underline the rapidly changing strategic realities in Asia. Relations between India and Japan have gathered momentum, with the two countries making a concerted attempt to interact at various levels—economic, political, and strategic. A recent survey of global attitudes suggests that a huge majority of Indians and Japanese, 65 and 60 per cent respectively, continue to view each other very favourably in stark contrast to their views about other regional actors, especially China.[2] As Indian Prime Minister Manmohan Singh put it, 'The time has come for India and Japan to build a strong contemporary relationship, one involving global and strategic partnership that will have a great significance for Asia and the world as a whole'.[3] In the words of the former Japanese PM Shinzo Abe, 'A strong India is in the best interest of Japan, and a strong Japan is in the best interest of India'.[4]

This new-found warmth represents a transformation of the two countries' past relationship, which, though never conflictual, was characterized by a lack of interest in each other's priorities. The two countries' increasing closeness represents a major transformation of their past relationship. This chapter argues that a convergence of structural, domestic, and individual leadership factors has transformed the India–Japan relationship in recent years. At the structural level, the rise of China in the Asia-Pacific and beyond has fundamentally altered the strategic calculus of India and Japan, forcing them to rethink their attitudes towards each other. At the domestic level,

India's booming economy is making it an attractive trading and business partner for Japan as the latter tries to get itself out of its long years of economic stagnation. Japan is also reassessing its role as a security provider in the region and beyond, and of all its neighbours India seems most willing to acknowledge Japan's centrality in shaping the evolving Asia-Pacific security architecture. At the individual level, a new generation of political leaders in India and Japan are viewing each other differently, breaking from past policies, thereby changing the trajectory of India–Japan relations.

This chapter begins with a brief historical overview of Indo-Japanese relations through the Cold War years. Subsequently, the increasing convergence between India and Japan at three levels—structural, domestic, and individual leadership—is examined in detail. Finally, the future prospects of this bilateral relationship are explicated with a focus on the factors that have the potential to derail further progress in the Indo-Japanese relationship.

COLD WAR BACKGROUND

Though cultural links between India and Japan date back to the sixth century with the spread of Buddhism from its birthplace in India to the rest of the region including Japan, the two states found themselves in uncharted territory as World War II came to an end. Japan's 1905 victory over Russia was viewed by many, including independent India's first PM Jawaharlal Nehru, as the beginning of Asian resurgence and Japan's anti-colonial contributions, including support to Netaji Subhash Chandra Bose and his Indian National Army, trumped reservations about its militarism that so bothered the rest of Asia.[5] India's independence in 1947 and Japan's defeat in World War II meant that the two sides had to start building their bilateral relationship by laying its very foundations anew. However, unlike Japan's tumultuous past with its other Asian neighbours, there were no historical grievances to impede the evolution of India–Japan ties.

As a result, one of the first treaties Japan signed after World War II was its peace treaty with India in 1952 that established diplomatic relations between the two states. In many ways, India was instrumental in bringing Japan into the mainstream of international and regional politics by inviting it to the first Asian Games in New Delhi in 1951 and encouraging Tokyo's participation in the Afro-Asian Conference in Bandung (Indonesia) in 1955. As Japan made its way to economic and industrial recovery, India's supply of important minerals, especially iron ore, went a long way in helping Japan make this transition.[6] The visits of Japanese PM Nobusuke Kishi to India and Indian PM Jawaharlal Nehru to Japan provided additional momentum to this bilateral relationship. Nehru was spurred by his belief in an Asian community of states while the Japanese leaders were looking for friends in a region where they were virtually isolated. India became the first recipient of the yen loan aid extended by the Japanese government, and by 1986 Japan had become India's largest aid donor.[7]

The structural realities of the Cold War soon ensured that this momentum in India–Japan bilateral ties could not be sustained; India declared itself a member of the Non-Aligned Movement, arguing that the best way for a developing Third World country to retain its independence and concentrate on domestic development was by maintaining an equidistance from the two superpowers and their blocs. Japan, on the other hand, was clearly and openly in alignment with the United States (US) and its foreign policy priorities. It perceived the Soviet Union to be its main security threat, and being a close ally of the US, thrust Japan directly into the cauldron of East–West confrontation.[8] As India's tilt away from the US and towards the erstwhile Soviet Union became more pronounced in practice, India's ties with the US and its allies, including Japan, suffered.

During the 1962 Sino-Indian war, Japan decided to stay neutral even though the US came out in public support of India's position on the border dispute and even supplied military equipment to India.[9] Japan's preferred neutrality during India's conflicts with Pakistan also contributed to alienation between New Delhi and Tokyo. Over time, as the Indian economy continued to follow the outmoded socialist economic developmental model and stagnated even as the Japanese economy galloped ahead, the two nations found few economic complementarities. Japan was soon deeply engaged economically in East and Southeast Asia while India remained marginal to Japanese economic priorities. Following America's lead, Japan enhanced its engagements with China and other Southeast Asian nations in its role as the one of the most powerful economies in the 1970s and 1980s. Meanwhile, India remained inward-looking both in its economic orientation and foreign policy priorities. While India dismissed Japan as a camp-follower of the US, the Japanese perceived India as a chaotic, dysfunctional, desperately poor country, and not as a potential partner.[10] Japan continued to regard India as a local power, always hyphenated with Pakistan. As the Japanese economy led the economic revival in East and Southeast Asia resulting in the formation of new institutional structures such as the Association of Southeast Asian Nations (ASEAN), India was perceived to be outside the scope of such institutions and somehow excluded from the very definition of Asia.[11]

Even as the structural constraints of the Cold War loosened with the demise of the bipolar global order and India embarked upon economic liberalization, the momentum in India–Japan ties was slow to pick up. Japan was largely preoccupied with its domestic situation as its economy started showing signs of weakening. India had other priorities, primarily making sure that it was getting Western, especially American, support in shoring up the economy from the dire straits it had sunk into. And then came the Indian nuclear tests of 1998 that marked the lowest point in bilateral relations, with Japan reacting strongly to the nuclearization of the subcontinent. Tokyo suspended economic assistance for three years as well as put on hold all political exchanges between the two nations. Japan's economic measures against India included freezing of grant aid for new projects, suspension of yen loans, withdrawal of Tokyo as a venue for India Development Forum, a 'cautious examination' of loans to India by international financial institutions, and imposition of strict control over technology transfers.[12] Japan took the lead in various international fora like the G-8 in condemning nuclear tests by India and Pakistan, while the Japanese Diet described the tests as constituting a threat to the very survival of human beings.[13]

This strong reaction from Japan was in many ways understandable, given that the Japanese are the only people to have experienced the brutality of nuclear weapons; that experience has continued to shape its world view.[14] Yet, many in India saw the Japanese reaction as hypocritical given that India's genuine security concerns were brushed aside even as Japan itself enjoyed the security guarantee of the US nuclear umbrella. As many in India see it, Japan's commitment to the Nuclear Non-Proliferation Treaty (NPT), in many ways, remains predicated upon its reliance on American nuclear deterrence.

As the major global powers re-evaluated their approach towards India post-Pokharan II, Japan also gradually came on board and the then PM, Yoshiro Mori, paid a symbolically important visit to India in 2000, envisaging a 'global partnership' between the two states, thereby putting the India–Japan relationship on an entirely new trajectory. Since then, a confluence of structural, domestic, and individual leadership factors has ensured that the India–Japan relationship would assume a dynamic not previously present.

STRUCTURAL FACTORS

Changing Balance of Power in the Asia-Pacific

It is almost conventional wisdom now that the centre of gravity of global politics is shifting from the Atlantic to the Pacific in recent years with the rise of China and India, gradual assertion by Japan of its military profile, and a significant shift in the US global force posture in favour of the Asia-Pacific.[15] The world seems to be entering a 'post-American' era, and the international system is trying to come to grips with the rise of China and all that it implies for global peace and stability.[16] While realizing fully well that it would take China decades to seriously compete with the US for true global hegemony, China has focused its strategic energies on Asia. Its foreign policy is aimed at enhancing its economic and military prowess to achieve regional hegemony in Asia. China's emphasis on projecting its rise as peaceful is aimed at allaying the concerns of its neighbours lest they try to counterbalance its growing influence.[17] Its readiness to negotiate with other regional states and to be an economically 'responsible' power is also a signal to other states that there are greater benefits in band-wagoning to China's growing regional weight rather than opposing its rise in any manner. China realizes that it has thrived because it devotes itself to economic development while letting the US police the region and the world. Even as it decries American hegemony, its leaders envision Pax Americana extending well towards the middle of this century, at least until China becomes a middle-class society and, if present trends continue, the world's largest economy.[18]

While the US still remains the predominant power in the Asia-Pacific, the rise of China is reshaping the strategic environment in the region. China, India, and Japan have long been viewed as the states with potential for great power status with inherent capacities to influence international economic, political, and military systems, but it is only in the last few years that these projections have come closer to being realized.[19] For more than a century it was Japan that dominated Asia first as an imperial power and more recently as the first Asian economy to achieve Western levels of economic development. It is China's turn now, which, while declaring that it will be focusing on internal socio-economic development for the next decade or so, is actively pursuing policies of preventing the rise of other regional powers such as India and Japan, or at least to limit their development relative to itself. China's resurgence is altering the power balance across the Asia-Pacific region, and in the absence of effective regional institutions the region is now at least as volatile as during the Cold War.[20]

Despite significant economic and trade ties between China and Japan underscored by China replacing the US as Japan's biggest trading partner in 2004, political tensions have increased in recent years, especially over the differing interpretations of history by the two nations.[21] There was public outcry in China in 2005 when Japan's education ministry approved history textbooks that were said to whitewash Japan's militarism in Asia during the first half of the last century. It is argued that about 2,00,000 to 3,00,000 Chinese were killed during the Japanese occupation of Nanjing that began in 1937. China asked Japan to take responsibility for the unrest in various Chinese cities that erupted with some subtle manipulation by the China's political establishment.[22] Japan, meanwhile, asked for an apology of its own from China for violent attacks against Japanese government offices and businesses in China. It also did not help when Tokyo's High Court rejected an appeal for compensation by Chinese survivors of biological warfare experiments conducted by Japan during the Second World War.[23]

But it would be a mistake to view these Sino-Japanese tensions merely through the prism of history. It is also about the future of Asian balance of power. At its foundation, what is fuelling these Sino-Japanese tensions is a burgeoning sense of strategic rivalry as China's power expands across Asia and Japan redefines its regional military role in close cooperation with the US and other regional actors.

Responding to the 'China Challenge'

The George W. Bush administration in the US backed the notion of a more assertive Japan, viewing Tokyo as an increasingly important partner at a time of dwindling support for the administration's policies among US allies. The US faces a prospect of an emerging power transition involving China, and the most consequential challenge for the US foreign policy in the coming decades will be to deal with this prospect. With this in mind, the US seems to be pursuing a policy of engaging China while simultaneously investing in increasing the power of other states located along China's periphery. This has involved not only reinvigorating its existing alliance with Japan but also reaching out to new partners such as India.[24] Japan and the US signed a pact to enhance cooperation on a ballistic missile defence system in 2004 that is due to be fully operational by 2011. The US has also encouraged Japan to forge close political and strategic ties with neighbouring states such as India and Australia.

India, meanwhile, is also gearing up to face China. India and China are two major powers in Asia with global aspirations and some significant conflicting interests. As a result, some amount of friction in their bilateral relationship is inevitable. The geopolitical reality of Asia makes sure that it will be extremely difficult, if not impossible, for *Hindi–Chini* to be *bhai-bhai* (brothers) in the foreseeable future.[25] If India and China continue to rise in the next few years, a security competition between the two regional giants will be all but inevitable. And if India is serious about its desire to emerge as a major global power, then it will have to tackle the challenge of China's rise. It is to tackle this challenge that Indian foreign policy is gearing up with its new approach towards the US and Japan.

India is now charting a new course in its foreign policy by getting closer to the US in recent years.[26] If India is indeed a 'swing state' in the international system, then it seems to have swung considerably towards the US. The demise of the Soviet Union liberated Indian and US attitudes towards each other from the structural confines of Cold War realities. As India pursued economic reforms and moved towards global integration, it was clear that the US and India will have to find a modus vivendi for a deeper engagement with each other. The Bush administration has transformed the nature of the US–India partnership by advocating civilian nuclear energy cooperation with India, thereby incorporating India into the global nuclear order as well as declaring that the US is committed to encouraging the growth of India as a great power.[27]

India's growing closeness to the US is also making Japan take India seriously and both are well aware of the Chinese strategy to contain the rise of its two most-likely challengers in the region. Both Tokyo and New Delhi seek to hedge against Chinese influence by trying to create stronger relations with other democracies in Asia. Both consider China a potential military threat that would have to be faced and countered in the coming years. The 2008 Defence White Paper of Japan expresses concern over the effects that the lack of transparency in China's defence policy and its military build-up will have on the regional state of affairs and on the security situation of Japan.[28] India's diplomatic and military posture is also increasingly geared towards countering China's rising profile.[29] The goal of Indo-Japanese cooperation is to ensure that China becomes less threatening and ultimately more cooperative.

India's ties with Japan have travelled a long way since May 1998 when a chill had set in after the former's nuclear tests with Japan imposing sanctions and suspending its Overseas Development Assistance (ODA). Since then, however, the changing strategic milieu in Asia-Pacific has brought the two countries together so much so that the last visit of the Indian PM Manmohan Singh to Japan in October 2008 resulted in the unfolding of a roadmap to transform a low-key relationship into a major strategic partnership. India and Japan have decided to invigorate all major aspects of their relationship ranging from investment, defence, science and technology, to civilian cooperation in space and energy security. The rise of China is a major factor in the evolution of Indo-Japanese ties as is the US attempt to build India into a major balancer in the region.

Both India and Japan are well aware of China's not so subtle attempts at preventing their rise. It is most clearly reflected in China's opposition to the expansion of the United Nations Security Council to include India and Japan as permanent members. China's status as a permanent member of the Security Council and as a nuclear weapons state is something that it would be loathe to share with any other state in Asia. India's 'Look East' policy of active engagement with ASEAN and East Asia remains largely predicated upon Japanese support. India's participation in the East Asia Summit was facilitated by Japan, and the East Asia Community proposed by Japan to counter China's proposal of an East Asia Free Trade Area also includes India. While China has resisted the inclusion of India, Australia, and New Zealand in ASEAN, Japan has strongly backed the entry of all three nations.

The massive structural changes taking place in the geopolitical balance of power in the Asia-Pacific are driving India and Japan into a relationship that is much closer than many could have anticipated even a few years back.

DOMESTIC-LEVEL FACTORS

Economic Complementarities and Trade Security

Domestic-level factors have also contributed to the recent convergence between Japan and India. The most important element is the change that the two economies have experienced in recent years, allowing them to focus on economic complementarities and exploit opportunities provided by each other. Japan is witnessing a steady decline as a major economic power, ranking twentieth among economies in gross domestic product (GDP) per capita as opposed to fourth 15 years ago. It remains the world's second-largest economy as measured by gross size even as some estimates suggest that by 2050 Japan's economy will be about the size of Indonesia's.[30] The current recession is forcing reforms and restructuring in the Japanese economy, and key sectors of the economy such as banking, securities, and telecommunications are opening up. Junichiro Koizumi moved more aggressively than any post-war Japanese leader to overhaul the banking system, deregulate big business, and open up the economy. His successors, however, have failed to follow through on the momentum he generated.[31] Despite its relative decline in recent years, Japan remains an economic giant rich in high technology and flush with investible capital. Japanese corporate culture is undergoing changes in light of the recent troubles and Japanese corporations are more willing to enter into global partnerships.

While China's image in Japan is one of cheap manufacturer and technological imitator, India's success in software development, internet business, and knowledge intensive industries is leading Japan to view India as the world's ascendant knowledge superpower.[32] For Japan, India has emerged as an attractive market, both for its growing consumer spending and cheap labour. Tokyo also has an interest in diversifying its Asian trading partners and reducing its dependence on China. Japan's modest growth over the past five years has been fuelled almost entirely by its exports to China with China–Japan trade now approaching $250 billion a year. Japan has invested more than $6 billion in China and has 20,000 companies operating there.[33] Japan's ability to invest any further in the Southeast Asian markets is also becoming limited even as a realization is growing that it has not benefited diplomatically from its role as the major trading partner and aid provider to Southeast Asia with China emerging as the dominant economic player in the region. Japan is seeking stable dependable destinations for large investment that India offers. India's remarkable economic growth over the last few years makes it ever more hungry for investments and technology. Though Japan has been India's biggest bilateral aid donor since 1986, India has now superseded China as the biggest recipient of such Japanese aid with 30 per cent of Japanese foreign aid coming to India.[34]

For long Japan continued to view India as a large and growing market for export of capital and technology but not foreign direct investment (FDI). India has made a strong push for more FDI and funds by providing guarantees on export finance, urging institutions such as the Japan Bank for International Cooperation to fund more infrastructure projects. Japan is gradually beginning to see the Indian market as an opportunity and Japanese investment in India is expected to reach $5.5 billion by 2011 from a meagre $515 million in 2006.[35]

Indo-Japanese trade has so far failed to reach full potential and much remains to be done. India has set up its first industrial park exclusive to Japanese investment to facilitate Japanese companies' entry into India. The conclusion of a bilateral Economic Partnership Agreement/ Comprehensive Economic Partnership Agreement (EPA/CEPA) is on the cards to boost bilateral trade which totalled about $10 billion in 2006–7.[36] Indian businesses, particularly in the information technology (IT) sector, in Japan have made great strides breaking into the market there in the last decade. The Japan–India economic relationship after stagnating for a while is finally infused with new energy. Companies such as Suzuki and Honda that have done well in India are doubling their production capacities with new Japanese companies following suit.[37] The most successful India–Japan business partnership to date is a venture by the automakers Suzuki and Maruti, which has become one of India's leading car-makers. India, which desperately needs more power generation, could be a particularly fertile market for Toshiba, which has bought the nuclear power plant manufacturer Westinghouse.

Infrastructure bottlenecks have often been cited by the Japanese businesses as a major obstacle to investing in India. Japanese investment in India is centred on manufacturing and needs infrastructure connectivity for export of goods manufactured inland. India is keen to learn from the experiences of Japan in infrastructure development as India's manufacturing and export potential are still crippled by an inability to move goods in and around the country. The most expensive development project in India—a $100 billion infrastructure project to create a hi-tech manufacturing and freight corridor between New Delhi and Mumbai—will have a third of its bill being paid by Japanese public and private money.

Both Japan and India rely on the security of the sea lanes of communication for their energy security and economic growth. They have a shared interest in guaranteeing the free transit of energy and trade between the Suez Canal and the Western Pacific. With this in mind, they are developing maritime capabilities to cooperate with each other and other regional powers. The navies of the two are now exercising regularly as well as the interactions between the coast guards is increasing with a view to combat piracy and terrorism and to cooperate on disaster relief operations. Japan feels that only the Indian Navy in the region can be trusted to secure the sea lanes in the Indian Ocean, vital for Japan's energy security.[38] It is also important for India to join hands with the much larger Japanese Navy, Asia's most powerful, to make sure that no adversarial power controls the regional waterways.

Changing Demographic Profiles

Japan's aging population and India's growing skilled workforce also make the two states ideal partners with great potential. Even as the proportion of population in the working age group will continue to rise in India, Japan's population will not only decline but the median age of its population will continue to increase. Japan has the world's highest population of elderly people and the lowest proportion of children. By 2050 population decline will have reduced economic growth to zero. Japan will lose 70 per cent of its workforce by 2050, and within 50 years the population, now 127 million, will fall by a third.[39] India, meanwhile, will be enjoying a 'demographic dividend' in the coming years as a big influx of young adults will give its labour force a boost with few children and elderly population to support. It is being suggested that the Japanese government should expand immigration to draw in more foreign workers with various skills, especially high-ability professionals who would stay in Japan longer and contribute to growth.[40] India will be a major beneficiary if the Japanese government does decide to undertake immigration reforms.

Changing Domestic Political Attitudes

Various Liberal Democratic Party (LDP) governments in recent years have been keen on amending the Japanese constitution, especially Article IX, so that Japan can possess armed forces like any other sovereign country and play its rightful role as a global power. The aim is to remove constitutional constraints that would allow Japan to engage in military activities beyond its current defensive activities. The LDP has stressed that Japan must fulfil its obligations in the global war and accept a security role commensurate with its economic clout. Since 11 September 2001, the Japanese military has undergone its most significant transformation since World War II, one that has brought it operationally closer to America's military even as it has generated concerns in northeast Asia.

Japan has begun to accept more responsibility for its own national defence and is seeking a more active role as an international security actor. Authorized by the country's so-called 'anti-terror' law implemented to provide logistical support for coalition forces operating in Afghanistan, Japan had refuelled US, United Kingdom (UK), and other nations' warships since November 2001. Japan's forces have been dispatched to the Indian Ocean and to Iraq as part of a more robust security policy. Japan has been providing at-sea refuelling to coalition vessels from several states performing maritime interdiction operations in the Indian Ocean. In Iraq, in accordance with a special law to aid in reconstruction, a symbolic ground force was deployed to a non-combat area in southern Iraq to engage in relief activities. After it left in 2006, Japanese planes began transporting American troops and cargo from Kuwait to Baghdad. The Japanese Self Defense Forces (SDF) engineering battalion is deployed in Samawah in Iraq and is working towards various reconstruction projects.[41] These Iraq missions have continued despite critics opposing these military dispatches as a violation of the country's constitution.[42] Japan now intends to withdraw its military airlift mission in Iraq in light of the security improvements there and a growing focus on Afghanistan. The Japanese government has now floated the idea of dispatching troops to Afghanistan.[43] As Japan moves forward in its attempt to redefine its security role in the region and beyond and to emerge as a 'normal' state, India will be only too willing to lend a helping hand, given the absence of conflicting interests between the two states. India–Japan defence and security cooperation will increase significantly as Japan takes on a greater share of providing regional security.

Unlike India's ties with China and the US, close relations with Japan have not been a political issue in India so far. Both the major political parties, the Congress and the Bharatiya Janata Party (BJP), have pursued similar policies vis-à-vis Japan in recent years. However, Japan's alliance with the US may become a contentious issue especially with the Left parties, if the Indo-Japanese strategic ties are seen to be cementing and taking on an anti-China posture.

Though both India and Japan continue to face serious economic and political challenges as they move on with their attempts to reform their economies and redefine their foreign and security policies, their evolving economic and security priorities are making it difficult for them to ignore each other as in the past.

INDIVIDUAL-LEVEL FACTORS

Individual leadership has also played a major role in facilitating enhanced India–Japan ties in recent years. Various Indian and Japanese leaders in the last few years have made significant contributions in this regard.

Indian Leaders Court Japan

The government of late P.V. Narasimha Rao not only unshackled the Indian economy but also gave a new direction to the Indian foreign policy. The 'Look East' policy was Rao's brain-child who had envisaged developing linkages with the ASEAN and its northern neighbours. The idea was to gain some political and economic space in a geopolitical environment where the former Soviet Union had imploded and Southeast Asia was growing rapidly. As a result, a degree of clarity, coherence, and progress was achieved in Delhi's relations with its eastern neighbours. As the then Finance Minister Manmohan Singh had acknowledged, India's 'Look East' policy was not just the gateway to trade for the region but a strategic shift in India's vision of the world as India sought greater engagement with hitherto neglected Asia-Pacific nations. Given that the region's rapid development was being underpinned by Japan's economic might, India also realized that one way to court Japan was by deepening its economic engagement with other Asia-Pacific states.[44] Rao visited Japan in 1992 and made it clear that Tokyo had garnered an important place in New Delhi's emerging foreign policy priorities.

Atal Bihari Vajpayee, the leader of the BJP-led government (1998 –2004), continued to pursue a proactive approach towards wooing India's east and southeast Asian neighbours. His visit to Japan in 2001 was crucial as it cemented the institutionalization of bilateral relations and widened their scope by including issues like global terrorism, Afghanistan, and economic and environmental issues. Vajpayee's visit also laid to rest the ghosts of Pokharan II as it was under his watch that India had conducted the nuclear tests resulting in a rapid deterioration in India–Japan ties. Vajpayee's successor, Manmohan Singh, has continued to work towards maintaining the momentum in Indo-Japanese ties. His last visit to Tokyo in 2008, resulted in India and Japan signing a significant declaration on security cooperation towards making their partnership 'an essential pillar for the future architecture of the region'. India is only the third country after the US and Australia with which Japan has decided to sign such an agreement. This security declaration essentially builds on the existing momentum in defence ties by focusing on Indo-Japanese joint efforts in counter-terrorism, piracy, non-proliferation, as well as policy coordination in regional affairs in the Asia-Pacific region.[45]

Japanese Leaders 'Rediscover' India

In a sign of evolving foreign policy priorities of Japan, all Japanese PMs since Mori, barring Fakuda who had a short tenure, have made it a point to visit India, and the two states have decided to hold annual talks at the prime ministerial level. Mori's visit to New Delhi in 2000, the first such visit in over a decade, broke the logjam in India–Japan ties since the Indian nuclear tests of 1998. Announcing a global partnership between India and Japan, Mori argued that the two states have a global responsibility in 'defending and spreading the values of democracy and freedom that India and Japan share'.[46] Mori continues to exert considerable influence in the ruling LDP, and his views have been embraced by other leaders of his party. His successor Koizumi, after taking charge in 2001, not only managed to convince the Japanese public of the need for painful economic reforms and restructuring but also reoriented Japanese foreign policy.[47] He continued to build on the gradual thawing of ties with India and led the initiative to bring India, Japan, Brazil, and Germany together to work towards their permanent membership in the United Nations Security Council. He worked with Indian PM Atal Bihari Vajpayee to give the relationship a strategic orientation.

But it was Shinzo Abe who was most enthusiastic about the future of India–Japan relationship and gave it an entirely new dimension. In his address to the joint session of the Indian Parliament in 2007, Abe talked about a 'broader Asia' [48]consisting of Pacific and Indian Ocean countries such as Japan, India, Australia, and the US that share common values of democracy, freedom, and respect for basic human rights. He argued for greater cooperation among these states. In his book, *Towards a Beautiful Country*, Abe makes the case about Japan advancing its national interests by strengthening its ties with India. He has argued: 'It will not be a surprise if in another decade Japan–India relations overtake Japan–US and Japan–China ties.'[49] Building on the idea of a triangular security dialogue between Washington, Tokyo, and Canberra initiated by his predecessor, Abe made known his desire to create a four-way strategic dialogue with the US, Australia, and India, a framework that Tokyo stresses will be based on their shared universal values such as freedom, democracy, human rights, and rule of law. This focus of Japanese leaders to frame their foreign policy on the basis of values is an attempt by the Japanese elites to adopt the tools that best help them enhance their influence and shape their security environment at any given time.[50] This has allowed India to emerge as a major foreign policy priority for Japan.

Abe's successor, Yasuo Fakuda, however, represented a break from the nationalist Abe and his predecessor Koizumi, and emphasized the importance of focusing on stronger ties with China. But with the coming to office of Taro Aso, who served as foreign minister under Abe, India–Japan ties, in all likelihood, will continue to follow the upward trajectory. The security declaration signed during Indian PM Manmohan Singh's last visit to Tokyo was largely a product of Aso's efforts to forge a new security architecture in the region.[51]

PROSPECTS FOR THE FUTURE

Due to a convergence of a range of factors in recent years, India and Japan seem to have rediscovered their common values and reaffirmed their proximity as ancient civilizations. Indian PM Manmohan Singh has aptly described India and Japan as 'civilizational neighbours'.[52] India and Japan are exemplars of how economic growth can be pursued in consonance with democratic values. A strategic partnership between Japan and India is also critical to the Asian power equilibrium. The rise of China and Japan's increasing strategic isolation in its own neighbourhood have motivated Japan to seek closer ties with India based not only on their interests but also on their shared liberal-democratic and free market values. For India, a strategic and economic partnership with Japan is central to its vision of a dynamic, multipolar Asia. Their democratic traditions, an absence of either any negative historical legacy or outstanding political issues, as well as a striking convergence of strategic interests in Asia and beyond provide a strong underpinning to Indo-Japanese bilateral ties.

Although bilateral relations appear to be extremely promising at the moment, a number of issues could slow or derail continued progress. India and Japan do share concerns about China's growing diplomatic weight, defence capability, and economic clout, but neither wishes to retrench or downgrade its own relations with China. The shadow of China will continue to loom large over the future trajectory of India–Japan ties, and neither would be too eager to form an open alliance against China. Immediately after signing a declaration on security cooperation during the last visit of Indian PM Manmohan Singh to Tokyo in 2008, both India and Japan sought to reassure China that their ties would not be at the cost of any third country, least of all China.[53]

Indian strategic elites crave for strategic autonomy in their nation's foreign policy. Therefore, while the US has played a crucial role in bringing India and Japan closer in recent years, any sign that India is courting Japan because of American pressures can be detrimental to the health of India–Japan bilateral partnership.[54] While the two main political parties in India remain well disposed towards Japan, their allies have often taken stridently anti-American postures largely for domestic political consumption. This reflexive anti-Americanism still retains its hold in a substantial part of Indian political establishment and can also hamper India's ties with Japan, especially if they are viewed as following too closely the pattern of Indo-US ties.

Domestic institutional constraints continue to operate as a major limitation on the potential of emerging Japanese foreign policy posture. One of the most influential determinants of Japanese foreign policy is the pre-eminence of Japanese career bureaucrats in the foreign ministry that makes radical shifts in policy difficult to accomplish. Though the capacity of national bureaucrats to maintain their traditional hold over policy is weakening as politicians are trying to get a stronger hold over the policy-making apparatus, the absence of strong political leadership continues to ensure that bureaucracy retains its decisive influence.[55] Weak political leadership and vertically divided administrations as well as fragmented domestic consensus will continue to adversely affect Japan's foreign policy. After five years of the charismatic Koizumi, Japan has now had two PMs fall from power without surviving a year in office. Japan needs still more reforms, and the present leadership does not seem to have the political capital to push them through. In the case of Japan's India policy, while the political leadership has provided the necessary momentum, the trade and security bureaucratic establishment continue to have a rather negative opinion of India.

The integration between Indian and Japanese economies remains shallow, and, since Japanese investments tend to follow Japanese trade as long as the India–Japan bilateral trade remains limited, Japanese investment is unlikely to pick up. For all the hype, India–Japan trade ties are growing at a glacial pace. The Japanese are falling significantly behind even when compared to the neighbouring South Korea.[56] In the services sector, the two countries have different demands on each other for opening up. For the Japanese, these are the maritime, insurance, civil aviation, and banking, while for India these include information technology, biotechnology, and medical. There remain differences on hi-tech trade with a number of Indian companies continuing to be on the blacklist of the Japanese government.[57] Japanese investors still find India's economic procedures a formidable barrier. Concerns that continue to plague Japanese investments in India include infrastructure inadequacy, a complicated legal and taxation system, and insufficient regulations for inter-state transactions. As a result, the vast opportunities provided by the financial and technological empowerment of India's expanding and highly skilled workforce along with India's huge market remain untapped.

This is despite the fact that FDI policies of India remain more attractive than China's and that over 80 per cent of foreign ventures in India remain profitable, earning above average returns. It has been suggested that Japanese businesses have focused too much on China and have failed to adequately appreciate India's rapid liberalization process and changing policy frameworks. The result has been that Japanese competitors from the US, the European Union (EU), and even South Korea have taken a lead over Japan in investing in India. The Indian PM Manmohan Singh in his address to the Diet in 2006[58] pointed out the disproportionately low levels of investments and underscored the need for more Japanese investment in India. India is seeking a shift in Japanese attitude from that of an aid giver to that of an investment partner for FDI, not ODA.

Though Japan has supported the US–India civilian nuclear energy cooperation treaty, there remain differences between Japan and India on the nuclear issue. Japan continues to insist that India sign the NPT and the Comprehensive Test Ban Treaty (CTBT) whereas India has no intention of doing so given its long-standing concerns regarding the discriminatory nature of these treaties. There has been a gradual evolution in the Japanese approach towards the Indian nuclear capability. It has refused to view the US–India nuclear pact as a danger to the global non-proliferation framework and was not an obstacle in the decision of the Nuclear Suppliers Group (NSG) to amend its guidelines enabling India to trade in nuclear technology and fuel. But the Japanese government has ruled out any civilian nuclear technology transfer to India, at least for the time being, as domestic sentiment in Japan remains strongly anti-nuclear.[59] Current Japanese law allows nuclear exports only to states that unlike India are either a party to the NPT or allow the International Atomic Energy Agency to safeguard all their nuclear facilities. If India decides to go in for more nuclear tests in the future, the Japanese government of the day would be forced to respond in a manner that may be inimical to India–Japan ties.

The regional security architecture in Asia still does not fully reflect current geo-economic realities. India is making a case that it is imperative for the wider Asian region to evolve within a cooperative framework if the region is to successfully meet the challenges of the twenty-first century. Yet, India has not found representation in agencies such as the Asia-Pacific Economic Cooperation (APEC), and its role in the ASEAN Regional Forum (ARF) and the ASEAN plus arrangements remains limited. Though Japan has helped India in its gradual integration into the Asia-Pacific regional order, India is still not viewed as an 'Asian' power. As Japan gets further integrated into the regional economic and political structures and India continues to lag behind, there is a real danger that the two states might not be able to realize the full potential of their relationship.

Japan's former PM Shinzo Abe is probably right that the 'Japan–India relationship is blessed with the largest potential for development of any bilateral relationship anywhere in the world'.[60] However, that potential will remain untapped if the two nations do not make the requisite effort in removing the remaining obstacles that continue to hamper their relationship.

NOTES

1.   This remark of a former American Ambassador is cited in William J. Long (2001), 'Nonproliferation as a Goal of Japanese Foreign Assistance', in Akitoshi Miyashita and Yoichiro Sato (eds), *Japanese Foreign Policy in Asia and the Pacific* (New York: Palgrave Macmillan), p. 132.

2.   See Pew Global Attitudes Project (2006), 'China's Neighbors Worry About Its Military Strength', 21 September, http://pewglobal.org/reports/pdf/255.pdf (accessed on 15 November 2008).

3.   See the Indian PM's Address to Joint Session of the Diet, 14 December 2006, http://pmindia.nic.in/visits.htm (accessed on 15 November 2008).

4. See the speech by the former Japanese PM Shinzo Abe at the Indian Parliament, 22 August 2007, http://www.mofa.go.jp/region/asia-paci/pmv0708/speech-2. html (accessed on 15 November 2008).

5. For a historical survey of India–Japan ties, see P.A. Narasimha Murthy (1986), *India and Japan: Dimensions of Their Relations* (New Delhi: ABC Publishing House), pp. 107–68.

6. Purnendra Jain (2008), 'Westward Ho! Japan Eyes India Strategically', *Japanese Studies*, 28 (2), pp. 14–19.

7. Details available at the Japanese Ministry of Foreign Affairs, http://www.mofa. go.jp/region/asia-paci/india/relation/relation.html (accessed on 15 November 2008).

8. B.M. Kaushik (1989), 'Japan's Defence Policy', in K.V. Kesavan (ed.), *Contemporary Japanese Politics and Foreign Policy* (London: Sangam Books Ltd), pp. 83–5.

9. Neville Maxwell (1970), *India's China War* (Dehra Dun: Natraj Publishers), pp. 270–1.

10. For a detailed examination of popular perceptions in Japan about India, see Purnendra Jain (2008), 'From Condemnation to Strategic Partnership: Japan's Changing View of India (1998–2007)', Working Paper No. 41, Institute of South Asian Studies, National University of Singapore, pp. 28–31.

11. Subrahmanyam Jaishankar (2000), 'India–Japan Relations After Pokharan-II', *Seminar*, 13 (3), March, http://www.india-seminar.com/2000/487/487%20 jaishankar.htm (accessed on 15 November 2008).

12. Ibid.

13. For a detailed explication of the role of non-proliferation in shaping Japan's foreign economic assistance, see Long, 'Nonproliferation as a Goal of Japanese Foreign Assistance', pp. 119–36.

14. On the evolution of the choices that confront Japan on the nuclear issue, see K. Ibo Singh (1989), 'Japan's Nuclear Policy', in Kesavan (ed.), *Contemporary Japanese Politics and Foreign Policy*, pp. 90–6.

15. For some of the most powerful articulations of this view, see Kishore Mahbubani (2008), *The New Asian Hemisphere: The Irresistible Shift of Global Power to the East* (New York: Public Affairs); Fareed Zakaria (2008), *The Post-American World* (New York: W.W. Norton & Co.).

16. Zakaria (2008), *The Post-American World*. The term 'post-American' has been used by Fareed Zakaria to describe his conception of the emerging global order.

17. For a discussion of the various interpretations of China's 'peaceful rise', see Evan S. Medeiros (2004), 'China Debates Its "Peaceful Rise" Strategy?', http://yaleglobal. yale.edu/display.article?id=4118 (accessed on 15 November 2008).

18. For a full explication of this argument, see Michael D. Swaine and Ashley J. Tellis (2000), *Interpreting China's Grand Strategy: Past, Present and Future* (Santa Monica, CA: Rand Corp.).

19. For an assessment of the great power potential of China, India, and Japan in the

1980s, see Stephen Cohen (1980), 'Toward a Great State in Asia?', in Onkar Marwah and Jonathan D. Pollack (eds), *Military Power and Policy in Asian States: China, India, and Japan* (Boulder, CO: Westview), pp. 9–41.

20. Bill Emmott (2008), *Rivals: How the Power Struggle between China, India and Japan will Shape Our Next Decade* (London: Allen Lane), pp. 1–24.

21. On the role of nationalism in the shaping of Japan–China ties, see Yutaka Kawashima (2003), *Japanese Foreign Policy at the Crossroads* (Washington, DC: Brookings Institution Press), pp. 104–6.

22. Robert Marquand (2005), 'Anti-Japan Protests Jar an Uneasy Asia', *The Christian Science Monitor*, 11 April.

23. 'Asian Row Turns to Wartime Past', *The BBC*, 19 April 2005, http://news.bbc.co.uk/1/hi/world/asia-pacific/4459243.stm (accessed on 15 November 2008).

24. Ashley Tellis (2007), 'India in Asian Geopolitics', in Prakash Nanda (ed.), *Rising India: Friends and Foes* (New Delhi: Lancer Publishers), pp. 123–7.

25. 'Hindi–Chini Bhai Bhai' (Indians and Chinese are Brothers) was a popular slogan during the 1950s, the heyday of Sino-Indian relationship, which became discredited after the 1962 Sino-Indian war.

26. Sumit Ganguly (2003–4), 'India's Foreign Policy Grows Up', *World Policy Journal*, 20 (4), pp. 41–7.

27. Harsh V. Pant (2008), *Contemporary Debates in Indian Foreign and Security Policy* (New York: Palgrave Macmillan), pp. 19–37.

28. Annual White Paper, Ministry of Defence, 2008, http://www.mod.go.jp/e/publ/w_paper/index.html (accessed on 15 November 2008).

29. Harsh V. Pant (2007), 'India in the Asia-Pacific: Rising Ambitions with an Eye on China', *Asia-Pacific Review*, 14 (1), pp. 54–71.

30. Blaine Harden (2008), 'Japan's Long, Slow Economic Slide', *Washington Post*, 3 February.

31. 'Another Lost Decade?', *Wall Street Journal*, 31 October 2008.

32. Martin Fackler (2008), 'Losing and Edge, Japanese Envy India's Schools', *New York Tmes*, 2 January.

33. Jim Hoagland (2008), 'New Allies in Asia', *Washington Post*, 11 May.

34. 'Striking a Balance', *The Hindu*, 24 October 2008.

35. Heather Timmons (2007), 'As Japan and India Forge Economic Ties, a Counterweight to China is Seen', *New York Times*, 21 August.

36. Shubhajit Roy (2008), 'PM invites Japan to Set Up Plants in India', *The Indian Express*, 29 October 2008.

37. Masanori Kondo (2008), 'India as an Emerging "Brain Power"', *The Asahi Shimbun*, 10 March.

38. Sandeep Dikshit (2007), 'Japanese Energy Security is Dependent on the Indian Navy', *The Hindu*, 1 September.

39. Blaine Harden (2008), 'Japan Steadily Becoming a Land of Few Children', *Washington Post*, 6 May.

40. Takeo Hoshi and Anil K. Kashyap (2008), 'A Blueprint for Reforming Japan', *Wall Street Journal*, 12 September.

41. See the testimony of Christopher R. Hill (2005), 'US Relations with Japan', Senate Foreign Relations Committee, 29 September, http://www.state.gov/p/eap/rls/rm/2005/54110.htm (accessed on 15 November 2008).

42. On the continuing domestic opposition to the LDP's plans to revise the constitution, see Leo Lewis (2007), 'Abe's Vision of a New Japan Prompts March', *The Times* (London), 4 May.

43. 'Japan Weighs Military Withdrawal from Iraq', *Associated Press*, 11 September 2008.

44. Purnendra Jain (2002), 'India's Calculus of Japan's Foreign Policy in Pacific Asia', in Takashi Inoguchi (ed.), *Japan's Asian Policy: Revival and Response* (New York: Palgrave Macmillan), pp. 220–7.

45. Details of India–Japan Joint Declaration on Security Cooperation are available at http://www.mofa.go.jp/region/asia-paci/india/pmv0810/joint_d.html (accessed on 15 November 2008).

46. Jain, 'India's Calculus of Japan's Foreign Policy in Pacific Asia', p. 231.

47. Michael Green (2008), 'After Fakuda', *Wall Street Journal*, 3 September.

48. See note 57.

49. Shinzo Abe (2006), *Utsukushii kuni e: jishin to hokori no moteru Nihon e* (Tokyo: Bungei Shunju), p. 160.

50. Michael J. Green (2007), 'Japan is Back: Why Tokyo's New Assertiveness is Good for Washington', *Foreign Affairs*, 86 (2) (March/April), pp.142–7.

51. Siddharth Varadarajan (2008), 'India, Japan Say New Security Ties Not Directed Against China', *The Hindu*, 23 October.

52. See note 3.

53. P. Vaidyanathan Iyer (2008), 'Eye on China, India and Japan Ink Security Pact', *The Indian Express*, 23 October.

54. For a view cautioning India against developing closer ties with Japan upon US prodding, see Achin Vanaik (2006), 'Containing China', *The Telegraph* (Kolkata), 26 December.

55. Tanaka Akihiko (2000), 'Domestic Politics and Foreign Policy', in Inoguchi Takashi and Purnendra Jain (eds), *Japanese Foreign Policy Today* (New York: Palgrave Macmillan), pp. 7–11.

56. See Walter Andersen's chapter in this volume for details.

57. See *Report of India–Japan Joint Study Group*, June 2006, http://www.mofa.go.jp/region/asiapaci/india/report0606.pdf (accessed on 15 November 2008).

58. See note 3.

59. P.S. Suryanarayana (2008), 'No Civil Nuclear Aid from Japan, for Now', *The Hindu*, 21 September.

60. See the speech by the former Japanese PM Shinzo Abe at the Indian Parliament, 22 August 2007, http://www.mofa.go.jp/region/asia-paci/pmv0708/speech-2.html (accessed on 15 November 2008).

11

The Evolution of India's Relations with Russia

Tried, Tested, and Searching for Balance

DEEPA M. OLLAPALLY

As the Cold War ended and the Soviet Union collapsed, India's most important strategic partnership seemed to be in danger as well. Indeed, in 1991 India faced an unprecedented twin challenge: first, its economy was in crisis with foreign exchange reserves hitting an unacceptably low level at only two weeks' worth of imports; second, the entire underpinning of its four-decades' old foreign policy was being destroyed with no easy replacement. Since then, Russia's importance to India has waxed and waned, never reaching the romantically high levels of years past, nor fading into irrelevance as some might have predicted in the early 1990s. What has driven India's policy towards this distant neighbour, and where are relations headed? Are the factors underlying Indian foreign policy constant or have they changed over time?

This chapter will consider three levels of analysis to assess Indian foreign policy towards the Soviet Union/Russia: the international system, the nation-state, and individual decision-making realms.[1] In considering these different explanations, it may be noted that from the 1950s to the current period, we have witnessed massive changes at all three levels: internationally, bipolarity has given way to unipolarity or multi-polarity; India has gone from a largely one-party democracy to coalitional democracy; and decision-makers at India's helm have come from a wide spectrum of ideological leanings. As for the Soviet Union, domestic and ideological changes are nothing less than epic.

I will first set up the theoretical framework and proceed to examine Indian foreign policy in light of the international, domestic, and ideological factors. The emphasis will be on the post-1991, post-Cold War period since it remains the least understood, but the Nehruvian and post-Nehruvian eras prior to 1991 have important historical markers. To anticipate, this chapter will argue that a combination of systemic and ideological factors motivated Indian foreign policy towards the Soviet Union, and that, somewhat surprisingly, similar elements explain Indian policy towards the new Russia. Relatively speaking, strategic factors at the systemic level prove to be primary, buttressed by ideational forces. The main difference in India's approach to the Soviet Union versus its successor Russia is a lack of clear commitment in the current period—something that can be said for both sides. We are also at a possible transitional moment: the September 2008 civil nuclear deal struck between India and the US could be a 'game changer' in that much of Russia's attractiveness having to do with sensitive technology sales and transfers to India under a regime of technology denial since the early 1970s spearheaded by the United States (US) is now being dismantled by the US itself.

THE DRIVERS OF INDIAN FOREIGN POLICY

In assessing the importance of the systemic, state, and decision-making levels to explain Indian foreign policy towards the Union of Soviet Socialist Republics (USSR)/Russia, it is useful to state what we would expect as evidence for each. For the systemic level, strategic factors and security concerns would be predominant, as realism would predict. For a strong systemic argument, we would see these factors dominate even at the expense of economic gain or ideological preferences. For a domestic-level argument, we would expect the calculation of political gains and losses to be determining the nature of policy. Finally, at the decision-making level, a number of factors might be at work: strength or weakness of the leadership, ideological preferences, or idiosyncrasies of a given leader.

None of the aforementioned variables has remained constant between the mid-1950s and now, and Indian policy itself has been shifting—most furiously since the nuclear tests of 1998. India's new ties with the US as well as its economic growth and rise to the status of a global economic player are the most obvious changes. But Indian foreign policy has also become more diversified and less predictable. In particular, relations between India and Russia have had to be significantly refashioned since the end of the Cold War.[2] The declining and uncertain relations of the 1990s have, however, given way to a more stable, if much weaker, relationship under Vladimir

Putin's leadership, spanning the diverse regimes led by the Bharatiya Janata Party and the Congress in India. What explains this?

EXAMINING THE INTERNATIONAL SYSTEM

The convergence of Indian and Russian interests is evident in three arenas: global, regional, and bilateral. In all of them, the incentives for closer relations are, by and large, strategic and military in nature. Increasingly though, narrow defence commerce is a primary factor—giving a less compelling basis for a durable relationship than before. India and the Soviet Union first found common ground in challenging and opposing American power under bipolarity from the 1950s well into the 1980s. Soon after independence in 1947, India's main objective was to protect its new-found freedom from colonial rule and to avoid falling into an asymmetrical power relationship with the world's pre-eminent power, the US.[3] Prime Minister Jawaharlal Nehru's strong inclination was to keep a fine balance of nonalignment between the US and the USSR, but the idea of nonalignment or equidistance proved particularly grating to the US. For the Americans, the bipolar order represented not just a power equation but a stark ideological and even moral choice between communism and capitalist democracy. Secretary of State John Foster Dulles is one of the most well-known US officials who showed frustration with India's stand. American frustration was no doubt compounded when in practice India tilted towards the Soviets.[4] India's outcry over the Western military response to Egypt's nationalization of the Suez Canal in 1956, but silence after the Soviet intervention against Hungary's anti-communist uprising the same year, is telling in this regard. Moreover, Nehru's own preference for socialist economics and a barely hidden anti-Westernism also marked the foundation of India's foreign policy. In contrast, Pakistan's willingness to join the American camp in the US–Soviet struggle and their close military ties from 1954 onwards more or less guaranteed that Indo-US relations would not be smooth or easy.

The Nehruvian legacy of close ties with the Soviets and statist economics outlasted Nehru's death in 1964 and well after, fully crumbling only by 1991. India's humiliating defeat in the war with China in 1962 and the clash between the Soviets and Chinese on their border in 1969 had given the USSR and India a common adversary in the wider Asian region. The US rapprochement with China in 1971 and Pakistan's role as facilitator, given its friendship with Beijing and Washington, were viewed as highly threatening by India.[5] As the Bangladesh crisis unfolded in March 1971 and the Americans were seen to be 'tilting' towards Pakistan, the importance of the Soviet Union to India increased dramatically. New Delhi finally signed a Treaty of Friendship and Cooperation with Moscow in August 1971, giving India a vital partner as the crisis escalated into war between India and Pakistan in December 1971.

Although the 1971 break-up of Pakistan led to India's undisputed predominance in South Asia, the international alliance structure was unfavourable for India and favourable for its arch rival Pakistan. This kept India 'hemmed in' in South Asia and prevented it from playing a bigger role on the international scene. The external system only became more polarized with the Soviet intervention in Afghanistan in 1979, with India standing by the Soviets and against the US that was viewed as bringing the Cold War back to India's neighbourhood. Indian PM Rajiv Gandhi and US President Ronald Reagan attempted to nudge Indo-US relations closer in the mid-1980s, taking off on Indira Gandhi's small steps in this direction. The hesitant liberalization by India during the 1980s had produced some results: average growth rates had increased to 5.5 per cent from the earlier perennial so-called Hindu growth rate of about 3.5 per cent.[6] This move proved to be politically unsustainable and Indian politicians after Rajiv Gandhi did not maintain the momentum. With such little change at the political and strategic levels, India's relations with the Soviet Union remained primary. Thus, at the end of the Cold War, India was hardly prepared for a world that was suddenly unipolar.

From the early 1990s onwards, American predominance led to experimentation by both India and Russia in dealing with unipolarity, sometimes in tandem, at other times, not. It is safe to say that neither was willing to concede American hegemony; their underlying beliefs were that the US was experiencing more of a 'unipolar moment' and that a more multipolar world was not impossible. The rise of Chinese power during the last 15 years has been an important, if unstated, catalyst for convergence of Indo-Russian interests on the regional stage. The common unease over China has taken on a very different form than it did under the Soviets, but the logic has not disappeared. At the same time, India's policies became increasingly tempered by the steady improvement in its relations with the US, beginning in earnest since 2001.

Coping with Unipolarity

In the aftermath of Soviet collapse in 1991 and a radical narrowing of Russia's strategic purview, India found itself cut adrift from its traditional foreign policy partner. Coming at a time when India was facing one of the most serious economic crisis in its history, the country was forced to craft an entirely new strategic framework with little confidence regarding Russia's reliability or a clear idea of its role vis-à-vis the subcontinent. Long accustomed to being defined by its superpower status on the global scene, Russia's search for a new identity initially seemed confused and caught in particular between the pulls of hard nationalism and some form of internationalism. From India's perspective, the central question was whether Russia would perceive itself first and foremost as a European power or a Eurasian one, and what its new role would be in a global system that went from being bipolar to unipolar.

Strictly speaking, the security environment did not present new threats per se for India. But the lack of a great power 'ally' did leave India exposed to any negative future developments. While Russia was 'collecting itself'[7] during the 1990s, India took several uncharacteristically bold steps in the changed global arena. These actions—weaponization of its nuclear capability; deep economic reforms amounting to an overhaul of the Nehruvian paradigm; and a diversification of its external ties such as PM Narasimha Rao's 'Look East' policy—may have been taken even if the Cold War had never ended. But there can be little doubt that the changed international environment played a key part. All these steps were also consistent with India's long-standing obsession to protect its strategic autonomy, which explained why India had never joined any military pacts or security alliances, even at the height of the Cold War.[8] Indeed, some might say that India's unwillingness to throw its lot decisively with one of the superpowers during that time left it vulnerable, revealing a lack of hard-headed realist thinking. Conversely, given that India did not have the capability to 'go it alone' militarily against a more powerful state in the 1950s and 1960s, internal balancing was not a viable option. Thus, we are compelled to see India's choice to stay aloof from alliances as pointing to the strength of its ideological preference for autonomy—something that is deeply rooted in its strategic culture. Such a preference is not just historical, as India's relations with Russia in recent years illustrate.

As the historic Russian transformation got underway, India found itself severely disadvantaged vis-à-vis Russia, having had close ties with the old Soviet Union and few friends among Russia's so-called new democrats who were swept into power with Boris Yeltsin in 1991.[9] Within the Russian establishment, the foreign ministry under pro-Western Andrei Kozyrev relegated India to a secondary position. President Yeltsin's clear tilt towards the Western world and the search for a European identity (continuing the trend begun by his predecessor Mikhail Gorbachev) were interpreted as turning his back on Russia's Eurasian identity. Yeltsin's gamble failed to pay off as envisioned: the country had expected rich dividends in the form of economic largesse and a nod to its great power status by the US. Instead, as Russia's economic health plunged, the leadership learnt the hard way that little relief would be forthcoming on its huge debt, of which an astounding $100 billion was simply inherited loans from the Soviet days. Domestic economics under the new market system did no better, with the resulting hybrid often described popularly as 'criminal capitalism'. In addition, the first stage of the expansion of the North Atlantic Treaty Organization (NATO) and the large-scale military action against Yugoslavia in spring 1999 were double shocks for those Russians who had expected greater sensitivity to Russia's security concerns despite its loss of international stature.[10] The upshot of Russia's disillusionment with the West was the landslide victory of Vladimir Putin in March 2000. Putin was surrounded by personnel from the country's intelligence services (former Committee for State Security (KGB) and then Federal Security Service of the Russian Federation (FSB) who held the view, fairly widespread among Russia's elite, that the drive towards the European community and the US had failed to produce adequate results.

Russia's search for a European identity thus suffered a loss of credibility, to be replaced in part by more realist notions of international power and a willingness to let pragmatism dictate foreign policy. Putin made it clear at the outset that 'pragmatism' was second only to 'national interests' as a key principle of Russian foreign policy, both followed by 'economic efficiency'.[11] Putin's conceptions of Russia's power have tended to hark back to its past great power and status as an independent power axis. Thus, rather than conforming to unipolarity as in the 1990s, Putin's regime sought to counter and even challenge it at times. This reorientation under Putin included a more robust relationship with non-European regional powers, in particular India and Iran. The receptivity of India's leadership across political parties to Russia's renewed overtures showed its own pragmatism. It also revealed a convergence of world views that chafed at unipolarity, although Putin's antipathy against it has been far more pronounced than India's.

BILATERALISM IN DEFENCE

During the Cold War years, India's defence ties reflected the reality that the Soviets were consistently more open to providing high technology and advanced military equipment than the US, which denied India items like the Cray supercomputer in 1987 because of its military and civilian dual-use capability. Historically, the Soviets had also accepted India's pre-eminence in South Asia, rather than seeing the region through the lens of

Indo-Pakistan relationship, as the US was repeatedly prone to do. From India's perspective, Pakistan's ability to 'borrow power' from the US not only denied New Delhi its rightful place in the region, but emboldened Pakistan militarily against India.

Putin's trip to India in October 2000 with a 70-member delegation and his high-profile stopover at the Bhabha Atomic Research Centre (BARC), India's premier nuclear research institution, symbolically underscored this type of attitude by Russia towards India even after the nuclear tests, distinguishable from American denunciation after the tests. Putin described BARC, the country's nuclear nerve centre, as a 'temple of science and technology', and struck a note of tolerance for India's decision to hold off on signing the Comprehensive Test Ban Treaty (CTBT).[12] The Russian president visited BARC with R. Chidambaram, the then Chairman of the Atomic Energy Commission, and Anil Kakodkar, Director of BARC, both closely connected to the 1998 Pokhran tests. The two sides signed the Declaration of Strategic Partnership during Putin's trip, providing critical impetus to the relationship. Against this backdrop was the fact that earlier in the year, US President Bill Clinton had also visited India, signalling that major changes were afoot in global perceptions of India, not just by Russia.

In response to Russia's prolonged indifference in the 1990s, India's foreign policy managers seem to have made a virtue out of necessity. Their drive for diversification of India's friends meant more foreign policy options. For example, New Delhi attempted to redress the long neglect of the Asia-Pacific region by cultivating ties with Singapore, South Korea, and, to a lesser extent, Japan (as Walter Andersen's chapter in this volume shows). The most dramatic shift was the breakthrough achieved in Indo-US relations, culminating in Bill Clinton's historic visit in 2000, despite India's nuclear tests two years earlier. Some termed this the beginning of an American 'India-first' policy (in contrast to a hyphenated Indo-Pakistan equation), bringing it closer to Russia's traditional view of India. As India's economic and military clout increased since the late 1990s, the urgency for a partnership with Russia receded for India. That Indian policymakers have not neglected relations with Russia suggests careful calculation about the role of Russia in India's foreign policy even as it moves closer to the US.

Arms Sales

One area in which Indo-Russian ties have been nearly unbroken is arms transfers, although India faced a crunch in getting spare parts and equipment immediately after the Soviet Union's collapse. Even without the strategic and ideological dimensions of the earlier ties, the two countries have maintained a fairly steady relationship in this techno-commercial sector. The Indian leadership perceives defence deals with Russia as holding the advantage of price competitiveness, cutting-edge technology, and the potential for technology transfers, as well as the Indian military's familiarity with Russian equipment. India's need to upgrade its Soviet-made conventional weapons arsenal and to step up the modernization and expansion of its defence capabilities (especially after the 1999 conflict with Pakistan in Kargil) led it back to the Russians. Besides, because Russia is not in a position to finance production of weapons on a large scale, it has more incentive to conduct joint development and production of weapons systems, something that India welcomes, given its own commitment to improving its defence industry.[13]

The stimulus for the arms trade since 1991 from the Russian side has been its pressing need to earn hard currency and safeguard its embattled defence industry. Russia's commercial imperatives in its defence sector are considerable: it inherited a huge military–industrial complex comprising 1,600 defence enterprises with nearly 2 million personnel. The stark reality was that without major outside markets, Russia's defence industries would languish. Large firms such as MiG MAPO were given the right to engage in arms transactions directly. Deputy PM Ilya Klebanov promised India that 'big contracts, joint work and joint production of arms are waiting for us [India and Russia] in the future'.[14] From India's point of view, this type of openness is extremely attractive given its persisting commitment to improve indigenous capability. The importance of India for Russia's defence industry may be gauged by the fact that Indians buy more military hardware from the Russian defence industry than Russia's own military forces.

Putin's visit to India in January 2007 (his fourth) was as India's chief guest at the Republic Day celebrations, an honour reserved for special friends. (His predecessor Yeltsin had visited India only once, in 1993.) A great deal of the military equipment on display during the ceremonies was of Russian origin, a reminder of the strong bonds. The agreements forged during his trip have cemented the ties that his regime rejuvenated and demonstrated that Delhi's growing ties with the US have not negatively impinged on Indo-Russian relations. In a joint statement after a meeting between Indian PM Manmohan Singh and Russian President Putin, Russia offered to build four new nuclear power plants in India, in addition to the two reactors that are already under construction.[15] Coming on the heels of the historic US legislation allowing Washington to cooperate with India on its civilian nuclear power programme, the dialogue on nuclear reactor sales between India and Russia was noteworthy. As one Indian expert put it, 'It tells the Indian population that we are not on the US bandwagon', harking back to popular and elite views on the importance of autonomy.[16] But the significance of Russia's offer went beyond atmospherics: so far, Indian defence scientists and sections of the foreign policy establishment continue to repose greater confidence in Russia's long-term reliability as a supplier of critical nuclear-related technology and equipment than the US. Thus, although it is the US policy shift allowing in effect 'an India exception' to the non-proliferation regime and Nuclear Suppliers Group (NSG) guidelines, Russia is better poised, at least for the moment, to take advantage of this potential market (an estimated high of $100 billion) thanks to its track record and perceived lack of political constraints unlike the US.

Moscow has favoured India in defence production as well. India was selected by Moscow in 2007 to jointly develop the fifth generation fighter aircraft and a multi-purpose transport aircraft. As early as 2000, Putin had assured the Indian leadership that Russia was willing to share any cutting-edge defence technologies that it had; this became evident in the subsequent joint development and production of weapons such as the Brahmos supersonic cruise missile, a highly advanced system.[17] Despite these favourable steps and long history, other developments suggest that Russia's near monopoly on arms sales to India may be coming to an end.

New US Opportunities

India is fast becoming a very attractive target for arms exporters from the West, with the addition of US firms into the fray since 2005. India is the developing world's largest arms importer; the value of its arms imports is expected to reach $30 billion by 2012 and a stunning $80 billion by 2022.[18] Although Russia remains the most important supplier at over 70 per cent, it is facing increasing competition in the Indian arms market and is thus trying to protect its market share. For example, in 2006, Russia set up a consignment warehouse and a service centre in India called Rosoboron Service as part of a joint venture, which is expected to meet India's significant demand for timely and uninterrupted supply of spare parts and repair and maintenance of Soviet and Russian equipment.[19] But on India's most lucrative proposed purchase—126 new fighter jets at approximately $11 billion to replace aging Russian MiGs—there is every chance that its traditional suppliers from Russia and France will be edged out by the US. This deal is touted as the biggest single fighter aircraft purchase in 30 years, since a combined European F-16 purchase in the mid-1970s.

The path for major American inroads into the Indian market is being rapidly paved. In 2007, India filled its need for military transport planes and helicopters by placing a $2 billion order with Lockheed Martin Corporation, the largest defence contractor in the US and the Pentagon's number one supplier. The six C-130J 'Super Hercules' aircraft transaction represents the first Indian purchase of US military aircraft and a major breakthrough for American companies.[20] In the longer term, Lockheed expects opportunities to open up for sales of command and control systems, Patriot Advanced Capability-3 missile interceptors, anti-tank guided missile systems, and other advanced weapons systems. To assist American companies Lockheed and Boeing in the race for India's order of 126 fighter jets, the US government cleared the way for them to offer cutting-edge radar technology as part of their bids.[21] Unlike the past, Russia cannot expect to have a clear advantage in its offer of MiG-35s in this high-stakes competition. Even on the question of cost competitiveness, as Lockheed's top executive on South Asia, Richard Kirkland argues, India will need to consider immediate cost savings of Russian equipment versus higher quality, better capability, and performance of US-made systems. As he puts it, 'It's a choice of mass versus precision.'[22]

India's turn to alternative providers is also spurred by defence transactions with Russia that have been nothing short of vexing. A high-profile and long-running deal that seems to defy an easy resolution is Russia's sale of a critical aircraft carrier to India. After years of negotiations beginning in the 1990s for the purchase of Russian aircraft carrier Admiral Gorshkov (*INS Vikramaditya*), to be retrofitted to Indian specifications, an agreement was finally signed in 2004. The price tag was given as $1.5 billion for the carrier along with a complement of deck aircraft (16 MiG 29K) and training for the crew. But in 2007, the deal became mired in controversy when the Russians announced that they could meet neither the original cost nor the delivery date of 2008.[23] Some reports suggested that the Russians were asking up to an additional $1.2 billion in unexpected cost increases, with India balking.[24] Since the Admiral Gorshkov would give the Indian Navy a much sought after capability, this was a huge blow. Despite public pledges by the Indian officials that they would not pay more than the agreed upon price, in March 2008 it was reported that India would give an additional $600–$800 million for delivery in 2010. Without another carrier, the Indian Navy's potential blue water capability would be seriously in question. There are no other suitors on this, although there was some public discussion about the US having offered its *Kitty Hawk* aircraft carrier in March 2008, dismissed by the

Navy as unfounded rumours. India is also holding out hopes for leasing nuclear-powered submarines, on which Russia has been equivocating, apparently in response to US pressure. With the progress made on the US–India nuclear deal (see later), this could change. A senior Russian official's prediction some years ago that 'the teeth of the Indian Navy will continue to be Russian' may hold only for the near term.[25]

Reliability Issue

India has a long memory, and it may be difficult for the US to live down its past disruption of low enriched uranium for India's Tarapore power plant after 1974, despite the existence of an Indo-US agreement that had the force of an international treaty. In contrast, Russia supplied 50 tons of low enriched uranium for Tarapore under the safety exception clause in 2005. At the time, the US had expressed its reservations regarding Russia supplying nuclear fuel to India. Nicholas Burns, Undersecretary of State for Political Affairs, had stated, 'We think the proper sequencing would be that if India needs nuclear fuel for its reactors in Tarapur, that the proper way to do this would be to have the U.S. Congress act, hopefully change our laws, have the NSG act and change NSG practices, then countries would be free to engage at that point in civil nuclear trade with India'.[26] Russia's decision to assist India *before* the NSG consensus and US Congressional approval of the historic US–India nuclear deal in September 2008, demonstrated a new assertiveness: in 1993 during the turbulent post-Soviet days, Moscow had been forced under US pressure to rescind its agreement to provide India cryogenic engine technology for its space programme. But then again, transactions like Lockheed's C-130J sale could change India's perceptions about the US. Lt General Jeffrey Kohler, the former top arms sales official at the Pentagon, believes that '... every sale helps all U.S. companies looking to enter the Indian market. It helps build trust and confidence'.[27]

In the broader energy sector, Russia's importance to India is likely to keep growing as the Indian economy expands at an unprecedented rate. By 2030, India is expected to become the third-largest energy consumer, behind the US and China, and ahead of Russia and Japan. At the 2007 summit, between President Putin who was visiting India as the chief guest at India's Republic Day celebrations and PM Singh, the Indian leader declared that, 'Energy security is the most important of the emerging dimensions of our strategic partnership.' He went on to add that 'Russia remains indispensable to India's strategic interests'.[28] Russia's oil output has risen dramatically (after dropping nearly 50 per cent from the Soviet era peak), making it the world's second-largest producer, behind only Saudi Arabia. Russia is the world's largest producer of natural gas and has the biggest share of the world's gas reserves (32 per cent).[29] India's Oil and Natural Gas Corporation (ONGC) Videsh (the external arm of the state-owned oil and gas company) is gaining an important foothold in Russia's oil and natural gas production, especially on Sakhalin Island. ONGC Videsh was allowed to acquire a 20 per cent stake in the Sakhalin I project totalling more than $2 billion, India's largest investment abroad. India is also slated to gain even greater access through Russia's planned Sakhalin 3 project—a much sought after prize. Coming at a time when Western companies are deliberately being shut out of Russia's hydrocarbon projects, this sends a strong message.[30]

Putin has been the key architect of what might be termed energy 'power politics', and his hand-picked successor, Dmitry Medvedev, who took over in May 2008 as president, was initially viewed as a more moderate face towards the West. Still, he was expected to retain Putin's assertive foreign policies that have proved to be popular at home. Medvedev himself headed Gazprom, Russia's gas monopoly, which came to symbolize Russia's hard-line foreign policy.[31] With Putin becoming PM, his influence is unlikely to disappear any time soon.[32] The crisis over Georgia and Russia's choice of swift military action over diplomacy in 2008 was a stark reminder that accommodating the West had its limits. Western commentators were left asking whether 'there was a return to the bad old Cold War days'. Coming at a critical period in the Indo-US negotiations over the nuclear deal, India was in an awkward position, but took the view that it was not a matter of concern to New Delhi.

This situation could become more complex as India has been given the all-important waiver allowing international nuclear trade with it—at the International Atomic Energy Agency (IAEA), the NSG, and the US Congress. At every stage of this historic accommodation of India (a non-signatory to the Nuclear Non-Proliferation Treaty with nuclear weapons capability), the US has taken the lead in prodding key states to go along with the exception. The US did this despite the very real possibility that its corporate sector will not be the biggest beneficiary of the projected $100–150 billion market in India for nuclear reactors and related material. Rather, France and, most importantly, Russia stand to gain the most. The US is expected to gain about 30 per cent of the market; according to experts at the US–India Business Council, the premier US business lobby for the historic agreement, even this share is extremely valuable, with estimates of up to 75,000 jobs in the US being created as a result.[33] The Bush administration's persistent efforts to extricate India from existing nuclear technology denial regimes—risking the credibility of the global non-proliferation framework—and its success in doing so, have hardly been lost on Indian decision-makers.[34]

Apart from the nuclear arena, another area that used to distinguish Indo-Russian cooperation was the space sector—considered by many Indian scientists and policymakers as India's 'crown jewel' in high technology. An agreement for long-term collaboration in the joint development, operation, and use of Russia's GLONASS global navigation system for peaceful purposes was signed during Putin's 2004 visit to India. This cooperation envisions the launching of new Russian satellites from Indian launch pads with the assistance of Indian launch vehicles. Its effect will be to reduce India's dependence on the American Global Positioning System. There is some opinion that even foresees Indo-Russian use of GLONASS extending into the military sector.[35] Whatever the ultimate use, space cooperation is being taken to a higher level than ever before, thus bringing together a critical and strategic sector in the two countries. Here too, however, the US is making inroads with India. In October 2008, India's maiden unmanned moon mission Chandrayan I's payloads included that of the US National Aeronautic Space Administration (NASA), something unimaginable just a few years earlier.

Beyond the realm of techno-commercial relationship, Indo-Russian relations have been deepening: in May 2003, the two countries held their first joint naval exercises in the Arabian Sea since the break-up of the Soviet Union. In an attempt to consolidate their relationship, annual summits between the Russian President and Indian PM have been held without fail since 2000, providing an excellent opportunity for talks at the highest levels. But for the Indian side, these are becoming commonplace with other powers as well, especially the US, thus robbing Russia of its earlier exclusive status.

STRATEGIC CONCERNS IN THE REGIONAL ENVIRONMENT

In the regional arena, India's concerns impinge mostly on Pakistan, China, and Iran. On all three, at first glance, India has more convergence on policy and world views with Russia than with any other major power. While this convergence is not as robust as in the earlier Indo-Soviet period, it is surprisingly resilient.[36] On Pakistan, Moscow did make some gestures in 2000 that suggested a possible change in a strategy that had from the 1950s put all its eggs on the subcontinent in the Indian basket. Although Pakistan took the initiative to reach out to Russia, reports that Putin's special envoy Sergei Yaztrzhemsy would visit Pakistan, and perhaps even Putin himself, gave India a jolt. On the Pakistani side, the military leadership had been seeking ways to overcome the international isolation it faced before 11 September 2001, especially as it saw the US move steadily closer to India. Recognizing Russia's vulnerability, Pakistani leader General Pervez Musharraf sent his Inter-Services Intelligence (ISI) chief Lt General Mahmood Ahmed to Russia in August 2001, signalling that Pakistan may be ready to address Russia's concerns on terrorism and drug trafficking originating in Afghanistan.

Post-9/11, both India and Russia are in agreement on curtailing Pakistan's influence in Afghanistan and regaining their own favourable position in Afghanistan prior to 1979. Indeed, American overthrow of the pro-Pakistan Taliban has benefited both Russia and India, and they would like to ensure that the new environment is not vitiated by Pakistan. Russia's short-lived responsiveness to Pakistan in 2001 was stimulated no doubt by the upswing in Indo-US relations since 2000, leading to questions about a purely India-centric approach for Moscow. But Russia's relations with Pakistan never took off the ground, and there has been no change in Moscow's long-standing commitment of not selling arms to India's adversary. Russia has also taken into account Indian concern about China providing Pakistan with fighter aircraft made with Russian engines. Moscow invoked the end-user provision in its agreement to stop China from supplying such aircraft.[37]

India and Russia share an unspoken but deep concern about China's rapid rise and growing influence. In the past, both have had periods of significant antagonism with China. China remains the only regional power that can seriously challenge or potentially deny a dominant Russian role in Eurasia, likewise for India in Asia. Despite the enormous defence sales with China and soaring trade, the Russian elite are ambivalent regarding China's increasing power. The same could be said of most of the Indian elite, with the exception of the leftist groups, especially the Communist Party of India (Marxist). India continues to be suspicious of China's intentions in its close relations with Pakistan; there is a strong sentiment in New Delhi that China seeks to hem Indian power and restrict it to the subcontinent. The development of the Gwadar port off the Baluchistan coast by China, China's growing ties with the military junta in Myanmar, its stepped up role in development projects in Bangladesh, and its ambition to be part of the South Asian Association for Regional Cooperation (SAARC) are all viewed with concern by New Delhi.

In Russia, there has been increasing debate about Moscow's military-technical cooperation (MTC) which includes Russian arms transfers to

China, as well as licence and technology transfers.[38] The main rationale for Russia's arms sales is economic and has been defended on the grounds that assistance is restricted to defensive capabilities and does not pose a threat to Russia itself. Russian analysts also tend to see China's security orientation as geared towards Taiwan and the South China Sea, rather than towards Russia and Central Asia. At the same time, these experts have urged greater caution. Indeed, some have argued that Russia's overall interests are better protected through arms sales to India rather than China.[39] The prospects of a Chinese threat via Russia's own arms are not lost on the Russian establishment. China, which has serious gaps in its military arsenal, lags behind Russia by 15 or more years; hence it could continue to absorb substantial amounts of Russian weaponry without shifting the balance. Meanwhile, India seems to be counting on Russia's own self-interest to ensure that China is not provided military equipment that would irrevocably upset the current balance of power. Russia's choice of India over China to jointly produce the fifth generation aircraft suggests as much.

IDEATIONAL CONVERGENCE IN THE REGIONAL ENVIRONMENT

There are, however, some signs of concerns and common worldviews that are bringing India, Russia, and China closer together—almost all of them relating to America's leadership role in the world. From concrete institutions like the Shanghai Cooperation Organization (SCO) to renewed rhetoric on multipolarity, their dissatisfaction with US unilateralism is evident. The informal growth of a trilateral dialogue between Russia, India, and China since 2005 stands in some contrast to the failed attempt by Russia to counter US hegemony and regain its lost ground with the 'Primakov Plan in the late 1990s'.[40] Russian PM Yevgeny Primakov's trial balloon had aimed to form a 'strategic triangle' comprising China, India, and Russia, a grouping that could be an antidote to American hyper-power. Although some experts have argued that the notion of triangular cooperation is unlikely to emerge due to the realities of the international balance of power or 'structural realism', a conclusion that most analysts would still agree with, it is then all the more notable that cooperation has come as far as it has.[41]

Ironically, it seems that apart from the underlying mutual distaste for America's unilateralism, each of the three is also concerned about the others' cultivation of ties with America itself. This is especially true of China, which cannot but notice the sea change in Indo-US relations since 2000, most recently the unprecedented nuclear deal designed by the Bush administration that amounts to 'an Indian exception' to the nuclear non-proliferation regime. By September 2008, America had put an enormous amount of diplomatic effort and pressure to get the IAEA and the NSG on board, a fact not lost on any observer. More pointedly, the underlying motivation for stepped up Indo-US ties and the increasing importance attached to India by US defence planners reflect a mutual concern with China, with the most extreme viewpoints in New Delhi and Washington seeing the need to 'contain' China. Thus, China may be seen as following a dual policy towards India: improving ties on the one hand to the extent that it is set to overtake the US as India's largest trading partner in the near future and, on the other hand, continuing to forge close ties with Pakistan to try and check Indian ambitions.[42]

In the past, China has resisted being drawn into negotiations or talks that elevated India's standing, such as including it in any non–South Asia nuclear dialogues in the 1990s. China was also extremely wary of engaging in talks of any nature that gave the appearance of India being on par with it. Thus, the reference to civil nuclear energy cooperation for the first time in the joint declaration after Chinese President Hu Jintao's visit to India in 2006 may be seen as a watershed.[43] China has increasingly shown greater openness to Indian participation in regional organizations in which Beijing may have harboured hopes of exerting significant influence. India's admittance into the SCO as an observer (along with Pakistan and Iran) in 2005 signalled that the group was on its way to potentially becoming a key Eurasian actor economically and strategically. Having begun as a Russian–Chinese creation in 1996 to demilitarize their borders, its agenda has clearly expanded. Indeed, in July 2005 the group grabbed international attention when it issued a time-line for US forces to pull out of Uzbekistan, a move that led some to jump to the conclusion that it had already become a potent anti-US bulwark.[44]

An incipient Russian–Chinese–Indian trilateralism is being displayed more openly since 2005, and by all accounts Russia's former President Putin has been the most instrumental broker. Putin can take much credit for institutionalizing the emerging trilateral dialogue among Russia, India, and China, despite initial scepticism, especially in Beijing. Russia's consistent view of India (with the exception of the late 1980s–90s interlude) has not been lost on observers. As K. Subrahmanyam, a leading Indian strategic analyst, put it, 'Russia has seen India as a key to Asian stability for the past 50 years, some four decades before George W. Bush's administration reached that conclusion'.[45] It was on Russian soil that the foreign ministers of the three countries met together for the first time in May 2005, separate from any international forum. In July 2006, a three-way summit took place on the sidelines of the G-8 meeting in St Petersburg, fuelling the notion that trilateralism was gaining ground.[46]

In February 2007, India took the lead and hosted its first high-level meeting of the three powers. The joint communiqué released on 14 February referred to the 'trilateral' nature of the meeting of the three foreign ministers and noted that they discussed 'the political, security and economic aspects of the current global system'. A centrepiece of their agenda was the need to build 'a more democratic multipolar world', not so obliquely challenging the US-dominated world order.[47] The fact that this declaration came only four days after Putin stunned Western leaders by denouncing American foreign policy during a security conference in Munich added to its significance. China hosted the third trilateral meeting in October 2007, and, unlike previously, the group took several small but crucial steps to institutionalize the annual meeting, including the establishment of a consultation mechanism at the level of director general/division head among the foreign ministries.[48] At the same time, the emphasis was said to be on 'pragmatic' cooperation in economic and cultural interactions, thus downplaying any notion of strategic alignment. Cooperation is likely to be in functional areas at lower levels, rather than converging on grand strategic visions. Still, with reference to India, it may be noted that the joint communiqué stated that the Foreign Ministers of China and Russia reiterated that their countries attach importance to the status of India in international affairs and understand and support India's aspirations to play a greater role in the United Nations.

Although Putin's Russia has been in the forefront of challenging US dominance, both China and India share the aversion to American interventionism and the Bush administration's activism. In 2003, at the height of delicate Indo-US bilateral efforts to strengthen their cooperation, India turned down America's request for troop support in Iraq. The Pentagon, which had hoped that India would deploy a division—15,000–20,000 soldiers—was apparently caught by surprise.[49] But this was entirely in keeping with long-held Indian preferences against external intervention, a position shared by Russia and China. Indeed, despite India's own prolonged fight against extremism and terrorism, and the US post-9/11 'war on terror', the strong belief in New Delhi is that American action in Iraq has[50] been a boost to Islamic radicalism. As one well-known commentator put it, 'We will pay for US mistakes in Iraq'.[51] Moreover, all three are opposed to outside interference in separatist conflicts, something on which they are all vulnerable, from Chechnya, Xinjiang, and Kashmir. This explains in large part the hesitancy of India to condemn Russia's high-handed response to Georgia's challenge to its power and influence.

Finally, the three countries also hold similar views on how to handle one of America's newest and stickiest challenges: Iran's nuclear programme. On the one hand, it is notable that China, Russia, and India have not openly challenged the US in its campaign to isolate Iran, despite all three countries having strong energy interests in Iran. (India has had the most difficult balancing act on Iran, given the concurrent deliberation of the civil nuclear deal in the US Congress since 2005.) There is clear convergence between the three against any military option by the US against Iran; their preference is for a negotiated settlement via the IAEA. The standoff between the US and Iran has, however, forced India, Russia, and China to clarify their own position on Iran and nuclear weapons, but their preferences are ambivalent. While it is becoming evident that none of the three are entirely comfortable in accommodating nuclear weapons for Iran, they are also not in favour of militarily foreclosing this option for Iran. Meanwhile, at this stage, their energy interests seem to dominate any concern over Iran's nuclearization.

India has resisted US efforts to divert it from the highly politicized proposed India–Pakistan–Iran gas pipeline.[52] The US aim is to isolate and economically punish Iran as part of America's broader strategy to pressure it on the nuclear front; the pipeline is seen as rewarding Iran. Rhetorically at least, India is keeping the project alive, moving ahead, for example, on negotiation over the price of gas with Iran. Russian–Indian energy cooperation is extending to this regional project as well. Gazprom has expressed its interest in taking part in the gas pipeline which has a price tag of $7 billion. It has indicated a willingness to be involved as a contractor to do feasibility studies and as an investor.[53] In an oblique reference to this controversial project during his 2007 visit, President Putin pointed to vast opportunities for cooperation 'in building facilities for gas production and transportation in India and the adjacent region'. Deputy PM Sergei Ivanov openly stated that 'We are pegging big hopes on Gazprom-GAIL strategic partnership, including joint efforts in building the Iran–Pakistan–India gas pipeline.'[54] As Christine Fair points out elsewhere in this volume, the need for regional energy supplies will keep India engaged with Iran in the foreseeable future, despite systemic constraints posed by American preferences.

EVALUATING THE MOTIVATIONS OF INDO-RUSSIAN RELATIONS
Whether we consider the bilateral, regional, or global levels, current Indo-Russian orientations reveal a considerable degree of consensus. Yet at the

same time, there are also no overarching strategic, domestic, or ideological interests that make the relationship compelling and primary for either state. A look at the major determinants of the convergence tells us why. As the preceding discussion shows, strategic as well as ideational factors draw the two states together. In pure power terms, Russia's resurgence and greater consolidation is indeed a favourable international outcome for New Delhi, but hardly essential for India's own rise. Globally, India has had a preference for a multipolar world, an objective which a weak and chaotic Russia could not contribute to. Russia's unwillingness to bend to US pressure and its drive to protect its position as an 'independent pole' in the international system fits in well with long-held Indian views. The Yukos standoff between Russia and the US was one of the most dramatic instances of Russia standing up to American pressure, and an early sign of its new-found assertiveness.[55] At the January 2007 meeting, Indian PM Singh and Russian President Putin once again made direct references to their commitment to a multipolar world. Shortly thereafter, at a trilateral meeting between the foreign ministers of India, Russia, and China, there were calls for a more multipolar world. Normatively, Indo-Russian preferences on the global world order show some meeting of the minds.

Beyond the normative level, Russia's renewed global power is viewed by many in India as facilitating India's pursuit of its own national interests, in a realist framework.[56] Bilaterally and regionally, a strengthened Russia is in a better position to play a useful role, from joint defence production to promoting India in the SCO. India accepts a large international role for Russia; conversely, Russia has continuously recognized India's dominance in South Asia, and is in favour of India emerging as a strong power in Asia and on the world stage. Indeed, President Medvedev has put forward a new 7,000-word foreign policy blueprint for a Pan-European Security structure (an implicit alternative to the NATO) which envisages a role for India in Euro-Atlantic affairs.[57] Despite the qualitatively improved ties between India and the US, India's discomfort with American unilateralism has not disappeared. Indian leaders do not want the cementing of relations with the US to come at a cost to the country's long-protected strategic autonomy or create unacceptable fallout such as intervention in regional conflict with Pakistan.[58] As S. Paul Kapur describes in this volume, Indo-US relations may still be frustrated by uncertainty regarding American relations with Pakistan. Russia's independence on the global stage offers India greater manoeuvring space as well. Russia clearly does not want to be relegated to the position of the weakest of the Western powers as it was in the 1990s, and it is searching for ways to reassert itself. Putin's more overt nationalism and his perceived autocratic style have led observers in the West to question Russia's commitment to democratic and cosmopolitan norms. From Moscow's point of view, a robust relationship with a democratic and plural India, whose global influence is rising, is symbolically attractive.

As in the previous Soviet period, ties are strongest in the defence field, with the economic sector nearly stagnant, pointing to the weakest link between the two countries. The volume of bilateral trade has increased only minimally, from $1.5 billion in 1996 to $2.7 billion in 2006, with an unimpressive target of $10 billion by 2010. In comparison, India's trade with China grew rapidly from $1 billion to $18 billion by 2006; Russia's trade with China was over $36 billion in 2006, and rising at more than 30 per cent annually.[59] Though this gap in the economic realm is not likely to improve quickly, Russia's energy role will be substantial in contributing to India's energy security objectives, a critical ingredient for sustaining rapid economic growth. For India, the relationship with Russia is by and large consistent with both its normative and realist conceptions of India's global role—interestingly, there are few voices of dissent in India on stronger ties with Russia; the same cannot be said for Indo-US or Sino-Indian relations.

Despite the convergences, there are signs that India cannot take relations with Russia for granted. As US–India ties reached new heights in 2007 (climaxing with the unprecedented 'quadrilateral' naval exercises between India, US, Japan, and Australia), some close observers saw a sudden chill in Russia's attitude towards India. New Delhi has described its burgeoning ties with the US as being parallel, not in opposition, to relations with other major powers.[60] On the other hand, episodes such as Russia's military campaign against Georgia in 2008 to protect the pro-Russian regions of South Ossetia and Abkhazia (the first time Russia intervened in this fashion in a sovereign country since 1990), in spite of strong American backing to Georgian leader Mikhell Saakashvili, portend future dilemmas for India. If Russia embarks on an ever more aggressively nationalist foreign policy aimed at the US—something that seems to be coming to pass with the combination of Putin and Medvedev at Russia's helm—India's ability to maintain a delicate balance between the US and Russia could be severely tested. However, the international system is no longer so polarized that India will be forced to make the kinds of choices it had to in the Cold War years, while its near great power status will ensure that neither Russia nor the US can impose their preferences at will.

* * *

Indo-Russian relations have recovered from the doldrums following the collapse of the Soviet Union and have become surprisingly robust once again. Indeed, it is difficult to identify any issue on which their interests significantly diverge, but at the same time there are clearly no longer the compelling strategic and ideological rationales that fused them during the Cold War era. On balance, India has more options in its foreign policy choices thanks partly to its unprecedented economic rise and its increasingly close ties with the US. India's major objective of achieving developed country status leaves Russia at a disadvantage since the economic attraction for India lies elsewhere. Developments in the regional arena are particularly important to both Russia and India, but are also likely to be the most unpredictable. In this regard, China and Iran are the key variables.

In the new global system, it has become necessary to diversify a country's ties: economic globalization and the breakdown of power blocs have given rise to cross-cutting and transnational issues. Thus, partnerships and coalitions have to be more tactical in nature, often made on a case-by-case basis. In this environment, India and Russia (and others like China) are learning to hedge their bets by not cultivating any exclusive ties. As this chapter shows, in Indo-Russian relations, the logic of today's international system reinforces some of their own enduring proclivities and interests and brings them closer together than ever imagined after the Soviet Union's demise. But it also shows that while Russia will be an important partner for India, it will be unlikely to regain a pivotal position in the foreseeable future.

NOTES

1. Kenneth N. Waltz (1979), *Theory of International Politics* (Reading, MA: Addison Wesley).

2. This article is based on Deepa M. Ollapally (2002), 'Indo-Russian Strategic Relations: New Choices and Constraints', in Sumit Ganguly (ed.), 'Special Issue on "India as an Emerging Power"', *The Journal of Strategic Studies*, 25 (4), pp. 135–56.

3. For an overview of India's early foreign relations, see Baldev Raj Nayar and T.V. Paul (2003), *India in the World Order: Searching for Major Power Status* (Cambridge: Cambridge University Press), pp. 115–58.

4. S. Paul Kapur and Sumit Ganguly (2007), 'The Transformation of U.S.–India Relations: An Explanation for the Rapprochement and Prospects for the Future', *Asian Survey*, 47 (4), pp. 642–56.

5. For background, see Robert C. Horn (1982), *Soviet–Indian Relations: Issues and Influence* (New York: Praeger) and Robert H. Donaldson (1974), *Soviet Policy Toward India: Ideology and Strategy* (Cambridge, MA: Harvard University Press).

6. Nayar and Paul, *India in the World Order*, p. 197.

7. This is a historical reference to Russian Prince Aleksandr Gorchakov's comment after the humiliating defeat in the Crimean War that: 'It is said that Russia sulks. Russia does not sulk. Russia is collecting itself.' Quoted in Celeste Bohlen (2001), 'Putting the Power Broker', *New York Times*, 26 August.

8. For a discussion of India's strategic autonomy goal, see Deepa M. Ollapally (2000), 'India's Strategic Doctrine and Practice: The Impact of Nuclear Testing', in Raju G.C. Thomas and Amit Gupta (eds), *India's Nuclear Security* (Boulder, CO: Lynne Rienner Publishers), pp. 67–85.

9. Hari Vasudevan (2001), 'Russia as a Neighbor: Indo-Russian Relations 1992–2001', Lecture at the Conference on 'Russia—Ten Years After', Carnegie Endowment for International Peace, Washington, DC, 7–9 June.

10. See, for example, Alexi Arbatov (2001), 'Russia and NATO—Ten Years After', Paper prepared for the Conference on 'Russia—Ten Years After', Carnegie Endowment for International Peace, Washington, DC, 7–9 June.

11. Hari Vasudevan, 'Russia as a Neighbor'.

12. *New York Times*, 6 October 2000.

13. Jyotsana Bakshi (2006), 'India–Russia Defence Cooperation', *Strategic Analysis*, 30 (2), pp. 449–56.

14. Baidya Bikash Basu (2000), 'Trends in Russian Arms Exports', *Strategic Analysis*, 23 (11), pp. 1919–32.

15. Amelia Gentleman (2007), 'Russia Offers to Build Four New Nuclear Reactors for India', *International Herald Tribune*, 25 January.

16. Ashok Mehta, quoted in Gentleman, 'Russia Offers to Build Four New Nuclear Reactors for India'.

17. Vladimir Radyuhin (2007), 'Putin Visit: Chance for Course Correction', *The Hindu*, 23 January.

18. Subhash Vohra (2008), 'India is Emerging as a New Major Market for U.S. Defense Industries', 25 March, http://www.voanews.com (accessed on 10 December 2008). See also Jan Cartwright (2007), 'India and Russia: Old Friends, New Friends', *South Asia Monitor*, Center for Strategic and International Studies, Washington DC, No. 104, 1 March, pp. 1–3.

19. Jyotsna Bakshi, 'India–Russia Defence Cooperation', p. 454.

20. *The Atlanta Journal-Constitution*, 12 November 2008.

21. SiliconIndia.com, 26 December 2007 http://www.siliconindia.com/shownews/US_eyes_40_Bn_arms_market_in_India-nid-38405.html (accessed on 10 December 2008).

22. Author's interview with Richard Kirkland, President, South Asia, Lockheed Martin, 11 December 2008.

23. Sudha Ramachandran (2007), 'India Takes a Hit Over Russian Fighters', *Asia Times Online*, 27 May, http://www.atimes.com (accessed on 15 September 2008).

24. See for example, Stratfor Global Intelligence, 'India, Russia: A No-Win Resolution on the Gorshkov', 20 February 2008. www. stratfor.com (accessed 5 May 2008).

25. Quoted in John Cherian (2000), 'The Defense Deals', *Frontline*, 17 (21), 14–27 October, http://www.hinduonnet.com/fline/fl1721/17210120.htm (accessed on 11 December 2008).

26. 'India and Russia in Energy Talks', BBC News, 17 March 2006, http://news.bbc.co.uk/2/hi/sough_asia/4815588.stm (accessed on 28 March 2007).

27. http://www.india-defence.com, Report 3725, 2 July 2008 (accessed on 10 December 2008).

28. Quoted in Gentleman, 'Russia Offers to Build Four New Nuclear Reactors for India'.

29. Vladimir Radyuhin (2004), 'Russia Plays Energy Card', *The Hindu*, 6 July.

30. Lisa Curtis (2007), 'India's Expanding Role in Asia: Adapting to Rising Power Status', *Backgrounder*, No. 2008, 20 February, p. 10; *Kyodo News*, 'India PM to Discuss Energy, Defense Contracts in Russia', 2 December 2005; and Cartwright, 'India and Russia'.

31. M.K. Bhadrakumar (2007), 'Putin's Choice', *Asia Times Online*, 14 December, http://www.atimes.com (accessed on 1 May 2008).

32. 'Russia's Medvedev Offers Foreign Policy Continuity', Reuters, 1 May 2008, http://www.reuters.com/article/idUSL0192315220080501 (accessed on 1 May 2008).

33. Ted Jones (2008), 'New Energy for the US–India Nuclear Deal: Business and Policy Implications', talk at the Sigur Center for Asian Studies, Washington DC, 18 September.

34. Interview with Michael Krepon, 'U.S.–India Nuclear Agreement Weakens Nonproliferation Efforts', Council on Foreign Relations, 17 September 2008, http://www.cfr.org (accessed on 19 November 2008).

35. Jyotsna Bakshi (2005), 'Prime Minister's Moscow Visit: Commentary', *Strategic Analysis*, 29 (4), pp. 732–7.

36. For an early recognition of prospects for cooperation at the regional level, see Madhavan Palat (2000), 'Jettison Past Baggage: Starting Fresh Relations with Russia', *The Times of India*, 3 October.

37. K. Subrahmanyam (2007), 'The Lessons from Putin's Visit', rediff.com, 29 January, http://www.rediff.com/news/2007/jan/29ks.htm (accessed on 19 November 2008).

38. For a good discussion, see Paradorn Rangsimaporn (2006), 'Russia's Debate on Military–Technical Cooperation with China', *Asian Survey*, XLVI (3), pp. 477–95.

39. Ibid., p. 482.

40. See, for example, Sunanda K. Datta-Ray (1999), 'Suppose Russia, India and China Could Really Get Together', *International Herald Tribune*, 5 January.

41. See, for example, Harsh V. Pant (2004), 'The Moscow–Beijing–Delhi "Strategic Triangle": An Idea Whose Time May Never Come', *Security Dialogue*, 35 (3), pp. 311–28.

42. China has been instrumental in building up Pakistan's civil nuclear sector. It built the 300 MW Chashma reactor and is building a second one. 'Editorial: India and Pakistan Get Their Nuclear Deals', *Daily Times*, 18 November 2006, www.dailytimes.com.pk (accessed on 18 November 2008).

43. Siddharth Varadarajan (2006), 'New Delhi, Beijing Talk Nuclear for the First Time', *The Hindu*, 22 November.

44. Lionel Beehner (2006), 'The Rise of the Shanghai Cooperation Organization', Council on Foreign Relations Backgrounder, 12 June, p. 2.

45. K. Subrahmanyam (2007), 'The Lessons from Putin's Visit', 29 January, rediff.com (accessed on 23 March 2007).

46. Radyuhin, 'Putin Visit'.

47. Jeremy Page (2007), 'Giants Meet to Counter U.S. Power', *The Times* (London), 15 February.

48. Yu Bin (2008), 'China–Russia Relations: Living with Putin's Unfading Glory and Dream', *Comparative Connections: A Quarterly E-Journal on East Asian Bilateral Relations*, January, http://www.csis.org/media/csis/pubs/0704qchina_russia.pdf (accessed on 12 December 2008).

49. See Deepa M. Ollapally (2005), *U.S.–India Relations: Ties That Bind?* The Sigur Center Asia Papers No. 22, The Elliott School of International Affairs, The George Washington University, Washington, DC, pp. 3–5.

50. Iranian President Mahmoud Ahmadinejad's meeting with Indian PM Manmohan Singh in April 2008 in New Delhi and their optimistic assessment of the Iran–Pakistan–India pipeline deal suggests that India has not shifted its position as much as the US would like. See *The Hindu*, 30 April 2008.

51. Swaminathan S. Anklesaria Aiyar (2004), 'Kush vs. Berry', *The Times of India*, 10 October.

52. Ibid.

53. M.K. Bhadrakumar, 'Gas: Iran Turns Up the Heat', *Asia Times Online*, 10 February 2007, http://www.atimes.com/atimes/Middle_East/IB10Ak02.html (accessed on 10 December 2008).

54. Quoted in Igor Tomberg (2007), 'Russia–India Energy Dialogue Traditions and Prospects', *Energy Daily*, 7 February, http://www.energy-daily.com (accessed on 23 March 2007).

55. This affair between 2004 and 2006 involved British and American oil companies trying to gain a controlling share in Russia's biggest oil company, Yukos, only to be thwarted by Putin's extreme measure of arresting the head of the company on charges of fraud and tax evasion.

56. See for example, M.K. Bhadrakumar (2007), 'Putin Comes to India Riding on Russia's Resurgence', 25 January, rediff.com (accessed on 23 March 2007).

57. P. Stobdan (2008), 'Russia's New Rules for Global Competition', IDSA Strategic Comments, 7 August, www.idsa.in/publications/stratcomments/pstobdan070808.htm (accessed on 11 December 2008).

58. For a discussion of the constancy of this view even with new schools of thought in foreign policy, see Deepa M. Ollapally (2008), 'Great Powers in Wonderland', *The National Interest*, No. 94 , pp. 57–9.

59. Radyuhin, 'Putin Visit'.

60. The uncharacteristically dismissive treatment of Indian Defence Minister A.K. Anthony during his visit to Moscow in October 2007 was seen as a sign of displeasure of India's 'embrace' of the US. Author's interview with senior Indian correspondent, 13 November 2007, Washington DC.

12

India and the United States from World War II to the Present

A Relationship Transformed

S. PAUL KAPUR[1]

Relations between the United States (US) and India are at an all-time high, with the two countries enjoying unprecedented levels of cooperation in the economic, strategic, and diplomatic spheres. As former US President George W. Bush put it, 'India and the United States are separated by half a globe. Yet today our two nations are closer than ever before.'[2] In Indian Prime Minister Manmohan Singh's words, India and the US 'share the common goal of making this one of the principal relationships of our countries'.[3] And US Undersecretary of State Nicholas Burns predicted that 'within a generation many Americans may view India as one of our two or three most important strategic partners'.[4]

However, Indo-US relations have not always been so cordial. Indeed, the two countries' increasing closeness represents a major transformation of their past relationship. In the following, I describe the nature of Indo-US relations from World War II through the end of the Cold War. As I explain, although the countries shared a number of important interests and values, their relationship was historically characterized more by suspicion and resentment than by cooperation. I then show how a convergence of structural, domestic, and individual leadership factors has transformed Indo-US relations. At the structural level, the end of the Cold War forced Indian leaders to rethink their attitude towards the US while freeing Americans from the need to view India through an anti-Soviet lens. At the domestic level, India's economic failings made clear that its socialist development model was no longer tenable, spurring a raft of market-oriented reforms that brought India closer to the US.

And at the individual level, Indian and American political leaders took the difficult and sometimes risky political steps necessary to create an environment in which an Indo-US partnership could take root. Together these factors radically altered the nature of Indo-US relations in the post-Cold War era.

HISTORICAL BACKGROUND

World War II and Independence

The US first began to take notice of India during World War II. Up to that point there had been remarkably little contact between the two countries. Only a handful of Indians lived in the US, and most Americans' knowledge of India was limited to exotic portrayals in film or fiction. India's status as a British colony made diplomatic relations cumbersome; communications between the two sides had to go through the India Office and the Foreign Office in London and the British Embassy in Washington. And given India's massive poverty and underdevelopment, the subcontinent held little strategic or economic interest for the US.[5]

Nonetheless, the Franklin D. Roosevelt administration viewed India as a potentially important player in the war effort. India could serve as a bulwark against Japanese aggression in Southeast Asia, a logistical hub for support of Chinese nationalist forces, and a source of raw materials and manpower for the allies. If these goals were to be realized, however, India's cooperation was essential.[6] Indian nationalist leaders were willing to support the British, but they demanded independence in return. Yet the British refused to give India a firm timetable for transition to self-rule.[7]

President Roosevelt feared that British intransigence would make the Indians unwilling to cooperate with the allies. Roosevelt also believed that British policy was morally repugnant; it denied Indians the fundamental rights and freedoms that the British and Americans held dear and the fact that they were fighting to secure against Nazi and Japanese fascism. Moreover, given the closeness of the US–UK relationship, British policy tainted the US, exposing it to charges of hypocrisy. This could have significant practical implications after the war, when Indians and other Asians would likely remember America's support for British colonialism. Roosevelt worried that the resulting resentment could create hundreds of millions of adversaries throughout the region. In addition to these strategic and ethical problems, Roosevelt faced domestic political pressure over the India issue. The American public was sympathetic to the Indian cause. A majority believed that Britain should negotiate with Indian nationalist leaders. And Republicans attacked

Roosevelt over the practical and ethical implications of his perceived association with British colonial policy in Asia.[8]

Roosevelt therefore undertook substantial efforts to establish direct ties with India and to persuade Churchill to give the Indians a clear timetable for independence in return for their cooperation in the war effort. In order to avoid the cumbersome process of communicating through the India and Foreign Offices, the US in 1941 sent a senior diplomat to serve as US Commissioner in New Delhi and simultaneously received a senior Indian civil servant, known as the Agent-General of India, in Washington. Roosevelt subsequently expanded the lines of Indo-US communication, naming former Assistant Secretary of War Louis Johnson as his Personal Representative to India in 1942.[9] Roosevelt also directly lobbied Churchill in favour of Indian independence, both in person[10] and in writing.[11]

Churchill angrily rebuffed Roosevelt's entreaties. The prime minister was unwilling to preside over the dissolution of the British Empire, particularly at the behest of the US.[12] Churchill also believed that the Indians were incapable of responsible self-rule and predicted that independence would result in large-scale communal violence.[13] Roosevelt's and Churchill's fundamental philosophical disagreement over India was perhaps best captured in their differing views of the Atlantic Charter. The Charter, which enunciated fundamental allied war aims, stated that 'all peoples' possessed the right to self-determination. Churchill argued in parliament that the Charter's commitment to self-determination applied only to people in Nazi-occupied territories and not to the overseas subjects of the British Empire. Roosevelt, by contrast, viewed the Charter as applying universally and believed that it included the right of colonial populations to seek independence.[14] Roosevelt's and Churchill's differences over India became a significant source of tension between the two leaders, with Churchill even threatening to resign in the face of Roosevelt's prodding.[15] The vehemence of the PM's objections persuaded Roosevelt not to pursue the Indian issue further, though he remained convinced that Britain's colonial policy was a major strategic blunder.[16]

Indian leaders were disappointed by America's failure to press the case for India's independence more vigorously. The Indians had long considered the US a potential ally in their freedom struggle. Indeed, Congress leader Jawaharlal Nehru had made the argument for Indian independence directly to the American foreign policy elite in articles in *Foreign Affairs* and the *Atlantic Monthly*.[17] However, in the end it became apparent to the Indians that the US was willing to tolerate its ally's colonial policy so as not to jeopardize larger American geostrategic aims. US officials, for their part, were critical of the Indians as well. The Americans believed that Indian independence leaders' tactics undermined the war effort. The Quit India civil disobedience movement, which was launched under Mahatma Gandhi's leadership in 1942, particularly rankled the Americans who believed that winning the war should be the top priority for all concerned. In the American view, the failings of British policy, though serious, could not justify an Indian refusal to support the allied cause against the evils of Japanese and Nazi fascism.[18]

In the end, the difference between the Americans and the Indians over the question of independence was less one of philosophy than one of priorities. Each side believed in the other's agenda. The Americans thought that Britain should grant India independence and pressed British leaders to do so. The Indians wanted the allies to win the war and provided them with men, material, and logistical support. However, the US' most urgent goal was prevailing against the Axis Powers. The achievement of Indian independence, though important, could not be allowed to interfere with that aim. And for the Indians, winning the war was secondary to the project of ending the British *Raj*. Thanks to this divergence of priorities, what could have been a promising start to the Indo-US relationship was, in fact, characterized by deep ambivalence on both sides.[19]

Indian–American relations deteriorated further immediately following India's achievement of independence in 1947. The source of the problem was US policy regarding the Indo-Pakistani dispute over Kashmir. Kashmir's Hindu ruler, Maharaja Hari Singh, had been uncertain as to whether the territory should join India or Pakistan when British India was partitioned. In October 1947, however, a tribal rebellion erupted, and soon a force of Pathan tribesmen and Pakistan Army personnel disguised as locals was marching on the Kashmiri capital of Srinagar. Hari Singh appealed to British Viceroy Lord Louis Mountbatten for help in repelling the attackers. Mountbatten and Indian PM Nehru agreed to support the Maharaja, provided that Kashmir would accede to India rather than join Pakistan. The accession would be ratified by a vote of the Kashmiri people at a future date, once the current hostilities had ended. Hari Singh agreed to the Indian terms, signing an instrument of accession on 26 October. Indian troops then deployed to Srinagar.[20]

The Indians adopted a two-pronged strategy for dealing with the Kashmir conflict. At one level, they employed diplomacy, formally complaining about the Pakistani attack to the United Nations (UN) Security Council on 1 January 1948. The Indians hoped that the UN would condemn Pakistani aggression and call for the withdrawal of intruding forces from Kashmir.[21] Simultaneously, India employed a military approach, launching extensive combat operations in Kashmir. The Indians also reserved the right to carry the fight into Pakistan proper if necessary, though they never made good on this threat.[22]

Neither India's diplomatic nor its military tactics succeeded in significantly changing the situation on the ground. When Indian forces arrived in Kashmir, the attackers had already captured about one-third of the territory. In the following months, the Indians defended Srinagar and engaged in a series of battles with both Pakistan-backed forces and regular Pakistan Army elements. And India engaged in extensive discussions regarding the Kashmir situation with Britain and other members of the Security Council. But despite periods of intense fighting and bouts of flurried diplomatic activity, the territorial balance remained roughly the same, with India controlling about two-thirds of Kashmir and Pakistan holding roughly one-third of the region. The war eventually ground to a stalemate and officially ended with a UN-sponsored ceasefire on 1 January 1949.[23]

India's pursuit of a diplomatic solution to the conflict through the UN, and its decision not to expand the fighting beyond Kashmir, resulted to a significant degree from international pressure to exercise restraint. The British in particular were anxious to prevent the outbreak of a wider war that could be injurious to Pakistan, and to reach a settlement on Kashmir that protected Pakistani interests. These concerns arose primarily out of the Kashmir conflict's potential ramifications for British interests in the Middle East. After World War II, Britain had relinquished its League of Nations mandate for Palestine and placed the Arab–Israeli dispute before the UN. The UN General Assembly had then adopted a measure calling for the partition of Palestine into Arab and Jewish states, triggering the outbreak of Arab–Israeli violence. Britain's actions had been deeply unpopular with the Palestinian Arabs. The British now feared that if they were seen to side with India against Pakistan in the Kashmir dispute, they would further inflame Arab opinion, creating legions of enemies in the Middle East and beyond.[24]

The British thus promoted policies in Kashmir that were supportive of the Pakistanis. For example, they strongly discouraged the Indians from widening the war and attacking Pakistan proper. Mountbatten pointedly warned Nehru that a larger conflict could be long, costly, and difficult to contain and pushed the PM to refer the matter to the UN. And British PM Clement Atlee suggested that an Indian expansion of the Kashmir war would violate international law.[25] British diplomats' specific proposals for resolution of the conflict reiterated Pakistani calls for a plebiscite in Kashmir, which would have allowed Pakistani forces to remain in the region until the two sides had reached a political settlement and the plebiscite had occurred, and sought to replace the Sheikh Abdullah government in Jammu and Kashmir.[26]

Although they were deeply concerned with achieving an acceptable outcome to the Kashmir dispute, British officials wished to avoid the appearance of overtly meddling in South Asian affairs. They therefore sought US backing for their positions and in fact encouraged the US to play a leading part in promoting them with the UN.[27] American diplomats were initially reluctant to support the British, believing their proposals to be overly biased in favour of the Pakistanis. They respected Britain's regional expertise, however, and did not wish to cause a rift with their close ally. Thus, the Americans eventually adopted a number of positions initially held by British diplomats, such as the necessity of replacing the Kashmiri government and the need to hold a plebiscite and reach a political settlement before tribal and Pakistani forces withdrew from the region. US officials went so far as to warn the Indians that failure to cooperate on these matters would jeopardize future Indo-American relations. This deeply offended Indian leaders. They rebuffed the American threat, stating that India did not require the goodwill of any particular country. The Indians also suggested that they might establish closer ties with the Soviet Union in the future.[28]

The UN Security Council ultimately adopted a resolution on Kashmir that was considerably more balanced than the earlier British and American proposals.[29] For example, it called on India to hold a plebiscite, but only after the attacking forces had withdrawn from Kashmir and peace had returned to the region. And the resolution did not seek to remove the Sheikh Abdullah regime from Jammu and Kashmir.[30] Nonetheless, the earlier manoeuvrings of British diplomats and eventual American support for them had significant effects on India—regarding not just Kashmir policy but also the tenor of Indo-US relations. In addition to convincing Nehru to pursue a diplomatic resolution to the Kashmir conflict and not to widen the war by attacking Pakistan proper, they led the Indians to see the US as insensitive to Indian interests. Indeed, in following the British lead on Kashmir policy, the US appeared to be assuming the mantle of Britain's colonial role.[31] Nehru later characterized Anglo-American policy towards Kashmir as 'highly objectionable', claiming that the US and Britain had 'completely lost the capacity to think and judge anything'.[32] Thus, suspicion and resentment characterized the US–India relationship not just during World War II but also in the years immediately following India's independence. It was a problem that would extend well beyond the 1940s. Indeed, Indo-US relations would deteriorate considerably further during the coming decades of the Cold War.

The Cold War

Despite American interest in India during World War II and its immediate aftermath, for most of the period after Indian independence the US viewed South Asia as a region largely peripheral to its strategic needs. This said, various American administrations did consider India to be a potentially important front in the Cold War contest, viewing the country as a fledgling democracy emerging in China's communist shadow. They surmised that India's fate could have important implications for other Asian states struggling to be free. To this end, the US gave India substantial economic assistance, particularly as American ties with China deteriorated. During the 1962 Sino-Indian war, the US publicly supported India's interpretation of its border with China in the eastern Himalayas and even ferried military equipment to India.[33] Despite India's potential importance, however, and occasional periods of Indo-US cooperation, it was clear from early on that India would not serve as an active US ally in the battle against global communism. India refused to join either the American or the Soviet side in the Cold War conflict and instead charted its own non-aligned course largely independent of either superpower.[34]

On one level, US policymakers sympathized with India's position of 'nonalignment'. After all, India risked becoming a target of the opposing camp if it openly took sides in the Cold War struggle. This was the reason that the US had been averse to joining military alliances for the first 150 years of its history. It was not surprising that India—a newly established and relatively weak country—had to do the same.[35] From the US perspective, the main problem with Indian policy was that 'nonalignment', in practice, did not translate into genuine neutrality. Instead, India tilted away from the US and more into the Soviet Union's ambit, especially after the early 1970s.

India's affinity for the Soviet Union was rooted both in subjective preferences and objective strategic factors. At the preferential level, Indians admired the Soviet Union's economic success. This also appealed to the socialist proclivities of PM Jawaharlal Nehru and subsequent generations of Indian elites, who deeply distrusted American-style free-market capitalism. In addition, Indians believed that the Soviet Union would not become a colonial power in the future because it lacked a colonial history; thus, it would not seek to expand its territory or influence at India's expense.[36]

At the strategic level, the Soviet Union afforded India crucial protection against regional adversaries. In 1971, New Delhi and Moscow signed a treaty of 'peace, friendship, and cooperation' under which the two parties promised to aid one another in the event of a perceived military threat.[37] After that, India came to rely on the Soviets to help protect it against the People's Republic of China, with which it had fought a bloody border war in 1962 and had an ongoing territorial dispute. During the early 1970s China also began to enjoy improved relations with the US, further exacerbating perceptions that Beijing was a threat to India. The Soviets responded by bolstering their relationship with India, providing sophisticated arms under highly favourable terms and taking supportive positions in the UN Security Council, particularly over the disputed territory of Kashmir.

In return, India continued to support the Soviet Union on a variety of controversial international issues. New Delhi withheld criticism of the Soviet invasion of Afghanistan in 1979, just as it had done with the Soviet invasion of Hungary in 1956 and Czechoslovakia in 1968. India also denied that the Eastern bloc's military capabilities endangered Western Europe.[38] India's non-aligned foreign policy thus became a source of considerable irritation to the US. Not only did the Indians refuse to assist the US in containing Soviet power but they also actively cooperated with the Soviet Union in significant ways. In the end India was not useful in achieving America's grand strategic goals and, in fact, was perceived as actually helping the Soviets to undermine them.

Beyond these strategic problems, India was economically unattractive during the Cold War. Given India's chronic underdevelopment, the US did not view it as a potentially serious trading partner, target for investment, or source of skilled labour. Thus, the US could reap few economic benefits through engagement with India. This economic weakness, in turn, severely constrained India's military capabilities and limited its ability to pose a direct challenge to American interests in South Asia, further reducing India's relevance. In essence, during the Cold War, India refused to promote US grand strategic goals and offered few economic benefits, while posing little military threat to American interests. India therefore was largely ignored.[39]

Any strategic interest that the US perceived in South Asia lay primarily with India's arch rival, Pakistan. Pakistan, at least notionally, supported American grand strategic goals and participated in anti-communist military alliances such as the Central Treaty Organization (CENTO) and the Southeast Asia Treaty Organization (SEATO).[40] Pakistan also allowed Washington to use its territory as a base for overflights to eavesdrop on the Soviet Union, in addition to serving as a vital conduit for American arms shipments to anti-Soviet forces in Afghanistan during the 1980s. In return, the Pakistanis received substantial American economic and military assistance.[41]

American ties with Pakistan exacerbated Indo-US estrangement, convincing the Indians of the US' malign intentions. India objected to the US–Pakistan relationship on a number of levels. Most fundamentally the Indians were angered by the US decision to favour small, dictatorial Pakistan over a major democratic state such as India. Also, American support allowed the Pakistanis to adopt confrontational policies, confident that their superior equipment, training, and doctrine would enable them to wring concessions from the Indians and, if necessary, prevail in any military conflict. Such inflated Pakistani confidence threatened Indian security and forced New Delhi to devote scarce resources to increased defence spending. Finally, American aid helped to reinforce the dominant position of the army in Pakistani politics, decreasing the likelihood that Pakistan would make serious efforts to settle its differences with India diplomatically. In the eyes of many Indians, America's support for Pakistan reached its zenith during the 1971 Bangladesh war, when US President Nixon 'tilted' towards the Pakistanis and dispatched the aircraft carrier *Enterprise* to the Bay of Bengal. This incident continued to engage and infuriate Indians for decades. The close relationship between the US and Pakistan thus had an exceedingly negative impact on Indo-US relations, convincing the Indians that the US sought to undermine their country by supporting its sworn enemy.[42]

Finally, India and the US spent several decades during the Cold War at loggerheads over the issue of nuclear weapons proliferation. In the wake of India's 1974 'peaceful nuclear explosion', the US made South Asia a centrepiece of its non-proliferation efforts, in part by crafting legislation such as the 1978 Nuclear Non-proliferation Act, the Pressler Amendment, and the Symington Amendment, designed to thwart India and Pakistan from acquiring nuclear weapons.[43] As Jason Kirk's chapter in this volume explains, Indians deeply resented this policy, which they viewed as discriminatory and hypocritical. If nuclear deterrence worked for the West, Indians reasoned, why should it be any less effective in South Asia? In 1998, the then Foreign Minister Jaswant Singh famously labelled the US non-proliferation policy as 'nuclear apartheid'.[44]

Thus, for most of the past six decades, relations between the US and India were frosty. Why then has their relationship changed so radically in recent years? I argue that a confluence of structural, domestic, and individual leadership factors has been responsible for this shift. At the structural level, the end of the Cold War fundamentally altered India's strategic calculus and broadened US foreign policy options. At the domestic level, India's economic reforms made it an attractive business and trading partner. And at the individual level, political leaders broke with past policies in ways that helped change the trajectory of Indo-US relations. In the following, I address each of these issues in turn.

FORGING A NEW INDO-US RELATIONSHIP

Structural Factors

Few American interests were directly impacted in South Asia as the Cold War came to a close. During the 1980s, the US had been drawn into the region to contest the expansion of Soviet power into Afghanistan. However, after the Soviet defeat, Washington ignored Afghanistan and virtually abandoned its erstwhile ally, Pakistan. In fact, the George H.W. Bush administration imposed sanctions against Pakistan under the aegis of the Pressler Amendment in 1990, saying it was unable to certify that Pakistan did not possess a nuclear explosive device. Relations with India—despite occasional signs of improvement—remained mired in differences over India's nuclear weapons programme as well as the Indo-Pakistani dispute over Kashmir.[45] The Indians, for their part, viewed the US as a quasi-colonial power, determined to deny India both its rightful dominant role in South Asia and its status as an important player on the larger global stage.[46]

The demise of the Soviet Union and the end of the Cold War had profound consequences for India's foreign and security policies. As noted earlier, despite its non-aligned status, India had maintained a close relationship with the Soviets. The collapse of the Soviet Union forced India's policymakers to recalculate their strategic options. No longer could they rely on their superpower ally's military and diplomatic protection. Nor, the Russians made clear, would the Indians be able to continue purchasing arms under exceptionally favourable Cold War terms. As a result, Indian officials began exploring other possibilities. Slowly they undertook measures to improve their relations with China. More importantly, the Indians largely abandoned their reflexive opposition to American strategic, economic, and diplomatic policies, evincing a new openness to the pursuit of mutually beneficial endeavours. While determined to avoid becoming a pawn in US efforts to contain China, the Indians realized that a closer relationship with the US could help them to fill the vacuum left by the Soviet

Union's fall and also to balance against rising Chinese power. The US, for its part, was no longer forced to view India in light of the latter's friendship with the Soviets and could re-evaluate Indo-US relations on their own merits.[47] Thus, the massive structural shift that resulted from the end of the Cold War foreclosed India's old Soviet-centric strategic policies and drove it to consider an approach more amenable to cooperation with the US. The shift also enabled the US to be more receptive to this new orientation.

Domestic Factors

Domestic-level factors also contributed to an Indo-US rapprochement in the post-Cold War era. The most important element was the severe financial crisis that gripped India in 1991, after the first Gulf War. The convergence of three distinct forces caused this crisis. First, India had badly depleted its foreign exchange reserves purchasing oil on the global spot market prior to the outbreak of the war. Second, the hostilities forced India to repatriate, at short notice, over 1,00,000 expatriate workers from the Persian Gulf region. Their return closed an important source of foreign exchange. Third, shortly after the war's end, a series of loan payments to multilateral banks came due. The combination of these three factors sent the Indian exchequer into a tailspin.[48]

Although its immediate cause was the Persian Gulf War, the roots of the financial crisis lay much deeper in the structural weakness of the Indian economy. As Rahul Mukherji explains in his chapter, this emanated from the failures of India's socialist development programme. For decades, India had hewed to a course of industrial regulation, import substitution, and central planning.[49] In the early 1990s, PM Narasimha Rao and his Finance Minister Manmohan Singh faced a stark choice. They could seek a short-term solution to India's financial crisis through multilateral loans, or they could try to address the deeper economic problems. Rao and Singh opted for the second approach and decided to use the crisis to make fundamental changes in India's economic growth strategy. They abandoned, for all practical purposes, India's atavistic commitment to 'import-substituting industrialization' and the labyrinthine regulatory system that it had spawned. Instead, they chose to move India towards more market friendly economic policies. Key aspects of this approach included adopting a structural adjustment regime, reducing tariffs and agricultural subsidies, loosening industrial regulations, and paring down India's massive public sector.[50]

Since then India's economic performance has improved dramatically. Its gross domestic product (GDP) of approximately $3 trillion (purchasing power parity) trails only that of the US, China, and Japan.[51] Moreover, India's GDP growth is no longer stuck at the traditional 'Hindu' rate of roughly 3 per cent. Instead, GDP grew 5.6 per cent in 1990 and 8.7 per cent in 2007. The Asian Development Bank (ADB) predicts 2008 and 2009 GDP growth rates of 8 per cent and 8.5 per cent, respectively. India has also emerged as a major player in the information technology sector and an important international source of skilled labour. Its burgeoning middle class offers a potentially vast market for foreign exports. Not surprisingly, Indo-US trade skyrocketed from approximately $4.5 billion in 1988 to roughly $27 billion in 2005.[52] Despite this progress, India continues to face serious economic challenges, particularly regarding inequality, education, infrastructure, and continued liberalization. As I explain later, these are potentially serious problems that could undermine India's economic progress—and the further expansion of its relationship with the US. Nonetheless, the new market-oriented approach has helped to spur India's economic growth. This has played a major role in India's rapprochement with the US. Both sides have much to gain from further cooperation in the future. They can no longer afford to ignore one another.

Individual Leadership Factors

In addition to these structural and domestic factors, individual leadership has also played a major role in facilitating enhanced Indo-US ties. Various Indian and American leaders have made significant contributions in this regard. For instance, the decision by Narasimha Rao and Manmohan Singh to break with India's autarkic development strategy and begin moving towards market reforms facilitated the growth that has made India such a valuable economic partner for the US. Even though these market reforms were triggered by the economic crisis emanating from the Gulf War, it still took considerable foresight and political courage for Rao and Singh to launch a policy that represented such a major departure from the past. This is particularly true given the entrenched interests within India that opposed any break with previous policy. For example, both labour and management in the industrial sector strenuously opposed the government's efforts to undo restrictions on investment and expansion that impeded the integration of Indian industry into the global economy. Elements of the foreign policy bureaucracy also opposed economic and political measures that they saw as too closely aligned with the US and the West. In addition, many commentators in the press and academe were severely critical of India's new direction. Efforts to implement the new economic policies have not been uniformly successful and powerful industrial groups and labour unions continue to thwart further reform.[53] Still, the changes in Indian economic policy have been significant. Other leaders more cautious than Rao and Singh might not have even attempted to introduce them.

US President Bill Clinton's leadership also played an important part in facilitating Indo-US rapprochement. The Clinton administration was committed to limiting the global spread of nuclear weapons; it imposed economic sanctions to punish India and Pakistan in the wake of their 1998 nuclear tests. This thoroughly vexed Indian leaders. However, in the Indians' view, Clinton's actions during their country's 1999 Kargil conflict with Pakistan largely atoned for his earlier policy. Indeed, American actions during the Kargil conflict helped begin undoing the deep distrust of the US that Indian leaders had acquired over the previous several decades. To explain, India discovered in the spring of 1999 that Pakistani forces had breached the Line of Control (LoC) dividing Indian- and Pakistani-controlled Kashmir in a sector called Kargil. The Pakistani positions enabled them to threaten Indian lines of communication into northern Kashmir. In the face of a large-scale Indian counter-offensive to beat back the intruders, Pakistani PM Nawaz Sharif travelled to Washington in July and asked Clinton to help him devise a solution to the conflict. Clinton refused to cooperate until all Pakistani forces had retreated to their side of the LoC. He also kept New Delhi informed of the progress of his discussions with Sharif. The PM eventually agreed to Clinton's terms and called for the withdrawal of all intruding forces back across the LoC.[54]

Clinton's actions were significant because they demonstrated to India that the US was not blind to Pakistani malfeasance and that it would not necessarily support its traditional ally at India's expense. Indeed, under the right circumstances the US was prepared to side with India even to the detriment of Pakistan. This signalling to India was not simply an accident but rather a deliberate goal of Clinton's approach to Kargil.[55] It proved tremendously important in demonstrating America's good faith to the Indians, suggesting that the two countries could work together as partners in the future. As Indian Foreign Minister Jaswant Singh told US Deputy Secretary of State Strobe Talbott in the wake of the Kargil crisis, 'Something terrible has happened these past several months between us and our neighbours. But something quite new and good has happened ... between our countries, yours and mine—something related to the matter of trust. My prime minister and I thank your president for that.'[56]

Another example of individual leadership's role in facilitating improved Indo-US relations is the George W. Bush administration's 2008 nuclear energy deal with India. The Nuclear Non-proliferation Treaty (NPT) offers assistance with civilian nuclear programmes only to states that join the treaty as non-nuclear powers. US law and Nuclear Suppliers Group (NSG) guidelines forbid the sharing of nuclear fuel and technology with countries classified as 'non-nuclear weapons states' under the NPT, unless those states accept full-scope International Atomic Energy Agency (IAEA) safeguards. Thus, India—which neither acceded to the NPT nor accepted full-scope IAEA safeguards—had been ineligible for civilian nuclear assistance under the NPT, US law, and NSG guidelines. Nonetheless, the Bush administration announced in July 2005 that it planned to offer India fuel and technical support for its civilian nuclear programme under specific conditions. India would have to separate its civilian and military programmes, allow inspections of its civilian programme, effectively secure its nuclear materials and technologies in order to prevent their proliferation, continue its moratorium on nuclear testing, and participate in negotiations for a Fissile Material Cut-off Treaty (FMCT).[57] The US Congress ratified the deal in 2008, following approval by the Indian government, the NSG, and the IAEA.

The Indo-US nuclear deal has spurred a contentious debate. Critics argue that the agreement badly undermines the NPT by rewarding India with nuclear assistance despite its refusal to sign the treaty and would encourage other supplier countries to provide nuclear technologies and materials to potential proliferators. By allowing India access to a ready international supply of civilian nuclear fuel, the deal also could enable the Indians to use their scarce indigenous uranium supplies to expand their nuclear weapons arsenal. This could lead to Pakistani and Chinese balancing behaviour, possibly destabilizing South Asia. Proponents of the deal argue that it actually strengthens nuclear non-proliferation goals by bringing India *into* the non-proliferation regime rather than keeping it isolated. In addition, the advocates argue that the deal will help reduce India's reliance on fossil fuels by increasing its access to clean energy sources and will recognize India's growing international stature and history of responsible nuclear stewardship, thus removing an important impediment to improved Indo-US relations.[58]

Regardless of one's views on the desirability of the agreement, two things seem clear. First, the nuclear deal, to a large degree, resulted from US President Bush's personal leadership. As the agreement's critics point out, the accord did not emerge from a protracted process of inter-agency policy formulation but rather from a very small group within the administration, including Secretary of State Condoleezza Rice, Undersecretary of State Nicholas Burns, counsellor Philip Zelikow, and President Bush himself.

These leaders 'had [apparently] made up their minds to lead a bold departure from long-standing policies towards India and towards U.S. and international rules governing nuclear technology commerce'.[59] The plan was subjected to minimal inter-agency and congressional review; Bush and Indian PM Manmohan Singh announced it as a surprise during the latter's July 2005 visit to Washington. Thus, presidential leadership was crucial to the formulation of the US–India nuclear agreement. It is questionable that a different administration—with a president less committed to a thorough transformation of Indo-US relations—would ever have offered such a deal.

Second, there is little doubt that the nuclear agreement has played an important role in facilitating the recent Indo-US rapprochement. As noted earlier, Indian leaders bitterly resented American efforts to keep India from acquiring nuclear weapons and the American punishment once it had done so. Indeed, the Indians viewed the entire nuclear non-proliferation regime as being deeply flawed. They believed that the regime perpetuated a world of inequality in which the existing nuclear powers enjoyed the benefits emanating from their possession of the ultimate weapon, while other states were forced to accept second-class status. This double standard was particularly offensive in light of India's colonial past. The Indians also perceived that the non-proliferation regime ignored legitimate security concerns of non-nuclear states. Many non-nuclear countries are located in extremely dangerous regions; these states can potentially benefit from nuclear weapons' deterrent effects. Thus, in the Indian view, the nuclear non-proliferation regime was both philosophically and strategically unsound.[60] As former Foreign Minister Jaswant Singh argued,

If the permanent five continue to employ nuclear weapons as an international currency of force and power, why should India voluntarily devalue its own state power and national security? Why admonish India ... for not falling in line behind a new international agenda of discriminatory non-proliferation ... Nuclear weapons powers continue to have, but preach to the have-nots to have even less.[61]

Indian leaders' resentment over America's non-proliferation policy broadly tainted the Indo-US relationship, impeding cooperation even in areas wholly unrelated to nuclear weapons.[62] Now, however, the US has radically altered its position, changing its domestic laws and convincing international agencies to alter their regulations in order to provide India with civil nuclear assistance. In doing so, the US has evinced a commitment not only to support India's continued economic progress but also to recognize it as a de facto nuclear weapons state. Therefore, as Ashley Tellis argues, the nuclear deal 'symbolizes, first and foremost, a renewed American commitment to assisting India [to] meet its enormous developmental goals and thereby take its place in the community of nations as a true great power'. The deal thus 'becomes the vehicle by which the Indian people are reassured that the United States is a true friend and ally responsive to their deepest aspirations'.[63] By clearly ending the past several decades of nuclear 'apartheid', the civilian nuclear agreement has helped to fundamentally change the tenor of Indo-US relations and promises to open new potential avenues of cooperation.

PROSPECTS FOR THE FUTURE

What does the future hold for the relationship between the US and India? Although bilateral relations appear to be promising at the moment, a number of difficulties could slow or derail continued progress. One problem is that American leaders may behave as if their willingness to cooperate on nuclear matters has bought them India's allegiance. Some American policymakers believe that in return for the nuclear agreement, India is obliged to support US global non-proliferation efforts. As Congressman Tom Lantos put it, 'There is quid pro quo in international relations. And if our Indian friends are interested in receiving all of the benefits of U.S. support, we have every right to expect that India will reciprocate in taking into account our concerns'.[64] Many Indians resent this view, believing that the price of cooperation with the US should not be Indian acceptance of American foreign policy goals.[65] A similar situation could emerge regarding US policy towards China. The US hopes that greater Indian economic and military prowess will offer a useful hedge against expanding Chinese power. India, for its part, also has reason to fear increased Chinese capabilities and ambitions. Nonetheless, India will formulate its China policy primarily from the standpoint of Indian interests. As a result, US and Indian objectives vis-à-vis China may not always be compatible. If the US assumes that they must be so, this could lead to discord over the long term.[66]

Another possible stumbling block is the Indian economy. Despite its impressive recent performance, significant weaknesses remain in a number of important areas that could impede continued economic growth. For example, India continues to suffer from massive inequality. Its economic boom has largely been an urban phenomenon, with much of the countryside—which accounts for roughly 70 per cent of the population—having been left out. Indeed, approximately 50 per cent of rural India still lacks access to electricity.[67] The Indian government estimates that over one-fifth of the population lives in poverty. And 46 per cent of Indian children suffer from malnutrition, in comparison to 35 per cent in sub-Saharan Africa and only 8 per cent in China.[68]

India's public education system, furthermore, is in shambles. About one-third of children fail to complete five years of primary school and roughly the same proportion of the population is illiterate.[69] Another challenge to continued economic growth lies in India's dilapidated physical infrastructure, which is in desperate need of large-scale investment. Experts estimate that in order to sustain robust economic expansion, the government must spend approximately five times the $30 billion it has currently earmarked for yearly infrastructure expenditure. This lack of solid infrastructure, including transportation facilities, has negatively affected India's agricultural sector, which loses between 30 per cent and 40 per cent of its produce to waste. Agricultural growth, in fact, shrank from 6 per cent to 2.7 per cent during 2006–7. Additionally, despite economic liberalization, the country remains hidebound by regulation. The World Bank in 2006 ranked the ease of doing business in India at 134 out of 175 countries in the world.[70] Thus, continued economic expansion is not a foregone conclusion. India's economic growth could stall if it fails to feed and educate its people, neglects to build and maintain the ports and roads necessary for easy movement of goods and services, and/or impedes wealth creation through punitive regulations. This would make India a much less attractive strategic partner for the US and would remove one of the main factors driving the current rapprochement.

Finally, continued conflict with Pakistan could impede further progress in the Indo-US relationship. Indo-Pakistani discord is rooted in the two countries' dispute over the territory of Kashmir, which has been divided between them since 1948 and which both sides claim wholly. India and Pakistan have fought three wars over the territory and Indian-controlled Kashmir has been wracked by a Pakistan-supported insurgency since the late 1980s. The Kashmir conflict has proved extremely costly for India, killing significant numbers of Indian security forces and diverting considerable military and economic resources from other uses. The conflict has severely tarnished India's international reputation, largely because New Delhi's efforts to combat the Kashmiri insurgents have led to large-scale human rights violations.[71]

Costs such as these could impede the future progress of Indo-US relations. They threaten to divert resources needed for continued economic development, distract policymakers' attention from managing India's emergence in the larger global arena, and damage the country's image.[72] The conflict could also trigger an outright Indo-Pakistani confrontation, putting India in the awkward position of fighting with a key US ally. Fortunately, the Kashmir conflict appears to be ebbing in the face of increasing Indian conventional military capacity, American pressure on Pakistan to rein in the insurgency, Pakistan's preoccupation with its own sectarian problems, and India's willingness to negotiate directly with separatist groups. In addition, as Rajesh Basrur argues in this volume, factors such as enhanced Indo-Pakistani trade, more inclusive conceptions of national identity, and a new-found flexibility amongst Indian and Pakistani leaders have facilitated a broad improvement in Indo-Pakistani relations. If India and Pakistan do manage to resolve their differences, it will enable India to avoid the risks discussed earlier and remove a potential stumbling block to continued progress in its ties with the US.

It is difficult to conclusively predict whether any of these problems will substantially impede further improvement of the Indo-US relationship. However, at present the signs appear to be hopeful overall. In the diplomatic sphere, even though American officials have touted the growing bilateral partnership, they have also taken great pains to acknowledge India's independent international stature and policy autonomy. American leaders thus seem unlikely to make the mistake of confusing India's friendship with servitude. On the economic front, most analyses call for continued robust Indian economic growth for the foreseeable future, despite the problems discussed earlier. This continued expansion may give policymakers a window of opportunity to address looming challenges before they become too much of a drag on the economy.

Perhaps the least predictable challenge to improved ties is India's relationship with Pakistan. As noted earlier, the situation in Kashmir has improved considerably. Insurgent violence and cross-border infiltration have declined; the Indo-Pakistani peace process continues to work towards achieving a mutually agreeable settlement to the dispute. However, the situation in Kashmir is fluid. Pakistan helped create and support the jihadi organizations seeking to oust India from Kashmir. Were they to launch a major attack in Kashmir or in India proper, New Delhi could be pressed to take a hard line against Pakistan, irrespective of any direct involvement by Islamabad. Alternatively, a major domestic upheaval in Pakistan—such as a takeover of the country by radical elements—could threaten India. This would put the two back in an adversarial role, possibly to the detriment of India's larger strategic aspirations—such as continued improvement in ties with the US. But such events could also bring India and the US closer together, reinforcing for both sides the commonality of their long-term strategic interests to contain a potentially dangerous situation. Even in the worst-case scenario, it will be difficult to completely stop the current momentum of the Indo-US relationship.

NOTES

1.   The views the author expresses here do not necessarily reflect those of the US government. This chapter is an expanded version of S. Paul Kapur and Sumit Ganguly (2007), 'The Transformation of Indo-US Relations: An Explanation for the Rapprochement and Prospects for the Future', *Asian Survey*, XLVII (4), (July/August), pp. 642–56.

2.   Roxanne Roberts (2005), 'A Bush Dinner as Rare as a Pink Elephant: President Hosts India's Leader at First Such Event in Two Years', *Washington Post*, 19 July.

3.   PM Manmohan Singh's Opening Statement at the Joint Press Conference at the White House, 18 July 2005, http://www.indianembassy.org/press_release/2005/July/22.htm (accessed on 8 December 2008).

4.   Nicholas Burns (2007), 'Heady Times for India and the U.S.', *Washington Post*, 29 April.

5.   Dennis Kux (1992), *India and the United States: Estranged Democracies, 1941–1991* (Washington, DC: National Defense University Press), pp. 3–4, 7; Harold A. Gould (2006), *Sikhs, Swamis, Students, and Spies: The India Lobby in the United States, 1900–1946* (New Delhi: Sage Publications), pp. 39–47.

6.   R.J. Moore (1979), *Churchill, Cripps, and India: 1939–1945* (Oxford: Oxford University Press), pp. 47–9.

7.   See Michael Greenberg (1942), 'India's Independence and the War', *Pacific Affairs*, 15 (2), pp. 179–81.

8.   See Kux, *India and the United States*, pp. 9, 18, 27, 37; Kenton J. Clymer (1988), 'Franklin D. Roosevelt, Louis Johnson, India, and Anticolonialism: Another Look', *Pacific Historical Review*, 57 (3), pp. 261–84; Warren F. Kimball (1997), *Forged in War: Roosevelt, Churchill, and the Second World War* (New York: William Morrow), pp. 138–40, 194–5, 301–5.

9.   Clymer, 'Franklin D. Roosevelt, Louis Johnson, India, and Anticolonialism', pp. 263, 279.

10. Moore, *Churchill, Cripps, and India*, pp. 47–9.

11. See Roosevelt to Churchill, 10 March 1942, and Roosevelt to Churchill, 11 April 1942, in Francis L. Loewenheim, Harold D. Langley, and Manfred Jonas (eds), *Roosevelt and Churchill: Their Secret Wartime Correspondence* (New York: E.P. Dutton & Co., 1975), pp. 191–2, 202–3.

12. Robert E. Sherwood (1948), *Roosevelt and Hopkins: An Intimate History* (New York: Harper & Brothers), p. 512.

13. Martin Gilbert (1988), *Winston S. Churchill: Volume VIII, Never Despair, 1945–1965* (Boston: Houghton Mifflin), pp. 252, 277, 293–5.

14. See text of the Atlantic Charter, http://www.yale.edu/lawweb/avalon/wwii/atlantic/at10.htm; Moore, *Churchill, Cripps, and India*, p. 42; Sherwood, *Roosevelt and Hopkins*, pp. 507–8.

15. See Sherwood, *Roosevelt and Hopkins*, p. 512; Clymer, 'Franklin D. Roosevelt, Louis Johnson, India, and Anticolonialism', p. 280. Churchill had resigned from the Tory leadership in 1931 over the party's plans to end British rule of the subcontinent. See William Manchester (1988), *Winston Spencer Churchill: The Last Lion, Alone 1932–1940* (New York: Dell Publishing), pp. xxxi, 102, 146.

16. Clymer, 'Franklin D. Roosevelt, Louis Johnson, India, and Anticolonialism', pp. 280–1.

17. See Jawaharlal Nehru (1938), 'The Unity of India', *Foreign Affairs*, 16 (2), pp. 231–43; and Nehru (1940), 'India's Demand and England's Answer', *Atlantic Monthly*, 165 (4), pp. 449–55. See also Sarvepalli Gopal (1976), *Jawaharlal Nehru: A Biography, Volume One, 1889–1947* (Cambridge: Harvard University Press), pp. 260, 290.

18. Kux, *India and the United States*, pp. 37–8.

19. Ibid., p. 38.

20. For detailed accounts of these events, see Prem Shankar Jha (1996), *Kashmir 1947: Rival Versions of History* (New Delhi: Oxford University Press); H.V. Hodson (1985), *The Great Divide: Britain–India–Pakistan* (Karachi: Oxford University Press); Robert G. Wirsing (1998), *India, Pakistan, and the Kashmir Dispute: On Regional Conflict and Its Resolution* (New York: St. Martin's Press).

21. For a discussion of the Indian complaint, see Josef Korbel (1954), *Danger in Kashmir* (Oxford: Oxford University Press), pp. 98–100.

22. See Jawaharlal Nehru, 'Facts Relating to Kashmir', Press Conference Statements in New Delhi, 2 January 1948, in *Jawaharlal Nehru, Independence and After: A Collection of Speeches, 1946–1949* (New York: John Day Company, 1950), pp. 66, 69.

23. Sumantra Bose (2003), *Kashmir: Roots of Conflict, Paths to Peace* (Cambridge, MA: Harvard University Press), p. 41. For a concise discussion of the first Kashmir War, see Sumit Ganguly (2002), *Conflict Unending: India–Pakistan Tensions Since 1947* (New Delhi: Oxford University Press), pp. 15–30.

24. Alex Von Tunzelmann (2007), *Indian Summer: The Secret History of the End of an Empire* (London: Simon & Schuster), pp. 306–7; C. Dasgupta (2002), *War and Diplomacy in Kashmir, 1947–1948* (New Delhi: Sage Publications), p. 111.

25. Von Tunzelmann, *Indian Summer*, pp. 295, 302–3. See also Philip Ziegler (1985), *Mountbatten* (New York: Alfred A. Knopf), pp. 447–50, 504; Narendra Singh Sarila (2008), *Once a Prince of Sarila: Of Palaces and Tiger Hunts, of Nehrus and Mountbattens* (London: I.B. Taurus), pp. 286–7. Note that Mountbatten later believed that Britain had gone too far in support of the Pakistanis and urged his government to adopt an approach more sensitive to Indian interests. See Ziegler, *Mountbatten*, p. 450.

26. Dasgupta, *War and Diplomacy in Kashmir*, p. 113. Maharaja Hari Singh had named Kashmiri National Conference leader Sheikh Abdullah as the head of an emergency administration in October 1947. Abdullah subsequently became prime minister of Kashmir in March 1948.

27. Dennis Kux (2001), *Disenchanted Allies: The United States and Pakistan 1947–2000* (Baltimore: The Johns Hopkins University Press), p. 23.

28. Dasgupta, *War and Diplomacy in Kashmir*, pp. 118, 123.

29. S/726 (21 April 1948). Available online at http://daccessdds.un.org/doc/RESOLUTION/GEN/NR0/047/72/IMG/NR004772.pdf?OpenElement (accessed on 8 December 2008).

30. The Indians were nonetheless disappointed with the resolution, as it called on both India and Pakistan to withdraw their forces from Kashmir, which in the Indian view wrongly equated India's defence of the territory with Pakistani aggression. The Pakistanis, for their part, were unhappy that the resolution required them to remove their forces from Kashmir before the Indians withdrew or held a plebiscite. See Von Tunzelmann, *Indian Summer*, p. 321; Korbel, *Danger in Kashmir*, pp. 112–13.

31. See Von Tunzelmann, *Indian Summer*, p. 307.

32. Quoted in Korbel, *Danger in Kashmir*, p. 182. See also Ziegler, *Mountbatten*, p. 450.

33. See Steven A. Hoffmann (1990), *India and the China Crisis* (Berkeley: University of California Press), pp. 196–200, 209; Neville Maxwell (1970), *India's China War* (Dehra Dun: Natraj Publishers), pp. 146, 270–1, 364, 378, 385.

34. Stephen P. Cohen (2001), *India: Emerging Power* (Washington, DC: Brookings Institution Press), p. 271.

35. John Lewis Gaddis (2005), *Strategies of Containment: A Critical Appraisal of American National Security Policy during the Cold War* (Oxford: Oxford University Press), p. 154.

36. Cohen, *India*, p. 272; Sumit Ganguly (2003/4), 'India's Foreign Policy Grows Up', *World Policy Journal*, XX (4), pp. 41–7.

37. For a discussion of the politics surrounding the treaty, see Robert Horn (1982), *Soviet–Indian Relations: Issues and Influence* (New York: Praeger).

38. Ganguly, 'India's Foreign Policy Grows Up', p. 41.

39. On this subject, see, Andrew Rotter (2000), *Comrades at Odds: The United States and India, 1947–1964* (Ithaca: Cornell University Press).

40. Pakistan was less concerned about a communist threat to its security than a possible attack from India. See Russell Brines (1968), *The Indo-Pakistani Conflict* (New York: Pall Mall).

41. See Kux, *Disenchanted Allies*, pp. 70–4, 91–2, 256–94. For a critique of American policy, see Robert J. McMohan (1996), *The Cold War on the Periphery: The United States, India and Pakistan* (New York: Columbia University Press).

42. See Cohen, *India*, pp. 273–4; Sumit Ganguly (1990), 'Deterrence Failure Revisited: The Indo-Pakistani Conflict of 1965', *Journal of Strategic Studies*, 13 (4), pp. 77–93.

43. For details, see Devin T. Hagerty (1998), *The Consequences of Nuclear Proliferation: Lessons from South Asia* (Cambridge, MA: Massachusetts Institute of Technology Press), pp. 74–5, 82–3. Note that the Pressler Amendment was directed specifically at Pakistan.

44. Jaswant Singh (1998), 'Against Nuclear Apartheid', *Foreign Affairs*, 77 (5), pp. 41–52.

45. On the fitful improvement in Indo-US relations, see Sunanda K. Datta-Ray (2002), *Waiting for America: India and the United States in the New Millennium* (New Delhi: HarperCollins).

46. Cohen, *India*, pp. 86–7, 272.

47. See John Garver (2000), *Protracted Contest: Sino-Indian Rivalry in the Twentieth Century* (Seattle: University of Washington Press); C. Raja Mohan (2003), *Crossing the Rubicon: The Shaping of India's New Foreign Policy* (New Delhi: Viking Publications).

48. Sumit Ganguly (1991), 'India Walks a Middle Path in Gulf Conflict', *Asian Wall Street Journal Weekly*, 4 March.

49. Jagdish Bhagwati and Padma Desai (1970), *India: Planning for Industrialization* (London: Oxford University Press).

50. T.N. Srinivasan (2000), *Eight Lectures on India's Economic Reforms* (New Delhi: Oxford University Press).

51. See https://www.cia.gov/library/publications/the-world-factbook/rankorder/2001rank.html (accessed on 8 December 2008).

52. See Asian Development Bank (2007), 'South Asia's Growth to Remain Strong in 2007–2008, Says ADB', 27 March, http://www.adb.org/Media/Articles/2007/11669-south-asian-developments-outlooks/; Asian Development Bank, 'Country Reports: Key Indicators, India', http://www.adb.org/Documents/Books/Key_Indicators/2006/pdf/IND.pdf; Asian Development Bank, 'Asian Development Outlook 2008', http://www.adb.org/Documents/Books/ADO/2008/IND.asp. The pun 'Hindu growth rate' plays on the term 'secular growth rate'. It was coined by the Indian economist Raj Krishna.

53. Ganguly, 'India's Foreign Policy Grows Up', pp. 42–3.

54. For inside accounts of Clinton's decision-making during the Kargil crisis, see Bruce Reidel (2002), 'American Diplomacy and the 1999 Kargil Summit at Blair House', Center for Advanced Study of India, University of Pennsylvania; Strobe Talbott (2004), *Engaging India: Diplomacy, Democracy and the Bomb* (New Delhi: Penguin Books).

55. Talbott, *Engaging India*, p. 163.

56. Ibid., p. 169.

57. For a detailed discussion of the terms of the agreement, see Fred McGoldrick, Harold Bengelsdorf, and Lawrence Scheinman (2005), 'The U.S.–India Nuclear Deal: Taking Stock', *Arms Control Today*, 35 (8), pp. 6–12.

58. This brief discussion does not purport fully to capture the arguments of the deal's

proponents or detractors. For detailed analysis see Ashton B. Carter (2005), *The India Deal: Looking at the Big Picture* (Testimony before the Committee on Foreign Relations, United States Senate), 2 November, http://bcsia.ksg. harvard.edu/publication.cfm?ctype=testimony&item_id=51; George Perkovich (2005), 'Faulty Promises: The U.S.–India Nuclear Deal', *Carnegie Policy Outlook* (September), pp. 1–14; Sumit Ganguly (2005), 'Giving India a Pass', *Foreign Affairs* (August), http://www.foreignaffairs.org; Zia Mian and M.V. Ramana (2005), 'Feeding the Nuclear Fire', *Foreign Policy in Focus*, 20 September.

59. Perkovich, 'Faulty Promises'.

60. S. Paul Kapur (2007), *Dangerous Deterrent: Nuclear Weapons Proliferation and Conflict in South Asia* (Stanford: Stanford University Press).

61. Singh, 'Against Nuclear Apartheid', p. 43.

62. Sumit Ganguly, Andrew Scobell, and Brian Shoup (eds) (2006), *Indo-U.S. Strategic Cooperation Into the Twenty-First Century: More than Words* (London: Routledge).

63. Ashley J. Tellis (2006), 'U.S.–India Atomic Cooperation: Strategic and Nonproliferation Implications', Testimony before the Committee on Foreign Relations, United States Senate, 26 April.

64. 'India, Iran, and the Congressional Hearings on the Indo-U.S. Nuclear Deal', *The Hindu*, 1 August 2005.

65. For example, see, Prakash Karat (2005), 'Betrayal on Iran: Costs of India–U.S. Partnership', *The Indian Express*, 30 September.

66. Perkovich, 'Faulty Promises'.

67. Adil Zainulbhai (2006), 'Equitable Growth Not Just a Dream', *Financial Times* (Asia Edition), 29 November.

68. Government of India, *Economic Survey 2006–2007*, http://indiabudget.nic.in/ es2006-07/esmain.htm (accessed on 4 February 2007); Jeremy Page (2007), 'India's Economy Fails to Benefit Children', *The Times* (London), 22 February. The Indian government bases its poverty estimates on data from state and sector-specific household surveys and price indexes. For a detailed discussion of this methodology, see Angus Deaton and Valerie Kozel (2005), 'Data and Dogma: The Great Indian Poverty Debate', *The World Bank Research Observer*, 20 (2), pp. 177–200.

69. Guy de Jonquieres (2007), 'Just Rolling Back India's State is Not Enough', *Financial Times*, 1 February; Jo Johnson (2007), 'Where All is Not Yet Equal India', *Financial Times*, 14 March.

70. Johnson, 'Where All is Not Yet Equal India'; 'Rs. 50,000 Crore Worth Farm Produce Going Waste Every Year', *The Hindu*, 20 June 2005; Shalini S. Dagar (2007), 'The Missing Chain', *Business Today*, 20 May; Government of India, *Economic Survey 2006–2007*. In addition to supply-chain problems, other causes of India's steep decline in agricultural growth include poor fertilizer use, low seed replacement rates, and low investment levels. See Government of India, *Economic Survey 2006–2007*.

71. See Kapur, *Dangerous Deterrent*. On the sources of the Kashmir insurgency, see Sumit Ganguly (1997), *The Crisis in Kashmir: Portents of War, Hopes of Peace* (Cambridge: Cambridge University Press).

72. Sumit Ganguly (2006), 'The Kashmir Conundrum', *Foreign Affairs*, 85 (4), pp. 45–57.

13

The Evolution of India's Nuclear Policies

JASON A. KIRK

Political change in India has been incremental over the six decades since independence. Although the very decision to embrace a democratic model of government was ground-breaking in the context of the poverty and social divisions confronting India in 1947, the path of social and economic reforms pursued since then has been characterized as a 'gradual revolution'.[1]

So it has been with India's nuclear programme. India's plodding path towards nuclear weapons capability was so long in the making that it might be presumed a predestined outcome, but that assumption would be a mistake. Pursuit of nuclear weapons has been the exception, not the norm, for states in the post-war world. Certainly, India faces real security threats that have shaped its nuclear policies, but other states in dangerous neighbourhoods have forsworn the nuclear option. Indeed, there was a time when India itself seriously pursued alternatives to nuclear weapons as a means to security. That such alternatives were ultimately foresworn does not mean that they could never have 'satisfied' an Indian leadership that was attuned to external security threats, but was also concerned with maintaining internal political stability, husbanding scarce resources towards economic development, and promoting a certain image of India on the international stage—as a country apart, a rightful entrant to the circle of great powers, but with a superior culture, time-honoured civilization, and special moral quality.

India ultimately went in for the deadliest instruments of unsentimental realpolitik, but a long view suggests that this policy was not so much purposefully conceived at the outset as it was incrementally advanced by successive political and scientific leadership. Important contextual factors gradually pushed India's leadership towards nuclear weapons development. Regional security considerations were crucial, but they do not fully account for India's policies, let alone the considerable pauses the country took en route to weaponization. Each era's policy choices shaped new material possibilities for subsequent decision-makers, even as a strong norm of nuclear restraint lived on—a legacy of India's non-violent independence movement and diplomatic opposition to nuclear proliferation during the long premiership of Jawaharlal Nehru (1947–64). The final 'crossing of the Rubicon'[2]—when India unambiguously announced its intention to become a nuclear weapons state—occurred only in the 1990s, and even today a significant strand of elite opinion in India remains strongly anti-nuclear.[3]

As Karsten Frey has argued, 'structural conditions of India's regional security environment were *permissive* to India's nuclear development, but not *sufficient* to make India's nuclearization imperative for its self-preservation'.[4] Understanding the evolution of India's nuclear policies calls for a 'levels-of-analysis' approach, which combines partial explanations at the *international* (systemic and regional), *state* (domestic politics), and *individual* (decision-making) levels, and above all, pays close attention to the context and conjuncture through which causal variables interact.

In contrast to this multi-level and ontologically diverse approach (emphasizing material incentives and ideational constraints), a 'structural realist' orthodoxy in international relations theory explains India's development of nuclear weapons in very simple terms: India inhabits a hostile security environment.[5] The structural realist, in a sense, already knows why India sought the bomb, and there is little to be gained apart from colourful 'story' elements from a more inductive investigation of India's nuclear history. But as India's strategic environment has changed, the justifications for nuclear weapons offered by the political leadership have shifted in subtle but significant ways, even while earlier rationales live on as totems of the security challenges India has confronted over the decades.

China remains a central referent for India's leaders, but in a much more multidimensional way than in the 1960s, when the sting of defeat in a 1962 border war was followed quickly by anxiety when China conducted a nuclear test two years later. China's role in India's nuclearization has been complex. In May 1998, the Indian Prime Minister, Atal Bihari Vajpayee, famously foregrounded the Chinese threat in a letter to United States (US) President Bill Clinton, explaining India's decision to conduct nuclear tests.[6] Yet, in studies of public opinion[7] and elite media reporting on nuclear issues in India,[8] the Chinese threat ranks surprisingly low in importance—behind the Pakistani threat, the discriminatory global non-proliferation regime, India's desire for great power status, and domestic politics. Even if we allow for potential methodological deficiencies in such studies and recognize that the impact of public opinion on India's nuclear policies has been indirect at best, it is telling that many Indians today seem to regard 'the China factor' as a *pro forma* justification. Clearly, the Chinese threat was the leading contributor to India's decision of more than four decades ago to pursue nuclear weapons development, but this chapter will argue that India's security motives must be understood in ways that transcend specific military threats from hostile neighbours, to encompass its desire to control its own destiny in an international system dominated by stronger states intent on preventing its acquisition of nuclear weapons.

There is by now a substantial literature on nuclear India, which this chapter cannot comprehensively summarize. The more modest goal is to show how existing scholarship has thought about India's nuclear evolution—selectively highlighting explanations at the international, state, and individual levels—and to refer the student of India's foreign policy who wishes to investigate the topic further to authoritative sources. The first part of the chapter will note key historical junctures and developments in India's nuclear policies, to the Pokhran II tests of May 1998, with reference to international-systemic, domestic-political, and individual-leadership factors. The second part will discuss India's nuclear doctrine in the post-1998 period and will examine in some detail the nuclear dimensions of a force mobilization episode in 2001–2, a serious nuclearized crisis in the long-running India–Pakistan conflict.

By tracing the entire arc of this still unfolding story—linking developments in the pre- and post-1998 periods—we will see that in addition to understanding India's nuclear policies as responses to specific threats from China and Pakistan, we should also understand them as reactions to the evolution of the global non-proliferation regime and, relatedly, to shifts in the international and regional balances of power: from Cold War bipolarity and Indian nonalignment to post-Cold War unipolarity and a new triangular South Asian security dynamic involving India, Pakistan, and the US.

THE LONG AND WINDING ROAD

From Independence to the Chinese Threat: The Origins of India's Nuclear Programme

India embarked on its atomic path almost at the moment of independence in August 1947, through scientific research that was oriented towards civilian energy applications but which held open the 'dual use' possibility of military application. The Indian Atomic Energy Commission (AEC) was inaugurated in 1948, exactly one year after independence; by 1954, the Department of Atomic Energy (DAE) was funding a fairly robust research and development programme.

Two individuals dominated this formative period. The key political actor (as in virtually every other major issue of state policy during the period) was Nehru; within the scientific establishment, the 'dominant historical figure' was nuclear physicist Homi Bhabha.[9] Ashok Kapur refers to the period from 1947 to 1964 in India's nuclear history as 'the Nehru–Bhabha years', in which 'Indian attitudes and policies were formed' that would go on to shape 'the parameters of India's nuclear behaviour in the coming decades'.[10]

Though the institutions founded by Nehru and Bhabha would later come to steer India's nuclear programme under conditions of high secrecy, the general question of nuclear energy—including its potential military application—was initially discussed in the Constituent Assembly. It is not excessively dramatic to emphasize that nuclear issues commingled with discussions that would define Indian statehood itself. The spirit of Mohandas Gandhi and his dedication to *ahimsa* (the avoidance of violence, which had defined the essence of the Mahatma's strategy for opposition to British rule) hung over these debates.[11] Gandhi himself had expressed abhorrence at the atomic bomb, believing that it 'would bring moral devastation on those who developed and used it'.[12]

Nehru's devotion to Gandhian principles, but simultaneous exaltation of scientific–technological development, would significantly shape the political discourse around nuclear energy, which wrestled with its destructive as well as developmental potentials.[13] Nehru's stance on nuclear weapons, like his non-aligned foreign policy generally, was linked to his vision that India 'would stake a claim for a moral stance which might serve and unite many Asian and African countries seeking a genuine independence of policy, and would work for peace by preventing the building up of antagonistic power blocs'.[14]

Against this conventional understanding of Nehru's nonalignment and anti-nuclear views, George Perkovich—the author of one of the most detailed accounts of the Indian bomb programme that appeared in the early wake of the 1998 nuclear tests[15]—argues for a more complicated reading of the prime minister's position. He explains,

Nehru sought to position India as a moral exemplar, a state that could lead the transformation of the international system away from over-militarized power politics and towards a more equitable global order...

However, notwithstanding his idealistic, antinuclear leanings, the worldly Nehru also recognized that India could gain international power, standing, and a measure of security if it acquired nuclear weapons capability. Thus, Nehru hedged many of his antibomb statements with qualifications that India could develop nuclear weapon capability and might choose to do so someday.[16]

Nehru clearly saw India's civilian nuclear programme in an international context—a competitive endeavour, a test of national mettle for a poor but proud country emerging out of a protracted colonial slumber. Whether latent dual-use potential was a significant objective is a more debatable question. In 1946, Nehru expressed 'his hope that India would develop atomic power for peaceful uses but [he also] warned that, so long as the world was constituted as it was, every country would have to develop and use the latest scientific devices for its protection'.[17] Though it is important to recognize in such a statement the suppleness and pragmatism in Nehru's views, the PM's desire to 'hedge' on the bomb option can be overstated. Little in the historical record suggests that his expressed revulsion towards the bomb—and the international power structure that it symbolized—was anything less than genuine. To be sure, Nehru's faith in nonalignment, non-proliferation, and many other things eventually would be damaged quite severely by the Chinese attack on India in 1962, as we will see later. But the most significant Nehruvian legacy to India's nuclear policy remains a principled commitment to global non-proliferation and disarmament, tethered to a forceful rejection of an existing order enshrining nuclear weapons possession by some states and proscribing the option for others.

Nehru and Bhabha secured the political support needed to establish a cluster of institutions that would advance nuclear research and policy through the 1950s (the AEC; a closely related Scientific Advisory Committee to the Ministry of Defence, later renamed the Defence Science Advisory Board; the DAE), largely insulated from democratic scrutiny and even from input by the Indian military. Itty Abraham argues that internal concerns as much as external threats dictated the need for high secrecy. As an apex achievement of the era, atomic energy was a potent symbol of state capability—for Indian citizens at least as much as foreign observers. But behind a cultivated mystique lay a more complicated picture. Though Indian rhetoric emphasized self-sufficiency, in fact external assistance—especially British, Canadian, American, and French—helped underwrite the endeavour.[18]

Secrecy permitted a coterie of political and scientific elites to shape India's nuclear programme in the 1950s. Bhabha, for his part, steered technical decisions so as to hold open dual-use potential. He lobbied, with some success, for diluted safeguards against nuclear proliferation under the International Atomic Energy Agency (IAEA). This represented a shift from the strong safeguard position that India had taken in support of the US-led Baruch Plan in 1946, in which the US would have submitted its arsenal to an atomic authority of the United Nations, in exchange for agreements that would have prevented other countries from acquiring nuclear weapons. When that approach foundered on Soviet suspicion that it was in fact intended to maintain America's atomic monopoly, Moscow pressed ahead to consummate its own weapons programme in 1949, and Washington in turn put aside significant arms control proposals for the years, returning to such efforts only after the Cuban missile crisis. India adopted a pragmatic course of action, which increasingly diverged from its continued official opposition to the spread of nuclear weapons. This inconsistency was not so much hypocrisy as a realistic resignation that so long as the most powerful states retained nuclear weapons, it would be imprudent for India to foreclose its options.

Thus, even before India adapted its nuclear programme in the face of a specific security threat from China, its general unease with a world ordered around the great powers' possession of the bomb led it to hold open the possibility of military application at some point in the future. In 1958, construction began on a reprocessing plant capable of extracting weapons-grade plutonium from spent fuel. Nehru maintained (not entirely correctly, it turned out) that India had the 'technical know-how for manufacturing the bomb', and could do so within 'three or four years' if it diverted resources towards the task, but qualified this statement with a moral claim that India would not do so.[19]

The 1962 border war with China, which a surprised and humiliated India lost badly, was a seminal event in the development of India's nuclear policies. Nehru had fashioned his government's approach to Sino-Indian relations during the 1950s around a view that the two great Asian civilizations 'shared many of the same problems and could learn from each other and work closely together to create a new Asian identity and role in the changing world'.[20] This hope may have led him to discount signs—such as the rendering of the inter-state border on some Chinese maps—that Mao's regime harboured irredentist territorial goals. After the war, Nehru's mordant pronouncement that India had been 'getting out of touch with reality in the modern world' and 'living in an artificial atmosphere of our own creation',[21] and the resignation of Defence Minister Krishna Menon over India's lack of military readiness, reflected the sense of shock.

Moreover, during the war, Nehru had panicked into soliciting military assistance from the John F. Kennedy administration, thus risking the exposure of nonalignment as an untenable policy. Kennedy promptly expressed 'support as well as sympathy', but was initially preoccupied by the October 1962 crisis over Soviet nuclear missiles in Cuba. The Sino-Indian conflict quickly escalated, and before Kennedy could make a decision in response to Nehru's plea for a US air intervention, the Chinese declared a ceasefire that would leave them in possession of territory in the Aksai Chin area of Ladakh, a region in India's Jammu and Kashmir state.[22]

Certainly, Nehru's authority and self-confidence were badly damaged by the war. According to Dennis Kux:

The Indian leader never recovered from the staggering psychological blow. Until mid-October 1962, Nehru, although aging, was still a towering international figure... A month later, Nehru was a beaten old man, his country seemingly dependent on the military support of the United States, his policy of nonalignment in shreds.[23]

Although his body would hold out until 27 May 1964, Nehru's spirit was broken, and he never regained the commanding heights he had traversed in domestic politics since independence.

1964–74: China's Nuclear Test, the NPT, and the Decade to Pokhran I

A month after the 1962 war, the Hindu right Jana Sangh party (a precursor to the Bharatiya Janata Party [BJP] that emerged in the 1980s and led governments in the 1990s) had called for India's development of nuclear weapons. After China's October 1964 nuclear test, this position found favour among some left rivals of the Congress as well. Others, such as the Swatantra Party, advocated the strengthening of ties between India and the West (effectively scrapping nonalignment).[24]

It is highly significant that, as noted earlier, the India–China war ran partially concurrent to the Cuban missile crisis: India's incentives to pursue a bomb were strengthened just as the superpowers stared into the abyss and pulled back to pursue arms control efforts with a new vigour. Initially, India welcomed the resumption of an international dialogue that had been basically dormant since the early Cold War years. In 1963, it signed the Partial Test Ban Treaty—which prohibited nuclear explosive tests in the atmosphere, in outer space, or underwater—'in the hope that the treaty would lead to further nuclear disarmament'.[25]

But contrasting reactions to the Chinese nuclear test of 1964 drove deeper the wedge between India and the great powers over non-proliferation. For the established nuclear weapons states, the Chinese test further increased incentives to establish a workable non-proliferation regime, whereas for India, it increased pressure to acquire a deterrent capability. A line in the sand was being drawn, and India was on the wrong side: a neighbour that had recently committed aggression against it was being accepted as one of the nuclear weapons states, whereas India was being excluded.

Nehru's successor as PM (from the Congress), Lal Bahadur Shastri, remained personally opposed to nuclear weapons development, but whereas Nehru and Bhabha had rarely clashed in public, India's top nuclear scientist now undermined the political leadership by publicly offering estimates that India could develop a bomb at a relatively low cost.[26] This was a significant political intervention by India's top nuclear scientist, since financial cost was 'one of the central issues' in the 1964–5 parliamentary deliberation on the nuclear option.[27]

Shastri privately explored 'the possibility of being given a formal guarantee of US assistance in the event of a nuclear attack by China, offering in return that India would not begin its own weapons program'.[28] But Bhabha sought to persuade the Americans that 'a nuclear India would be a good idea'.[29] A physicist drawn to geopolitics, he argued that the Chinese test had intensified the challenge to India to demonstrate its scientific prowess. Since this contest would be closely watched by other emerging Third World regimes as a symbol of communist versus democratic development, he believed the West had a stake in India's triumph. For Washington, however, this particular Asian drama seemed to matter less than the general goal of stopping the spread of nuclear weapons.

Separately, but also significantly for the course of nuclear policy in India, the US–Pakistan relationship complicated any Indian effort to obtain an American security guarantee. Cold War-era American policies in South Asia attempted to balance Pakistan's explicit interest in alliance with the West (in contrast to New Delhi's non-aligned policy) against India's larger size and longer-term strategic significance as an uncommon Asian democracy. This bearing was not easy to maintain. During the 1965 war—the second major India–Pakistan conflict after 1947–8 hostilities following Partition—the Lyndon Johnson administration suspended American military aid to both the countries. In fact, Pakistan had provoked renewed conflict with India, after a long and basically fruitless period of American-led diplomatic efforts to resolve the Kashmir dispute (in line with UN Security Council resolutions that had ended the 1947–8 war). While the strong-willed Johnson may have believed that this even-handed US policy represented Solomonic wisdom, many Indians perceived it as typical American short-sightedness and perfidy, and it undermined political support for the idea of a security pact with the US.

Thus, even as China continued to loom large in India's nuclear debate, the iniquities of the global order re-emerged as the broader context confronting the leadership. The Nuclear Non-Proliferation Treaty (NPT) that opened for signature in July 1968

created two classes of states: those that had tested a nuclear device before January 1967 and those that had not done so by that date. The treaty would not only legitimize the nuclear capabilities of the five states that conducted such tests, including China's [the others were the US, USSR, UK, and France], but would prevent India from developing nuclear weapon capability even in the face of a major nuclear threat arising...

Although India cited the norm of sovereign equality of all states while arguing against the treaty, self-interest deriving from the treaty's constraining of its own nuclear options was the paramount reason for the opposition.[30]

In sum, two interrelated international factors strengthened India's incentive to pursue the bomb during the 1960s. One was the crystallization of a specific threat from China. The other was the emergence of a global non-proliferation regime that sought to freeze a nuclear status quo that was deeply unsatisfactory for India, in that it reaffirmed the inequitable global and regional balance of power, shut out India, and contained 'no room for rising powers to acquire nuclear weapons'.[31]

This much is straightforward. But to understand India's development of a 'peaceful nuclear explosive' (PNE) device, it is necessary to supplement systemic explanations by taking domestic politics and individual leadership into account. The period after Nehru's passing was marked by political fragmentation and policy muddle. The Congress began to factionalize and had to fend off challenges, both from the ideological left and from the right, as well as from regional parties whose priorities that had little to do with international statecraft. Stephen Cohen calls the policy consensus that emerged in the late 1960s 'the option': India would keep open the possibility of developing a military nuclear programme, while deferring any explicit decision 'that might prove to be politically risky, unpopular, or unnecessary'.[32] This course, he suggests, represented a compromise—de facto more than deliberate—among three groups: nuclear abolitionists, hawks, and 'contingent hawks' who advocated weaponization but only in the face of an intensified specific threat, such as conflict with China. A PNE could be used for major engineering projects such as tunnelling, but in reality 'little technical difference existed between a peaceful nuclear explosive and a bomb'.[33]

When both Shastri and Bhabha unexpectedly passed from the scene in January 1966 (Shastri died of a heart attack during an India–Pakistan summit in the Soviet city of Tashkent; Bhabha died in a plane crash), nuclear decision-making became even more muddled. Shastri's successor was Indira Gandhi, Nehru's daughter, who was put forth by the regional Congress bosses—the so-called 'Syndicate'—in the expectation that she would be a pliant figurehead. Her government almost immediately confronted an economic crisis that would result in the devaluation of the rupee under US and World Bank pressure, which in turn strained her relations with the regional party leaders. Thus, during her early premiership, internal economic and political struggles took priority over security policy. Even so, her experience with external pressure to change India's economic policies made her particularly sensitive to the whiff of imperialism, and when it became clear that the emerging global non-proliferation regime would treat India as a nuclear have-not, her government condemned the draft NPT as 'nuclear apartheid'.[34]

The scientific establishment itself became fragmented and less subject to political oversight. Bhabha's successor Vikram Sarabhai opposed continuing work on the bomb, ordering an end to explosive design work. But he did not enjoy the same authority that Bhabha had within the nuclear establishment, and 'behind the scenes, and without prime ministerial authorization', subordinates continued work on nuclear explosives 'in large part to demonstrate to themselves, their countrymen, and the world that they could do it'.[35] By the time of Sarabhai's death in 1971, substantial explosive work had been completed. According to Perkovich, though basic designs were in place by 1971, all of the requisite technical components for an explosive were only completed in 1974.[36]

India conducted its first 'peaceful' nuclear test in May 1974, near Pokhran in the Rajasthan desert. The test represented the culmination of the scientists' work on an explosive device and a permissive political environment. It was not a proximate response to any deterioration in India's security situation. Ironically, in fact, India's position had somewhat improved in the period before the nuclear test. A war with Pakistan in 1971 resulted in the independence of Bangladesh (formerly East Pakistan), and 'India emerged as the dominant power on the subcontinent'[37]—though, over the longer run, Pakistan's devastating loss spurred it to intensify its own quest for a bomb. The Nixon–Kissinger 'tilt' in favour of Pakistan during that conflict was a new nadir in US–India relations, but India's consummation of a Treaty of Friendship with the Soviet Union 'served as a vital guarantee against possible Chinese misbehaviour'[38] given the, by then, well-established enmity between Moscow and Beijing. India's victory in the 1971 war was politically advantageous to Indira Gandhi, and it encouraged an image of a determined leader that complemented her populist strategy for consolidating power. She apparently gave the political authorization for the nuclear test in 1972; the decision, like many taken by her government, was made behind closed doors in consultation with nuclear scientists and a few trusted political advisors, with even the military kept out of the loop.[39]

India thus stumbled into the first Pokhran test and emerged 'with the demonstrable capacity to build nuclear explosives, but with no policy actually to go ahead and do so',[40] let alone an outline of how nuclear weapons would relate to military doctrine and grand strategy. International reaction to the Indian test was mixed but generally critical and over time—led by the US—it would intensify.

The Hiatus and the Road Back to Pokhran

The most anomalous period in India's nuclear weapons development is the protracted pause between Pokhran I and Pokhran II. The decision to test in 1974 had intimated a shift 'from nuclear *moralpolitik* to a policy of "hesitant nuclear *realpolitik*"',[41] but the other shoe failed to drop. One reason related to economic sanctions that India would have confronted had it followed through on a weapons programme; another economic crisis loomed in 1974 and would have sharpened the pain that external sanctions would have meted out.

Leadership vagaries also played a role; in 1975, political rivals put Indira Gandhi's government in jeopardy, and she retaliated with the imposition of Emergency rule, which again shifted her priorities away from foreign policy. Morarji Desai, who led a coalition government (1977–80) following the Emergency, expressed strong opposition to nuclear weapons in moralistic terms reminiscent of Mahatma Gandhi. Indira Gandhi again led a government from 1980 until her assassination in 1984, and it remains a puzzle that India did not conduct another nuclear test under her leadership, given that the nuclear scientists apparently asked for authorization to do so (she did, however, 'approve an ambitious program to develop, test, and produce ballistic missiles').[42] Her second premiership, and that of Rajiv Gandhi (1984–9), confronted new regional security concerns that might have provoked a more deliberate effort at bomb production—the Soviet war in Afghanistan from December 1979 (which contributed to the superpower's overstretch and eventual decline, weakening the protection that Moscow might have offered) and the advancement of Pakistan's own

China-assisted nuclear weapons programme. But both Gandhis were surprisingly ambivalent towards India's bomb project.

The domestic political trend that transcended individual leaders, however, was the continuing fragmentation of power: away from the Centre and towards the states, away from the Congress and towards an array of smaller parties championing sub-national interests or distinct ideological platforms. An overt weaponization policy would have required bold leadership, but India's political system increasingly did not reward risk-taking; thus, the nuclear halfway house that India had built for itself endured. Scientific progress on bomb design continued, but only incrementally in the absence of new explosive testing.

But by the late 1980s, Indian capabilities were reaching a point such that, though New Delhi did not possess an assembled, at-the-ready arsenal, it was generally understood both within and outside South Asia that nuclear weapons could figure in a significant conflict with Pakistan. After a period of relative quiet, the two countries' relations sharply deteriorated as India confronted an indigenous insurgency in Kashmir, which Pakistan abetted in a bid to slowly bleed its rival and advance its revisionist goals. Though the Kashmiri uprising was essentially home-grown, Islamabad actively supported it as 'an opportunity to begin redressing the enormous material discrepancies'[43] that favoured India. Pakistan further believed that its own incipient nuclear capability would dissuade India from mounting any serious conventional military response and would ultimately 'lead India and the international community to revisit the Kashmir dispute'.[44] By 1988, both nations could have manufactured within a few weeks nuclear weapons for deployment by aircraft—a nuclear capabilities profile variously described as 'opaque,' 'recessed,' or 'de facto'.

But it was not simply the renewal of tensions over Kashmir, or even the specific Pakistani nuclear threat, that led India back to Pokhran. In the mid-1990s, the NPT underwent a review for extension as part of a new non-proliferation push led by the Clinton administration. In connection with another Clinton priority, the achievement of a long-mooted Comprehensive Test Ban Treaty (CTBT),[45] many Indians perceived a US-led international effort to 'permanently foreclose India's nuclear option'.[46] As we have seen, Indian attitudes towards the bomb have ranged from moralistic opposition to unapologetic advocacy. One attitude that has always resonated across the political spectrum, however, has been intolerance towards the discriminatory principles embodied in the global non-proliferation regime. As this discrimination once again became the most salient issue in India's debate over the nuclear option, 'new alliances and partnerships [formed] in the Indian strategic community'.[47] One of the most fascinating individual realignment stories involved George Fernandes, a former leftist trade union leader and strident critic of the 1974 nuclear test, who transformed into one of India's most outspoken hawks—and would eventually serve as defence minister in the Indian government that tested nuclear weapons in 1998.

In the late 1960s, it had rankled Indian leaders that the NPT was drawn to include China as a nuclear weapons state but to exclude India. Now, it was an outrage that even as this disparity remained, India was being treated as if its nuclear programme was the moral equivalent of Pakistan's—which the Chinese had materially assisted and which the US had turned a blind eye to for so many years (during the Soviet war in Afghanistan). Thus, in updated forms, the basic external stimuli to India's earlier forward-lean in nuclear weapons development were again present a quarter century later: the 1998 tests were in part a reaction to changing security threats in the preceding years, but even more to a tightening of the global non-proliferation regime.

But the final, necessary ingredient behind the tests lay in the change of India's political dispensation in early 1998. The BJP—a descendent of the Jana Sangh, which, as noted, had advocated nuclear weapons development in the 1960s—headed a new coalition government (though a previous BJP effort to form a government in 1996 had collapsed in under two weeks, the party leadership had considered conducting a nuclear test even at that time).[48] The BJP, to attract allies, had had to drop key elements of its platform relating to Hindu identity politics that many minority and regional interests found either intimidating or irrelevant. But watering down its agenda threatened to alienate the BJP from its core support base as party of a family of Hindu-right organizations. In retaining the nuclear plank, the BJP partially placated its more hard-line supporters, while also mobilizing (or at least not alienating) supporters of new Indian nuclear testing from other points on the political spectrum.

It was not that it *had* to be the BJP, specifically—though its strident nationalism and long history of bomb advocacy certainly fit. Earlier in the 1990s, a Congress government led by P.V. Narasimha Rao had apparently come close to conducting nuclear tests (physical work on underground shafts was completed).[49] But Rao's major preoccupation was confronting a serious balance-of-payments crisis and securing the political space needed for economic liberalization (leaving little political capital to expend on the bomb impulse). But, by the late 1990s the Indian economy had stabilized, and there was a sense that 'the money would be there if the nuclear option were exercised', even to ride out likely sanctions from the US and other parties.[50]

On 11 May 1998, Vajpayee 'tersely announced that India had conducted three nuclear tests, one of which involved the detonation of a thermonuclear device'[51] with a yield significantly greater than that of the 1974 test. Two days later, even as US intelligence scrambled to understand how it had missed Indian preparations for the test, India conducted two more blasts. Pakistan would respond with its own nuclear tests—a total of six detonations, for good measure—in just over a fortnight. The US, China, Japan, and other countries condemned both countries' nuclear tests, and a range of economic sanctions went into effect. Yet India, as Vajpayee would put it before the country's Parliament two weeks after the tests, had announced its intention to become a 'nuclear weapons state'. It would be for the rest of the world—and especially for the existing closed circle of nuclear weapons states—to reconcile to this new reality.

NUCLEAR DOCTRINE AND CRISIS BEHAVIOUR IN THE POST-1998 PERIOD

The 'Minimal Credible Deterrent' Doctrine

In the aftermath of Pokhran II, India moved to announce a formal nuclear doctrine. A kind of informal doctrine had begun taking shape in the 1980s as Indian capabilities had matured, but it had been wrapped in layers of secrecy and an ad hoc process for consultation between the military and the civilian leadership. Now India proclaimed a doctrine of 'minimum credible deterrence'; even in the explicit possession of nuclear weapons, it still sought to project the image of restraint. According to Rajesh Basrur:

In essence, the Indian conception of minimum deterrence encompasses the understanding that it is not necessary to have large numbers of sophisticated weapons to deter nuclear adversaries; that nuclear 'balances' are not meaningful; and that weapons need not be deployed and kept in a high state of readiness in order that deterrence be effective.[52]

This doctrine implied that India intended to 'acquire a nuclear deterrent configured as a force-in-being, rather than [a] robust and ready arsenal'.[53] Ashley Tellis suggests that minimum credible deterrence was 'a *compromise* choice on the part of Indian policymakers that seeks to serve many external demands and internal constraints simultaneously'.[54] It is a posture to provide some protection against nuclear blackmail by Pakistan or China, while retaining some of the character of restraint that India has traditionally sought to project diplomatically; it must also be noted that after Pokhran

II, India declared a nuclear doctrine of no-first-use. It is a pragmatic stance given that India's budgetary resources—though considerably less constrained nowadays—are not unlimited, and the country can scarcely hope to build into its nuclear arsenal the almost absurd redundancy that the Cold War-era US and Soviet Union did. This doctrine is not the only way in which India's nuclear policies have diverged significantly from the earlier superpower models.

Nuclearized Crisis Behaviour: 'Trilateral Compellence' and 'Pivotal Deterrence' in 2001–2

A declared nuclear doctrine is important to transparency and strategic stability. But crisis behaviour offers an opportunity to discover dimensions of nuclear statecraft that leaders might think about, but not directly talk about, in quieter times.[55] In a 1990 crisis over Kashmir, even as 'opaque' nuclear weapons states, Pakistan and India realized that the US had a strong interest in preventing a conflict in the subcontinent that might lead to nuclear war. After overt nuclearization in 1998, a strategy of nuclear-tinged *trilateral compellence* emerged in two subsequent crises—by Pakistan in the 1999 Kargil imbroglio and by India in a major 2001–2 military mobilization that brought the two sides closer to high-intensity conflict than at any time since 1971. Both states sought to use the threat of conflict escalation to encourage Washington to pay more heed to their respective grievances, relating to their long-standing dispute over Kashmir. This put the US in the position of formulating a response based on *pivotal deterrence*—an under-recognized but important concept that merits particular attention in the South Asian context.

Understandably, analysis of nuclear dynamics in the India–Pakistan rivalry has been strongly conditioned by theoretical frameworks inherited from the US–Soviet rivalry. But unlike the bipolar superpower order of the Cold War, the regional security architecture in South Asia is essentially *triangular*, comprising the two principals but also the US as the pre-eminent extra-regional power (this regional configuration, in turn, is connected to the emergence of a US-led *unipolar* global politico-military order after the Cold War). The US shares certain interests with both India and Pakistan, and has the potential to exert significant diplomatic, economic, and even military influence in the region.

As Rajesh Basrur, a contributor to this volume, has observed, 'South Asia's nuclear rivals have added a new dimension' to the generally bilateral politics of nuclear weapons 'by involving a third country'.[56] Basrur labels the strategy, in which one principal uses nuclear-tinged threats in an effort to affect simultaneously both the behaviour of its adversary and of the extra-regional superpower, *trilateral compellence*. As the weaker conventional power, Pakistan would appear to have stronger incentives than India to manipulate the threat of nuclear escalation in order to elicit US diplomatic intervention, and indeed, elements of such a strategy were evident in the 1999 Kargil confrontation initiated by Pakistan. But the 2001–2 war mobilization crisis demonstrated that India, too, might employ such a strategy to compel Washington to put pressure on Pakistan to end its policy of low-intensity aggression across the Line of Control (LoC) in Kashmir.

A conceptual corollary to trilateral compellence, in terms of the predicament such a strategy creates for the US, is *pivotal deterrence*, which Timothy Crawford defines as 'the manipulation of threats and promises in order to prevent war'.[57] As Crawford explains, pivotal deterrence 'tries to prevent war by making potential belligerents fear the costs, by confronting them with risks they do not want to run'. To be successful, the third-party state 'must hold a "pivotal" position between the adversaries, which means that it can significantly influence who will win in a war between them'; this is more likely to be the case when the adversaries' alternative alignment options are limited (as the only superpower in today's international system, the US is likely to face scenarios calling for such diplomacy). 'A pivotal deterrer,' Crawford explains, 'will try to maintain flexibility and avoid consistent alignment in relation to the adversaries, and therefore avoid firm commitments to either side'.

The 2001–2 crisis unfolded against the backdrop of shifting American priorities in South Asia, following the terrorist attacks of 11 September 2001 against them. The George W. Bush administration enlisted the cooperation of Pakistan in prosecuting Operation Enduring Freedom against the Taliban regime in Afghanistan, which harboured the al Qaeda leadership responsible for the 9/11 attacks. Nevertheless, India saw an opportunity to a gain a more sympathetic hearing for its long-standing accusation that Pakistan actively supported the flow of militants across the LoC—a chance to file the Kashmir issue under the Bush administration's sweeping pronouncement of a Global War on Terrorism. 'Indian decision-makers', Ganguly and Hagerty suggest, 'sought to depict Pakistan as a state that was actively harbouring terrorist organizations and thereby providing a breeding ground for terror in South Asia and beyond.'[58]

Moreover, India's indignation at Pakistani provocation had finally reached a boiling point by late 2001. India's leaders had become determined that Pakistan should not believe that it could use its nuclear capability to deter India from responding militarily to low-intensity aggression; this belief, they perceived, had encouraged the Pakistani provocation at Kargil in 1999.[59] As Indian analyst C. Raja Mohan put it at the time, 'There is a growing belief in New Delhi that the time has come to call Pakistan's nuclear bluff. If it does not, India places itself in permanent vulnerability to cross-border terrorism from Pakistan.'[60] Further (and ironically), the Kargil episode had demonstrated that military engagement with Pakistan would not necessarily provoke a nuclear response—conventional war could still be waged in a nuclear South Asia. As Michael Krepon put it, now 'India too was a state dissatisfied with the status quo. It was now ready to play the stability-instability game as well, and would try to reshape the rules in its own favour.'[61]

Kargil had also demonstrated that Washington took very seriously the threat of a nuclear war and would take strong diplomatic action to prevent one. The Clinton administration's intervention had basically favoured India even then, and the overall US–India relationship had warmed considerably since. As Mohan commented at the onset of the new crisis:

Though Indian analysts of foreign affairs used to bristle every time a visiting American scholar or policymaker mentioned the phrase that Kashmir is a 'nuclear flashpoint'... since the Kargil crisis in 1999, the American concerns on the dangers of a 'nuclear flashpoint' in the subcontinent have worked against Pakistan and in India's favour.[62]

The crisis began with a brazen strike to the heart of India's democracy. On 13 December 2001, the Lok Sabha (the lower house of Parliament) was attacked while in session in New Delhi. While no lawmakers were affected, eight Indian security personnel and six attackers died in an exchange of gunfire on the grounds outside.[63] India blamed two Pakistan-based militant groups, Lashkar-e-Taiba (LeT) and Jaish-e-Mohammed (JeM), for the attack, even alleging that they had 'acted at Pakistan's behest'.[64] New Delhi demanded that Pakistan ban the two groups, put a firm and indefinite end to militant incursions across the LoC, and extradite 20 individuals in its custody that India suspected of terrorist acts.

India backed up its demands with a sustained strategy of compellence. Beginning within a week of the attack, Operation Parakram mobilized Indian forces along the LoC and international border. By the following spring, nearly *half a million* Indian military personnel would be deployed and Pakistan would mount its own enormous force build-up in response. India deliberately sought to project a break from its previous policy of restraint.[65] The Indian leadership 'had three distinct audiences in mind when they set forth their demands': first, President Pervez Musharraf in Pakistan; second, India's own public; and third, the global community in general and 'the US in particular'.[66]

Indian leaders pre-empted the usual nuclear rhetoric from Pakistan. On 25 December, the president of the BJP, Jana Krishnamurthy, warned that if Pakistan attempted to use nuclear weapons, 'its existence itself would be wiped out of the world map'. Four days later, Defence Minister George Fernandes warned, 'Pakistan can't think of using nuclear weapons despite the fact that they are not committed to the doctrine of no first use like we are. We could take a strike, survive, and then hit back. Pakistan would be finished'. On 11 January 2002, in a comment widely reported in an international press now galvanized by the escalating crisis, Indian army chief General S. Padmanabhan said simply, 'If we have to go to war, jolly good.'[67]

In the Indian view, however, a mix of long-term and short-term incentives for the Bush administration would require the US to put pressure on Pakistan. Washington would take much more seriously the threat of militant extremism that India had long confronted and would demand that Pakistan desist in its support to *jihadi* groups. At the same time, the American military presence to Pakistan's west created additional insurance for India: as Basrur argues, 'the physical presence of US military forces in the region was seen as an effective firebreak against escalation: it made full-scale war very unlikely, and it was expected that if fighting did break out, the United States would immediately intervene and enforce a ceasefire.'[68]

On 12 January, Musharraf gave a televised address pledging that Pakistan 'must rebuild', and mount a vigorous attack on militant extremism. He announced a formal ban on the LeT and JeM and threatened to 'punish hard anyone responsible for extremism in Indian-administered Kashmir or involved in religious intolerance within Pakistan'. He rejected India's demand to extradite the 20 suspects, however, and stood firm in Pakistan's traditional diplomatic position on Kashmir.[69] US Secretary of State Colin Powell immediately praised Musharraf's 'explicit statements against terrorism'.[70] He travelled to the region to support Pakistan's commitments and to urge India's restraint, assuring New Delhi that Musharraf was taking concrete steps to rein in terrorist activity and was considering handing over a number of non-Pakistani fugitives.[71]

But Indian forces remained forward deployed, and an atmosphere of high tension persisted through early 2002. India tested a new nuclear-capable missile with a range of over 600 kilometres, and its army chief professed that 'the message was part of the strategy... [of] coercive diplomacy'.[72] The crisis threatened to escalate again in May, when militants attacked an Indian Army camp, killing 32 soldiers. Visiting the scene, the then Indian PM Vajpayee declared that India should prepare for a 'decisive battle' against Pakistan.[73] Impending monsoon rains implied a narrowing window of opportunity for a major Indian thrust into Pakistan, adding to perceptions 'that war might be imminent.[74] On 30 May, Musharraf said he would begin a significant redeployment of Pakistani forces away from the Afghan front, to Kashmir and the India–Pakistan border.[75]

The Bush administration interceded more assertively. On 30 May, Bush announced plans to send Secretary of Defence Donald Rumsfeld to the region in June. He also put Musharraf on notice in a statement to the press: 'He must stop the incursions across the Line of Control. He must do so. He said he would do so. We and others are making it clear to him that he must live up to his word'.[76] The next day, the US Department of State upped the ante. It issued a travel advisory warning that 'tensions have risen to serious levels' and urging an estimated 60,000 Americans in India for business, study, or tourism to leave immediately, and advising all but essential diplomatic staff to evacuate (a similar advisory had already been issued for Pakistan in March, after a church bombing in Islamabad that killed two Americans). The warning stopped short of a formal evacuation order, but nevertheless served as a clear signal to India that its strategy of coercive diplomacy risked not only a spiral into war, but could also damage burgeoning US–India economic ties and the warming bilateral diplomatic relationship. Pentagon and State Department officials said, 'the warning resulted from a decision that the administration cannot err too much on the side of caution, given the substantial nuclear arsenals on both sides and the deep passions over the disputed region of Kashmir'.[77]

America's diplomacy was noteworthy for its equipoise—its *pivotal* quality. It pressed Islamabad firmly on cross-LoC militant activity. At the same time, the Bush administration apparently recognized that some of the 'huffing and bluffing' from New Delhi was designed to compel precisely such an exercise of its leverage over Pakistan. While aware that perceived American submission to India's coercive nuclear diplomacy might set an undesirable precedent, the administration decided, 'the risks were too great to ignore'.[78] Bush therefore responded, but in a way that signalled to Indian leaders that the US was also willing to exercise economic and diplomatic leverage against India if the latter persisted on its precarious course.

In early June, Deputy Secretary of State Richard Armitage extracted a promise from Musharraf not only 'to staunch the flow of terrorist infiltration into Indian Kashmir but to end infiltration "permanently"'. Armitage then conveyed Musharraf's pledge to Indian officials, leading them to believe that 'coercive pressure was working'.[79] India did not immediately demobilize—most of its forces would remain in deployment until October—but by July, the sense of acute crisis had begun to abate. Rumsfeld's visit a week later 'put a seal on the new situation'.[80] Indian spokespersons publicly justified demobilization on the grounds that the purposes of the general mobilization had been served. They contended that the international community had taken cognizance of Pakistan's involvement with terror and so India could now afford to return its military units to their peace-time stations. Such an argument, however, was mostly self-serving; India had, in fact, failed to accomplish the stated goals of its dramatic military mobilization.[81]

Indeed, New Delhi had backed itself into something of a corner. Ganguly and Hagerty argue, 'the central Indian demand—the end to all infiltration into Indian-controlled Kashmir—set an extraordinarily high standard for Pakistani compliance'.[82] The demand *did* set an important standard, and the fact that the US upheld it was symbolically significant in defining Pakistan's politico-military establishment as both part of the terrorist problem in South Asia (the Indian argument) as well as a key to its resolution (the preferred American framing). Yet India's demand was essentially open-ended, ignoring one of the fundamental principles of compellence—such a strategy must make specific and time-bound demands of a target state, but in a way that does not lead to humiliation for either side.[83] This is a very fine balance—and a very difficult one to achieve.

On balance, given that Pakistan already had been subjected to uncompromising American demands—to withdraw from Kargil in 1999 and to ally against the Taliban in 2001—the 2001–2 crisis and US intervention were probably more of a blow to India's image and pride than to Pakistan's, and represented a chastening of New Delhi's attempt at trilateral compellence. Suddenly, this rising power and dynamic emerging market risked looking dangerously unstable and as though it too, like Pakistan, needed Washington's help to 'pull its chestnuts out of the fire', as Edward Luce put it.[84] Basrur argues, 'It would be hard to claim that the mobilization achieved a significant measure of success in relation to the political objective of transforming India's strategic position vis-à-vis Pakistan by projection of a compellence threat'.[85]

Timothy Hoyt offers a mixed assessment of trilateral compellence in nuclear South Asia:

In a nuclearized region and a unipolar international system ... US involvement promises both a buffer against escalation and a third-party channel of communications in a crisis...

Both [Pakistan and India], however, have also been exposed to the limitations of the US role. Pakistan relied on US support in the Kargil war and was rudely disappointed. India hoped for significant support at the height of the [2001–2] crisis and was surprised by the US recommendation to evacuate all non-essential personnel and all US civilians from India and Pakistan in late May, 2002.[86]

India's high-wire mobilization act had succeeded in triggering an intervention of sorts by the US, but the response was focused on the immediate crisis. The American leadership had signalled that the US did not, in any event, intend to broker a diplomatic resolution to the underlying political conflict between India and Pakistan. Whether future American leadership will commit to such a goal remains to be seen.

* * *

To make sense of India's long march to becoming a nuclear weapons state and to understand how India's nuclear doctrine and crisis behaviour have evolved in the decade since Pokhran II, we must bring to bear factors at the three levels of analysis long central to the study of international relations: the international system, domestic politics, and individual leadership. The structural realist theory of international politics—which privileges systemic factors and discounts unit-level explanations for state behaviour—locates the motives for India's nuclear programme in specific security threats from hostile neighbours. Though conflicts with China and more recently Pakistan have been necessary drivers, these security threats alone do not fully account for India's nuclear weaponization, nor for the unusually protracted course that it followed. The evolution of India's domestic politics and the personal imprints of individual leaders from the political and scientific establishments also have driven the outcomes.

India's nuclear programme has always been related to its search for recognition and respect in the eyes of the world. It sought to unlock the power of the atom in service of development even before the crystallization of the threat from China and for long held open the nuclear bomb option as much to defy a discriminatory international regime that sought to restrict it from doing so as to balance against hostile neighbours. It moved to a declared nuclear weapons state status when it perceived that regime to be closing in around its closeted programme.

Linking developments across the pre- and post-1998 periods, this chapter finds that India's nuclear policies have as much to do with the global power structure—defined, since the end of the Cold War, by American politico-military unipolarity—as with China or Pakistan. Indian crisis behaviour under the shadow of nuclear weapons has confronted the role that the US plays at the fulcrum of what is now a triangular security architecture in South Asia. India has tried using brinkmanship to scare Washington into taking diplomatic action against Pakistan in the long-running conflict over Kashmir. While this new form of nuclear statecraft has paid limited dividends, it has also carried risks, and both scholars and policymakers alike must seek to better understand its dynamics.

This chapter has not addressed the major nuclear agreement between India and the US that emerged in 2005 out of a dialogue between the Manmohan Singh government and the Bush administration. The agreement would open up for India civilian nuclear trade and cooperation normally proscribed by US export laws and would effectively legitimize India's nuclear capability outside of the NPT. The dramatic shift in American attitudes towards India's programme has represented an enormous strategic victory for India. Remarkably, one of the most politically challenging aspects of this agreement has been India's domestic politics, as the left parties that provided support to Singh's Congress-led coalition government resisted the deal precisely *because* it represented a deepening of ties between India and the US—which the left saw as reducing rather than increasing India's freedom of action. India now stands on the threshold of a transformed relationship with the US and the global non-proliferation regime. And yet, there could be no clearer illustration that domestic politics and individual leadership also continue to play central roles in shaping its nuclear policies.

NOTES

1. Francine R. Frankel (2005), *India's Political Economy, 1947–2004: The Gradual Revolution*, 2nd edition (New Delhi: Oxford University Press).

2. C. Raja Mohan (2003), *Crossing the Rubicon: The Shaping of India's New Foreign Policy* (New York: Palgrave Macmillan).

3. See, for example, Amartya Sen (2005), *The Argumentative Indian: Writings on Indian History, Culture, and Identity* (New York: Farrar, Straus, and Giroux).

4. Karsten Frey (2006), *India's Nuclear Bomb and National Security* (Oxon, UK: Routledge).

5. See, for example, Waltz's explanation in Scott D. Sagan and Kenneth N. Waltz (2002), *The Spread of Nuclear Weapons: A Debate Renewed*, 2nd edition (New York: W.W. Norton & Co.).

6. For the text and a discussion of the letter, see Jaswant Singh (2007), *In Service of Emergent India: A Call to Honor* (Bloomington, IN: Indiana University Press), p. 117.

7. David Cortright and Amitabh Mattoo (eds) (1996), *India and the Bomb: Public Opinion and Nuclear Options* (Notre Dame, Indjana: University of Notre Dame Press).

8. Frey, *India's Nuclear Bomb.*

9. George Perkovich (2002), 'What Makes the Indian Bomb Tick?', in D.R. SarDesai and Raju G.C. Thomas (eds), *Nuclear India in the Twenty-First Century* (New York: Palgrave-Macmillan), pp. 25–62.

10. Ashok Kapur (2000), *Pokhran and Beyond: India's Nuclear Behaviour* (New Delhi: Oxford University Press), p. 45.

11. Gandhi had largely absented himself from decision-making by this time. In January 1948, he would be assassinated by a fellow Hindu at a prayer meeting in New Delhi.

12. Cortright and Mattoo, *India and the Bomb*, p. 6.

13. Itty Abraham (1998), *The Making of the Indian Atomic Bomb: Science, Secrecy and the Postcolonial State* (New York: Zed Books).

14. Judith M. Brown (2003), *Nehru: A Political Life* (New Haven and London: Yale University Press), p. 257.

15. George Perkovich (1999), *India's Nuclear Bomb: The Impact on Global Proliferation* (Berkeley: University of California Press).

16. Perkovich, 'What Makes the Indian Bomb Tick?', p. 27.

17. Lorne J. Kavic (1967), *India's Quest for Security: Defence Policies, 1947–1965* (Berkeley: University of California Press), pp. 27–8, n. 19.

18. Abraham, *Making of the Indian Atomic Bomb*, p. 10.

19. Perkovich, 'What Makes the Indian Bomb Tick?', p. 27.

20. Brown, *Nehru*, p. 267.

21. Quoted in Dennis Kux (1992), *India and the United States: Estranged Democracies, 1947–1991* (Washington, DC: National Defense University Press), p. 204.

22. Ibid., pp. 207–8.

23. Ibid., p. 208.

24. Perkovich, 'What Makes the Indian Bomb Tick?', pp. 28–9.

25. T.V. Paul (2002), 'India, the International System, and Nuclear Weapons', in SarDesai and Thomas (eds), *Nuclear India in the Twenty-First Century*, pp. 85–104.

26. Perkovich, 'What Makes the Indian Bomb Tick?', pp. 28–9.

27. Stephen P. Cohen (2000), 'Why Did India "Go Nuclear"?', in Raju G.C. Thomas and Amit Gupta (eds), *India's Nuclear Security* (Boulder, CO: Lynne Rienner), pp. 13–36.

28. Abraham, *The Making of the Indian Atomic Bomb*, pp. 125–6.

29. Ibid.

30. Paul, 'India, the International System, and Nuclear Weapons', p. 92.

31. Ibid., p. 86.
32. Stephen P. Cohen (2001), *India: Emerging Power* (New Delhi: Oxford University Press), p. 163.
33. Perkovich, 'What Makes the Indian Bomb Tick?', p. 29.
34. Perkovich, *India's Nuclear Bomb*, p. 138.
35. Perkovich, 'What Makes the Indian Bomb Tick?', p. 32.
36. Perkovich, *India's Nuclear Bomb*, pp. 171–3.
37. Sumit Ganguly (2002), *Conflict Unending: India–Pakistan Tensions Since 1947* (New Delhi: Oxford University Press), p. 71.
38. Ibid., p. 73.
39. Perkovich, *India's Nuclear Bomb*, pp. 177–8.
40. Perkovich, 'What Makes the Indian Bomb Tick?', p. 34.
41. Bharat Karnad (2002), *Nuclear Weapons and Indian Security: The Realist Foundations of Strategy* (New Delhi: Macmillan India Ltd), p. xxxii.
42. In 1982, according to Perkovich, Indira Gandhi authorized a nuclear test at the scientists' request, but within 24 hours she reversed her decision without explanation; 'What Makes the Indian Bomb Tick?', p. 36.
43. S. Paul Kapur (2007), *Dangerous Deterrent: Nuclear Weapons Proliferation and Conflict in South Asia* (Stanford, CA: Stanford University Press), p. 99.
44. Ibid.
45. On India's rejection of the CTBT, see Dinshaw Mistry (2003), 'The Unrealized Promise of International Institutions: The Test Ban Treaty and India's Nuclear Breakout', *Security Studies*, 12 (4), pp. 116–51.
46. Cohen, *India*, p. 173.
47. Ibid., p. 174.
48. Singh, *In Service of Emergent India*.
49. Ibid.
50. Cohen, *India*, p. 177.
51. Ashley J. Tellis (2003), 'Toward a "Force-in-Being": The Logic, Structure, and Utility of India's Emerging Nuclear Posture', in Sumit Ganguly (ed.), *India as an Emerging Power* (London: Frank Cass Publishers), pp. 61–108.
52. Rajesh M. Basrur (2006), *Minimum Deterrence and India's Nuclear Security* (Stanford, CA: Stanford University Press), p. 1.
53. Tellis, 'Toward a "Force-in-Being"', p. 63.
54. Ibid.
55. Dinshaw Mistry (2009) (also a contributor to this volume) offers an excellent discussion of the multiple dimensions of nuclear statecraft in South Asia, in 'The Complexity of Deterrence among New Nuclear States: The India-Pakistan Case', in T.V. Paul, Patrick Morgan, and James Wirtz (eds), *Complex Deterrence: Theory and Practice in a Complex Era* (Chicago: University of Chicago Press).
56. Basrur, *Minimum Deterrence*, p. 90.

57. Timothy Crawford (2003), *Pivotal Deterrence: Third-Party Statecraft and the Pursuit of Peace* (Ithaca, NY: Cornell University Press), p. 5.

58. Sumit Ganguly and Devin T. Hagerty (2005), *Fearful Symmetry: India–Pakistan Crises in the Shadow of Nuclear Weapons* (New Delhi: Oxford University Press), p. 169.

59. Basrur, *Minimum Deterrence*, p. 84.

60. C. Raja Mohan (2001), 'Between War and Peace', *The Hindu*, 20 December.

61. Michael Krepon (2002), 'Last-Minute Diplomacy', *Outlook*, 29 April, p. 24.

62. C. Raja Mohan (2001), 'Managing the "Nuclear Flashpoint"', *The Hindu*, 17 December.

63. Ganguly and Hagerty, *Fearful Symmetry*, p. 167.

64. Ibid., p. 168.

65. Kapur, *Dangerous Deterrent*, p. 133.

66. Ganguly and Hagerty, *Fearful Symmetry*, p. 172.

67. Basrur, *Minimum Deterrence*, p. 87.

68. Ibid.

69. Musharraf Declares War on Extremism,' BBC News, 12 January 2002, http://news.bbc.co.uk/2/hi/south_asia/ 1756965.stm (accessed on 11 March 2008).

70. Ibid.

71. Kapur, *Dangerous Deterrent*, p. 134.

72. Ganguly and Hagerty, *Fearful Symmetry*, p. 175.

73. Rahul Bedi and Anton La Guardia (2002), 'India Ready for "Decisive Battle"', *Daily Telegraph*, 23 May, p. 1.

74. Kapur, *Dangerous Deterrent*, p. 135.

75. Seth Mydans (2002), 'Pakistan to Pull Troops from Afghan Front', *The New York Times*, 31 May.

76. Elisabeth Bumiller and Thom Shanker (2002), 'Bush Presses Pakistan and Orders Rumsfeld to Region', *The New York Times*, 31 May.

77. Thom Shanker and Elisabeth Bumiller (2002), 'State Department Advises 60,000 Americans to Leave India', *The New York Times*, 31 May. Australia, Britain, Canada, and Japan issued similar advisories. In New Delhi, a Japanese foreign ministry spokesman warned, 'It has the possibility of developing into a full-scale war. Nuclear weapons will be used, which will lead to massive tragedy'. Available at http://www.nytimes.com/2002/05/31/politics/31CND-PREX.html?scp=1&sq=state%20department%20advises%2060,000%20americans%20to%20leave%20India&st=cse.

78. Basrur, *Minimum Deterrence*, p. 92.

79. Kapur, *Dangerous Deterrent*, p. 135.

80. Edward Luce (2007), *In Spite of the Gods: The Strange Rise of Modern India* (New York: Doubleday), p. 271.

81. Ganguly and Hagerty, *Fearful Symmetry*, p. 168.

82. Ibid., p. 180.

83. Robert J. Art (1980), 'To What Ends Military Power?', *International Security*, 4 (4), pp. 3–35.

84. Luce, *In Spite of the Gods*, p. 271.

85. Basrur, *Minimum Deterrence*, p. 94.

86. Timothy D. Hoyt (2003), 'Politics, Proximity and Paranoia: The Evolution of Kashmir as a Nuclear Flashpoint', *India Review*, 2 (3), pp. 117–44, n. 78.

14

India's Foreign Economic Policies

RAHUL MUKHERJI[1]

This chapter argues that international and domestic factors were important for determining the course of India's foreign economic policy. The strategic nature of the bipolar balance of power affected India's economic relations.[2] Bipolarity during the Cold War forced India to veer closer to the Soviet Union from the late 1960s to the late 1990s. The end of the Cold War enabled India to engage with the United States (US) and its allies in a manner that was not possible during the Cold War. Second, international structural considerations were mediated by domestic political considerations. India's foreign relations were affected by the idea of nonalignment till the mid-1960s, which was premised on a policy of not veering too close to the US or the USSR, so as to preserve India's autonomy in external relations. Third, the political power of economic ideas—such as self-reliance and trade promotion—made an impact on India's foreign economic relations. Fourth, the power of political factions within Indian democracy also affected the nature of support for either the US or the Union of Soviet Socialist Republics (USSR).

The chapter divides India's foreign economic policy in five Cold War phases and the post–Cold War phase. The first one from 1947 to 1954 was a period when neither the US nor the USSR showed much interest in India. Both were sceptical of India's policy of nonalignment. The second era from 1956 to 1962 was one where nonalignment spurred competition between the superpowers, and India attracted substantial foreign aid from the US as well as the USSR.[3] The third phase from 1963 to 1966 witnessed the deterioration of economic relations with the US. The fourth period from 1967 to 1977 was a time when India and the USSR enjoyed special security and economic relations, which worked to the detriment of Indo-US relations. The fifth and the last Cold War phase, which lasted till 1990, found India in a situation where its resolve to improve relations with the

US was not rewarded because it could not give up its preferred relationship with the USSR. Nor could India improve its economic relations with the allies of the US during the Cold War.

The international structural imperative of the end of the Cold War coincided with strengthening of Indo-US economic relations and India's economic liberalization. The chapter argues that India's economic liberalization was affected by international and domestic factors. These factors led to an economic engagement with the US, the International Monetary Fund (IMF), China, and countries in Southeast Asia. Economic engagement within the South Asian region, however, was not fundamentally altered by the end of the Cold War. This chapter locates the causes for the twists and turns in India's economic relations at the international and domestic levels of analysis.

THE COLD WAR

The Cost of Nonalignment: 1947–54

The immediate aftermath of India's independence witnessed a gradual warming of strategic and economic relations with the USSR, to which the US responded in a limited manner. Relations with the superpowers were affected by two domestic-level factors. The first was India's policy of economic self-reliance, and the second was its choice to follow a policy of nonalignment rather than balance of power. The policy of economic self-reliance made it tough to establish close economic ties with the US, and was appreciated by the USSR over time. Second, nonalignment frustrated the Americans and gradually reassured the Soviets that India was not a camp follower of the US.

India's goal of self-reliant development hurt the prospects of a preferential Indo-US economic relationship. The British Indian government had opposed the most favoured nation status for the US in its trade with India, as this would have hurt Britain's preferential economic relations with India. The US was keen to conclude a preferential treaty of economic cooperation with India after the British departed in 1947. The US Ambassador, Henry Grady, presented the 'Draft Treaty of Friendship, Commerce and Navigation between the United States of America and India', in February 1948. This treaty sought the most favoured nation treatment in trade and national treatment for US investments in India.[4] The Americans were unhappy about the Industrial Policy Resolution of 1948 and the Industrial Development and Regulation Act of 1951, which brought certain sectors of Indian industry within the control of the state.[5] India also signalled to the US that national industrialists were to be promoted preferentially within India's private sector. The possibility of nationalizing private sector assets and the inability of the Indian government to treat Indian and US firms at par made it tough for India and the US to conclude the treaty.[6]

India's policy of nonalignment was not appreciated by the US in the early years of the Cold War. India was attempting to build an Asian solidarity based on nonalignment from the politics of great powers—at a time when the US desired anti-communist allies in Asia. The then Indian Prime Minister Jawaharlal Nehru was unhappy with the US and British treatment of the Kashmir issue in the United Nations (UN). He had hoped that they would take a position closer to India's, justifying Kashmir as part of India.[7] India's positions on the Korean War and the admission of China to the UN diverged from the US' anti-communist stance. India was unhappy to note the special relationship between Japan and the US that did not include other Asian countries.

Stalin's views about India's ability to serve Soviet interests began to change towards the end of his tenure. Stalin had refused to meet Nehru's sister Vijaya Laxmi Pandit who was sent to Moscow as India's first ambassador to the Soviet Union.[8] The late Stalin years began to witness an appreciation for India's interests, as its policy of nonalignment began to frustrate the Americans. The Soviet position on Kashmir after 1952 was closer to the Indian one. Stalin met Indian Ambassador Krishna Menon in 1953, which was unusual of the leader.[9]

Closer ties with the USSR gradually nudged the US to engage with India's economic development. The US did not wish to lose the world's largest democracy to the Soviet bloc. It was only after the USSR agreed to lend 50,000 tons of wheat to India in a moment of crisis that the US shipped 2 million tons in 1951. The US Ambassador Chester Bowles' effort to obtain a more substantial amount of aid for India was largely a failure.[10]

Jerome Cohen has aptly described the prickly relationship between India and the US at this time. The US was India's most significant donor. It provided India with $500 million worth of aid between 1950 and 1955. Yet, India complained to the US that its economic assistance came with strings attached. American corporations found Indian screening procedures to be unfriendly. India could exploit the Cold War to garner substantial American aid during the next phase, which lasted from 1956 to 1962.[11]

1955–62: Nonalignment and External Assistance

India's preference for nonalignment, self-reliant industrialization, and democracy interacted with the international structural imperative of bipolarity between 1956 and 1962. First, India's policy of nonalignment created competition between the US and the USSR, and India received substantial financial aid from both. The US wished to ensure that India would not be lost to the Soviet camp. Second, India's preference for import-substituting industrialization won the approval of both the Cold Warriors. Third, the US wished to support India's democracy and make it the model for economic development in the developing world. India was in dire need of development funds for its Second Five Year Plan (SFYP, 1956–61). These three domestic-level factors interacted with the Cold War to generate these funds.

India's policy of nonalignment appealed to the new Soviet premier, Nikita Khrushchev. Nehru's successful trip to the USSR was followed by Khrushchev and Bulganin's (prime minister of USSR from 8 February 1955–27 March 1958) joint visit to India in December the same year. During his visit to India, Khrushchev noted the similarity of views between India and the USSR on issues such as disarmament, Indo-China, and China's right to membership in the UN and its right over Taiwan. India was portrayed as a great power whose rise would be opposed by the imperialists. The Soviets also appreciated India's efforts to promote decolonization.[12]

The Soviet Union was happy to note that in its annual session in Avadi in January 1955, the Indian National Congress agreed to pursue economic planning to promote a socialist pattern of society. India's SFYP had been inspired by the Soviet planning experiment. The Soviet Union decided to fund a steel plant in Bhilai in 1955 on favourable terms. This was an iconic decision because the Western countries were less willing to provide assistance for capital-intensive projects, which were the hallmark of the SFYP. The Soviet Union was willing to support planned development consistent with India's needs.[13] Even though external assistance from the Eastern bloc constituted only 8 per cent of the total assistance between 1951 and 1968, and trade with Eastern Europe was around 20 per cent of India's total trade, its impact on relations with the US was quite significant. The Soviets wanted to end the monopoly of Western firms. In a significant speech, Khrushchev announced that Western aid was a form of Soviet aid because the West would not part with large sums of development assistance to the developing world in the absence of Soviet financial assistance to these countries.[14]

The US paid serious attention to long-term assistance for India after 1956 for three significant reasons. The first was competition with the USSR. Second, the US wanted to promote India's democracy and showcase a model of development within a democratic polity. Third, US policy favouring aid for economic self-reliance had support within the policy community. The US' Development Loan Fund, the World Bank affiliate International Development Association, and the World Bank's efforts to create an Aid India Consortium all constituted a substantial effort at providing aid assistance to India. Between 1951 and 1966, 51 per cent of India's external assistance came from the US while 11 per cent came from the USSR and Eastern Europe.[15] In January 1957, the National Security Council of the US reviewed its position on India and found that the security risks from a weak and vulnerable India would be greater than the risks posed by a strong India because a vulnerable India would increase the appeal of communist China.[16]

The US wanted to promote economic development within India's democracy, as a contrast to the development experience within communist China. During his second visit to the US in 1956, PM Nehru spent fourteen-and-a-half hours with US President Eisenhower in his private farm in Gettysburg, Pennsylvania. Even though the President and the PM differed on the impact of communist countries on world order, the American President developed a healthy respect for the Indian PM and the planning experiment.[17]

Second, there was growing sympathy for Indian planning among the leading US economists. Walt W. Rostow and Max F. Millikan of the Massachusetts Institute of Technology (MIT) wielded enormous influence on US-aid policies. Development economics of the West was supportive of the 'big push' or an industrial 'take off', both of which required finance for rapid heavy industrialization.[18] India's SFYP was consistent with this approach. It was a model of self-reliant heavy industrialization based on the growth of the capital goods sector, which neglected investment in agriculture and consumption goods. Such a strategy of rapid industrialization seemed a wise decision for the doyens of development economics—who argued that India should be given all help to ensure the economic 'take off' of a democracy. One of India's pre-eminent technocrats I.G. Patel, posted in Washington, reports that the MIT team of Rodan, Millikan, and Rostow did a signal service to India by supporting Indian planning in the late 1950s.[19]

Political and intellectual support for Indian planning in the US aided the planning process. India's self-reliant industrialization, which was consolidated during the SFYP, became heavily aid-dependent. The SFYP was more than double the size of the First FYP (1951–6). It ran into financial difficulties in 1957 because India lacked the foreign exchange to finance the imports required for implementing the plan. President Eisenhower aided by Democratic Senator John F. Kennedy and Republican Senator Sherman Cooper in March 1958 urged the Senate to participate actively in India's development.[20] In 1958, the State Department with Undersecretary Douglas Dillon and later Secretary Christian Herter (1959),[21] and the World Bank under the presidency of Eugene Black successfully crafted the Aid India Consortium. Kennedy's ascent to presidency in 1960 and his announcement of the 1960s as the Development Decade helped matters further. Ambassador John Kenneth Galbraith, the Harvard economist, became a friend and sympathetic advisor of India, who won the respect of Nehru.

The competition to support India produced generous aid packages from the US and the USSR after 1958. Bipartisan support for India in the US saw the aid figure grow from $400 million in 1957 to $822 million in 1960. In May 1959, there were reports that even Moscow was willing to pledge $1 billion to India. Kennedy became interested in funding India's Third FYP (TFYP, 1961–6) to the tune of about $1 billion per year, of which $500 million could go as food assistance under the Public Law (PL) 480 programme.[22]

The Indian agricultural strategy of the SFYP, which depended on investments in heavy industry but not agriculture, increased the country's dependence on US food aid. Farm price support in the US had led to massive overproduction and food stock worth $6 billion in 1958. The US used these stocks for pushing the democratic development agenda in India by moving the wheat surplus to India at the time of scarcity. The US Ambassador Sherman Coopers negotiated a three-year food agreement with India in 1956, which was renewed in 1960 by the Eisenhower administration. Food shipped to India under the PL 480 programme became the basis of food policy in India. It helped keep food prices under control in India.[23]

1963–6: Differences with the US

Domestic and international factors changed the aid dynamic between 1963 and 1966. At the domestic level, the US was less convinced about the success of India's planning after 1963. At the international level, the war with Pakistan in 1965 and India's criticism of the US involvement in Vietnam made it tough for India to draw on US funds. Under these circumstances, the USSR remained a friend whose financial contribution was more symbolic than substantial.

The US became critical of Indian planning after 1963. The Aid India Consortium became worried about the lack of private sector participation in the development process, inefficiency, and problems of plan implementation. Aid pledges were less than $1 billion even though the Indian government had sought more in order to finance the TFYP. Despite Ambassador Galbraith's best efforts and the support of President Kennedy in 1963, US aid for the $900 million public sector steel plant at Bokaro failed to materialize.[24]

The Soviet Union seized the opportunity and decided to support the construction of the steel plant in Bokaro in 1964. It wanted to build a 'second Aswan' and promote India's public sector-oriented heavy industrialization at a time when the US was becoming sceptical about it. The Soviets spent less on foreign aid than the Americans and used their money on highly visible projects. The two steel plants in Bhilai and Bokaro constituted 33 per cent of the total Soviet credit from 1956 to 1965.[25]

The US' aid weariness became evident in the manner in which it dealt with India at the time of a balance-of-payments crisis in 1966. Driven by the failure of monsoons in 1965 and 1966 and rising food price inflation, India direly needed subsidized foodgrains from the US in 1966. The US used the food crisis lever to achieve three objectives. It induced the Government of India to devalue the Indian rupee, to reduce tariffs and export subsidies, and to invest more in agriculture. The devaluation of the rupee and reduction in import duties and export subsidies met with widespread political opposition. Despite this bold Indian move to honour US conditions, President Lyndon Johnson put India on a policy of 'short-tether', which ensured that US shipments would require presidential assent.[26]

These measures humiliated the Indian political establishment. Indira Gandhi had just become the PM in 1966 and was not politically secure at that time. Her critical remarks on US action in Vietnam infuriated President Johnson. The US government, on the other hand, felt that India was being ungrateful, considering the substantial economic and food support that it had received. Despite oral pledges in 1966 by the US and the World Bank of providing aid worth $900 million per year for several years, the aid amount fell after the first year. This approach of the US towards foreign aid to India did not augur well for Indo-US relations in the future. The US' help in making India self-sufficient in foodgrains was one area where India heeded the advice—once bitten, it was shy of having to go begging to the US again for food.[27]

1967–77: Drawing Closer to the Soviet Union

Domestic and international factors accounted for a clear Indian policy tilt towards the USSR after 1967. Indira Gandhi needed the support of the

Communist Party of India and the left within the Congress to consolidate her position as the PM. Moreover, the experience with US President Johnson in 1966 convinced her of the problems of depending on the US for financial assistance. India decided to play Cold War politics by aligning itself more closely with the USSR than the US.

The period from 1969 to 1974 is when India developed close ties with the USSR and curbed private sector commercial activity more stringently than ever before. Indira Gandhi aligned the Congress with the Communist Party of India in order to consolidate her position with respect to the senior conservative members of the Congress. This was her way of successfully contesting the senior right-wing leadership within the Congress.[28] India signed a peace treaty with the Soviets (1971) that gave it security guarantees—a factor that enabled India to score its first decisive victory over Pakistan in a major war in South Asia in 1971.[29] Nehru's planned industrialization looked liberal in comparison with the rise of statism during this period. Big business houses were regulated more stringently than before. Banks, wheat, steel, coal, and various other sectors of the Indian economy were nationalized. Multinational corporations were discouraged by reducing their maximum permissible equity limit from 51 per cent to 40 per cent. Foreign economic relations with the US were at an all-time low.[30]

Aid figures tell the story of India's economic policy adjusting to lack of support from the US very clearly. External assistance from the US, which was 51 per cent of the total external assistance received by India between 1951 and 1966, fell to 1 per cent in 1975. The same figures for World Bank (International Bank for Reconstruction and Development and the International Development Association) rose from 13 per cent to 30 per cent. The figures for the USSR, which were 11 per cent in the first period (1951–66), are not clearly known for the second period (1975–6).[31] In 1972, there were rumours that India would join the Council of Mutual Economic Assistance and there developed a close rapport between the Soviet Gosplan and the Indian Planning Commission.[32]

One can conclude that the loss of the US as a major donor in 1951–66 was compensated to some extent by the World Bank lending. Second, the green revolution of the early 1970s that was aided by home-grown technocratic conviction within the Indian policy community and US technical assistance was a great boon at a time when India was no longer going to receive concessional food assistance. When the food stocks plummeted in 1972, Indira Gandhi purchased wheat commercially from the US.

Despite India's warming up to the Soviet Union, American goodwill was not entirely lost at this time. The US was accumulating huge rupee reserves resulting from the sale of wheat under PL 480, which amounted to over $3 billion in 1971. The Americans could only make a limited use of these reserves as they could only be deployed for supporting the American Embassy in New Delhi and for US multinationals in India, which would not consume such a hefty amount easily. Thanks to the goodwill of Ambassador Moynihan and the support of President Nixon, in 1974, the US waived interest payments which could amount to $4 billion in future. This was a substantial achievement in the aftermath of the Indo-Pakistan war at a time when India had entered into a close partnership with the Soviet Union. Nixon's support for the waiver reveals that he was not entirely averse to engaging with India.[33]

1977–90: Soviet Tilt despite Attempts to Befriend the US

Close links with the USSR came in the way of Indian and US efforts at the domestic level to improve their foreign economic relations. It was expected that the Janata Party government in 1977, led by PM Morarji Desai, would work towards warmer Indo-US relations, with a liberal democrat, President Jimmy Carter, at the helm. If domestic-level factors such as Indira Gandhi's political manoeuvres and the Congress were responsible for India's close association with the USSR, then the arrival of new governments in India and the US, respectively, should have made a difference. These expectations were not realized when the Janata Party government independently came to the conclusion that the Indo-Soviet Treaty of 1971 remained an important instrument of India's foreign policy. This view was asserted during Soviet Foreign Minister Andrei Gromyko's visit to India in April 1977.[34]

The Gromyko visit led to a generous offer of credit worth Rs 2.25 billion on terms that were more lenient than in the past. The rate of interest was fixed at 2.5 per cent, and the amortization period was 20 years, which compared favourably with the 12-year period offered in previous years. This was also the first time that the Soviets had offered non-project aid, which meant that the Government of India could use these credits in whichever way it pleased.[35]

Discussions about US economic aid to India resurfaced. Sceptics in the US argued that the US food aid had kept food prices down but had also led to the neglect of Indian agriculture for a long time. Second, economic assistance had been used by India to expand its public sector rather than increase efficient economic activity via private sector orientation. Third, foreign assistance helped to promote a policy of import substitution that had sheltered inefficient Indian industries in the public and private sectors. Fourth, a renewal of assistance would come with performance requirements that would be opposed by the Indian government. For all these reasons, the sceptics argued, renewing economic assistance to India would not be a good idea.[36] The proponents of the US aid to India, on the other hand, had argued that American failure to deal with India largely wrested with the manner in which President Johnson dealt with India in 1966. With better handling of aid, the positive sum in Indo-US relations could have been realized.[37] This debate did not result in the renewal of any significant aid relationship with the US.

India expressed its pro-Soviet tilt when the Soviets invaded Afghanistan in 1979. India did not condemn the Soviet invasion of Afghanistan in the UN in January 1980. Pakistan became a frontline state in the Cold War, and the US and Pakistani interests converged at this time. The US agreed to a $3.2 billion military and economic package to Pakistan, which caused much dismay within the Indian policy community. India believed that this package would destabilize the region, whereas the US argued that the destabilizing factor was the Soviet Union's presence in Afghanistan, rather than the aid package.[38]

India and the US diverged on substantial economic policy issues, despite a non-Congress government coming to power between 1977 and 1979. Industry Minister George Fernandes, who was both a socialist and an economic nationalist, implemented the Foreign Exchange Regulation Act (1974), which had restricted foreign equity in India to 40 per cent, rather stringently. IBM and Coke left India during this period. The US–India Business Councils could not make any progress. The US became India's largest trading partner during this period, despite these developments.[39]

The IMF was willing to engage with India but the US was not. When India successfully sought Special Drawing Rights (SDR) of $5 billion loan from the IMF in the aftermath of the second oil shock in 1979, the IMF supported the request. The US abstained from voting in India's favour. It worried that the home-grown conditionality approach of this reform package was inadequate. India's decision to favour the Soviet Union at the UN, helping to legitimize the invasion of Afghanistan, and purchase of the French Mirage fighter aircraft had discouraged the US from voting in India's favour.[40]

India became interested in high technology cooperation with the US after Indira Gandhi returned to power in 1980 and subsequently after her son Rajiv Gandhi became the PM in 1984. A memorandum of understanding on high technology cooperation between India and the US signed in 1985 met with limited success. The US feared that these technologies could reach the Soviet Union. Differences on the supply of nuclear fuel for the power plant in Tarapur continued. When India desired the powerful Cray supercomputer XMP-24, it was only able to get an inferior machine—the XMP-14. The US refused to part with the $1.2 million Combined Acceleration Vibration Climatic Test System (CAVTS), a sophisticated rocket testing device.[41]

Trade disputes occurred between India and the US at this time, which led to the US' threat to sanction India's trade under the Omnibus Trade Competitiveness Act of 1988. The US opposed the Foreign Exchange Regulation Act (1974). US foreign direct investment in India was a miniscule $19 million in 1990. US pharmaceutical multinationals favoured more stringent patent protection laws in India. They worried that Indian companies were becoming competitive as a result of the low level of protection accorded to intellectual property in India. When matters came to a head, Indian Ambassador Abid Hussein successfully shifted the venue of deliberations to the World Trade Organization (WTO). This helped to avert US economic sanctions on India.[42]

India's strategic relations with the USSR and Vietnam affected its economic relations with Southeast Asia during the Cold War. India supported the Heng Samrin regime in Vietnam and could not take positions that satisfied US allies and friends in Southeast Asia. The result was that India could not forge close economic ties with the region. Dialogue partnership with the Association of Southeast Asian Nations (ASEAN) would have to wait till the end of Cold War and the initiation of friendly ties with the US.[43]

INDIA'S FOREIGN ECONOMIC RELATIONS AFTER THE COLD WAR
International and domestic factors affecting India's foreign relations underwent major changes after the Cold War. At the international level, the collapse of the USSR made it possible for India to relate with the US, IMF, and US' friends in a manner that was impossible in the past. At the domestic level, India's preference for the public sector and economic self-reliance was replaced by greater private sector and trade orientation. These two changes significantly transformed the character of India's foreign economic relations. Trade and foreign investment, which became important aspects of India's development strategy, have contributed to India's high growth trajectory.

Important international-level factors affected India's foreign economic policies after the Cold War. First, the end of the Cold War considerably improved the strategic relations between India and the US. Change in security relations after the Cold War was quite dramatic. The withdrawal of the Soviet Union from Afghanistan in 1988 and the disintegration of the USSR removed a major strategic irritant in Indo-US relations. Trade in sophisticated dual-use technologies ensued at a time when Russia did not possess this technology.[44] These relations have withstood the Indian nuclear tests (1998), and India signed a significant civilian nuclear deal with the US in 2008.[45]

Second, Russia's value as an economic partner declined rapidly. India was unable to participate in the preferential rupee trade. While Indian exports were being delivered on time, imports from Russia suffered from procurement delays. The preferential demand for Indian products ceased to exist. As the two countries moved away from the rupee–ruble barter arrangement, settlement issues became complicated. The declining ruble at this time meant that India's imports from the USSR had become much cheaper. The USSR wanted India to honour the 1978 ruble rate, which was opposed by the Indian government. By August 1991, the Indian Ministry of Commerce took measures to curb India's exports to the USSR. In 1991/2, traditional crude oil supplies from the former Soviet Union (FSU) declined, and India's hard currency bill arising from oil imports rose considerably.[46] India's exports to Russia and later the FSU, as a percentage of its total exports, declined from 20.4 per cent to 16.1 per cent to 3.6 per cent in 1985, 1990, and 1995, respectively. The corresponding figures for Indian imports were 9.6 per cent to 5.5 per cent to 3.2 per cent.[47]

At the domestic level, after years of import substitution, the balance of payments crisis of 1991 convinced Indian policymakers of the need for promoting trade and investment. India and the IMF ran one of the most successful stabilization programmes in the 1990s that aided the government to decisively change the course of economic policy in India. It is these policies that have contributed to growth rates that are among the highest in the world. India grew at the rate of about 5.4 per cent per annum between 1975 and 1990, and at a rate greater than 6 per cent per annum after 1991. Its growth rate beyond 2003 has surpassed 8.5 per cent per annum, making it the fastest growing economy in the world, after China. The combination of private sector orientation and high rates of economic growth within a democratic polity is precisely what the US had wished for India in the 1950s and the 1960s. The end of the Cold War and India's private sector-oriented globalization spurred a paradigm shift in India's economic relations with the rest of the world.

External pressure at the time of a crisis combined with internal technocratic conviction to drive the Indian economy towards trade, foreign investment, and private sector orientation. Owing to a combination of rising fiscal deficit and the exogenous shock of the Gulf War in 1990, India's precarious foreign exchange situation found the country two weeks away from a default in 1991. India approached the IMF at the time of a dire financial crisis. A convinced technocratic-executive team of PM Narasimha Rao and Finance Minister Manmohan Singh made virtue of necessity and transformed the course of India's economic policy. The Government of India had experimented with industrial reforms in the 1980s, but bold moves towards embracing globalization were not possible due to opposition from a variety of interest groups. India embraced global economic integration in 1991, even though it had opposed it in 1966. Years of import substitution within a closed economy and the demonstration effect of the Asian success stories had driven home virtues of economic integration to the technocrats at the helm at this time. The India–IMF interaction highlighted the success of home-grown conditionality—where the IMF and the World Bank respected India's sophisticated approach to economic stabilization and structural adjustment. India kept government spending and the fiscal deficit at a reasonably high level, acknowledging the fact that democratic polities have little toleration for an economic shock treatment due to fiscal contraction. Second, the political power of Indian trade unions ensured that flexible labour laws, where firing workers would be easier, could not be implemented.[48]

A number of policy decisions since 1991 have produced far-reaching changes in India's foreign economic policy. The Foreign Exchange Regulation Act (1974) was abolished and foreign investors were encouraged to invest in India. The rupee was devalued and made convertible on the trade account. India's tariffs, which were among the highest in the world, were slashed to a considerable extent. Private investment in India, which had suffered from licensing regulations, was largely freed of this bottleneck. India's telecommunications, stock markets, and banks became efficient by world standards, even though there was less progress in the area of physical infrastructure such as roads, ports, and power. These policy changes constituted a silent revolution in Indian economic policy, which made an impact on Indian productivity and competitiveness.[49]

Institutional changes favouring economic globalization followed as India strengthened its capacity to engage with the WTO. The profile of the Ministry of Commerce and Industry was raised in relation to the Ministry of Finance and the Ministry of External Affairs, and its capacity to deal with WTO-related issues was enhanced considerably. The Trade Policy Division within the Ministry of Commerce and Industry became an important department. In 1991, India was ill-equipped to deal with trade issues—it had even opposed service sector liberalization, which was its area of comparative advantage in trade. India's institutional capacity to deal with trade-related issues changed considerably by 2001, and it began to be respected as an important player within the WTO. India's economic diplomats became adept at dealing with trade policy issues. The interaction between the Ministry of Commerce and Industry and think-tanks increased considerably. Inter-ministerial coordination on issues such as agricultural price support and intellectual property improved considerably, a contrast from an earlier era dominated by turf wars and bureaucratic conflict. India abolished quantitative restrictions in 2001 and has complied with the Trade Related Intellectual Property Rights regime within the WTO. It is keen on aggressive service sector liberalization and has taken a forceful position in the area of agricultural subsidies.[50]

Intra-regional trade in South Asia has historically been affected by the India–Pakistan rivalry. Many of India's neighbours worry about its hegemonic role by virtue of the fact that more than 80 per cent of South Asia's gross domestic product (GDP) resides in India. Intra-South Asia trade was less than 5 per cent of its total trade in recent years. Even though India's trade with Pakistan and Bangladesh is far below its potential, India's bilateral trade with both the countries has grown in the last few years. Despite this, India's exports to South Asia at $6.4 billion in 2006/7 were only marginally greater than its exports to Singapore during the same year.[51] The fact that Sri Lanka, Nepal, and Bhutan have preferential trade agreements with India has not promoted South Asian trade to a considerable extent.[52] A substantial informal trade compensated for formal trade in the absence of friendly security and commercial relations with the other two large South Asian neighbours, Pakistan and Bangladesh.

India's trade with the US became extremely important because it became the primary destination for India's information technology (IT) and information technology enabled services (ITES) exports.[53] More than 60 per cent of India's service trade in these areas has been with the US. Quality higher education and low wages gave India a comparative advantage in service trade. First, most of this trade was web-enabled and was not affected by the poor quality of Indian roads and ports. Indian programmers began visiting richer countries on a temporary basis for trouble-shooting software problems. This new type of service activity has famously been called 'body shopping'. Second, another type of service—the ITES—blossomed. Indians could export services ranging from call centres and settling insurance claims, to conducting high-end research in a variety of areas from India via the Internet. The father of ITES revolution is Jack Welch, the former chief operating officer of General Electric (GE), who first visualized the idea of India's comparative advantage in ITES when he visited the city of Gurgaon in the early 1990s. Subsequently, Indian entrepreneurs have learnt this trick and excelled. Such has been the success in this area of trade that if China is the world's manufacturing hub then India is its back office.

The end of the Cold War and India's trade and investment promotion propelled its 'Look East' policy. India wished to participate in the process of Asian economic integration at a time when South Asian economic integration was riddled with political bottlenecks. India could not secure the status of a Dialogue Partner with the ASEAN during the Cold War. Security and commercial relations between India and Southeast Asia were transformed after the Cold War. India became a sectoral Dialogue Partner of ASEAN in 1992 and a full Dialogue Partner in 1995. In 1996, India was invited to the ASEAN Regional Forum—a platform for security dialogue in Southeast Asia. In December 2005, India was invited to the East Asia Summit, which comprised of the member states of the ASEAN and India, China, Japan, Australia, and New Zealand. This summit diplomacy charts out a path of Asian regional economic integration to counter regionalism in Europe and the Americas.[54]

The most tangible institutionalization of economic relations between India and other Asian countries is the Comprehensive Economic Cooperation Agreement (CECA) signed between India and Singapore in 2005. This was the first comprehensive agreement between India and a country outside South Asia. Trade between the two countries has surged ever since. The $2.8 billion trade in 2002/3 shot to $11.54 billion in 2006/7.[55] Second, Singapore is the Southeast Asian headquarters of many Indian companies. CECA governs the liberalization of trade in goods and services between India and Singapore.

This agreement was possible because Singapore agreed to stringent rules-of-origin criteria, which would make it tough for third countries to export to India by using Singapore as a base. CECA reflected Singapore's pre-eminent role in helping India to become a part of various regional clubs in Asia. A similar agreement between India and the ASEAN has been bogged down over the size of the Indian negative list of goods and rules-of-origin issues. India has a less comprehensive agreement with Thailand, and its efforts to bring together the Bay of Bengal region including Bangladesh, Myanmar, Thailand, and Nepal have not met with much success.[56]

India and China have learnt not to let their border dispute over parts of eastern India—especially Arunachal Pradesh—interfere with their trade. India's trade with China has grown from $4.7 billion in 2002/3 to $25.7 billion in 2006/7.[57] The most recent estimates suggest that China has surpassed the US as India's leading trading partner.[58] Will economic interdependence keep the peace and even produce accommodation of differences on the Sino-Indian border issue? Or, will the trade and the security dynamic follow different and unrelated paths? While normal trade between the two giant neighbours with rapidly growing economies is surging, India is hesitant to enter into a preferential trading agreement with China.

* * *

The interaction of domestic and international factors produced a variety of foreign economic policy outcomes for India. International structural factors such as the Cold War or its aftermath provided a context within which domestic-level choice was exercised by India and the major partners. Given India's size and its experience with colonialism, it responded to the international structural imperative of the Cold War by actively seeking an autonomous foreign policy that stressed nonalignment and economic self-reliance. Nonalignment did not yield substantial economic assistance during the first phase from 1947 to 1955, when both the superpowers were sceptical of India's independent positions in security and economic affairs.

Soviet appreciation of India's nonalignment and economic planning drove the US to support India's FYPs from 1955 to 1962. At the domestic level, American social scientists supported capital-intensive import substitution, and there was appreciation for India's democratic experiment. The Cold War and domestic-level considerations helped secure funds for India's FYPs. The third phase from 1963 to 1966 witnessed growing US disenchantment with India's nonalignment and economic planning.

India largely abandoned its policy of nonalignment during the fourth phase from 1967 to 1977 after it signed a treaty with the Soviet Union in 1971. At the domestic level, PM Indira Gandhi's need for support from the Indian left for political survival aided this alliance formation. The US response to India's aid requirements during President Lyndon Johnson's tenure had fuelled scepticism about the utility of the Indo-US relationship. The Cold War alliance system remained so potent that India could not substantially improve its economic relations with the US till the end of Cold War in 1990. At the individual level, PMs Morarji Desai, Indira Gandhi, and Rajiv

Gandhi could not substantially improve Indo-US economic relations, in the context of India's special relationship with the USSR.

The end of the Cold War at the international level and India's rejection of economic self-reliance in favour of trade promotion at the domestic level transformed India's foreign economic relations. This led to substantial economic engagement with the US, IMF, WTO, Southeast Asia, and China. India's economic relationship with Russia became relatively less significant. India's globalization has resulted in one of the highest rates of economic growth in the world.

Economic integration within the South Asian region continued to be conspicuous by its absence. This had more to do with perceptions of vulnerability and hegemonic domination by India in a region where more than 80 per cent of the gross domestic product is produced within India. India's economic strategy has been to bypass its immediate neighbourhood and integrate its economy with East Asia.

NOTES

1. I thank Sumit Ganguly, Walter Anderson, Sanjaya Baru, Vasudha Dhingra, and Anjali Mukherji for comments. Sitaram Kumbhar's timely research assistance is gratefully acknowledged.

2. For accounts that suggest a relationship between trade and security relations, see Kenneth N. Waltz (1979), *Theory of International Politics* (Reading: Addison-Wesley), Chapter 7; Edward D. Mansfield and Rachel Bronson (1997), 'Alliances, Preferential Trading Arrangements, and International Trade', *American Political Science Review*, 91 (1), pp. 94–107; Edward D. Mansfield and Rachel Bronson (1997), 'The Political Economy of Major Power Trade Flows', in Edward D. Mansfield and Helen V. Milner (eds), *The Political Economy of Regionalism* (New York: Columbia University Press), pp. 188–208. For the best discussion of the levels of analysis problem in international relations, see Arnold Wolfers (1962), *Discord and Collaboration: Essays on International Politics* (Baltimore: Johns Hopkins University Press), pp. 3–24.

3. See Robert H. Donaldson (1974), *Soviet Policy toward India* (Cambridge: Harvard University Press), Chapter 4.

4. National treatment implied that US firms would be treated in the same way in India as Indian firms and vice versa. See R.C. Jauhari (1994), 'The American Quest for a Treaty of Commerce with India—1939–55', in A.P. Rana (ed.), *Four Decades of Indo-US Relations* (New Delhi: Har Anand), pp. 213–30.

5. The Industrial Policy Resolution (1948) and the Industrial Development and Regulation Act (1951) took a more benign view of the private sector than the Industrial Policy Resolution (1956).

6. For an account of the US' early initiatives to have a preferential trade agreement

with India, see Dennis Merril (1994), 'The Political Economy of Foreign Aid', in A.P. Rana (ed.), *Four Decades of Indo-US Relations* (New Delhi: Har Anand), pp. 213–60. See also, Dennis Merril (1990), *Bread and the Ballot* (Chapel Hill: University of North Carolina Press), Chapter 2.

7.   Kashmir was a Muslim-majority province that had come to India by virtue of its Hindu ruler acceding to it. Its popular leader Sheikh Abdullah had also sided with India. Moreover, when neighbouring Pakistan sent troops to secure this province in October 1947, Indian troops succeeded in keeping a substantial part of the territory. It was finally decided that the Kashmir issue would be resolved via a plebiscite after peace returned to the region. Nehru was unhappy when the US and the UK set up the United Nations Commission on India and Pakistan (UNCIP) in 1948. Subsequent action by the US within the UNCIP also pained Nehru.

8.   S. Nihal Singh (1986), *The Yogi and the Bear: Story of Indo-Soviet Relations* (London: Mansell Publishing Limited), pp. 1–22; Dennis Kux (1992), *India and the United States: Estranged Democracies 1941–1991* (Washington DC: National Defense University Press), pp. 44–78.

9.   Donaldson, *Soviet Policy toward India*, p. 108.

10. Kux, *India and the United States*, pp. 78–84; Donaldson, *Soviet Policy toward India*, p. 109; Sanjaya Baru (2006), *Strategic Consequences of India's Economic Performance* (New Delhi: Academic Foundation), p. 62.

11. Jerome B. Cohen (1955), 'India's Foreign Economic Policies', *World Politics*, 7 (4), pp. 546–71.

12. Donaldson, *Soviet Policy toward India*, pp. 114–18.

13. Both India and China neglected investment in agriculture and focused on heavy industrialization. India was influenced by China's experiment with collectivization and tried to implement it rather unsuccessfully. See Francine R. Frankel (1978), *India's Political Economy, 1947–1977* (New Delhi: Oxford University Press), pp. 124–55.

14. On change in the Soviet attitude towards India, see Asha L. Datar (1972), *India's Economic Relations with the USSR and Eastern Europe: 1953–1969* (Cambridge: Cambridge University Press), pp. 1–32. Donaldson, *Soviet Foreign Policy toward India*, pp. 114–19.

15. On the rise of US' interest in India's development, see Nick Cullather (2007), 'Hunger and Containment: How India Became Important in US Cold War Strategy', *India Review*, 6 (2), pp. 59–90; Kux, *India and the United States*, pp. 139–54; Lloyd I. Rudolph and Susanne H. Rudolph (2008), *Explaining Indian Democracy—A Fifty Year Perspective, 1956–2006, Volume III: The Realm of the Public Sphere* (New Delhi: Oxford University Press), pp. 217–22.

16. Kux, *India and the United States*, pp. 154–60.

17. Ibid., pp. 140–4.

18. Influential economists such as Paul N. Rosenstein-Rodan, Ragnar Nurkse, and Albert O Hirschman—all argued for the importance of government intervention

and heavy investments for industrialization in developing countries. Rostow's work on the economic 'take off' suggested the importance of sectors such as manufacturing, engineering, power generation, and mass communication, which required the support of urban elites. Agriculture was not an important sector and much of development economics acknowledged the importance of protecting domestic industry till it matured. The MIT's Centre for International Studies played an important role in producing a soft power strategy during the Cold War, which would keep friends by playing a crucial role in the development strategy. See Cullather, 'Hunger and Containment', pp. 73–8; Jagdish Bhagwati (2007), 'What Went Wrong?', in Rahul Mukherji (ed.), *India's Economic Transition: The Politics of Reforms* (New Delhi: Oxford University Press), pp. 36–9; I.G. Patel (2003), *Glimpses of Indian Economic Policy* (New Delhi: Oxford University Press), pp. 76–7.

19. See Patel, *Glimpses of Indian Economic Policy*, pp. 69–80. On the Mayflower Hotel conference, see Kux, *India and the United States*, pp. 149–52.

20. John F Kennedy, 'A Democrat Looks at Foreign Policy', *Foreign Affairs*, 36 (October 1957), p. 57. This is taken from Kux (1992), p. 174. Kennedy had argued for India's role as a middle broker in a *Foreign Affairs* article in 1957. Kux, *India and the United States*, pp. 147–8.

21. Herter became Secretary of State after John Foster Dulles in 1959. He was much more positive about India than Dulles. Kux, *India and the United States*, p. 150.

22. The Public Law 480 was a way of providing food aid to friendly countries out of the excess stock of US wheat. On the generous aid packages, see Kux, *India and the United States*, pp. 150–4, 186–90.

23. Cullather, 'Hunger and Containment', pp. 68–73.

24. On US aid weariness after 1962, see Bruce Muirhead (2005), 'Differing Perspectives: The World Bank and the 1963 Aid-India Negotiations', *India Review*, 4 (1), pp. 1–22; Medha M. Kudaisya (2002), '"Reforms by Stealth": Indian Economic Policy, Big Business and the Promise of the Shastri Years, 1964–1966', *South Asia*, 35 (2), pp. 205–29. At the time of the Bokaro deal, the US was hoping to install a Voice of America transmitter that did not materialize. A $80 million assistance for the nuclear power plant at Tarapur was approved by the US in 1963. Kux, *India and the United States*, pp. 152, 188–9; John K. Galbraith (1969), *Ambassador's Journal* (New York: Paragon House), pp. 562–3.

25. Datar, *India's Economic Relations with the USSR*, p. 45; Donaldson, *Soviet Policy toward India*, pp. 119–20.

26. On the food crisis in 1966 and the policy of short-tether, see Rahul Mukherji (2000), 'India's Aborted Liberalization—1966', *Pacific Affairs*, 73 (3), pp. 375–92; Robert L. Paarlberg (1985), *Food, Trade and Foreign Policy: India, the Soviet Union and the United States* (Ithaca: Cornell University Press), p. 146; James Warner Bjorkman (2008), 'Public Law 480 and the Policies of Self-Help and Short-Tether: Indo-American Relations, 1965–68', in Lloyd I. Rudolph

and Susanne H. Rudolph (eds), *The Regional Imperative: The Administration of US Foreign Policy Towards South Asian States under Presidents Johnson and Nixon* (Bloomington: Indiana University Press), pp. 359–424.

27. On Indira Gandhi's political situation at this time, see Mukherji, 'India's Aborted Liberalization', pp. 381–2; Francine R. Frankel (2005), *India's Political Economy 1947–2004* (New Delhi: Oxford University Press), pp. 289–92. On how the US did not meet the expectations of Indian policymakers, considering the bold moves they had made to meet US conditions, see Arvind Panagariya (2008), *India: The Emerging Giant* (New York and New Delhi: Oxford University Press), pp. 49–50. On the initiation of the green revolution in India and the US contribution towards it, see Ashutosh Varshney (1998), *Democracy, Development and the Countryside* (New York: Cambridge University Press), pp. 48–80.

28. Frankel, *India's Political Economy, 1947–1977*, Chapter 10.

29. On the treaty with the Soviet Union that preceded the Indo-Pakistan war of 1971, see Sumit Ganguly (2002), *Conflict Unending: India–Pakistan Tensions since 1947* (New Delhi: Oxford University Press), pp. 50–78.

30. On economic policies of this period, see Baldev Raj Nayar (2006), 'When did the Hindu Rate of Growth End?', *Economic and Political Weekly*, 41 (19), 13 May, p. 1886; Baldev Raj Nayar (1989), *India's Mixed Economy* (Bombay: Popular Prakashan), Chapter 7; Rahul Mukherji (2007), 'Introduction: The State and Private Initiative in India', in Rahul Mukherji (ed.), *India's Economic Transition*, pp. 1–24.

31. Rudolph and Rudolph, *Explaining Indian Democracy*, p. 220.

32. Singh, *The Yogi and the Bear*, pp. 101–2.

33. Kux, *India and the United States*, pp. 312–14.

34. Baldev R. Nayar (1977), 'India and the Super Powers', *Economic and Political Weekly*, 12 (30) (23 July), pp. 1185–9; Kux, *India and the United States*, pp. 344–66.

35. Santosh K. Mehrotra and Patrick Lawson (1979), 'Soviet Economic Relations with India and Other Third World Countries', *Economic and Political Weekly*, 14 (30/32) (August), pp. 1367–92.

36. On the renewed debates on foreign aid to India during the Carter administration, see Myron Weiner (1979), 'Assessing the Impact of Foreign Assistance', in John W. Mellor and Philips Talbot (eds), *India: A Rising Middle Power* (Colorado: Westview Press), pp. 49–68.

37. Lloyd I. Rudolph (1979), 'Comment', in Mellor and Talbot (eds), *India*, pp. 69–76.

38. Kux, *India and the United States*, pp. 367–71.

39. Ibid., pp. 362–4.

40. Praveen K. Chaudhry, Vijay L. Kelkar, and Vikash Yadav (2004), 'The Evolution of "Homegrown Conditionality" in India: IMF Relations', *Journal of Development Studies*, 40 (6), pp. 59–81.

41. On India's high technology cooperation with the US in the 1980s, see Kux, *India and the United States*, pp. 404–12; Devin T. Hagerty (2006), 'Are We Present

at the Creation? Alliance Theory and the Indo-US Strategic Convergence', in Sumit Ganguly, Brian Shoup, and Andrew Scobel (eds), *US–Indian Strategic Cooperation: Into The 21st Century* (London: Routledge), pp. 11–37.

42. Kux, *India and the United States*, pp. 434–8.

43. Rahul Mukherji (2008), 'Appraising the Legacy of Bandung', in See Seng Tan and Amitav Acharya (eds), *Bandung Revisited: The Legacy of the 1956 Asian–African Conference for International Order* (Singapore: NUS Press), pp. 170–3; Kripa Sridharan (1996), *The ASEAN Region in India's Foreign Policy* (Aldershot: Dartmouth Publishing Co. Ltd), Chapters 2–4.

44. On greater strategic convergence and sensitive dual-use high technology cooperation beyond the Cold War, see Hagerty, 'Are We Present at the Creation?', pp. 16–31; Varun Sahni (2006), 'Limited Cooperation between Limited Allies: India's Strategic Programs and the India–US Strategic Trade', in Ganguly, Shoup, and Scobel (eds), *US–Indian Strategic Cooperation*, pp. 173–91.

45. For an account of the India lobby in the US that facilitated this deal, see Jason A. Kirk (2008), 'Indian-Americans and the US–India Nuclear Agreement: Consolidation of an Ethnic Lobby', *Foreign Policy Analysis*, 4 (3), pp. 275–300.

46. Ramesh Thakur (1994), *The Politics and Economics of India's Foreign Policy* (London: Hurst and Company), pp. 116–23.

47. Vinod K. Aggarwal and Rahul Mukherji (2008), 'Shifts in India's Trade Policy: South Asia and Beyond', in Vinod K. Aggarwal and Min Gyo Koo (eds), *Asia's New Institutional Architecture: Evolving Structures for Managing Trade, Financial and Security Relations* (Heidelberg: Springer), pp. 125–58.

48. On India's economic transition initiated in a big way in 1991, see Rahul Mukherji (2007), 'Economic Transition in a Plural Polity: India', in Rahul Mukherji (ed.), *India's Economic Transition*, pp. 118–45; Panagariya, *India*, pp. 95–109; Vijay Joshi and I.M.D. Little (1994), *India: Macroeconomic and Political Economy* (New Delhi: Oxford University Press), pp. 181–200.

49. Rahul Mukherji (2008), 'The Political Economy of India's Economic Reforms', *Asian Economic Policy Review*, 3 (2), pp. 315–31.

50. Aseema Sinha (2007), 'Global Linkages and Domestic Politics: Trade Reform and Institution Building in India in Comparative Perspective', *Comparative Political Studies*, 40 (10), pp. 1191–204.

51. Between 2002/3 and 2006/7 India's trade with Pakistan and Bangladesh grew from $251 million to $1.6 billion and $1.2 billion to $1.8 billion, respectively. These figures were obtained from the website of the Department of Commerce, Government of India. See http://commerce.nic.in/eidb/iecnt.asp. Kishore C. Dash (2008), *Regionalism in South Asia* (London: Routledge), pp. 142–69.

52. Aggarwal and Mukherji, 'Shifts in India's Trade Policy', pp. 237–8.

53. India's total trade with the US grew from $15.3 billion in 2002/3 to $30.5 billion in 2006/7. The US has been India's most important trading partner—a figure that has just been surpassed this year. India's total exports to the European Union

amounted to $26.7 billion in 2006/7. The same figure for the US alone was $18.8 billion. These figures were obtained from different searches of the website of the Department of Commerce, Government of India.

54. Aggarwal and Mukherji, 'Shifts in India's Trade Policy', pp. 165–74.

55. These figures were obtained from the website of the Department of Commerce, Government of India. See http://commerce.nic.in/eidb/iecnt.asp.

56. Aggarwal and Mukherji, 'Shifts in India's Trade Policy', pp. 240–4.

57. These figures were obtained from the website of the Department of Commerce, Government of India. See http://commerce.nic.in/eidb/iecnt.asp.

58. In 2007–8, the Department of Commerce website stated that total trade between India and US, and India and China were $ 41.7 billion and $ 37.9 billion, respectively. (http://commerce.nic.in/eidb/iecntq.asp) Let us go with these figures and say that China is India's second largest trading partner.

15

Domestic and International Influences on India's Energy Policy, 1947–2008

DINSHAW MISTRY

India obtains its energy from a number of sources such as coal, oil, gas, hydropower, and nuclear power. Much of this energy is produced domestically, and India's energy policies are made by the government ministry responsible for each energy source. Thus, domestic and bureaucratic factors primarily shape India's energy policy. However, India relies on foreign suppliers for most of its oil requirements and has also sought international suppliers for gas and nuclear energy. Not surprisingly, international political factors have significantly influenced India's energy policy in these areas.

Further, after it initiated economic reforms in 1991, India's economic growth rates increased (annual economic growth averaged 6 per cent during 1992–2001 and 8 per cent during 2002–7), and its consumption of energy also increased. Domestic producers were unable to meet this growing demand (especially for oil, where domestic production did not significantly increase but consumption more than doubled in the decade after 1991) and foreign suppliers then contributed a greater share of India's energy needs (see Table 15.1). In 1991, imports accounted for about 18 per cent of India's commercial energy requirements; by 2001, their share had risen to 25 per cent; and by 2007, their share was close to 30 per cent.[1] Accordingly, energy issues became more important in India's foreign policy and India's political leaders and foreign affairs bureaucracy sought to pursue 'robust and multifaceted engagements across the world to promote India's energy security interests'.[2] Thus, one additional bureaucratic–diplomatic factor—involvement by India's foreign policy bureaucracy and high-level diplomacy by India's political leaders—began influencing India's energy policy in the 2000s.

TABLE 15.1: India's Oil and Total Energy Production and Consumption

	1991	2001	2007
Total Primary Energy			
Consumption	8.4	13.9	16.2
Production	7.2	10.3	11.7
Imports	1.2	3.6	4.5
Oil			
Consumption	58.9	107.0	128.5
Production	33.1	36.0	37.3
Imports	25.8	70.9	91.2

Source: US Department of Energy, Energy Information Administration, *Country Energy Profiles: India* (2008); British Petroleum, *BP Statistical Review of World Energy* (June 2008). *Note*: Total primary energy is measured in Quadrillion Btu; Oil is measured in million tons.

This chapter discusses the aforementioned issues in Indian energy policy. The chapter first clarifies India's main sources of energy and energy policy. It then reviews India's policies on oil, gas, and nuclear energy, which are significantly influenced by international factors. On oil policy, it shows how India's choice of oil suppliers was influenced by the colonial legacy and then by socialist economic policies and India's relations with the Soviet Union. The chapter also discusses how India's relations with Russia and the states in Central Asia, the Middle East, and Africa influenced India's attempts to acquire oil assets in these states in the 2000s. On gas policy, the chapter discusses how India's relations with regional and neighbouring states, such as Pakistan, Iran, Myanmar, and Bangladesh, influenced its attempts to acquire gas from or transiting through these states. Finally, on nuclear energy, the chapter analyses the manner in which international economic, security, and environmental regimes influenced India's civilian nuclear imports.

MULTIPLE SOURCES OF ENERGY AND ENERGY POLICY

India's main sources of energy are coal (which accounts for about 50 per cent of primary commercial energy consumption and generates about two-thirds of India's electricity), oil (which accounts for approximately 30 per cent of commercial energy consumption), and gas (which accounts for approximately 8 per cent of commercial energy consumption).[3] India's two other important energy sources are hydroelectricity (which accounts for 5 per cent of commercial energy consumption and generates about one-fourth of India's electricity) and nuclear energy (which accounts for 1 per cent of commercial energy consumption and generates about 3 per cent of

India's electricity). Foreign suppliers are crucial to India's energy mix, but mainly in the areas of oil and gas. India imports about 70 per cent of its oil and 15–20 per cent of its gas, as shown in Table 15.2.

TABLE 15.2: India's Domestic Production and Imports of Energy in 2005

	Coal	Crude Oil	Gas	Nuclear	Hydroelectric	Renewable	Total
Domestic Production	186	37	24	4.5	8.6	158	419
Imports	26	101	5	0	0	0	144
Percentage of Imports	12	73	17				25

Source: International Energy Agency, *IEA Statistics, 2005 Energy Balances for India*.
Notes: All figures in million tons of oil equivalent (MTOE). Other energy sources are solar and geothermal (0.5 MTOE, domestic production) and petroleum products (11 MTOE, imported).

Indian government's policy for each energy source is developed by a ministry, such as the Ministry of Petroleum and Natural Gas, the Ministry of Coal, the Ministry of Non-Conventional Energy Sources, the Department of Atomic Energy, and the Ministry of Power. India's foreign ministry also plays a role in its energy policy. While energy issues were always important in Indian foreign policy—for example, New Delhi sought to maintain strong ties with the Middle Eastern states that were the source of its oil imports—energy became more prominent in Indian foreign policy in and since the late 1990s. In 1996, the Indian government began recognizing the significance of acquiring energy assets abroad. It established a new firm, ONGC Videsh Limited (OVL), a subsidiary of the state-owned Oil and Natural Gas Corporation (ONGC), to acquire oil assets overseas.

In the subsequent years, India's government recognized the need for an overarching energy policy. It sought institutional coordination among the different government ministries dealing with energy policy.[4] The Prime Minister's (PM) Office set up an inter-ministerial group to focus on energy policy, which produced a report in early 2000 titled *Hydrocarbon Vision 2025*. Further, India's policymakers began viewing energy as a security issue, and the concept of energy security increasingly entered government discourse on foreign policy and security policy.

Hydrocarbon Vision 2025 and reports by India's Planning Commission (such as the Five Year Plans and its Integrated Energy Policy that was drafted in 2005 and approved in 2008) noted that one route to energy security was through the diversification of foreign suppliers. They noted that another means to energy security was for Indian firms to invest in oil and gas ventures overseas. In short, by the early and mid-2000s, India's energy policies were concerned with diversifying its foreign sources of energy—particularly in the areas of oil and gas, and also in the area of nuclear energy.

OIL

India's foreign energy policy in the area of oil can be analysed in three phases—a first phase from India's independence to the 1960s, a second phase from the 1960s to the end of the Cold War, and a third phase thereafter. The colonial legacy, domestic factors (such as a socialist economic policy in the 1960s and 1970s), and international factors (such as India's stronger ties with the Soviet Union since the 1960s) influenced India's choice of suppliers in the first two phases. In the third phase, especially in the 2000s, India sought to diversify its sources of oil by acquiring oil assets overseas. High-level diplomacy by Indian government officials and a variety of technical, bureaucratic, and international factors influenced these attempts to purchase oil assets overseas.

Phases One and Two: Western Oil Firms, the Soviet Union, and Middle Eastern States

India's oil policy for some two decades after its independence was shaped by a historical–international factor—the colonial legacy. Its oil industry was largely controlled by the British-owned Burmah (that had a joint venture with Shell to form Burmah-Shell) and American companies Standard-Vacuum and Caltex. These firms imported oil from their fields in the Middle East; thus, from the 1940s to the 1960s, most of India's imported oil came from Iran and Saudi Arabia, with smaller amounts coming from Kuwait and Indonesia.[5] The Western oil companies also owned most of the refineries in India. Until the early 1960s, all four refineries in India were foreign-owned, and in the late 1960s foreign ownership was still considerable. For example, in 1967, of the nine refineries in India, five drew supplies from abroad, and only 5.7 million tons of a total of 14.4 million tons of India's crude oil consumption came from India's public sector refineries.[6]

During the second phase of India's oil policy, from the 1960s onwards, a domestic economic factor (India's socialist economic policy that was most strongly implemented from 1965–81)[7] and an international factor (its stronger ties with the Soviet Union) resulted in changes in India's oil suppliers. At the time, India's government had major disputes with Western oil firms over the price of oil and the refining of imported oil. Specifically, in 1960, New Delhi signed an agreement with Moscow to import Soviet oil at prices below those prevailing in world markets. The Western oil firms refused to refine this oil, causing the Indian government to hold back on the Soviet contract. The government then built public sector refineries with Soviet and Romanian support beginning in 1962, and it also banned Western oil companies from expanding their refineries in India.[8] Eventually, the state-owned Indian Oil Corporation was given a monopoly on oil imports; India expanded its domestic production with Soviet and Romanian assistance; in 1976, the Burmah-Shell and Caltex refineries were nationalized. As a result, India was no longer reliant on Western oil firms.

In 1977, New Delhi requested and Moscow agreed to supply crude oil to India, which was paid for in rupees. The Soviet Union accounted for 5–15 per cent of India's crude oil imports from 1977 to 1982, and its share increased to 23 per cent by 1984, after India requested an increase in Soviet supplies during the Iran–Iraq war.[9] The remainder of India's crude oil imports came from the Middle East, as shown in Table 15.3 (the table also shows how India's oil supplies from Kuwait, Iran, and Iraq were affected by war and international sanctions in these countries). In addition, of the 10 public sector refineries in India by 1984, three were built with Soviet assistance (and accounted for 16 million tons of India's total refining capacity of 34 million tons), and two were built with Romanian assistance.[10]

TABLE 15.3: Percentage Share of India's Foreign Suppliers of Oil

	1984–5	1985–6	1989–90	1992–3	2005–6
USSR/Russia	23	17	17		
Iran	13	23	9	11	10
Iraq	19	14	10		9
Kuwait	3	2	11	17	12
Nigeria				15	16
Saudi Arabia	33	16	25	30	25
United Arab Emirates	4	14	26	23	
Oman	4	10			

Source: *Monthly Statistics of the Foreign Trade of India*, various years.

The Third Phase: Oil Asset Acquisition in the Twenty-first Century

During the third phase of India's oil policy, since the 1990s, its oil suppliers again changed. With the collapse of the Soviet Union and the end of the rupee–ruble trading arrangements, Russia's oil supplies to India largely ended. India then purchased most of its oil on the world market, from Nigeria and the Middle East, as noted in Table 15.3. Thus, in 2005, India's main oil suppliers were Saudi Arabia (which supplied 25 per cent of its oil), Nigeria (16 per cent), Kuwait (12 per cent), Iran (10 per cent), and Iraq (9 per cent).[11] That year, foreign suppliers accounted for over 70 per cent of India's oil supply—domestic production by ONGC was only 26 million tons compared to India's total oil demand of 120 million tons, with the difference being purchased on the world market. To augment commercial purchases on the world market, India's government and oil firms sought to secure oilfields abroad—these assets added 3 to 5 million tons annually to India's oil supply in the mid- and late 2000s.[12]

India's government assumed that overseas production by Indian companies would enhance its energy security.[13] Accordingly, the state-owned OVL made several attempts to secure assets overseas. In the first decade after it was set up, OVL's two main foreign investments, on the order of $2 billion each, were the acquisition of assets in Sudan (beginning in 2002) and Russia (2001).

In 2002, OVL invested approximately $700 million for a 25 per cent share in the Greater Nile Oil Project in Sudan. It subsequently expanded investments in Sudan to some $2 billion, and by 2006 India was obtaining some 3 million tons of crude oil annually from its Sudanese investments. OVL also invested over $2 billion for a 20 per cent share of the Sakhalin-1 oil and gas field in Russia. India received its first oil shipments from Sakhalin-1 in 2006, and expected to obtain 2 million tons of oil annually from this field when it reached its full production level.[14]

Diplomacy involving India's senior-most political leaders influenced its investments in the Russian oil fields. In 2001, Finance Minister Yashwant Sinha discussed the Sakhalin-1 agreement during a visit to Moscow on 15 January, and Russian President Vladimir Putin spoke to Prime Minister Atal Bihari Vajpayee seeking more favourable terms for Russia. The Sakhalin agreement was signed on 10 February 2001.[15] In the subsequent years, India's political leaders had to lobby more actively for investments in Russia. Thus, during an October 2006 visit to Moscow, India's petroleum minister offered Russian companies participation in India's downstream energy sector, including a stake in a $4 billion refinery and petrochemical project in Orissa, in return for Indian investments in the Sakhalin-3 oil project. India's petroleum minister further discussed the Sakhalin-3 project with Putin during his visit to India in January 2007.[16]

High-level diplomacy, along with bureaucratic politics and the absence of international competitors, also influenced India's acquisition of oil assets in Sudan. In 2002, during Sudan's civil war, Canada's Talisman Energy was the target of a divestment campaign by Western human rights groups. It then sold its stake in the Greater Nile Petroleum Operating Company (GNPOC) to OVL (the other partners in GNPOC were the China National Petroleum Corporation and Malaysia's Petronas). Sections of the Indian government opposed investing in Sudan because of the political instability in that country. However, India's Ministry for Petroleum and Natural Gas and others in the government favoured the Sudanese investment. Further, Sudan's ambassador to India called attention to long-standing bilateral ties, noting that Indian investments in Sudan would be 'within the old framework of bilateral relationship and south–south partnership' and that such investments would 'enthuse the entire African continent'.[17] Eventually, India's government went ahead with the Sudanese investment, and senior Indian officials persuaded Sudan's leader to accept OVL's participation and to reject a rival bid by Petronas.

Beyond its investments in Russia and Sudan, OVL and other Indian firms signed agreements for the exploration, and in some cases development, of oil and gas blocks in Libya, Nigeria, East Timor, Vietnam, Iran, Syria, and Brazil, but most of these are relatively small projects. In the 2000s, OVL also failed to secure several investments.

Technical, bureaucratic, and international factors hindered OVL's attempts to acquire oil assets in some instances. On technical grounds, OVL lacked internationally competitive capabilities.[18] On bureaucratic grounds, hindrance from Indian government agencies prevented OVL from acquiring assets abroad. In 2004, OVL lost out to Chinese firms acquiring assets in Ecuador when India's government did not raise its bid of $1.4 billion. In 2005, India's government blocked OVL from acquiring assets in Nigeria on security grounds, and these were then procured by Chinese firms.[19] Also, OVL could not acquire PetroKazhstan despite making a higher bid of $3.6 billion compared to $3.2 billion offered by Chinese firms—China's political ties with and geographic proximity to Kazakhstan probably influenced Kazakhstan's decisions on this issue.[20]

In the 2000s, the Indian government recognized that more active diplomacy, financing, and economic assistance would be needed to secure oil agreements. Thus, in 2006, New Delhi signed an energy cooperation agreement with Beijing whereby both countries would cooperate, rather than compete against each other, in acquiring and developing oil assets overseas. Also, Indian ministers and officials increased their visits to oil-rich countries and began inviting leaders of these countries to India. This oil diplomacy, whereby foreign ministry diplomats and petroleum ministry officials worked together, produced a few successes. For example, in 2005, Indian firms won small contracts for oil and gas exploration or refineries in Saudi Arabia, Oman, and Venezuela.[21] India also lobbied for its oil firms in securing investments in Iraq. In 2000–1, Saddam Hussein's government had awarded oil exploration contracts for the Block 8 oil field to OVL and had negotiated with OVL and Reliance Industries for another oil block at Tuba. These contracts were suspended by the new Iraqi government in 2003. Indian diplomats persuaded this government to revive the Block 8 contract, though Indian firms had to make fresh bids for the Tuba oil field.[22]

India's government and public and private firms sometimes deployed military and economic tools towards oil diplomacy. They offered military cooperation, economic financing, and help in infrastructure development to secure oil and gas agreements in Kazakhstan, Nigeria, Uzbekistan, and other states.[23] For example, in 2005, ONGC and the private firm Mittal signed an agreement with Nigeria's Ministry of Energy to explore two oil blocks, in return for investing $6 billion in a refinery, a 2000-megawatt power plant, and a railway line in Nigeria.[24]

To summarize, in the 2000s, India's oil policies moved beyond commercial purchases on the international market and included the securing of oil investments overseas. High-level diplomacy, public–private partnerships, and military and economic cooperation initiatives influenced these attempts to purchase oil assets abroad.

Gas

India was not a major consumer of gas until the mid-1980s, when the Bombay High gas field went into production. By 2005, gas comprised 8 per cent of India's commercial energy consumption, and gas consumption was growing. India's domestic supplies were insufficient to meet this demand, and India began importing gas in 2004. It sought to import gas in two ways—via pipelines and through liquefied natural gas (LNG) shipped from the Middle East. International political factors significantly influenced these attempts to acquire gas from abroad.

LNG from Qatar and Iran

India's first LNG imports were from Qatar in 2004. Thereafter, in June 2005, a consortium of Indian firms—the Gas Authority of India Limited (GAIL), Indian Oil, and Bharat Petroleum—signed a contract with the National Iranian Gas Export Company (NIGEC) to import 5 to 7.5 million tons of LNG each year beginning in 2009. Technical obstacles and international political factors held up the implementation of this contract.

On technical grounds, Iran did not have the capacity to produce LNG and relied on foreign firms to set up LNG facilities in Iran. Yet Indian and foreign firms were reluctant to set up such facilities until any contract was confirmed and because of possible US sanctions (under the Iran–Libya Sanctions Act). More significantly, India–Iran relations somewhat cooled in 2005–6, and in 2006 the LNG project was held up after Iran sought higher prices.[25] Although the pricing issue was subsequently resolved, the LNG project was still held up as of 2009, as Indian and Iranian officials were unable to make further progress on this project.

Gas Pipelines via Iran–Pakistan, Myanmar–Bangladesh, and Turkmenistan–Afghanistan

To augment the Qatar and Iran LNG projects, India's Ministry of Petroleum and Natural Gas considered three transnational gas pipeline projects—an Iran–Pakistan–India project, a pipeline involving Turkmenistan and Afghanistan, and a Myanmar–Bangladesh–India project. Indian government officials at the senior-most levels were involved in advancing these projects, but technical and international political factors considerably delayed them. Further, India's government sought to ensure the security of gas supplies, but this was difficult given the political uncertainty in, or uncertainty in India's relations with, the countries through which the gas pipelines transited. As a result, by 2008, India had not concluded firm agreements for these gas pipeline projects.

The Iran–Pakistan–India pipeline was first discussed in the mid-1990s. It was proposed in July 1993 during the Iranian oil minister's visit to India, and in 1997 all three countries agreed in principle to pursue the pipeline. In 1999–2000, Indian and Iranian government officials held several meetings which resulted in the formation of committees to further discuss the pipeline. International political factors delayed the project for the next decade.

One international political factor was tension between India and Pakistan—the pipeline talks stalled in 2001–3 for this reason. India's Bharatiya Janata Party (BJP)-led government then linked pipeline negotiations with Pakistan granting most-favoured-nation (MFN) status to India. In 2004–5, in conjunction with a thaw in Pakistan–India relations, the two countries revived discussions on the pipeline. In mid-2004, India's new government led by the Congress did not link the pipeline with the MFN issue, and this resulted in a positive response from Pakistan.[26] India's petroleum minister led a delegation to Pakistan in early June 2005, and an Indian delegation also visited Iran in mid-June 2005.[27] In March 2006, Pakistan, India, and Iran held their first tripartite governmental talks in Tehran. Still, other political factors delayed the project.

A second political factor delaying the pipeline was the strain in Iran–India relations after India's September 2005 vote against Iran at the International Atomic Energy Agency (IAEA). (Earlier, India–Iran relations were advancing after President Khatami visited India in 2003—see the chapter on Iran in this volume.) Tehran then seemed to hold back on the pipeline project, also relating this delay to the cost of the project. In July 2006, it sought a price of $7.20 per million British thermal unit of gas against India's offer of $4.20. In early 2007, all three countries agreed to a price of $4.93.[28] Yet Indian officials could not finalize an agreement, and by September 2007 Tehran warned that it would go ahead with Pakistan bilaterally if India delayed on the project. High-level diplomacy prevented the pipeline project from collapsing in 2008—the oil ministers of India and Pakistan met in Islamabad on 25 April 2008 to resolve remaining price issues, and the Iranian president visited both India and Pakistan the following week, which helped to further discussions on the pipeline project.[29]

A third factor behind the delay of the Iran pipeline was United States (US) opposition, especially during the negotiations for and after Washington and New Delhi agreed to a civil nuclear cooperation initiative in July 2005. Washington had long-standing concerns about any foreign investment in Iran's oil and gas sector, and it repeatedly conveyed these concerns to Indian officials. Thus, in March 2005, Secretary of State Condoleeza Rice noted that the US had conveyed its 'concerns' to India, and the same day (whether by coincidence or not) India's petroleum minister asked Tehran to set a reasonable price for the pipeline.[30] Later, Rice unambiguously clarified that 'The United States has made very clear to India that we have concerns about their relationship with Iran', including over the gas pipeline issue.[31] In May 2007, press reports noted that although India's Ministry of Petroleum had worked out pricing issues with Pakistan and Iran, the PM's Office sought to go slow on the Iran pipeline while it was negotiating a nuclear agreement with Washington (this was the legally-binding '123' agreement that was finalized in July 2007).[32]

Although some groups in the US noted that the gas pipeline could advance the India–Pakistan peace process—it could bind the two countries in economic linkages that would be hard to cut off for political reasons[33]—Washington still opposed the Iran pipeline. It tacitly endorsed the Turkmenistan–Afghanistan–Pakistan–India pipeline and a US–India civil nuclear energy deal as alternatives to the Iran–Pakistan–India pipeline.[34]

India's second gas pipeline proposal was a Turkmenistan–Afghanistan–Pakistan–India project. This concept originated in a 1995 memorandum of understanding between the governments of Turkmenistan and Pakistan for a pipeline through Afghanistan, and another agreement between Afghanistan's new government and Turkmenistan and Pakistan in 2002. India joined the pipeline project thereafter. In 2005, the ADB submitted a feasibility study (designed by the British company Penspen) to the oil ministers of Turkmenistan, Afghanistan, Pakistan, and India.[35] The pipeline was a major agenda item at the second Regional Economic Cooperation Conference on Afghanistan—a meeting of Afghan donors—in November 2006 in New Delhi. In May 2007, India joined a four-party agreement with the ADB on this proposed pipeline. In April 2008, at a meeting facilitated by the ADB, the four participating countries signed a framework agreement seeking to begin construction by 2010, with gas supplies commencing by 2015.

In summary, despite the considerable logistical and technical difficulties of building a four-country pipeline, as well as political problems of coordination between the countries (especially due to strains between Afghanistan and Pakistan), the idea of a four-country pipeline was advanced from 2005 to 2008 due to somewhat favourable international political considerations. It was supported by the ADB and Western states because it could make a significant contribution to Afghanistan's development; it could reduce Russian influence in Turkmenistan; and it was a potential rival to the Iran–Pakistan–India pipeline.[36] While neither pipeline was finalized by 2008, political factors considerably delayed the Iran–Pakistan pipeline, and, relatively speaking, advanced prospects for the Turkmenistan–Afghanistan pipeline.

India's third gas pipeline project involved the Myanmar–Bangladesh–India pipeline, which would bring gas from Myanmar to Kolkata and east India via Bangladesh. The then Foreign Minister Jaswant Singh discussed this project during his visit to Myanmar in 2001.[37] The project had not just an energy component but also a political aspect—under a BJP-led government in the early 2000s, India sought to build ties with Myanmar to counter Chinese influence in that country.[38] In January 2005, the ministers of India, Myanmar, and Bangladesh discussed the pipeline. Still, international political factors related to Bangladesh's attempts to seek concessions from India—which India's foreign ministry had warned about[39]—delayed the pipeline project.

Specifically, Bangladesh linked the gas pipeline to economic concessions from India. It sought the removal of Indian non-tariff barriers; a trade and transport corridor linking Nepal and Bangladesh through Indian territory; and access to hydroelectric power generated in Bhutan.[40] Given this opposition from Bangladesh, India then considered a bilateral gas agreement with Myanmar, even though a pipeline routed through India's northeastern states bypassing Bangladesh would be more expensive than a pipeline routed through Bangladesh.[41] Thus, in the period 2005–8, the India–Bangladesh–Myanmar pipeline did not advance due to opposition from Bangladesh.

NUCLEAR ENERGY

India's nuclear energy policies can be differentiated into three phases. In the first phase, from the 1950s until its 1974 nuclear test, imported nuclear reactors were the main component of India's nuclear energy sector. In a second phase, from 1974 to the mid-2000s, civilian nuclear imports into India essentially ended. Thereafter, India built its domestic nuclear industry to offset the loss of nuclear imports. In a third phase, that began in the mid-2000s, the slow development of its indigenous nuclear sector, the growth of its economy, and a major US foreign policy initiative all contributed to India's revival of interest in nuclear energy imports. Also, prevailing international regimes in the areas of economics, security, and environment influenced India's nuclear energy policies during these three phases.

The First Phase: Civilian Nuclear Reactor Imports

India's first nuclear energy reactors were provided by foreign suppliers— two US-built 160-megawatt reactors at Tarapur commenced operation in 1969, and a Canadian-built 100-megawatt Canada Deuterium Uranium (CANDU) reactor commenced operation in 1973. Thereafter, with the exception of a second Canadian-built CANDU that commenced operation in 1981, India faced an international embargo on nuclear reactor imports. Domestic and international factors influenced India's nuclear energy policies at this time.

At the domestic and decision-making level, PM Jawaharlal Nehru and India's political leaders, as well as nuclear scientist Homi Bhabha (who headed India's Atomic Energy Commission), sought to use science and technology to advance India's economic development. They recognized the limitations of India's domestic industry and therefore sought nuclear imports to develop India's energy sector.[42] Internationally, an economic regime, based on the same notion of science and technology cooperation to promote development, influenced the US and Canada to supply reactors to India. Thus, guided by its 'Atoms for Peace' initiative of civilian nuclear energy cooperation and also for political reasons (to strengthen ties with India), the US provided the Tarapur reactors to India. Partially financed by the Colombo Plan for Cooperative Economic Development in South and Southeast Asia, Canada provided the 40-megawatt Canada India Reactor United States (CIRUS) reactor to India, after which it supplied two CANDU reactors, partly financed by the Canadian Export Credit Insurance Corporation.

The Second Phase: The Cessation of Imports with Minor Exceptions

After its 1974 nuclear test, India faced an international embargo on nuclear technology imports. The US and its Western allies reversed the 'Atoms for Peace' approach and constructed a security regime that tightened restrictions on nuclear technology transfers. These initiatives, centred around the Nuclear Suppliers Group (NSG), were a direct response to India's nuclear test. This international embargo affected and impeded the growth of India's nuclear energy sector.[43] Thus, after the Canadian-supplied CANDU in 1973, no other nuclear reactor entered India's energy grid in the 1970s, and only three reactors were completed in the 1980s (one of which was another Canadian-supplied CANDU). Although eight more reactors were completed in the 1990s, these Indian-built reactors, based on the CANDU design, had small 220-megawatt capacities and provided less than 3 per cent of India's electricity. During these decades, nuclear imports dropped off India's energy policy agenda, with two exceptions.

First, India still required enriched uranium fuel for the Tarapur reactors. India's political leaders were not confident in claims by Indian nuclear scientists that they could fuel this reactor through indigenously-produced mixed oxide. They, therefore, negotiated with the US, and then with other countries, to provide fuel for Tarapur. Accordingly, this fuel was supplied by the US (until 1982), which then agreed that it could be supplied by France, after which it was supplied by China (in 1995) and Russia (in 2001).

Second, in 1988, India signed an agreement with Russia for two 1,000-megawatt light water reactors. One main international factor—India's political ties with Moscow and their mutual interest in high technology cooperation—led to the signing of this agreement. However, other international factors—US opposition, as well as the collapse of the Soviet Union which resulted in problems in financing—held up the agreement for over a decade.[44] It was only in 1998 that the agreement was revived. By then, New Delhi and Moscow resolved financing problems after Russia extended a $2.6 billion credit at a low 4 per cent interest rate, to be paid back in hard currency after the first reactor was commissioned. Also, the US dropped its opposition by conceding to Russia's position that the original reactor agreement was signed in 1988, well before NSG guidelines of 1992 prohibited reactor sales to countries such as India that did not have full-scope safeguards. Russian technicians began constructing the reactors in 2002 and expected to complete them by 2009–10. By then, the NSG restrictions on India had been lifted.

The Third Phase: The Revival of Nuclear Energy Imports
In the mid-2000s, domestic factors (the slow development of its indigenous nuclear sector) and international factors (a US foreign policy initiative to reverse NSG guidelines, which was supported by other nations partly out of environmental considerations) contributed to India's revival of interest in nuclear energy imports.

In terms of domestic factors, although India's indigenous nuclear industry had matured and had built higher capacity 540-megawatt reactors (compared to its earlier low capacity 220-megawatt reactors), it was still some two decades away from realizing its ambitious three-phase programme of generating nuclear power from indigenous thorium reserves on a large scale. Also, India's indigenous nuclear sector could not attain crucial short-term and medium-term targets. For the short term, it was not supplying enough uranium to fuel its existing reactors, which were therefore operating at only 50 per cent of their capacity. And in the middle term, it was unlikely to attain its goals of generating 20,000 megawatts of nuclear energy by 2020 (by 2009, India's indigenous reactors had a capacity of only about 4,400 megawatts, two Russian reactors would add 2,000 megawatts, and even if India built eight new 700-megawatt reactors in the subsequent decade as planned it would be well short of its 20,000 megawatt target). Thus, India could only make up its nuclear energy deficit through imports of uranium fuel and of reactors, but it faced a long-standing embargo on such imports.

International factors, in the form of a major US foreign policy initiative in 2005, began the process of lifting this embargo. In a July 2005 meeting with PM Manmohan Singh, US President George W. Bush announced a commitment to civilian nuclear energy cooperation with India. Such nuclear cooperation was intended to boost the US strategic partnership with India, a partnership that was an important priority for the Bush administration as it sought to balance a rising China.[45] Indeed, it was only after the July 2005 announcement that the aforementioned domestic factor became more prominent—it was only thereafter that India's elites and policymakers more closely examined and recognized the shortcomings in India's indigenous nuclear sector, and this made international civilian nuclear cooperation more appealing to India's policymakers.

US policy was the main, but not the only, international factor enabling the lifting of nuclear technology embargoes on India. Washington still required the approval of the NSG. The NSG members were willing to lift trade restrictions against India for a few key reasons. Some, particularly France and Russia, had commercial interests in supplying reactors and fuel to India. Just as important, the NSG and international community recognized that India, the world's fifth-largest carbon emitter in 2005 and expected to become the third largest by 2015,[46] could help against global warming by increasing its reliance on nuclear power.[47] This issue of civilian nuclear energy in India helping the global environment was first raised in India's discussions with the European Union (EU), rather than with the US, in late 2004 at the India–EU strategic partnership discussions.[48] Thereafter, this environmental issue entered US and international discourse concerning civilian nuclear cooperation with India.[49]

In short, international factors such as a key US foreign policy initiative, furthered by a global recognition of the positive environmental impact of nuclear cooperation with India, helped in lifting the international nuclear technology embargo on India by 2008. This allowed India to import reactors and uranium fuel for its reactors and to acquire uranium assets abroad.[50] Such nuclear imports would enable India to attain its target of generating some 20,000 megawatts of electricity from nuclear reactors by 2020.

* * *

This chapter has discussed various bureaucratic, domestic, and international factors influencing India's energy policy since its independence. Similar factors are likely to influence India's future energy policy. Bureaucratically, by the late 2000s, India's foreign ministry had established institutional links with other government agencies responsible for securing energy supplies from abroad. In 2007, it formed an Energy Security Unit within the foreign ministry for this purpose. Thus, India's foreign ministry could considerably influence the country's future foreign energy policy. It would generally favour securing energy supplies from countries having good political ties with India. It would be cautious about energy investments in certain countries if these investments strain India's ties with other states.

Domestically, high economic growth rates would considerably increase India's demand for energy and its quest for energy from abroad—India may then more aggressively seek a larger number of energy investments with a wider range of countries. Conversely, reduced economic growth would lessen the magnitude and intensity of India's quest for energy imports. These domestic factors may combine with bureaucratic factors—a less internationally oriented oil minister may, especially during a time of economic slowdown, shift his ministry's focus homewards and rely more on state-run refineries and oil companies rather than on foreign suppliers to meet India's energy requirements.

Internationally, the prevailing economic, security, and environmental regimes will significantly influence India's energy policy. In particular, global environmental considerations will cause India to seek clean sources of energy. India may then opt for greater foreign technological collaboration in its energy sector; for example, seeking a range of clean—coal, nuclear, and non-fossil—fuel technologies from Western countries.

To summarize, some key domestic and international factors are likely to influence India's energy policy in the twenty-first century. Domestically, if India's economy maintains high growth rates, India could intensify its quest for energy from abroad, and its energy policy would then be significantly affected by international political factors. Internationally, India is likely to keep all its energy options open—it is likely to continue to maintain a diverse portfolio of foreign suppliers and sources for its energy requirements.

NOTES

1. Planning Commission of India, *Tenth Five-Year Plan*, Section 7.3, p. 765.
2. Talmiz Ahmad (2005), 'Oil Diplomacy for India's Energy Security', in Atish Sinha and Madhup Mohta (ed.), *Indian Foreign Policy: Challenges and Opportunities* (New Delhi: Foreign Service Institute), p. 1095.
3. Refer to the 2009 edition, British Petroleum (2009), *BP Statistical Review of World Energy* (June). These figures exclude renewable sources of energy that are shown in Table 15.2.
4. Planning Commission of India, *Tenth Five Year Plan*, Section 7.3.4. The PM's Office set up a formal inter-ministerial body, the Energy Coordination Committee, which held its first meeting in July 2005.

5. Biplab Dasgupta (1971), *The Oil Industry in India* (London: Frank Cass), p. 202.

6. Ibid., pp. 184–7.

7. Arvind Panagariya (2008), *India: The Emerging Giant* (New York: Oxford University Press).

8. Fariborz Ghadar (1982), *The Petroleum Industry in Oil Importing Developing Countries* (Lexington, MA: Lexington Books), pp. 137–8.

9. Santosh Mehrotra (1990), *India and the Soviet Union: Trade and Technology Transfer* (Cambridge: Cambridge University Press), pp. 178–80.

10. Ibid., pp. 116–17.

11. Tanvi Madan (2006), *The Brookings Foreign Policy Studies Energy Security Series: India* (Washington, DC: Brookings Institution), p. 54.

12. The production of oil and gas from OVL assets (mainly the Sakhalin-1 and Sudan oil fields), in million tons of oil equivalent, was 3.3 (oil) and 0.5 (gas) in 2004; 3.7 (oil) and 1.3 (gas) in 2005; 4.6 (oil) and 1.8 (gas) in 2006; and 5.8 (oil) and 2.1 (gas) in 2007; increases each year were due to increased production at existing fields rather than the acquisition of new fields.

13. This notion is sometimes flawed for a fungible commodity such as oil. Equity-oil assets abroad can enhance energy security only if this oil can be transported to the home country at lower costs and with greater reliability than from open-market sources. Jeremy Carl, Varun Rai, David Victor (2008), 'Energy and India's Foreign Policy', Working Paper No. 75, Program on Energy and Sustainable Development, Stanford, California (May), pp. 15, 20.

14. 'First Cargo of Crude from Sakhalin-1 Arrives', *Business Line*, 2 December 2006; 'Sakhalin-1 Output Drops', *Energy Tribune*, 24 April 2008.

15. T. Subramanium (2005), 'The Sakhalin Venture', *Frontline*, 22 (22), 22 October.

16. 'India will Demand Stake in Sakhalin', *The Times of India*, 25 January 2007.

17. John Cherian (2002), 'A Promising Deal', *Frontline*, 19 (15), 20 July.

18. Carl, Rai, and Victor, 'Energy and India's Foreign Policy', p. 20.

19. Madan, *The Brookings Foreign Policy Studies Energy Security Series: India*, pp. 42–3.

20. Keith Bradsher and Christopher Pala (2005), 'China Beat India for Kazakh Oil Field', *International Herald Tribune*, 23 August 2005; 'Kazakh Oil Coup for China, India Cries Foul', *Asia Times*, 24 August 2005.

21. Madan, *The Brookings Foreign Policy Studies Energy Security Series: India*, p. 46.

22. 'Indian Oil Cos will have to Bid Anew for Iraqi Blocks', *Business Line*, 26 May 2007.

23. Madan, *The Brookings Foreign Policy Studies Energy Security Series: India*, p. 48.

24. 'ONGC Mittal Energy Signs MoU with Nigeria', *Business Line*, 11 November 2005.

25. 'India, Iran Agree to Renegotiate LNG Price', *Tribune India*, 17 November 2006.

26. Sudha Mahalingam (2005), 'Politics of the Iran–Pakistan–India gas pipeline project', in I.P. Khosla (ed.), *Energy and Diplomacy* (New Delhi: Konark), pp. 74–85.

27. Government of India, Ministry of Petroleum, Factsheet, 'Import of Natural Gas to India through Transnational Gas Pipelines'.

28. 'Peace Pipeline Contract Soon, Gas Flow by 2011', *Iran Daily*, 1 July 2008.

29. 'Energy Crisis Forces India to Join Iran Gas Pipeline', *Dawn*, 26 April 2008.

30. Sudha Mahalingam (2005), 'Politics of the Iran–Pakistan–India gas pipeline project', in I.P. Khosla (ed.), *Energy and Diplomacy* (New Delhi: Konark Publishers), p. 87.

31. See *The U.S.–India Global Partnership: Hearing Before the Committee on International Relations, House of Representatives, April 5, 2006* (United States Congress, House Committee on International Relations, 2006). Washington also opposed Pakistan's involvement—in April 2007, US embassy officials in Pakistan noted that 'we will continue our opposition [to the pipeline]. At the same time, Pakistan should put more focus on finding means for alternate energy resources, such as from coal or wind or solar energy'. David Montero (2007), 'Pipeline would Extend Iran's Reach', *Christian Science Monitor*, 31 May.

32. 'UPA to go Slow on Iran Gas Pipeline', rediff.com, 21 May 2007. Later, Indian and Iranian officials discussed the pipeline during President Ahmadinejad's visit to Delhi in April 2008, and New Delhi outlined a number of issues to which Tehran responded in July. New Delhi then delayed the pipeline dialogue while the US Congress was voting to finalize a civilian nuclear agreement with India. It resumed pipeline discussions in November 2008, when India's foreign minister visited Tehran for the fifteenth meeting of the India–Iran joint commission. http://www.rediff.com/money/2007/may/21pipeline.htm.

33. Michael Krepon and Z. Haider (2005), 'A Pipeline for Peace?', *The Indian Express*, 19 April; S.G. Pandian (2005), 'Energy Trade as a Confidence-Building Measure between India and Pakistan: A Study of the Indo-Iran Trans-Pakistan Pipeline Project', *Contemporary South Asia*, 14 (3), pp. 307–20.

34. Ariel Cohen, Lisa Curtis, and Owen Graham (2008), *The Proposed Iran–Pakistan–India Gas Pipeline: An Unacceptable Risk to Regional Security* (Washington, DC: The Heritage Foundation, 30 May); K. Alan Kronstadt and Kenneth Katzman (2006), *India–Iran Relations and US Interests* (Washington, DC: CRS Report for Congress, 2 August).

35. 'Gas Pipeline Project Turkmenistan–Afghanistan–Pakistan–India Approved', *Turkmenistan.ru*, 20 November 2006.

36. Stephen Blank (2008), *India's Energy Options in Central Asia* (London: South Asian Strategic Stability Unit), p. 34; John Foster (2008), *A Pipeline through a Troubled Land: Afghanistan, Canada, and the New Great Energy Game*, Center for Policy Alternatives, Foreign Policy Series, 3 (1), 19 June.

37. 'Delegation to Visit Myanmar for Oil Deal', *Hindustan Times*, 18 February 2001.

38. Marie Lall (2006), 'Indo-Myanmar Relations in the Era of Pipeline Diplomacy', *Contemporary Southeast Asia*, 28 (3), pp. 424–46.

39. Mani Shankar Aiyar (2005), 'Energy Cooperation: India and its Neighbors', in Khosla (ed.), *Energy and Diplomacy*, p. 37.

40. *Energy Politics: India–Bangladesh–Myanmar Relations*, IPCS Special Report, July 2007 (Institute of Peace and Conflict Studies: New Delhi).

41. 'India, Myanmar may Bypass Bangladesh for Gas Pipeline—Other Options to be Explored', *Business Line*, 7 July 2005.

42. Accordingly, in nuclear energy plans of 1954 and 1961, India aimed to have 600 megawatts of nuclear power by 1970 (by that year, the two reactors at Tarapur provided a capacity of 320 megawatts), and 8,000 megawatts by 1980; a revised plan in 1970 called for 2,700 megawatts by 1980, which would be just sufficient to fuel one breeder reactor. George Perkovich (1999), *India's Nuclear Bomb: The Impact on Global Proliferation* (Berkeley: University of California Press), p.153; Atomic Energy Commission (1970), Government of India, *Atomic Energy and Space Research: A Profile for the Decade 1970–80* (Bombay: Atomic Energy Commission); and 'Plan for 2,700 MW of Nuclear Power by 1980 Urged', *The Times of India*, 26 May 1970.

43. Domestic factors also hindered India's nuclear industry. In 1987, because of inadequate government financing, a new company, the NPCIL was set up to raise capital from bonds and loans. Thereafter, India installed eight reactors in the 1990s (in the early and mid-1990s, India's government still did not provide sufficient financing to India's nuclear sector). A much earlier domestic policy, the 1962 Atomic Energy Act, which barred private sector investment in the nuclear sector, also impeded the development of this sector.

44. R. Adam Moody (1997), 'The Indian–Russian Light Water Reactor Deal', *The Nonproliferation Review*, 5 (1), pp. 112–22.

45. This priority was outlined well before the Bush administration took office. See Condoleezza Rice (2000), 'Promoting the National Interest', *Foreign Affairs*, 79 (1), pp. 45–62.

46. *World Energy Outlook* expected India's carbon dioxide emissions (in Gigatons) to be 1.1 Gt (2005), 1.8 Gt (2015), and 3.3 Gt (2030), compared to the United States' 5.8 Gt (2005), 6.4 Gt (2015), and 6.9 Gt (2030), and China's 5.1 Gt (2005), 8.6 Gt (2015), and 11.4 Gt (2030). International Energy Agency, *World Energy Outlook 2007*, p. 200.

47. The *World Energy Outlook 2007* (p. 538), noted that of India's projected greenhouse gas emission savings by 2030, most would come from efficiency in the end-use of electricity (18 per cent), use of renewables and biofuels (24 per cent), and switching from coal to gas (24 per cent), with only 5 per cent coming from the increased use of nuclear plants.

48. At this time, both sides noted that the issues of energy and the environment were a shared global and strategic challenge. This was the first instance in decades that India and its Western partners revisited the issue of cooperation on nuclear energy. See 'Address by [India's Foreign Secretary] Shyam Saran at the Japan Institute of

International Affairs', 15 January 2007. See, Ministry of External Affairs website, http://mea.gov.in/speech/2007/01/15ss01.htm.

49. Reflecting this theme, the IAEA safeguards agreement with India began by 'recognizing the significance India attaches to civilian nuclear energy as an efficient, clean and sustainable energy source for meeting global energy demand', and noted that India's civilian nuclear programme would 'meet the twin challenges of energy security and protection of the environment'. See International Atomic Energy Agency, 'IAEA Safeguards Agreement with India', 7 July 2008, p. 1.

50. In 2008, India modified its *Integrated Energy Policy* to include seeking uranium assets abroad for India's nuclear energy sector. See 'Govt to Build N-Buffer Stocks, Overseas Assets', *Financial Express*, 3 October 2008.

Select Further Readings

Aaron, Sushil J. (2003), *Straddling Faultlines: India's Foreign Policy Towards the Greater Middle East*, CSH Occasional Paper, No. 7, Centre de Sciences Humaines de New Delhi, New Delhi, August.

Ayoob, Mohammed (1990), *India and Southeast Asia: Indian Perceptions and Policies* (London: Routledge).

Bajpai, Kanti (2003), 'Indian Strategic Culture', in Michael R. Chambers (ed.), *Future Strategic Balances and Alliances* (Carlisle, Penn: Strategic Studies Institute).

Bandyopadhyaya, Jayantanuja (1979), *The Making of India's Foreign Policy: Determinants, Institutions, Processes and Personalities*, revised edition (New Delhi: Allied Publishers).

Basrur, Rajesh M. (2006), *Minimum Deterrence and India's Nuclear Security* (Stanford, CA: Stanford University Press).

—— (2008), *South Asia's Cold War: Nuclear Weapons and Conflict in Comparative Perspective* (Abingdon and New York: Routledge).

Brecher, Michael (1968), *India and World Politics* (London: Oxford University Press).

Brines, Russell (1968), *The Indo-Pakistani Conflict* (New York: Pall Mall).

Cohen, Stephen P. (2001), *India: Emerging Power* (Washington DC: Brookings Institution Press).

Cortright, David and Amitabh Mattoo (eds) (1996), *India and the Bomb: Public Opinion and Nuclear Options* (Notre Dame, Indiana: University of Notre Dame Press).

Dasgupta, C. (2002), *War and Diplomacy in Kashmir, 1947–1948* (New Delhi: Sage Publications).

Dixit, J.N. (1996), *My South Block Years: Memoirs of a Foreign Secretary* (New Delhi: UBS Publishers).

—— (2003), *India's Foreign Policy 1947–2003* (New Delhi: Picus Books).

Donaldson, Robert H. (1974), *Soviet Foreign Policy toward India: Ideology and Strategy* (Cambridge: Harvard University Press).

Dutt, V.P. (1984), *India's Foreign Policy* (New Delhi: Vikas Publishing House Pvt Ltd).

Ganguly, Sumit (1999), 'India's Pathway to Pokhran II: The Sources and Prospects of India's Nuclear Weapons Program', *International Security*, 23 (4).

—— (2001), *Conflict Unending: India–Pakistan Tensions Since 1947* (New York: Columbia University Press).

—— (ed.) (2003), *India as an Emerging Power* (London: Frank Cass Publishers).

—— (2008), 'Nuclear Stability in South Asia', *International Security*, 33 (2).

Ganguly, Sumit and Devin T. Hagerty (2005), *Fearful Symmetry: India–Pakistan Crises in the Shadow of Nuclear Weapons* (New Delhi: Oxford University Press).

Ganguly, Sumit, Brian Shoup, and Andrew Scobel (eds) (2006), *US–Indian Strategic Cooperation: Into The 21st Century* (London: Routledge).

Garver, John (2001), *Protracted Contest: Sino-Indian Rivalry in the Twentieth Century* (Seattle: University of Washington Press).

Gordon, Sandy (1995), *India's Rise to Power in the Twentieth Century and Beyond* (London: St. Martin's Press).

Heimsath, Charles H. (1956), *India's Role in the Korean War* (New Haven: Yale University Press).

Heimsath, Charles H. and Surjit Mansingh (1971), *A Diplomatic History of Modern India* (Calcutta: Allied Publishers).

Hoffman, Steven (1990), *India and the China Crisis* (Berkeley: University of California Press).

Horn, Robert C. (1982), *Soviet–Indian Relations: Issues and Influence* (New York: Praeger).

Kapur, S. Paul (2007), *Dangerous Deterrent: Nuclear Weapons Proliferation and Conflict in South Asia* (Stanford, CA: Stanford University Press).

—— (2008), 'Ten Years of Instability in a Nuclear South Asia', *International Security*, 33 (2).

Kapur, S. Paul and Sumit Ganguly (2007), 'The Transformation of U.S.–India Relations: An Explanation for the Rapprochement and Prospects for the Future', *Asian Survey*, 47 (4).

Kavic, Lorne J. (1967), *India's Quest for Security: Defence Policies, 1947–1965* (Berkeley: University of California Press).

Kux, Dennis (1992), *India and the United States: Estranged Democracies* (Washington, DC: National Defense University Press).

Mansingh, Surjit (1984), *India's Search for Power: Indira Gandhi's Foreign Policy, 1966–1982* (New Delhi: Sage Publications).

Maxwell, Neville (1970), *India's China War* (Dehra Dun: Natraj Publishers).

McMahon, Robert J. (1994), *The Cold War on the Periphery: The United States, India, and Pakistan* (New York: Columbia University Press).

Mellor, John W. and Philips Talbot (eds) (1979), *India: A Rising Middle Power* (Colorado: Westview Press).

Muni, S.D. (1993), *Pangs of Proximity: India's and Sri Lanka's Ethnic Crisis* (New Delhi: Sage Publications).

Nayar, Baldev Raj and T.V. Paul (2003), *India in the World Order: Searching for Major Power Status* (Cambridge: Cambridge University Press).

Panikkar, K.M. (1945), *India and the Indian Ocean* (London: G. Allen & Unwin).

Pant, Harsh (2009), *Indian Foreign Policy in Unipolar World* (New Delhi: Routledge).

Perkovich, George (1999), *India's Nuclear Bomb: The Impact on Global Proliferation* (Berkeley: University of California Press).

Racioppi, Linda (1994), *Soviet Policy toward South Asia since 1970* (Cambridge: Cambridge University Press).

Raja Mohan, C. (2003), *Crossing the Rubicon: The Shaping of India's New Foreign Policy* (New Delhi: Viking Publishers).

Rajan, M.S. (ed.) (1976), *India's Foreign Relations during the Nehru Era: Some Studies* (Bombay: Asia Publishing House).

Saint-Mézard, Isabelle (2006), *Eastward Bound: India's New Positioning in Asia* (New Delhi: Manohar and Centre de Sciences Humaines).

SarDesai, D.R. (1968), *Indian Foreign Policy in Cambodia, Laos, and Vietnam, 1947–1964* (Berkeley: University of California Press).

SarDesai, D.R. and Raju G.C. Thomas (eds) (2002), *Nuclear India in the Twenty-First Century* (New York: Palgrave Macmillan).

Sen Gupta, Bhabani (1970), *The Fulcrum of Asia; Relations among China, India, Pakistan, and the USSR* (New York: Pegasus).

Singh, S. Nihal (1986), *The Yogi and the Bear: Story of Indo-Soviet Relations* (London: Mansell Publishing Ltd).

Sisson, Richard and Leo E. Rose (1990), *War and Secession* (Berkeley: University of California Press).

Sridharan, Kripa (1996), *The ASEAN Region in India's Foreign Policy* (Aldershot: Dartmouth Publishing Company Limited).

Talbott, Strobe (2000), *Engaging India* (Washington, DC: The Brookings Institution).

Thakur, Ramesh and Carlyle Thayer (1992), *Soviet Relations with India and Vietnam* (London: Palgrave Macmillan and St. Martin's Press).

Thakur, Ramesh (1994), *The Politics and Economics of India's Foreign Policy* (London: Hurst & Co. Publishers Ltd).

Contributors

WALTER ANDERSEN is Associate Director of the South Asian Studies Programme and a Professorial Lecturer at the School of Advanced International Studies of Johns Hopkins University, Washington DC.

RAJESH M. BASRUR is Associate Professor at the S. Rajaratnam School of International Studies, Nanyang Technological University.

NICOLAS BLAREL is a PhD student, Department of Political Science, Indiana University, Bloomington.

NEIL DEVOTTA is Associate Professor of Political Science at Wake Forest University.

C. CHRISTINE FAIR is Assistant Professor at Edmund A. Walsh School of Foreign Service, Center for Peace and Security Studies, Georgetown University.

SUMIT GANGULY is Professor of Political Science and holds the Rabindranath Tagore Chair in Indian Cultures and Civilizations at Indiana University, Bloomington.

JOHN W. GARVER is Professor, Sam Nunn School of International Affairs, Georgia Institute of Technology.

S. PAUL KAPUR is Associate Professor in the Department of National Security Affairs at the US Naval Postgraduate School, and Faculty Affiliate at Stanford University's Center for International Security and Cooperation.

JASON A. KIRK is Assistant Professor of Political Science at Elon University, North Carolina.

DINSHAW MISTRY is Associate Professor, Department of Politics, University of Cincinnati.

RAHUL MUKHERJI is Associate Professor, South Asian Studies Programme, Faculty of Arts and Social Sciences, National University of Singapore.

DEEPA M. OLLAPALLY is Associate Director, Sigur Center for Asian Studies, and a Professorial Lecturer, Elliott School of International Affairs, George Washington University.

HARSH V. PANT teaches in the Department of Defence Studies, King's College London, and is also an associate with the King's Centre for Science and Security Studies.

MANJEET S. PARDESI is a PhD student, Department of Political Science, Indiana University, Bloomington.

MILIND THAKAR is Associate Professor of International Relations, University of Indianapolis.